'This is an important book at a crucial time. It is important because it is a rare anthropological study of how traditional courts function in one part of the country, Msinga. It comes at a crucial time as the question of how to regulate traditional courts has perplexed South African policy-makers for decades and attempts at doing so have so far failed. A key insight of the book is that traditional courts should not be equated to courts but are better understood as vernacular forums for local dispute resolution. The author argues persuasively that regulation of these fora should seek to foster their capacity to be successful mediators of community conflict.'

Kate O'Regan, *University of Oxford, UK, and former Judge, Constitutional Court of South Africa*

'The lasting contribution of the book lies in the author's ability to demonstrate the complexities of traditional justice mechanisms and the dilemmas of rural people who depend on them, especially women, while offering some hope that these mechanisms, and the core values underpinning them, can be strengthened to make these systems a viable component of the states' strategies to provide real access to justice for these communities.'

Thandabantu Nhlapo, *University of Cape Town, South Africa*

'This book is a must-read for anyone concerned with access to justice by the rural poor in the developing world. Combining ethnography and political economy to good effect, and informed by a sophisticated conceptual framework, the book provides compelling arguments on the contradictory nature of 'traditional' mechanisms for resolving disputes in rural South Africa. It also outlines convincing arguments for a co-operative governance model of dispute resolution. A *tour de force . . .*'

Ben Cousins, *Institute for Poverty, Land and Agrarian Studies, University of the Western Cape, South Africa*

Access to Justice and Human Security

For most people in rural South Africa, traditional justice mechanisms provide the only feasible means of accessing any form of justice. These mechanisms are popularly associated with restorative justice, reconciliation and harmony in rural communities. Yet, this ethnographic study grounded in the political economy of rural South Africa reveals how historical conditions and contemporary pressures have strained these mechanisms' ability to deliver the high normative ideals with which they are notionally linked. In places such as Msinga access to justice is made especially precarious by the reality that human insecurity – a composite of physical, social and material insecurity – is high for both ordinary people and the authorities who staff local justice forums; cooperation is low between traditional justice mechanisms and the criminal and social justice mechanisms the state is meant to provide; and competition from purportedly more effective 'twilight institutions', like vigilante associations, is rife. Further contradictions are presented by profoundly gendered social relations premised on delicate social trust that is closely monitored by one's community and enforced through self-help measures like witchcraft accusations in a context in which violence is, culturally and practically, a highly plausible strategy for dispute management.

These contextual considerations compel us to ask what justice we can reasonably speak of access to in such an insecure context and what solutions are viable under such volatile human conditions? The book concludes with a vision for access to justice in rural South Africa that takes seriously ordinary people's circumstances and traditional authorities' lived experiences as documented in this detailed study. The author proposes a cooperative governance model that would maximise the resources and capacity of both traditional and state justice apparatus for delivering the legal and social justice – namely, peace and protection from violence as well as mitigation of poverty and destitution – that rural people genuinely need.

Sindiso Mnisi Weeks is Assistant Professor in Public Policy of Excluded Populations in the School for Global Inclusion and Social Development at the University of Massachusetts Boston, USA. She previously served as a senior researcher in the Centre for Law and Society at the University of Cape Town, where she worked on the Rural Women's Action Research Programme combining research, advocacy and policy work on women, property, governance and participation under customary law and the South African Constitution. She holds a BA and LLB from the University of Cape Town and received her DPhil in Law (with a focus on socio-legal studies) from the University of Oxford, where she was a Rhodes Scholar. Prior to Oxford, she clerked for then Deputy Chief Justice of the Constitutional Court of South Africa, Dikgang Moseneke. She co-authored *African Customary Law in South Africa: Post-Apartheid and Living Law Perspectives*, published in 2015 by Oxford University Press Southern Africa.

Cultural Diversity and Law

Series Editor: Prakash Shah, School of Law, Queen Mary University of London, UK

For a full list of titles in this series, please visit www.routledge.com/Cultural-Diversity-and-Law/book-series/CULTDIV

Around the world, most states are faced with difficult issues arising out of cultural diversity in their territories. Within the legal field, such issues span across matters of private law through to public and constitutional law. At international level too there is now considerable jurisprudence regarding ethnic, religious and cultural diversity. In addition, there are several layers of legal control – from communal and religious regulation to state and international regulation. This multiplicity of norm setting has been variously termed legal pluralism, inter-legality or internormativity and provides a fascinating lens for academic analysis that links up to cultural diversity in new and interesting ways. The umbrella of cultural diversity encompasses various population groups throughout the world ranging from national, ethnic, religious or indigenous groupings. This series particularly welcomes work that is of comparative interest, concerning various state jurisdictions as well as different population groups.

Also in the series

Legal Pluralism in the Holy City
Competing Courts, Forum Shopping, and Institutional Dynamics in Jerusalem
Ido Shahar

Muslim Families, Politics and the Law
A Legal Industry in Multicultural Britain
Ralph Grillo

State and Legal Practice in the Caucasus
Anthropological Perspectives on Law and Politics
Edited by Stéphane Voell and Iwona Kaliszewska

Declarations of Interdependence
A Legal Pluralist Approach to Indigenous Rights
Kirsten Anker

Access to Justice and Human Security

Cultural Contradictions in Rural South Africa

Sindiso Mnisi Weeks

Routledge
Taylor & Francis Group
LONDON AND NEW YORK

First published 2018 by Routledge

2 Park Square, Milton Park, Abingdon, Oxfordshire OX14 4RN
52 Vanderbilt Avenue, New York, NY 10017

Routledge is an imprint of the Taylor & Francis Group, an informa business

First issued in paperback 2019

British Library Cataloguing-in-Publication Data
A catalogue record for this book is available from the British Library

Library of Congress Cataloging-in-Publication Data
Names: Weeks, Sindiso Mnisi, 1980–, author.
Title: Access to justice and human security : cultural contradictions in rural South Africa / Sindiso Mnisi Weeks.
Description: New York, NY : Routledge, 2017. | Series: Cultural diversity and law | Includes index.
Identifiers: LCCN 2017031662 | ISBN 9781138060777 (hardback)
Subjects: LCSH: Justice, Administration of—South Africa. | Law reform—South Africa. | Restorative justice—South Africa. | Dispute resolution (Law)—South Africa. | Rule of law—South Africa
Classification: LCC KTL470 .W44 2017 | DDC 347.68—dc23
LC record available at https://lccn.loc.gov/2017031662

ISBN: 978-1-138-06077-7 (hbk)
ISBN: 978-0-367-88911-1 (pbk)

Typeset in Galliard
by Apex CoVantage, LLC

Isethulo | Dedication

Kubo bonke abazinikezele ekulandeleleni ubulungiswa nalabo abahlukunyezwayo, abangaphephile.

To all who are dedicated to the pursuit of justice and to those suffering injustice, eluded by security.

The empirical research for this book was largely completed while Senior Researcher, Rural Women's Action-Research Programme, Centre for Law and Society, University of Cape Town.

Contents

Acknowledgements

As you will shortly read, the central dispute in this book features a woman who said that her reason for not initiating proceedings to unearth which members of her community were threatening her life was that the Bible teaches that 'ukuthula kudala ukuthula, izinkulumo zidala izinkulumo' (quiet breeds peace, talk breeds discord). I have tried to locate this enjoinment under this precise wording and have come up short. Yet, I have found a plethora of scriptural verses that could be summarised as such. The most pointed of these excerpts, found in 1 Peter 3:9–18 (ESV), reads as follows:

> Do not repay evil for evil or reviling for reviling, but on the contrary, bless, for to this you were called, that you may obtain a blessing. For 'Whoever desires to love life and see good days, let him keep his tongue from evil and his lips from speaking deceit; let him turn away from evil and do good; let him seek peace and pursue it. For the eyes of the Lord are on the righteous, and his ears are open to their prayer. But the face of the Lord is against those who do evil.' Now who is there to harm you if you are zealous for what is good? But even if you should suffer for righteousness' sake, you will be blessed. Have no fear of them, nor be troubled, but in your hearts honor Christ the Lord as holy, always being prepared to make a defense to anyone who asks you for a reason for the hope that is in you; yet do it with gentleness and respect, having a good conscience, so that, when you are slandered, those who revile your good behavior in Christ may be put to shame. For it is better to suffer for doing good, if that should be God's will, than for doing evil. For Christ also suffered once for sins, the righteous for the unrighteous, that he might bring us to God, being put to death in the flesh but made alive in the spirit.

This biblical injunction perhaps represents what could be described as the central question in this book: might it be possible that understandings of justice and security, as well as the lengths to which people will *and should* go to ensure these perceived goods, are far from universally agreed upon and thus vary even within a single, seemingly unified and harmonious milieu?

In keeping with the above question, in my journey to and through this book, I have spent much time thinking about community as it manifests both in the places studied and in my life. This reflection has only been deepened through the partnerships, collaborations, support and encouragement that have constituted the multiyear project culminating in this book. This research project was initially conceived with my colleague and mentor Aninka Claassens, spurred by the oppressive challenges and experiences of millions of rural men and women throughout the country whose stories she had documented and sought to help address with Henk Smith (and later Wilmien Wicomb) prior to my joining the Rural Women's Action-Research project (RWAR) in 2009. In thought partnership with my other colleague and mentor, Dee Smythe – and with the invaluable conceptual and strategic assistance of Debbie Budlender and Ben Cousins – the project grew into a plan for how we might execute it practically.

A crucial role was played by Mdukatshani Rural Development Trust – most notably Rauri "Makhonya" and Creina "Magogo" Alcock – who helped us operationalise the idea by developing it for the specific context and benefit of Msinga. Mdukatshani also helped us negotiate and gain access and acceptance in the area. I am very grateful to the two traditional areas' Nkosis for their receptivity and welcome. Likewise, I am immensely appreciative of the whole Mdukatshani team (particularly Ngididi Dladla, Gugu Mbatha, Baba Masondo and Sindi Ngubane) for all the on-the-ground assistance they provided with identifying, recruiting and managing our partner headmen, volunteer fieldworkers, research assistants, cultural interpreters, focus group participants, interviewees, and local service providers who delivered transport and catered events, among other support activities. Of course, none of these research activities could have been carried out without the generous financial support provided to RWAR by Atlantic Philanthropies and that given to the research project in particular by the Open Society Foundation.

A handful of Stanford Law students – particularly, Karli Baumgardner, Angel Chan, Anna Gardea, Sarah Greer, and Shirin Taherzadeh – who interned at the Centre for Law and Society and worked in RWAR provided desk-based research support. Some of the historical literature, legislation and case law that appears in this book is with thanks to them. Similarly, three students at the University of Cape Town – Paula Jackson, Moyo Ngubula and Wandisa Phama – supplemented this research with additional literature and data sorting. Least dispensable to the project's success, however, were the eight volunteer fieldworkers who helped gather the data for this project, and my field research assistant, Thabisile Nkosi. In part, I dedicate this book to them who have shown resilience in extremely difficult life circumstances. Moreover, my highest gratitude goes to the six wards' Ndunas (whose names I withhold so as to protect participants' identities) and the many ordinary people who allowed my data collection team and me to pry into their lives in order to gain a better understanding of their circumstances. As promised, I share their stories in this book in hopes that I might help to open the eyes of policy makers as they legislate to regulate the lives of those poor who are most remote from the urban centres.

Further afield, I must thank my two African Customary Law professors, Chuma Himonga and Thandabantu Nhlapo, who were among the first people I thought to consult for advice when, during preliminary fieldwork, I stumbled upon the startling case I lead with in the book. For years they have fostered me as a budding scholar, and for that I am immensely grateful. I am also thankful for the many other mentors I have been blessed to have, both professionally and personally, who have all played a vital role both directly and indirectly in making my completion of this project possible. Among them are Justices John Broderick, Edwin Cameron, Dennis Davis, Gary Hicks, Dikgang Moseneke, Kate O'Regan and Albie Sachs; Profs Penelope Andrews, John Comaroff, Hugh Corder, Stephen Ellmann, Harry Garuba, Bill Kiernan, Heinz Klug, Kay McCormick, Tjakie Naude, Pauline Peters and Rajini Srikanth; the ACR family, Advocate Geoff Budlender and Lew Feldstein; as well as my many esteemed colleagues at the Universities of Cape Town, New Hampshire (Law School) and Massachusetts Boston, especially Monica De Souza Louw, Diane Jefthas, Nolundi Luwaya, Gillian MacNaughton and Leah Plunkett.

I appreciate the contributions made by my students by indulging my bringing elements of my research to class in order to challenge them and obtain their input. I also greatly value how colleagues who have heard parts of this project (re)presented at conferences and workshops have helped to sharpen my thinking on aspects of the whole. Furthermore, each opportunity I have had to articulate the implications of this work in editorials, media interviews, speeches and at dinner parties has improved my ability to do so in this book. I would be remiss in not mentioning that, over various drafts, this book has been greatly benefitted by the editorial feedback of several critical readers named above, as well as Martha Carlson-Bradley.

Finally, the global community that has inspired and sustained this project encompasses mentors and peers through the Mellon Mays Undergraduate Fellowship Program and SSRC-Mellon Mays Graduate Initiatives Program (most notably, Kathy Erasmus, Gideon Nomdo, Cally Waite, and "the Braids"), as well as the Rhodes Scholarship. It also includes very dear friends both near and far – among whom my Constitutional Court sisters (Lalie Moraba, Lise Smit and Carmel Van Niekerk), my law school sisters (Pamhidzai Bamu-Chipunza, Tarisai Gonyora, Twaambo Muleza, Precillar Moyo, Tapiwa Nkhoma and Nicole Nieman), my Oxford sisters (Rachel Pfeifer and Wendy Quay Honeycutt) and the Race and Church family (especially Denise Gray, Andrew Kerr and Nokwanda Khumalo) warrant special mention. This wide-ranging community comprises my devoted parents, sister and nephew, as well as my late grandparents, my wider family, and my "in-loves" (in-laws). Most of all, my deepest thanks goes to my beloved husband and now our boy and girl, the naming of whom we have used to signal the need for our earth to become a gracious and compassionate home for *all* people. I thank God for all of these, "my people", my community. Ngibonga konke abangiphe kona; ngalokho nginikeza lomnikelo kuNkulunkulu ngethemba lokuthi umphakathi uyozuza ngawo. (With thanks for all they have given to me, I give this offering in hopes that it might serve the public good.)

1 Introduction

In conventional legal discourse today, access to justice is regarded as a moral and social imperative – at least, rhetorically. Accordingly, the South African government has settled on the policy of regulating traditional justice mechanisms with a view to maximising this 'imperative'. The government's assumption – implicit in legislation like the Traditional Courts Bill (B1-2017) – is that ordinary rural people do not possess much access to justice, at least not through the state courts, and that so-called traditional courts provide much more access to justice to their poor, rural patrons than do the relatively inaccessible state courts. Yet this is an empirical question: how much of this purportedly universal good do ordinary people in Msinga and similar deep rural areas in South Africa have?

To answer it, we must begin by responding to a few prior questions. First, what is meant by 'access' – that which the government means to maximise? Does it suffice for there to simply be a legally recognised forum within a half hour's walk of one's home, regardless of whether the forum is adequately resourced or the well party supported in bringing his or her dispute to that forum and obtaining a meaningful remedy and enforcement from it? Second, what is meant by 'justice' – that to which the government seeks to maximise access? Is the supposed justice to which traditional courts provide Msinga residents access the kind that would be universally recognised as such – and does it bear any relationship to human security as a similarly universal ideal? If not, what is the significance of its deviation from the 'model' understanding of justice and how should we respond to such variance?

Existing scholarship would lead us to ask of Msinga's traditional courts: what roles do gender and age play in determining the nature of disputes that concern residents? In turn, how do social expectations, attitudes, and capital influence the way traditional courts perceive and respond to complainants and their complaints? How do practices like the spread of rumours affect the seriousness of conflicts and the ways that traditional courts determine and place culpability? How do disputes transform over the course of their existence and shift even during a single hearing? And what impact have history and agents of the state (particularly police and civil courts) had on the way traditional courts review, interpret, and attempt to resolve local people's conflicts? This book addresses these questions.

A shot in the night

A bullet pierced through the window and shattered not only the window itself but also the quiet of that night.

MaThembile[1] momentarily thought it must be some neighbourhood children playing with fireworks in her yard. She was in her bedroom ready to turn in for the night.

But then, in rapid succession, another shot followed.

She could feel the burning in her thigh. She had been shot.

Crying out loud, she fled from her room, concerned for the wellbeing of her two children.

She thought to herself, 'I am going to die and leave my children behind!'

As she reached the second bedroom, she heard a third shot. The bullet went through the window of the bedroom to which she had fled.

She felt helpless. Her thought then was that there was nothing she could do as a woman and one who lives alone with her children.

Huddled in a corner with her children, she phoned her birth family to ask them to call the police to come to the scene; she had been shot.

The police arrived with her brothers. In her statement to the police, she told them that she had not seen the person who shot her.

≈≈≈≈≈

'Ima lapho ke, Mama.' [Pause there then, Mother.]

Ndunankulu (the chief headman) interjected to draw to the attention of the middle-aged shooting victim who sat as a witness before him the fact that the case had come into being because of her. He advised MaThembile, in this second forum in which the case was being heard, that she had paid money (as a participant in the case) and would have to answer for herself to those who had shot her.

MaThembile quickly retorted that she had not said that the parties before her had had anything to do with her shooting. For the second time in her testimony she said, 'I did not say that Mfana shot me having been bought by [MaLula along with] MakaSfanele.'

She continued that she knew both the father and mother of Mfana and father and mother of Sfanele – they are her neighbours – and she had never said that any of them were responsible for her shooting.

'What I did say, when [my nephew] Mbuzo came to visit me in the hospital . . . and asked, "Aunt, the person who shot you, did you really not see them?" . . . I said I really didn't see them – because, I really didn't see them.'

MaThembile described that Mbuzo later came to visit her at home, after she had been released from hospital, and pressed on with his questioning, asking if

1 All names of individuals in this book have been changed to protect study participants' identities.

she had not had differences with anyone who might want to do her harm. She said she had told Mbuzo that she had not had any such differences. He insisted that there is no one who has never had differences with anyone, even having a little problem with them.

'I then said, "concerning a problem (and I'm not saying it's them), I had a problem with Mfana, who hit my child while he was playing." The father of another child that was with my child went to Mfana and asked Mfana why he had hit the children.'

Based on prior conflict, the brief exchange had escalated to the point where the father of the other child, Mr. Zungu, had beaten Mfana. Mr. Zungu then took Mfana to the young man who had assaulted the children along with Mfana and beat that young man up also who was drunk at the time.

'So, what I said to Mbuzo, then, was that we have had conflict but it is not Mfana [who shot me].' MaThembile repeated, 'That's what I said, "It is not Mfana."'

She added that she had also had differences with the people whose goats had died on her property, where the goats basically lived. Mbuzo, who was her nephew only because they share the same surname, not because they are blood relations, had asked how the goat matter related to the shooting.

She explained to the chief's court attendees before her that the matter concerning the goats had arisen in the first hearing of this matter, 'under the tree', but ended there.

She added, 'The person who is concerned in that matter was there at that discussion, which is why I had asked then if I was the target of shooting because of the goats that it was said I was killing; but now I am speaking about a person who is not even present.'

As for Mfana, MaThembile noted, she had defended him, saying that it was not him who had shot her.

'After all, I did not beat him up; if he had a gun, he would have shot the person who beat him, not me. I don't know if I'm wrong in that assessment?!'

≈≈≈≈≈

Mfana was a drinking buddy of MaThembile's nephew-by-name. When her nephew-by-name, Mbuzo, was drinking with Mfana following his discussions with his aunt, he blurted out to Mfana, 'I'm not like you: one of those guys who shoots women'.

When he had testified earlier in the proceedings, Mfana claimed that Mbuzo had actually said 'I'm not like you guys who shoot women . . . for hire'. Mfana said that Mbuzo made the same claim days later, again while they were drinking together: 'Don't look at me, I'm not one of those women that you guys shoot'. When Mfana then asked Mbuzo why he was repeating this allegation and which women he was referring to, Mbuzo added, 'Isn't it true that you are hired by women?'

Mfana reported that he deduced from what Mbuzo had said that he must have been referring to MaThembile, who was the only woman who he knew had been shot. (Because they were neighbours, he had also heard the shots being fired). He had gone home and told his mother that this had happened again, and she advised him not to keep something this big to himself, so he went to report Mbuzo's allegation to the headman's policeman, at whose tree the matter was then discussed on two occasions.

From Mfana's family (namely, his mother), the rumour seems to have later developed that there were two women in particular – his mother, MaLula, and MakaSfanele – who were thought to have hired this young man to shoot the victim. The two women's husbands were the ones who had brought the case to the chief's court, where it was now being heard.

The two husbands had initially had the matter discussed by their local headman's policeman. They were objecting to Mbuzo's having defamed his friend and, at least according to the rumour that followed, their wives. *Iphoyisa*, the headman's policeman, had gathered the parties to discuss the matter under his tree – his dispute management forum.

Iphoyisa told the members of the chief's court that MaThembile had been present for the first hearing, at which she had testified that she had not seen who had shot her and therefore could not contribute anything to the proceedings. *Iphoyisa* had accepted her explanation and proceeded to hear the matter with the remaining parties in attendance. At the subsequent hearing, therefore, she had been absent, because the matter needing to be resolved was between the young men who had exchanged words.

There had been no resolution to the dispute. The two men who had brought the matter on behalf of their wives therefore appealed it to *Induna*, the headman, who said he would not hear it. *Induna* said it should go directly to the chief's court. It was there that *Iphoyisa* was taken to task by the court for not having compelled MaThembile to come to the second, and main, hearing as the one whose shooting had given rise to the conflict.

≈≈≈≈≈

The chief headman, *Ndunankulu*, acknowledged a member of the legislative-administrative body, the Traditional Council. The Traditional Councillor rose to make his comment. After greeting the house, he began: 'It seems problematic to me that *Iphoyisa*, uMtshali, did not have uMama [the woman/mother, MaThembile] attend the hearing. After all, the problem began with loMama [this woman/mother]; she was the one who was shot. She should have been there for discussion of this matter to respond for herself.'

He continued, 'Mtshali, you made an error there. This problem originates with uMama; the whole thing is uMama's problem. Mtshali should have asked her, "Mama, how could all of these goats die on your property?"'

The Traditional Councillor then acknowledged the chief, in thanks, and sat down.

Iphoyisa (Mtshali) responded that he had called a meeting to discuss 'uMama' – her shooting in the community. Nobody had emerged who had shot her, so the matter had ended there.

He observed that the goats matter came afterwards. In his view, and one of the headmen present spoke up in agreement, it was incumbent on MaThembile to bring the fact that someone had threatened her life to a community meeting.

≈≈≈≈≈

What then quickly became murky in the chief's court proceedings was whether MaThembile, who had been shot, was a witness or a party to the dispute. This murkiness was first apparent when, at the start of the hearing, *Ndunankulu* (the chief headman) called all the parties to pay R30 for the dispute to be heard.

MaThembile was asked to pay R30 among them, which she enquired about at the time. She told the court she had not understood herself to be a party to the dispute but a mere victim, and to thus be attending the hearing as nothing but a witness. Without offering a substantive explanation, the chief headman said that she had to pay the R30 also. Begrudgingly, or so it seemed, she did.

Later in the hearing before the chief's court, what had first appeared a side issue became central: as she had briefly mentioned in her testimony to the court, MaThembile had had several goats die on her property before her shooting and the alleged defamation took place – and these goats belonged to other people. One of the goats had belonged to the family of the young man, Mfana, who was allegedly accused of shooting her. The reason why this initially appeared to be an auxiliary matter was that it seemed to emerge only as a potential reason why people might have wanted to harm MaThembile.

≈≈≈≈≈

The court's attention was on MaThembile.

She described how she had first heard a gunshot fired outside of her house a year before she had been shot. At the time, she had thought that she was going to die – that she was going to be killed because, as she had learned, people said that she killed their goats with Tamaron (a lethal substance technically known as *methamidophos*).

Not long afterwards, a woman she worked with at the irrigation scheme farms at the time, MaLwazi, had told her that she knew the person who had fired the shot outside MaThembile's house. MaLwazi, a resident of the same ward as MaThembile, had been the one who had fully alerted MaThembile to the fact that people said that she was poisoning their goats.

MaLwazi now said that she was going to tell the person who had fired the shot outside of MaThembile's house not to do so, because MaThembile had said that the person wanted to kill her. MaLwazi observed that if said person had intended to kill MaThembile, that person would have fired at her rather than just outside her house. The implication seemed that the person had fired the shot in order to warn MaThembile off of further killing people's goats as she was suspected of doing.

MaThembile went to MaLwazi the following day and told her that she was going to report her knowledge to *Iphoyisa*, her family and the state police so that they would know that, if any harm came upon her, MaLwazi knew who was the likely suspect. MaLwazi refused to answer MaThembile alone; instead, MaLwazi took MaThembile to the person who had said that MaThembile killed people's goats with poison.

In that discussion, MaSmumu, the neighbour to whom MaLwazi had taken MaThembile, observed that three men and two women had gathered to discuss the dying of the neighbourhood goats on MaThembile's property. MaSmumu told MaThembile that there was no point in going to her family, the headman's policeman, and the state police, because the real culprit was MaThembile, who was killing people's goats. The conversation ended with MaSmumu warning MaThembile that '[If any of her son's goats die,] *umthofu uzogcwala esiswini*' (literally, lead will fill up the stomach). MaThembile – and apparently the chief's court – understood this to be a threat to her life.

MaThembile had not gone and told *Iphoyisa* or the state police of this threat.

'How many goats were there?' One of the local headmen was interrogating MaThembile.

'A few – four died that I knew about.' She listed them and described the circumstances of their deaths: in three of the four instances, she and her kids had shouted out for the neighbours to come see. Rather than being killed by puddles of sweet water she had poisoned on her property to tempt and kill the goats, as was claimed, according to MaThembile, the goats had come ailing to her property and died there. She said she did not have any Tamaron at home; only at the irrigation scheme farms.

There was some disagreement between MaThembile and the family who had brought her to the chief's court about the number of goats. The suggestion was made that the number may even be as high as 11. The members of the court ultimately accepted that the number was around nine.

Attention now turned to the need for the women who were witnesses to the threat made to MaThembile's life, MaLwazi and MaSmumu, to come give their testimonies. The most vocal headman in the proceedings seemed to expect that they were there, but MaThembile had not brought them with her. She was instructed to notify them of their being summonsed to the chief's court and the proceedings were postponed until these witnesses could be interrogated. A date was set for the next week.

≈≈≈≈≈

MaThembile seemed mildly distressed. Her older brother, who was there to represent her, did not seem to be putting up a very strong defence. He had only stood up twice during the proceedings: first, when MaThembile had been asked if there was anyone there with her to represent her and he stated that he was her older brother; and second, when the case was postponed and he expressed that it would be difficult for him to miss work again. Even when MaThembile had raised objection to her being asked to pay R30 along with the complainants in the case, he had not objected on her behalf. (He had, however, given her the money to pay because she had not brought money with her.)

MaThembile also seemed somewhat surprised – mainly, it would seem, because she had been under the impression that she was called to the matter as a witness, but it was starting to feel like she was the one on trial.

I was perplexed along with her.

I was attending the hearing because I was interested in observing how traditional courts function in practice. I was relatively new to the Msinga area and was just starting to develop my methodology for data collection on a substantial ethnographic study that I would conduct there.

The bulk of literature and my experience on the subject had prepared me for slow-paced dispute resolution (what I call dispute management) proceedings – and, in many ways, this was that kind of proceeding. Yet, this matter was also very fast-moving: it had transformed before my very eyes in ways that made little sense to me. Specifically, the focus of the matter had very quickly seemed to shift to the reasons why the victim had not told anyone about the deaths of the goats and to take on undertones of placing culpability for attempted murder on the victim, due to her silence.

MaThembile was substantially challenged in the chief's court for her not having reported the goat deaths to anyone long before her shooting. Those authorities and attendants who raised their voices in her matter before the chief's court were of the belief that her speaking up ahead of time might have prevented her shooting. They wanted to know more about this aspect of the dispute, thus adjourning the matter until they could get further witnesses to testify.

MaThembile and I had exchanged phone numbers when the rest of the hearing was postponed to the following week, when I would not be able to attend. I told her that I was interested in learning the outcome of the dispute. She had then called me a few days later to say that she had picked up a rumour (from people who were not even present at the case hearing on Tuesday) that she was going to be fined by the chief's court. She told me that she did not understand why she would be the one to be fined because she was innocent and was just a lone woman with no problems or differences with anyone. She asked me to investigate the legality of the situation and advise her of any solutions that might suit. I recommended that she wait until the judgment was handed down (rather than act on a rumour) then let me know and I would then see what I could do.

I was still in Msinga completing the same field research visit when she called me. If the rumour was true, then I shared her confusion at the case's outcome. Yet, even if the rumour was not true, I was still perplexed by the entire dispute proceedings that I had observed. My local research assistant, however, was not. He helped me to get clarity and a better understanding of what had happened in that case. He took me to some ordinary residents in the Msinga area to hear their thoughts on the dispute.

In the words of an older man whom I interviewed, 'A person's livestock is like a person – would you keep quiet about a person's death on your property?' He and the middle-aged woman I was interviewing together were of the view that, after the death of the second animal at the latest, the victim should have gone to her neighbours to ask them to help her enquire into what had happened and why these animals had died on her property. Her failure to do this – especially as a single woman who, they assumed, would ordinarily count on her neighbours to help her in any eventuality (the implication being that she should) – was understood to strongly suggest that she must be guilty of killing the goats with Tamaron, as she had been suspected of doing.

Why did the victim remain relatively silent rather than solicit an investigation into the numerous goats' deaths when the social expectation was that she would initiate an investigation after the second, if not the first, and thereby avoid personal suspicion? The victim herself claimed that her Christian beliefs led her to keep to herself and not talk too much, because she believes that '***ukuthula kudala ukuthula; izinkulumo zidala izinkulumo***' (quiet breeds peace while talk breeds dissension/discord).

By contrast, living 'as an island', as the community members saw it, was not an option that was to be entertained. In their view, living this way just is not done, no matter what one's beliefs. Thus, as far as the chief's court and ordinary community members were concerned, the victim's fault was not so much in that she had remained silent about the threat made against her but in that she had not widely publicised each of the livestock deaths that preceded it. Therefore, whatever the outcome of the case in the chief's court for any other parties to the dispute(s), the woman who was shot would likely have to pay a fine, as well as MaSmumu, who issued the threat (presuming that MaLwazi, who witnessed this, would testify that she had heard it said).

I later learned from the victim by phone that MaLwazi had appeared before the court but had not told the court from whom she had heard the threat. MaSmumu refused to appear before the court.

In the end, according to the shooting victim, in December 2014, the matter lay unresolved. The court had asked the primary witness, MaLwazi, to pay money to the court to close the case. MaThembile said she was not contented. She still wanted to know from MaLwazi who the person was who MaLwazi claimed to know had fired his gun outside MaThembile's house. MaThembile victim told me that (almost four years later) she still felt fearful and insecure, as a consequence of this unsatisfactory failure to properly resolve the matter. She also bemoaned the chief's court's receipt of money when she had gone uncompensated, although she was the one who had suffered personal harm.

This case in wider context

We cannot understand relationships – and, by extension, dispute management – in Msinga outside of their noteworthy historical, politico-legal and socio-economic context. Though it is surely unique to Msinga in some ways, this context relates to the political economy of South Africa at large – especially the systems of capitalist oppression that prevailed under colonialism and apartheid. These systems had devastating long-term effects on black families and communities, especially those in rural areas.

Scholars have described the dispossession of land and productive capacity, the forced participation in the modern economy of which migrant black male labour was the primary backbone, and the consequent fragmentation of family, community, and society that all resulted from the oppressive colonial system(s) and social engineering of apartheid.[2] They have described the implications of all this for several aspects of the lives of black people living in rural areas.

Land and leadership

Msinga was one of the first areas to be designated a reserve (or reservation) of the British-ruled Natal Colony in 1848.[3] Such a designation meant that black people were assigned to live there under the policy of 'indirect rule'.[4] This designation also subjected the exclusively black residents to discriminatory state laws that denied them the right to vote nationally, allowed traditional leaders to govern almost despotically over black residents, and made black residents wholly available to serve the labour needs of the industrialising colonial economy. The apartheid government reconceived the reserves on an artificially 'tribal' basis. From the 1950s, the government speciously named the reserves 'independent homelands' (or 'Bantustans'). 'Zululand' was designated such.[5] Though Msinga was never incorporated into 'Zululand', as a magisterial district, it was effectively managed like a Bantustan.[6]

2 Chanock, Martin (2001) *The Making of South African Legal Culture 1902–1936: Fear, Favour and Prejudice.* Cambridge, UK, Cambridge University Press; Cousins, Ben, Rauri Alcock, Ngididi Dladla, Donna Hornby, Mphethethi Masondo, Gugu Mbatha, Makhosi Mweli and Creina Alcock (2011) '*Imithetho yomhlaba yaseMsinga:* The Living Law of Land in Msinga District, KwaZulu-Natal'. PLAAS Research Report 43, The University of the Western Cape, Cape Town; Hunter, Mark (2005) 'Cultural Politics and Masculinities: Multiple-Partners in Historical Perspective in KwaZulu-Natal' in G. Reid and L. Walker (eds.) *Men Behaving Differently: South African Men since 1994.* Cape Town, Juta, 139–160; Mager, Anne (1999) *Gender and the Making of a South African Bantustan: A Social History of the Ciskei, 1945–1959.* Portsmouth, NH, Heinemann/Oxford, James Currey/Cape Town, David Philip; Marks, Shula (1989) 'Patriotism, Patriarchy and Purity: Natal and the Politics of Zulu Ethnic Consciousness' in L. Vail (ed.) *The Creation of Tribalism in Southern Africa.* Berkeley, CA, University of California Press, 215–240; O'laughlin, Bridget, Henry Bernstein, Ben Cousins and Pauline E. Peters (2013) 'Introduction: Agrarian Change, Rural Poverty and Land Reform in South Africa since 1994' *Journal of Agrarian Change*, 13(1): 1–15; Redding, Sean (2004) 'Death in the Family: Domestic Violence, Witchcraft Accusations and Political Militancy in Transkei, South Africa, 1904–1965' *Journal of South African Studies*, 30(3): 519–538.

3 Meintjes, Louise (2017) *Dust of the Zulu: Ngoma Aesthetics after Apartheid.* Durham, NC, Duke University Press at 3–5.

4 Mamdani, Mahmood (1996) *Citizen and Subject: Contemporary Africa and the Legacy of Late Colonialism.* Princeton, NJ, Princeton University Press.

5 Ibid. at 102, states that, by 1990, 50% of black South Africans were residing in Bantustans (so called 'independent homelands', though they were actually enforced reserves) that covered only 14% of the nation's land territory.

6 Meintjes (above) at 61–62.

With respect to the governance of rural communities like Msinga, scholars have depicted the ways in which the legitimacy of traditional leadership is in question after having been co-opted, distorted, and undermined by the apartheid government. They describe how this relationship between traditional leadership and oppressive government has led to traditional leaders' loss of the legitimacy they once had, based on reciprocity and mutual accountability with the communities they served.[7] Msinga itself is unique in this regard, as the traditional leadership there maintains a relatively high level of legitimacy and respect. People can still trace the bloodlines of the traditional leaders and largely continue to see the traditional leadership as their own.

The distortion of traditional leadership in rural areas was intimately linked with the land dispossession that rural communities also experienced. The government tried to reverse urbanisation by forcing black people to relocate to demarcated areas that were placed under the formal administration of traditional leaders.[8] Only those black people who were needed to perform labour in the urban areas were granted permission to stay in urban townships and hostels.[9] The remainder were legally restricted to increasingly overcrowded, overburdened and desperately poor reserved landholdings such as Bantustans and Msinga.[10]

7 Delius, Peter (2008) 'Contested Terrain: Land Rights and Chiefly Power in Historical Perspective' in Aninka Claassens and Ben Cousins (eds.) *Land, Power & Custom: Controversies Generated by South Africa's Communal Land Rights Act.* Cape Town, UCT Press, 211–235; Ntsebeza, Lungisile (2006) *Democracy Compromised: Chiefs and the Politics of Land in South Africa*, African edn. Cape Town, HSRC Press; Mamdani (above); Mnisi Weeks, Sindiso (2011) 'Securing Women's Property Inheritance in the Context of Plurality: Negotiations of Law and Authority in Mbuzini Customary Courts and Beyond' *Acta Juridica*, 140–173; Oomen, Barbara (2005) *Chiefs in South Africa: Law, Power and Culture in the Post-Apartheid Era.* Oxford, James Currey.

8 Native Administration Act 38 of 1927 and Bantu Authorities Act 68 of 1951.

9 Mamdani (above) at 96–102; Chanock (above) at 34–35, 329. According to Mamdani (above) at 97, by 1947, at least one million informal settlers were in the cities, accounting for 57.5% of the black urban population.

10 Note that the municipality of Msinga comprises six traditional communities or 'tribes' and a population that is 99.5% rural, black and isiZulu speaking. According to Lehohla, Pali (Statistician-General) (2012) *Census 2011 Municipal Report – KwaZulu-Natal.* Statistics South Africa Report No. 03–01–53 at 65, of Msinga's total population of 177,577 in 2011, only 796 were recorded as being of a race other than 'Black (African)'. Of the total population at that time, 101,399 were aged 19 and under. The present study is based in six wards in two deep rural traditional communities in the municipality; five of which are located in Msinga District and one in Muden. Lehohla (above) at 161, says that the Census shows that in 2011 there were 37,724 households in Msinga (with a total household population size of 174,855). The studied population largely resides in the subset of 25,142 households whose main dwelling is a 'traditional dwelling' (at 163), the subset of 20,520 households that have 'no access to piped (tap) water' (at 172), the subset of 27,911 households who have access to only a 'communal/own refuse dump' with no municipal or private refuse removal (at 174), and the subset of 23,183 households whose toilet facility is a pit latrine (at 176). At 178–189, the average household income in Msinga in 2011 was recorded as R35,939 as compared to R112,830 in the state's largest city of Durban (the third largest city in South Africa).

Gender and the economy

A well-researched aspect of the political economy of rural areas like Msinga relates to prevailing notions of masculinity and femininity. The latter half of this book draws heavily on this research to understand and contextualise the ways in which black men and women's socio-economic positions and identities have been placed in perpetual crisis by the very severe poverty and social disruption that their families and communities have endured.[11] Linked to that is the fact that, since 1921, marriage rates have been recorded as steadily declining under these arrangements, with notable implications for social stability and attitudes.[12]

Emasculated and infantilised by an oppressive system of government and unjust social experiment that deprived them of autonomy, material and physical security, as well as dignity, black men were still in a somewhat better position than black women. The early consequences of colonialism and apartheid for women – who were also denied the very goods that men were – included the denial of any independence they might have had under their traditional cultures. The extremely conservative colonial and apartheid governments perpetually fretted over women's purportedly loose morals and, later, their rapid urbanisation.[13]

Men were generally co-opted by the state to use the levers of the colonial and apartheid state's power to strengthen their own position against women. One of these levers was the government's explicit legislation of patriarchy. Consider the provisions of the KwaZulu Act on the Code of Zulu Law and Natal Code of Zulu Law.[14] Their very similar sections 20 prescribed that:

> The family head is the owner of all family property in his family home. He has charge, custody and control of the property attaching to the houses of his several wives and may in his discretion use the same for his personal

11 Hunter, Mark (2005) 'Cultural Politics and Masculinities: Multiple-Partners in Historical Perspective in KwaZulu-Natal' in G. Reid and L. Walker (eds.) *Men Behaving Differently: South African Men since 1994.* Cape Town, Juta, 139–160; McClendon, Thomas (1995) 'Tradition and Domestic Struggle in the Courtroom: Customary Law and the Control of Women in Segregation-Era Natal' *International Journal of African Historical Studies*, 28(3): 527–561.

12 Claassens, Aninka (2013) 'Recent Changes in Women's Land Rights and Contested Customary Law in South Africa' *Journal of Agrarian Change*, 13(1): 71–92; Hosegood, Victoria, Nuala McGrath and Tom Moultrie (2009) 'Dispensing with Marriage: Marital and Partnership Trends in Rural KwaZulu-Natal, South Africa 2000–2006' *Demographic Research*, 20(13): 279–312; Mhongo, Christine and Debbie Budlender (2013) 'Declining Rates of Marriage in South Africa: What Do the Numbers and Analysts Say?' *Acta Juridica*, 181–196. Also see Yarbrough, Michael W. (2017) 'Very Long Engagements: The Persistent Authority of Bridewealth in a Post-Apartheid South African Community' *Law and Social Inquiry.*

13 Mamdani (above) at 81, describes how a British native commissioner expressed horror in finding that Ndebele women were so liberated as to be permitted to choose their own spouses unrestricted and went on to recommend that the Natal Code of 1891 be applied to the Ndebele in order to limit such practices. Also see Marks (above); McClendon (above).

14 First legislated in 1876–78, this was ultimately published in Proclamation R151 of 1987, GG No. 10966. See McClendon (above) at 527 for further discussion of the history and impact of this legislative intervention.

> wants and necessities, or for general family purposes or for the entertainment of visitors. He may use, exchange, loan or otherwise alienate or deal with such property for the benefit of or in the interests of the house to which it attaches . . . .[15]

Section 22 of the Natal Code goes on to say that '[t]he *inmates* of a family home irrespective of sex or age shall in respect of all family matters be *under the control of and owe obedience to* the family head.'[16]

The nationally applicable Native Administration Act[17] similarly provided that women were to be perpetual minors, bound by the control of their fathers, then that of their husbands.[18] Likewise, section 3 of the same Act excluded women from participating in the decision-making by what were then called 'tribes'.[19] It specifically required that 'a majority of the adult male members of the tribe present at a public meeting convened for the purpose of considering such contract or liability' as the traditional leader (then referred to as 'Chief') was undertaking on behalf of the 'tribe' make the decision on behalf of all community members.

Of course, the decisions men could really make under a racist and paternalistic order were limited, and men had meaningful restrictions on their own movements and other rights. But those on women were greater because women were not only under the control of the government but also under that of the men in their lives.[20]

These historic interventions have had lasting consequences for communities like Msinga, where change with respect to women's rights and freedoms is

15 KwaZulu Act on the Code of Zulu Law 16 of 1985.

16 Emphasis added.

17 Native Administration Act 38 of 1927 (later renamed the Black Administration Act).

18 Section 11(3)(b). Also see McClendon (above) at 539; Chanock (above).

19 The term, 'tribe', is no longer considered politically correct because tribal boundaries and identity were imposed by the apartheid government under legislation such as the Black Administration Act 38 of 1927 and Black Authorities Act 68 of 1951. Under the Traditional Leadership and Governance Framework Act 41 of 2003, these socio-politically constructed communal entities are now legally referred to as 'traditional communities'. However, the definition of a 'traditional community' is highly controversial. In Msinga, the traditional authorities translated the local term for a 'traditional community' – '*isizwe*' – as 'tribe'. In this book, I translate izizwe (plural) as 'vernacular groupings' or 'nations'. When on occasion I refer to a nation's formal delineation in colonial or apartheid legislation, I use the historical term 'tribe' in inverted commas; and periodically, when referring to isizwe as it is defined in contemporary legislation, I use the legal descriptor, 'traditional community'. See Claassens, Aninka (2005) 'Women, Customary Law and Discrimination: The Impact of the Communal Land Rights Act' *Acta Juridica*, 42; Claassens, Aninka and Sindiso Mnisi (2009) 'Rural Women Redefining Land Rights in the Context of Living Customary Law' *South African Journal on Human Rights*, 25(3): 491–516; Mnisi Weeks, Sindiso (Summer 2012) 'Regulating Vernacular Dispute Resolution Forums: Controversy Concerning the Process, Substance and Implications of South Africa's Traditional Courts Bill' *Oxford University Commonwealth Law Journal*, 12(1): 133–155 for further discussion.

20 See McClendon (above) at 539; Chanock (above).

happening slowly. For instance, in one of the two communities studied – *Nezikhathi*,[21] a community of approximately 80,000 people – the legislative council made the decision in 2010 that single women (particularly those with children) would be allowed to acquire plots of land and thus live independently. In the other community studied (about 50,000 strong), commitment to these restrictions remains.[22]

Migrant labour and taxation

The challenges named in the subsections above are deeply linked with the tightly controlled movements of black people, which were most significantly affected by the migrant labour system set up by the colonial and apartheid governments. Under this system, black men were used as cheap labour in mining, agriculture and industry in the formal economy. Several researchers have shown how employment, income, and wealth were severely defined and impacted by the structure of the economy under apartheid, in which black people were at extreme disadvantage.[23]

Along with poverty and deprivation,[24] government-instituted taxes that were not to be used to serve and develop the otherwise neglected 'native' communities forced rural men into formal employment, which was the only place where they could earn the currency required to pay state taxes. Later, traditional leaders developed the ability to use government sanctions to enforce independent levies – these sanctions included denying their 'subjects' requisite stamps in their passes and thus preventing them from travelling to the cities where they had employment.[25] These 'tribal levies' persist as a source of income for traditional institutions today, even in Msinga.

In terms of the imposed migrant labour system, black men were required to leave their families for six months to two years at a time in order to go and work for the mines, farms and industries that provided their employment. Yet, their cultural value system maintained that the mark of a man is that he

21 The two Traditional Communities studied in this book project are partially anonymised by changing their names to *Nezikhathi* and *Nakudala*.

22 Seemingly regardless of the formal rules made by the Traditional Councils, according to Lehohla (above), in 2011, the percentage of female-headed households in Msinga was 66.7 and child-headed households was 1.7.

23 Campbell, Catherine (1992) 'Learning to Kill? Masculinity, the Family and Violence in Natal' *Journal of Southern African Studies* (Special Issue Political Violence in Southern Africa), 18(3): 614–628; Cross, Catherine (2002) 'Peri-Urban Land Tenure in the Age of AIDS: Report on the KwaNyuswa Case Studies' *The Impact of HIV/AIDS on Land Issues in KwaZulu-Natal Province South Africa*. Pretoria, South Africa, Integrated Rural and Regional Development, Human Sciences Research Council; Hunter (above); Marks (above).

24 Meintjes (above) at 36, 62–63.

25 Claassens, Aninka (2011) 'Resurgence of Tribal Levies: Double Taxation for the Rural Poor' *SA Crime Quarterly*, 35: 11–16.

maintains a strong household, even as it became increasingly difficult for them to achieve this.

As Mark Hunter observes, this equivocal set of circumstances placed men in a double bind:

> Certainly, one can easily underestimate the extent that aspiring for manhood in the mid-century placed men in an extremely ambiguous position; building a rural home and family forced men to work in towns and yet the consequences of this separation often undermined the very institution men sought to construct.[26]

Hunter explains that this led to an identity crisis that was suffered by black men and backlash against increasingly independent and (albeit barely) self-sufficient black women.[27]

Economic and social decline

It did not help when the rural economy collapsed in the 1980s and early 1990s. Indeed, in the context of the massive decline then suffered by the rural economy, which was built on disappearing migrant labour jobs, a deep poverty set in. As a consequence, we continue to see tremendous income and wealth disparities between black people – especially those in rural areas – and the rest of the South African population.

Msinga is no different in this respect.[28] Once a feeder for the migrant labour needs of mines and factories, mostly in Johannesburg, Msinga had once had a dedicated employment office situated there. Now, the employment office is gone, and deep rural Msinga allegedly experiences levels of real unemployment approaching 80% and poverty rates in excess of 72%.[29]

As part of the tools of oppressive state control under colonialism, forced removals and relocations left the people of Msinga on largely barren, thorny,

26 Hunter (above) at 394. Also see Meintjes (above) at 45; Waetjen, Thembisa (2004) *Workers and Warriors: Masculinity and the Struggle for Nation in South Africa*. Urbana, University of Illinois Press.

27 Hunter (above) at 397–398. Also see McClendon (above) at 539.

28 Meintjes (above), at 22 and 41, records growth in unemployment from the 1970s.

29 These numbers are estimates based on census data, from Demography SA and empirical research. Lehohla (above) at 159 notes a formal unemployment rate of 49.5% (down from 78.7% in 2001 and 79.8% in 1996). Ben Cousins and Donna Hornby *with* Makhosi Mweli, Rauri Alcock, Mphethethi Masondo, Gugu Mbatha, Ngididi Dladla (October 2009) '*Imithetho yomhlaba yaseMsinga:* The Land Laws of Msinga and Potential Impacts of the Communal Land Rights Act', unpublished report of the Church Agricultural Projects (CAP) and the Learning and Action Project (LEAP) at 9 observe that, in 1991, the Msinga municipality as a whole had an unemployment rate of 63% among the 39% of Msinga residents who are economically active (a low number reflected in the fact that 42% of Msinga residents are aged 5–20). Also see Meintjes (above) at 5–6, and Smythe, Dee (2015) *Rape Unresolved: Policing Sexual Offences In South Africa*. Cape Town, University of Cape Town Press at 62–66.

unproductive terrain, where agriculture is a very limited option on which people are required to build their livelihoods and sustain their precarious existence.[30] Though many maintain livestock, overgrazing, climate change and the growing frequency and duration of droughts in the Msinga microclimate (which was already prone to dryness) repeatedly undercut this form of wealth creation.[31] The one rapidly growing form of economic activity – marijuana cultivation – is illegal.[32]

The economic crash left men unemployed and women predominantly responsible for child-rearing. With respect to the former, young men in Msinga are faced with chronic and severe unemployment. They consequently continue to experience the effects of colonialism and apartheid on their identities and ability to fully participate in their communities. According to Louise Meintjes:

> In the new millennium, it is a challenge to accumulate the authority of proper Zulu men without knowing 'the nice of the world'. To reach maturity, men must negotiate the discrepancies between the lingering hegemonic idea of Zulu manhood promoted by Zulu nationalist discourse and its seeming unattainability.[33]

Put differently, while proper Zulu manhood remains acutely difficult to sustain, young men must still negotiate a pathway into mature adulthood within the community, albeit that it is a challenge to acquire 'proper' Zulu male authority without any real prospects of income generation. In this respect, young men share the struggles progressively experienced by their fathers and grandfathers as colonialism and apartheid systematically restricted their ability to accumulate wealth and acquire the independence they needed to become recognised as "adult men" according to their culture.

On the latter point of women bearing primary responsibility for providing for children, the democratic government intervened to provide some support through social grants. These grants are primarily delivered to families through women in two ways. First, women receive the childcare grants as the presumed primary caregivers of children. Second, since women live longer than men and grandmothers are often providing some primary care to their grandchildren, women's pension grants contribute to sustaining families also. Men are commonly accused of drinking any money they have away. Indeed, alcohol plays a big role in disputes in which men (and sometimes women) are the primary actors in Msinga. In the sessions in which we reported back to the traditional authorities after the research period, members of the traditional councils bemoaned the negative impact alcohol has on the local community.

30 Cousins et al. (above).

31 Meintjes (above) at 42–43 notes that these challenges, accompanied by livestock disease and the encroachment of industrial agriculture, were also contributors to men's joining the formal economy in the 1920s and 1930s as well.

32 Ibid. at 6.

33 Ibid. at 41–42.

In keeping with these gendered realities, the Community Agency for Social Enquiry (CASE) found, in a 2010 study,[34] that social grants are the main source of income in Msinga. With female-headed households making up significant proportions,[35] children are substantially raised by their mothers, with the children's fathers in the picture to a relatively limited degree. If one looks at those household members who are substantially present throughout the year, 36% of households in Msinga are effectively female-headed – as opposed to the 10% reported by survey respondents when initially asked about this phenomenon.[36]

The predominance of children being raised by their mothers is probably greater than the numbers of female-headed households would indicate: according to the CASE data, just because children grow up in homes with males does not necessarily mean that they grow up in homes with males who are their fathers. Often their mothers are still living at home with their birth families. In fact, according to the study, women living with their kinsmen as opposed to their spouses or partners make up a meaningful proportion of Msinga society.

Forty-six per cent of adult women in Msinga reported that they were married, 1.7% that they were separated or divorced, and 29.6% that they were widowed. Hence, though Msinga maintains higher rates of marriage and has lower rates of female-headed households than the other two rural areas with which it was compared in the CASE study,[37] it remains true of Msinga that women are most likely to be independent of spouses. By contrast with the other areas, however, women in Msinga are unlikely to be independent of men.[38]

Health and violence

If one understands violence comprehensively and therefore as not only physical,[39] then health and violence in rural South Africa are wholly connected. Regarding this, Meintjes writes:

34 Budlender, Debbie, Sibongile Mgweba, Ketleetso Motsepe and Leilanie Williams (2011) *Women, Land and Customary Law*. South Africa, Community Agency for Social Enquiry.

35 Cf. Lehohla (above) at 180 – based on Census data, female-headed households made up 66.7% in Msinga District in 2011 – and Walker, Cheryl (2009) 'Elusive Equality: Women, Property Rights and Land Reform in South Africa' *South African Journal on Human Rights*, 25(3): 467 at 476 states that they average around 44% in rural areas in general. Also see Debbie Budlender's analysis in Claassens, Aninka and Sizani Ngubane (2008) 'Women, Land and Power: The Impact of the Communal Land Rights Act' in Aninka Claassens and Ben Cousins (eds.) *Land, Power & Custom: Controversies Generated by South Africa's Communal Land Rights Act*. Cape Town, Juta at 154–183 at 168 fn 22., which concludes that women form 58.9% of those living in rural areas.

36 Budlender et al. (above) at 49.

37 Keiskammahoek, Eastern Cape, and Ramatlabama, North West Province.

38 See Mnisi Weeks, Sindiso (2013) 'Women's Eviction in Msinga: The Uncertainties of Seeking Justice' *Acta Juridica*, 118–142.

39 Spivak, Gayatri Chakravorty (1988) 'Can the Subaltern Speak?' in Cary Nelson (ed.) *Marxism and the Interpretation of Culture*. Illinois, University of Illinois Press at 271–316 developed the concept of 'epistemic violence'. Also see Gramsci, Antonio (1971) *The*

> The trajectories that render young African bodies vulnerable post apartheid stretch back through apartheid, through South African state building over the course of the twentieth century, through colonialism in southern Africa. Forms of violence are present throughout. Inattention to African disease and radically unequal health facilities are components of colonialism and apartheid as they are in the new era. Radical unemployment began in the 1970s, struggles to earn and to secure wages were present alongside industrialization through the twentieth century, and the struggle to subsist prior to this forced men and women to enter the cash economy of wage labor.[40]

Hence, the ill health that plagues people in places like Msinga is deeply linked with the epistemic, political and socio-economic violence they suffered at the hands of the state.

As shown, a major consequence of the various injustices suffered by black, rural families and communities under state-perpetrated violence has been social decay. Scholars have demonstrated that severe decline in physical health is another consequence of this same violence. Specifically, they have shown the severe inequity of affliction that existed throughout the colonial and apartheid period and how this persists in the diseases that present in these impoverished communities today.[41] In Msinga, HIV/AIDS[42] and tuberculosis present notable challenges that are slowly being overcome by systematic intervention by the local (research) hospital.

To understand Msinga fully, a final aspect of its political economy requires explaining. Msinga has a very heavy presence of (mostly illegal) firearms. Creina Alcock reports that, in 1868, men who had walked over 600km to work as diamond miners in Kimberley earned guns as part of their wages.[43] She notes that there was a rumour at the time that Zulu men already possessed thousands of firearms. These rumours seemed to be borne out by 1932, when guns were increasingly being used in the place of spears in local fighting, with bullet wounds bearing testimony.[44]

The critical thing to observe here is that guns are a significant part of the comprehensively violent conflict landscape in Msinga[45] and, hence, one of the

---

Philosophy of Praxis: Selections from the Prison Notebooks of Antonio Gramsci. New York, International Publishers Co.; Niebuhr, Reinhold (2013) *Moral Man and Immoral Society: A Study in Ethics and Politics*. Louisville, Kentucky, Westminster John Knox Press; Said, Edward (1979) *Orientalism*. New York, Vintage, 1994.

40 Meintjes (above) at 22.

41 O'laughlin, Bridget (2013) 'Land, Labour and the Production of Affliction in Rural Southern Africa' *Journal of Agrarian Change*, 13(1): 175–196; Cross (above).

42 Cousins, et al. (above) at 9.

43 Ibid. at 25.

44 Ibid.

45 Meintjes (above) at 288 fn 30 says 'Consider what it might mean to be a gun trade center in a gun-ridden nation. At the millennium's turn, there were 4.2 million licensed firearms in South Africa (Cock 2001, 48). This figure is high for a country of about forty million people, giving some indication of the density of weapon ownership in a hotspot like Msinga.

dimensions of disputing that local forums are continuously required to manage. This observation relates to the shooting that was at the centre of the dispute that opened this chapter.

Lessons to be drawn from the case of MaThembile

Of several jarring disputes that I have come across in the process of completing this project, the case of MaThembile has haunted me more than any other. Yet it has also probably taught me the most about the nature of disputing and its management in Msinga.

At numerous points, I have found myself returning to this case as a reference point – either to ground me again in the basics of what I learned early, through it, about disputing in Msinga or to compare and contrast disputes that presented what at least looked like or were notable differences. I open this book with it because it holds a plethora of meaning in it and therefore, by it, I can show the reader the essence of what I hope they too will learn about disputing and dispute management in vernacular groupings in reading this book.

Nature of disputes

First of all, this case reveals a multitude of key points about the *nature* of disputes in Msinga. To begin with, it can help the reader appreciate the setting of disputes in Msinga. People's lives are very entwined, but often people live in relatively dispersed arrangements. In one sense Msinga is crowded because, pre-colonially, people had much more space and territorial freedom. It was with forced removals during colonialism and apartheid that people were compelled into closer living arrangements – particularly compelled into and confined to the so-called 'homelands'.[46] Yet, the area is also very spacious, as there are often vast distances between clusters of homes, especially considering that people must typically walk between them because there is limited transportation available in the area.

People's homesteads tend to be arranged in clusters with a few neighbours' homesteads surrounding them or nearby. Individual homesteads are comprised of a handful of brightly coloured, individual rondavels (small huts) spread out on the family property. While still rare, more modern houses are becoming a more common feature – as complements to the huts on some people's properties – and government-supplied outside toilets have become commonplace.

Such easy availability of guns ups the opportunities and perhaps the felt necessities of gun ownership as well as the potential for serious injury (Cock 2001), while the display of weaponry, as well as its use, is a product of years of opposition to apartheid. (Xaba 2001).'Also see Cock, Jacklyn (2001) 'Gun Violence and Masculinity in South Africa' in Robert Morrell (ed.) *Changing Men in South Africa*. London, Zed Books, 43–56 and Smythe, Dee (2015) *Rape Unresolved: Policing Sexual Offences In South Africa*. Cape Town, University of Cape Town Press at 73.

46 Delius (above); Meintjes (above) at 3–5, 41–43.

There are no street lamps and mostly only unpaved, gravel roads or footpaths. With these spatial arrangements, one can understand how an assassin could easily reach a lone woman who slept in a small house on her own or with her two children, her neighbours at some distance, and attempt to kill her around 11 p.m., when most people had gone to sleep. As it happens, in the actual case, the neighbours were definitely within earshot and one neighbour was a mere stone's throw away. MaThembile also lives quite close to a major arterial road that leads to the nearby town of Tugela Ferry.

The next thing that stands out as important is the effect of people's lives being very enmeshed with those of their neighbours and kin: disputes are almost always between people who know one another.[47] In addition, because of the regularity of their interaction with those nearby, it is common for there to be long-existing tensions and differences between people that can then take a malicious turn. One sees this assumed tension in the nephew-by-name's first asking MaThembile who might have done this to her and in his insisting that her shooting could not have been random.

Arguably, the nephew was so acutely aware of the commonality of personal tensions as a source of conflict that he insisted that the victim think of acquaintances of hers who might have a grudge against her and might, therefore, have sought to harm her. She notes two sets of people with whom she had had what – in her testimony – were minor differences in the past.

Of course, the fact that MaThembile did not perceive a shared experience to be injurious to another does not preclude that other person from perceiving the incident as injurious to him or her. The goats' deaths are an instance of precisely this: if we temporarily take MaThembile at her word that she had not deliberately killed the goats, she had not perceived their deaths as an injurious experience that would warrant her murder. Yet it would seem that, for at least one party, the death of the goats had been such an injury.

Within this socio-legal context, it is unsurprising that some prior wrong surfaced as grounds for the present wrong of MaThembile's shooting. This fact of wrongs building on prior ones is in keeping with the relational nature of conflict in Msinga.[48] Also consistent with this deep-seated relationality of conflict, what escalated the disagreement was the nephew's accusing his drinking buddy.

Several factors can be highlighted here: first, the escalation of the conflict by means of the spoken word, especially an accusation; second, the role played by alcohol in many conflicts, especially those to do with verbal offences, with such altercations often escalating to the use of firearms; and, third, the profiles of

47 Hammond-Tooke, David (1989) *Rituals and Medicines: Indigenous Healing in South Africa*. Johannesburg, Ad. Donker; Redding, Sean (September 2004) 'Death in the Family: Domestic Violence, Witchcraft Accusations and Political Militancy in Transkei, South Africa, 1904–1965' *Journal of South African Studies*, 30(3); Van Beek, Walter E. A. (2006) 'The Escalation of Witchcraft Accusations' in Gerrie Ter Haar (ed.) *Imagining Evil: Witchcraft and Accusations in Contemporary Africa*.

48 Ibid.

those involved in the escalation of the conflict – namely, young men and older women. Let me address these each in turn.

One finds that, in Msinga, conflicts often rapidly scale up to interpersonal violence because of the wide availability of illegal guns. The reality that a person who is only suspected and not yet proven to be guilty might be punished in the alleged manner that MaThembile was can also be linked to the fragility of life in Msinga. Very often what escalates the conflict is something someone says. Rumour plays a substantial role in conflict – that is, often people will end up in an outright dispute because of something someone said to someone else. It is most frequently the case that 'the something that was said' was said by an adult woman. Thus, it is in keeping with the rest of the empirical findings presented in this book that the dispute here was escalated, at least in part, by the mother of the drinking buddy who it seems spread the rumour that she and another female relation of hers were the ones accused of hiring her son to kill the shooting victim.

Yet it is not absolutely out of the pale that the young men should have participated in escalating the dispute by what the nephew said to his drinking buddy. In fact, this study shows that, where alcohol is concerned, both young men (aged 16–25) and adult or grown men (roughly aged 26–59)[49] are most often involved and, when violence is combined with alcohol, young men are the common actors or, at least, the most commonly accused. Indeed, it is young men who are often hired as assassins,[50] even if I find that they are not the only ones in possession of (usually illegal) firearms, which are often owned by adult men too.

It is important to note the potency here of rumour.[51] In my naïveté, when MaThembile had called me for assistance because she was concerned about the

49 As distinct from boys (up to age 15) and old men (aged 60 and older). These are age categories that emerge from the data as being important. They are roughly consistent with the meaning, symbolism and significance that Msinga people ascribe to age, though there is some ambiguity and overlap between ages 25 and 30, wherein men can be considered both young men and adult (that is, grown) men. Part of what can influence in which category men between the ages of 25 and 30 are included is whether or not they are married and therefore head up their own family or home. Young men are generally referred to, by adult men, as 'boys'. I apply the same general categories to women, a subset of whom (young women, roughly aged 16–25) are generally referred to by adult women (approximately between the ages of 26 and 59) and older women (aged 60 and above) – as well as by all men – as 'girls'.

50 Also see Mthembu, Bhekuyise Isaac (October 1994) *Faction Fighting in Msinga District from 1874 to 1906* – A Dissertation submitted to the Faculty of Arts in the fulfillment of the requirements for the degree of Master of Arts in the Department of History at the University of Zululand Kwa-Dlangezwa. (Supervisor: Prof. S. J. Maphalala) at vi–vii. Mthembu writes that young men 'are used as hired killers only to meet the same fate themselves eventually.'

51 Stewart, Pamela J. and Andrew Strathern (2003) *Witchcraft, Sorcery, Rumors and Gossip.* West Nyack, NY, USA, Cambridge University Press. Speaking of the role of witchcraft, rumours and gossip in Zambia, Stewart and Strathern observe at 61–62: 'Public opinion, however – for which we may read rumor and gossip – had made of many of these objects

rumour that she would be fined by the chief's court, I had told her to wait until the judgment was handed down (rather than act on a rumour). I gave this advice before I had developed a better appreciation for just how much potency rumours carry in Msinga. It would seem that she had only recently developed that same appreciation: after all, she had not reported the alleged murder threat made against her a year before her shooting.

Put simply, accusatory rumours can be enough to get a person killed.[52] The first attempt on MaThembile's life had, it would seem, been the consequence of a rumour that she had killed the goats that had died on her property. She had then heard through a third party a rumour that some known person had fired the initial shot outside of her home a year earlier, an action that she interpreted to be based on a contract on her life made in response to the rumoured offence of killing people's goats. She was then directly threatened that if a goat belonging to her neighbour's son were to die, real harm would come upon her. She was now hearing a rumour that she was going to be fined by the chief's court – a rumoured outcome that my sources confirmed was likely and even reasonable.

It is interesting that, though I never heard that MaThembile was directly accused of witchcraft, her case presents as a classic witchcraft accusation case.[53] MaThembile was a socially marginalised woman who, it seemed, would not wholly conform to her neighbourhood's expectations.[54] Of this, Gordon Chavunduka explains that witchcraft accusations may be a tool for achieving social control:

> The [witchcraft] accusation may be a response to a situation of anxiety and stress or a means for the expression of social strain and tensions. These accusations, then, often act as a force buttressing the moral code of society. . . . Although these are not legal issues, they are cultural, social and psychological issues that nonetheless often call for legal attention because the consequence to the person named as a witch can be serious; violent reaction may follow.[55]

---

the irrefutable signs of the actions of witches and sorcerers. The whole ritual process instituted by the witch-finders therefore acted both as a kind of stimulus to public imagination and as a form of therapy to remove the fear of witchcraft heightened in the campaign against it.'

52 Ibid. at 64–65: 'As the chiefs' control and group cohesion decline, gossip and rumor, with their potential for violence, increase in intensity and scope.'

53 See Redding (above). Also see Comaroff, Jean and John L. Comaroff, eds. (1993) *Modernity and Its Malcontents: Ritual and Power in Postcolonial Africa*. Chicago, IL, Chicago University Press.

54 Van Beek (above) at 300. Also see Chavunduka, Gordon L. (2000) 'Notes on African Witchcraft' in John Hund (ed.) *Witchcraft Violence and the Law in South Africa*. Pretoria, Protea Book House at 137.

55 Ibid. Also see Van Beek (above) at 304: 'Witchcraft accusations result from stress, often within important relationships at the local level: kinship relations, neighbourhood relations,

The consequent risk of harm is evidently very real.

It is reasonable to deduce that, to the extent that people saw that the misfortune befalling them was MaThembile's doing and felt that their explanation was true and valid,[56] they saw that she was 'the enemy within the gates'.[57] On that basis, someone saw resorting to violence in return as a fully justified and equal measure.[58]

As Sean Redding describes (albeit with respect to the history of the Eastern Cape):

> [P]eople acted violently according to their own assessment of their problems and their causes. The principal problems that people tried to resolve through witchcraft accusations and violence often stemmed from broader social issues that they then analysed in very intimate terms. Many rural people needed an explanation for why they were unable to establish a minimum viable homestead.[59]

There is no evidence to prove it, but this explanation appears to be compelling within the context of the social issues I have discussed with reference to the political economy of South African rural areas such as Msinga. In the present instance, poverty and inequality as well as the devastating economic effects of climate change may have played a particularly important role.

When asked for an explanation of why the goats died on her property, MaThembile said that they had died from several causes beyond her control (and some beyond explanation) – most notably the severe drought with which Msinga was faced. The goats had died on *her* property because they had spent plenty

---

relations between old and young etc. The way in which these relations are defined, and how vulnerable they prove, are issues that shape witchcraft accusations. In effect, witchcraft accusations erupt when the need for explanation of personal mishap is larger than the linking relationship with the suspected witch.'

56 Redding (above) at 521; Ashforth, Adam (2005) *Witchcraft, Violence, and Democracy in South Africa*. Chicago, University of Chicago Press at 11, 116–121; Ellis, Stephen and Gerrie Ter Haar (September 2007) 'Religion and Politics: Taking African Epistemologies Seriously' *The Journal of Modern African Studies*, 45(3): 385–401 at 390. Furthermore, Ellis, Stephen and Gerrie Ter Haar (1998) 'Religion and Politics in Sub- Saharan Africa' *The Journal of Modern African Studies*, 36(2): 175–201 at 177 comment on how, for many Africans in vulnerable political circumstances, their world is one 'in which power is seen as being too often an instrument of evil people who use it to destroy peace and harmony'. Ellis and Ter Haar comment at 196 on the centrality of power that is improperly controlled causing moral confusion and making it difficult for people to distinguish good from evil.

57 Van Beek (above) at 302. Also see Hammond-Tooke (above) at 81: 'The witch or sorcerer, then, is a feared and hated figure. He or she is the very image of a traitor within the gates, as Mayer (1954) puts it, the quisling, the heretic. Witches as a category are veritable fifth column within society. As such, they must be identified and eradicated as soon as possible.'

58 Redding (above) at 522, 527; Ashforth (above).

59 Redding (above) at 536.

of time there as a matter of course. She would regularly throw out old food (gone bad because she did not own a refrigerator), and the goats had gotten accustomed to eating and relaxing on her property. After the dispute, she reported that she had stopped throwing the food out in her yard and no goats had died there since.

MaThembile suggests that people might have been envious[60] of the building she had done on her property in recent years: adding two new rooms to her old house and tearing down a hut that was falling apart. Amidst the general poverty of her community (which she said actually included her own), those renovations could have been a source of envy.[61] I cannot confirm whether that was the case, but many scholars show that poverty and inequality are significant contributors to witchcraft accusations in several different ways.[62] As Pamela Stewart and Andrew Strathern articulate the point, 'Those who are successful fear the jealousy of those less fortunate than themselves, while the latter think that only by witchcraft and magic could the rich and powerful have attained their position.'[63]

The fact that those who were seemingly most vocal in accusing MaThembile were themselves women also makes her situation consistent with most witchcraft cases recorded by researchers in different places.[64] Scholars have shown that women are most often those making witchcraft accusations. In contexts in which women's social power is limited, such accusations are a means by which women exercise a substantial amount of influence.[65] This is so especially because the buildup of gossip (rumour) is often sufficient to indict an accused person.[66]

To an outsider, it might seem strange that a woman should possibly be killed for the suspected killing of people's goats, as it initially did to me. Yet, when one takes into account the fact that goats are an essential commodity – in fact, all livestock are an important source of livelihood and wealth – one appreciates their value to people in Msinga. In addition, the extreme poverty that is prevalent in Msinga makes such a response even more understandable, even if not

60 Hammond-Tooke (above) at 81.

61 Kgatla, Selaelo Thias (2006) 'Containment of Witchcraft in South Africa: A Search for a Transformational Approach to Curb the Problem' in Gerrie Ter Haar (ed.) *Imagining Evil: Witchcraft and Accusations in Contemporary Africa*. Trenton, New Jersey, Africa World Press at 285–286.

62 Harnischfeger, Johannes (2000) 'Witchcraft and the State in South Africa' in John Hund (ed.) *Witchcraft Violence and the Law in South Africa*. Pretoria, Protea Book House at 48–49; Kgatla (above) at 270.

63 Stewart and Strathern (above) at 66. They conclude: 'Witchcraft fears work in a two-way shuttle, keeping suspicion between people at a high level. Rumor and gossip fill in the blanks in people's knowledge of what 'the others' do.'

64 Wilson, Monica (1964) *Reaction to Conquest*. London, OUP at 43, as quoted in Redding (above) at 524; Hammond-Tooke (above) at 87; Ashforth (above).

65 Redding (above) at 535.

66 Van Beek (above) at 301 says, '[a] groundswell of gossip can lead to a public voicing of the accusations and a communal outcry; accusation and condemning then easily blend.'

justifiable. Thus, indeed, her suspected killing of goats was a potential reason why people might have wanted to harm her. As the older man that I interviewed so clearly stated, 'a person's livestock is like a person'.

Local attitudes and social expectations

This brings me to the second major set of revelations of this case: namely, local attitudes towards disputes and culpability, and the social expectations that surround disputes. Social expectations, especially, are typically highly gendered. These considerations also arise as important in the wider set of observations of this research. In their manifestation in the case of MaThembile specifically, we see how naïve it seems she was about her circumstances. When asked why she had not initiated a public investigation into the deaths of the goats, she answered that she had thought that if she minded her own business, then she would stay out of any problems with other people. This was a significant error of judgment on her part.

What my informants said, when I interviewed them about the case, essentially expressed the overwhelming importance placed on community and membership. Underlying their observations was that, for them, the shooting victim's situation was really one about inclusion and reliance on the community for a multitude of purposes (above all, protection) versus exclusion and marginality. By keeping to herself, she said, MaThembile believed herself to be keeping out of trouble with her neighbours. Instead, she was keeping herself out of community and the protections that come with it.

While MaThembile perceived herself as just a lone woman with no problems or differences with anyone, she was actually very vulnerable by being a single, middle-aged woman. Community members thus assumed that she should lean heavily on her surrounding neighbours for support and assistance; but, instead, she had rendered herself even more vulnerable by not doing so. Being a Christian, as she claimed, led her to keep to herself and in that way stay out of trouble, but in her neighbours' eyes this did not excuse her from this obligation.[67] She was perceived as isolating herself, and anyone who does that is thought to have something dark to hide. This is the seedbed of witchcraft accusations.

In her community's view, she was most likely culpable of something nefarious. Hence, when she was accused by rumour of killing the goats, she was presumed guilty of what she was rumoured to have done and had no one – certainly, no one powerful or credible – to defend her. As the chief's court and ordinary

67 Stewart and Strathern (above) at 61 note of Malawi in the mid-1930s that: 'The [witch-finding] movement claimed the support of the administration but was openly hostile to the Christian missionaries, who instructed their adherents not to participate in the rituals.' Opting out of cultural and religious practices is a trend in often legalistic and conservative Christian communities that reject syncretism – in which many African Christians take part.

community members insisted, the victim could have done a great deal to protect herself by going to her neighbours, as soon as the first or second goat had inexplicably died on her property, to ask them to help her enquire into what had happened and why.

Yet, even if she had not gone to report her concerns to her neighbours early on when the goats started dying on her property, there was another positive intervention that she could have later made to advocate on her own behalf. Namely, she could have brought the matter of the threat against her life to a public forum.

This strategy of publicity as a form of protection presented itself repeatedly in the current study – specifically in the context of accusations of publicly detested activities such as witchcraft, whistle-blowing and large-scale stock theft. In essence, those accused or sometimes the community that believed it was being wronged by the accused brought the matter to the headman for investigation. Indeed, the importance of this strategy was something Mfana's mother understood when she prompted Mfana to take the matter of Mbuzo's accusation that Mfana shot women for hire to *Iphoyisa*.

In most instances of these disputes brought to a vernacular forum for publicity's sake, the accusations failed on grounds of there not being sufficient evidence. While this strategy of seeking to publicise a wrong was by no means foolproof, and depended on the extent of the accused's social capital, it often served to de-marginalise the accused somewhat, which is very helpful in the circumstances of such a fatal accusation of social wrong. It is in this way that publicity served as a form – albeit modest – of protection.

Dispute management process: initiation and representation

This leads me to the final category of lessons demonstrated by the case under discussion: those pertaining to the dispute resolution process. Since access to justice is the primary focus of this book, one would probably expect that I would delve into the process by which disputes are resolved in greater detail than any of the other sets of points I draw out of the case. However, as you will find in this book, I choose to give equal attention to the question of how disputes arise in Msinga (and what causes and contributes to their regularity) as to the dispute management process. Indeed, I argue that this wider context is critical to understanding and regulating dispute management for the purposes of advancing access to justice in rural communities like Msinga.

One of the things that stands out in this case is that it was initiated in a formal dispute management forum at the behest of the husbands of the two women who were allegedly accused of hiring MaThembile's would-be assassin. While the matter that initially presents – that of defamation – actually pertains to the women, it is the men who bring the matter as a case.

Moreover, at least in the chief's court, the shooting victim was represented by her older brother. In the witness stand, MaThembile spoke for herself – but she was still not very successful at defending herself, partly because of her ambivalent position as witness and defendant. Witnesses are only supposed to answer the questions asked of them. Unfortunately for MaThembile, the one who was meant to defend her ended up putting up what seemed a weak defence. Incidentally, such ambivalence as to the role in which a party is participating in a dispute – whether as witness or defendant – is not unique to this case.

The gendered pattern is very common: conventionally, men are the ones who get to make the decision of whether to bring a dispute to a forum and are required to provide representation. Women really only have the right to appear as witnesses or supports. Yet, this is mainly the 'normative ideal' from which people in Msinga deviate in practice. Thus, I recorded several instances of women making the decision of whether to bring a matter to a forum and representing themselves and their children.

However, this deviation from the ideal norm happened mostly at the lower levels – in the headmen's policemen's and headmen's forums. In the chief's court, there was greater compliance with the normative ideal, though even there deviation sometimes occurred. Even in this case, when the chief's court had said they wanted to postpone the case, the shooting victim and her brother expressed concern around the fact that her brother worked. He would therefore have difficulty attending her case on the date that the court had scheduled continuation of the hearing. When deviation in the chief's court did occur in another case, however, the case did not turn out well for the young woman concerned (though this was also due to other reasons pertaining specifically to her unfavourable identity and the bad reputation of her brothers).

Dispute management process: postponement and escalation

The manner in which MaThembile's case was adjourned on the day that I observed it was not unusual. It happened numerous times that disputes were postponed in order to bring in the appropriate witnesses. In several instances, disputes ended with the request for witnesses, who either could not be found or refused to appear. Indeed, the same happened in this case where one of the female witnesses, MaSmumu, would not appear because she said she did not remember the pertinent conversation. The shooting victim had effectively done the same in the forum of first instance, when she had told the headman's policeman that she had nothing to say to the forum because she had not seen her shooter.

In other instances, matters terminated because the dispute management forum could not get the primary witness to tell it what she knew, such as where she had heard of the threat on another's life. MaLwazi's refusal to identify MaSmumu, in the present case, was one of a handful of such examples.

The reader can imagine that this resistance would contribute to the frustration of management forums' ability to resolve disputes. This is exactly what happened in the hearing before the local headman's policeman. And, when the matter went to the chief's court (not having been heard in the headman's forum because he said he wanted it directly escalated to the chief's court), there was no real resolution arrived at there either, for similar reasons as in the court of first instance.

This is interesting if for no other reason than this 'normative ideal': the higher the forum, the greater its ability to resolve a matter. Yet, as one sees in this case and a few others, headmen sometimes pass cases on directly to the chief's court without hearing them. This occurrence then means that some cases do not get discussed in the forums that deal with the largest proportion of disputes in the area.

This action by the lower forums is significant because the lower forums use much fewer formal dispute management methods than do the chiefs' courts. This action therefore also means that people might be disincentivised from pursuing their matters further because the chief's court is more geographically and socially removed from them. (One sees this disincentive even in the pattern of intended – or threatened – appeals from the headmen's courts to the chief's courts that are not followed through.) That said, relatively few cases are passed up by the headmen. Because of this, the disincentive that results from the headmen's action in this regard is less important than that which might be caused by the fact that the chiefs' courts do not manage to settle all disputes even when they have followed the ideal route through the headmen's courts.

Dispute management process: resolution and roles

The reality as revealed by MaThembile's case is that the chiefs' courts successfully resolve only a fraction of the cases that come before them. Though they are the highest vernacular dispute management forums, when they fail to finalise a dispute, they refer it to either the family council or the state police. The family council is technically at the bottom of the forum hierarchy, while people in the area typically find the police alienating or do not quite know how to effectively use police services to meet their justice and security needs. The police are themselves unreliable in their attempts to resolve complaints that come to them.

In the least successful of instances, disputes not finally resolved by the highest vernacular forum take on a more destructive turn. The parties either appeal to self-help measures, which can include relocation or violence, or turn to vigilante groups. The same responses sometimes occur when matters terminate at the headman's forum level but are not resolved to the complainants' satisfaction.

With respect to the proceedings in the chief's court, I observe that – contrary to the conventional wisdom of today – the 'chief' did not play a role like that of a judge. Instead, questions were asked of the parties and witnesses by the chief headman and headmen (especially one very outspoken local headman). A few questions also came from the audience made up of members of the legislative-administrative Traditional Council constituted under the Traditional Leadership and Governance Framework Act 41 of 2003 and some ordinary community members (a number of whom were there for different cases). As twentieth century ethnographers report of vernacular dispute management forums around the country, the 'chief' spoke only toward the end.[68] He handed down the decision to adjourn after it had become clear that the matter had to be postponed because forum members had said they wanted a witness.

Dispute management process: transformations

I have already mentioned that the matter of MaThembile very quickly transformed before my eyes from one focusing on defamation to one focusing on the killing of people's goats. While this is one of the most radical transformations that I saw take place in the course of a dispute, it is not the only transformation of a dispute in the qualitative data we collected. It happens that transformation of disputes – either before coming to the forum or during a forum's proceedings – is rather common.

This frequency of transformation is underscored in the focal case by the articulation by MaThembile of her lack of satisfaction once the case ended. She said she still wanted to know who had accused her of killing people's goats and had probably hired someone to try to kill her. She was also feeling afraid and insecure. In other words, the case may have been over, but the conflict was not.

This tension that regularly occurs when a case is concluded while leaving the conflict unresolved is the reason why anthropologists espouse the 'case method' for researching conflict.[69] This method of study follows conflicts from their inception in their social environment of origin to their entry into a dispute management forum (if they ever enter one) to their unfolding after any attempt at formal resolution. Within the limited time frame of February 2011 to January 2012 – and in some instances beyond that (when I conducted preliminary and follow-up interviews outside of that time period) – I have attempted to incorporate this 'case method' into my data collection methodology.

68 Comaroff, John and Simon Roberts (1981) *Rules and Processes: The Cultural Logic of Dispute in an African Context.* Chicago and London, University of Chicago at 80–83, 180; Cook, Peter Alan Wilson (1931) *Social Organisation and Ceremonial Institutions of the Bomvana.* Cape Town and Johannesburg, Juta & Co. Ltd. at 146; Dutton, Major E. A. T. (1923) *The Basuto of Basutoland.* London, Jonathan Cape at 59–60; Hammond-Tooke, William David (1975) *Command or Consensus: The Development of Transkeian Local Government.* Cape Town, David Philip at 67–68, 74; Reader, Desmond H. (1966) *Zulu Tribe in Transition: The Makhanya of Southern Natal.* Manchester, Manchester University Press at 259–260.

69 Merry, Sally Engle (1979) 'Going to Court: Strategies of Dispute Management in an American Urban Neighborhood' *Law & Society Review*, 13: 891; Miller, Richard and Austin Sarat (1980) 'Grievances, Claims, and Disputes: Assessing the Adversary Culture' *Law and Society Review*, 15: 525; Nader, Laura (2002) *The Life of the Law: Anthropological Projects.* Berkeley, CA, University of California Press; Norgren, Jill and Serena Nanda (1996) *American Cultural Pluralism and Law.* Westport, Connecticut, Praeger.

Dispute management process: costs

In the chief's court proceedings, we see that money is significant. For the matter to be heard in the chief's court as a case (rather than as a mere mediation), each party had to pay R30. As I noted, MaThembile was disturbed by being required to pay that sum – this sum very clearly flagged her as a party (or, at least, a potential party) to the dispute rather than a mere witness.

At the end of the case (from the chief's court's perspective, that is), the court asked the primary witness, MaLwazi, who refused to disclose who had issued the potentially fatal threat against MaThembile, to pay money to the court to close the case. Happily for the victim, MaThembile was spared. Yet she still bemoaned the court's demand of money in the absence of her having been compensated for her injuries, pain and suffering.

The issue of money paid to the forums, though I explore it only to a very limited degree in this book, is actually important and requires further discussion elsewhere. In communities where people are poor, it is a matter of substantial tension how high legal costs are in some areas: in one of the two chiefs' courts, the 'chief' often fined the losing party in a dispute an additional cow (valued at about R1,500 at the time), which would go to the court's coffers. This fine was the source of some disgruntlement in this traditional community.

At the time of my doing the research, headmen (and sometimes headmen's policemen) received money for the opening of cases to be heard in their forums, but they reported that they did not keep the money – it went to the courts' coffers. The headmen also did not earn an income from the government though they did much administrative, support and mediatory work in their areas of jurisdiction. Many of them were absolutely poor and were taking extremely limited resources from their families to put toward this honourable task of being a 'chief's headman' (*induna yenkosi*).

Of those headmen who were not as poor as most, one was a medicineman (*inyanga*) and another sold snacks out of the back of his bakkie (small truck). Their engagement in their other income-generating enterprises both took them away from their duties as headmen which, in turn, made them less able to pursue their income-generating enterprises. Since then, the government has decided to pay headmen a standard sum.[70] Yet, in June 2015, these payments had not yet begun,[71] and it remains unclear that all of the headmen would equally qualify for salaries.

70 R80,875 a year with benefits.

71 The headmen reported having participated in protest marches against the provincial government to demand that their gazetted salaries be paid. Several media stories appeared on this: Madlala, Mpume 'Backdated Pay Hikes for Officials', 15 January 2014 (accessible at www.iol.co.za/news/south-africa/kwazulu-natal/backdated-pay-hikes-for-officials-1.1631758); Ndaliso, Chris 'Unpaid Headmen Threaten to Disrupt Polls', 29 June 2015 (accessible at www.iol.co.za/news/politics/unpaid-headmen-threaten-to-disrupt-polls-1.1877939#.VZqDX2CFFzd).

With respect to damages and compensation, it is the party found to have been wronged who gets to demand an amount that would satisfy them. Some of the monies at stake in lower forums were substantial – even from the perspective of an outsider like myself. But, in these instances, people would typically negotiate the damages or compensation amount demanded by the relevant party down. Hence, the one found to be in the wrong would often end up paying a more manageable – albeit, usually still substantial – amount (for instance, R2,000 in damages for a false witchcraft accusation).

Monies owed would often also only be paid in installments. This, of course, made it that much more difficult for the headmen to enforce the decisions handed down by their forums – especially considering that they have to claim payment from people who often are short on money, to hear many cases and mediations and to handle other administrative obligations as well. What was interesting in some cases was that the full or partial sum owed as damages or compensation for a wrong would be paid on 'pension day'. In other words, the money would be paid out of the party's limited social grant income from the government.

Dispute management process: evidence

The final element of the dispute management process pointed to by the case used as an entry into the book's themes and findings is the courts' treatment of evidence. The clearest facet of this treatment is that evidence rests heavily on people. As mentioned earlier, adult women tend to make up the largest proportion of witnesses to what they themselves have said as well as to what others have told them that they have done or intend to do. In this very limited sense, women have a substantial amount of power, as well as responsibility and even vulnerability.

Their power and responsibility can be seen in how they can put a person's life at risk by means of direct accusation or rumour. This power is very evident in the MaThembile case but also played out, for instance, in two matters in which young men were (it seemed, falsely) accused of raping young women.[72] Women's vulnerability is visible in their common refusal to tell the forums where they heard, for example, of a threat to another's life: should the women reveal this information, the risk to their own lives as 'snitches' would be immense.

In evidentiary terms, the community also has a significant amount of social capital and credibility. Take, for instance, the social belief that MaThembile's speaking up ahead of time might have prevented her shooting. Additionally, one observes the local emphasis on her having not initiated a substantive community-wide enquiry into the livestock deaths that preceded the threat made to her life. Finally, we should note Msinga residents' regular use of the publicity defence: that is, publicising an accusation against oneself by bringing it to a

72 See cases of MaMsolile and MaMsukela.

forum in the form of a challenge of that accusation and thereby requiring that the accuser provide evidence of the truth of his or her accusation.

Access to justice – or access to human security?

This book project began with an interest in the pursuit of justice and the extent to which, and ways in which, ordinary rural people can achieve this apparently patent good. In the end, the research process has led me to question the meaning of justice and what forms of it are realistically available to people like those in Msinga, given the comprehensively challenging circumstances in which they live.

This process has consequently moved me far beyond the simple question with which I began this research, of whether the Traditional Courts Bill (B8–2008/B1–2012) or legislation like it could effectively regulate vernacular dispute management forums so as to ensure ordinary rural people adequate access to dispute resolution services. I have had to understand that disputes and the processes through which they are mediated in pursuit of solutions are means to a variety of goods that people hold dear, as well as processes of apportioning power.[73] Disputes and mediation are therefore spaces of notable 'meaning-making'.[74]

I suppose the question to which I have progressively gravitated is whether 'access to justice' in the simplistic form in which lawyers typically mean it – namely, access to a legal remedy through the courts[75] – is achievable or, perhaps, even desirable on its own. The answer I have come to is 'no'.

The reason is simple: though ordinary people in Msinga would undoubtedly benefit from vernacular forums improving their dispute management strategies and tools, the relatively limited practical changes that such forums can make are insufficient to ensure the satisfaction of the enormous needs that underlie the repeated interpersonal conflicts that arise for people in the area.

At the end of the book, I make suggestions for what changes the vernacular dispute management forums should ideally make, but the ultimate solution lies in wider systemic change. Put differently, the solution ultimately depends on changes to the system of cooperative governance to which the vernacular forums are a party, as well as the provision of greater resource support by the state. With that being the conclusion to which the empirical evidence has led me, the project at hand seems significantly broader than access to 'justice' in narrow terms. It seems to me that the wider project is one of access to 'social justice'.

Looking squarely at the conditions in which ordinary people in Msinga live, this book makes the case that access to 'justice', narrowly construed, is virtually

73 Felstiner, William, Richard Abel and Austin Sarat (1980) 'The Emergence and Transformation of Disputes: Naming, Blaming, Claiming . . .' *Law and Society Review*, 15: 631; Merry (above); Miller and Sarat (above).

74 Geertz, Clifford (1973) *The Interpretation of Cultures: Selected Essays*. New York, Basic Books.

75 Felstiner, Abel and Sarat (above) at 639.

impossible for people in Msinga without their being ensured access to justice in the comprehensive form of 'social justice'. I refer to this comprehensive social justice as 'human security'.[76]

While 'human security' – especially as used by the United Nations – has become a controversial term,[77] I can find no other concept that lends itself as well to being shaped to accommodate the totality of needs that surfaced as a precondition to 'justice' in the narrow sense for people in Msinga. This does, however, mean that I am mobilising a very particular understanding of human security – namely, that put forward by Sabina Alkire,[78] in which human security is a contextually determined subset of human development. This understanding focuses on the 'capabilities or freedoms that people enjoy' and the factors that define those capabilities and freedoms in the long term.[79] In this sense, 'human security explicitly includes responses to violence and often studies how poverty causes violence and how violence contributes to poverty.'[80] Its achievement requires the joint engagement of affected individuals and institutional actors as agents in the protection (and advancement) of the fundamental capabilities people need.[81]

The 'human security' that I describe as a fundamental need for people in Msinga is therefore not just a *physical* security (that is, freedom from violence) – though they certainly need that. Rather, it is also *social* and *material* security. Thus, I consider 'human security' to encompass *freedom from fear*, and yet argue in this book that in areas like Msinga such security depends heavily on *freedom from want* (relative economic security).[82] This is consistent with the origins of the concept. As Alkire describes it:

76 Alkire, Sabina (June 2010) *Human Development: Definitions, Critiques, and Related Concepts*. United Nations Development Program Report observes at 59 that, '[t]he idea of human security directly parallels human development and addresses a different community: those focused on defending national security.' However, the concept is still applicable here because of how comprehensive it is of physical, social, political and material security. In this vein, see Ogata, Sadako and Amartya Sen (2003) *Human Security Now: Commission on Human Security*. New York (accessible at www.resdal.org/ultimos-documentos/com-seg-hum.pdf) at iv: 'Human security is concerned with safeguarding and expanding people's vital freedoms. It requires both shielding people from acute threats and empowering people to take charge of their own lives. Needed are integrated policies that focus on people's survival, livelihood and dignity, during downturns as well as in prosperity. The demands of human security involve a broad range of interconnected issues.'

77 Alkire, Sabina (2003) *A Conceptual Framework for Human Security*, CRISE Working Paper, Centre for Research on Inequality, Human Security and Ethnicity, CRISE, Queen Elizabeth House, University of Oxford at 13–23.

78 Alkire (June 2010) at 60–61.

79 Ibid. at 60.

80 Ibid. at 61.

81 Ibid.

82 The Preamble to the Universal Declaration of Human Rights (1948) announces: 'the advent of a world in which human beings shall enjoy freedom of speech and belief and *freedom from fear and want* has been proclaimed as the highest aspiration of the common people' (my emphasis).

> This particular phrase, "human security," is most often associated with the 1994 *Human Development Report* on Human Security drafted and championed by Mahbub ul Haq, even though the term itself was in circulation earlier. The intent of human security was to bridge the freedom from want and freedom from fear, freedoms that lay at the heart of the United Nations . . . As this discussion suggests, the phrase "freedom from fear" is intended to indicate freedom from violence, and the phrase "freedom from want", freedom from poverty. It is important to bear this mental equation in mind, because of course people also fear poverty and destitution; they also want peace and police protection.[83]

Put differently, physical or personal security and social or community security demand material security. This fact points to the intimate relationship between development and security insofar as security refers to defence or protection. This book therefore makes the case for why access to justice for individuals in places like Msinga is not realistically possible without access to such sufficient resources (for individuals and communities) as will render the people who live there materially secure.

The contribution of this book: chapter outline

The book is divided into four sections. The first section focuses on vernacular forums in historical and theoretical context. It comprises Chapter 2, which initially answers the question, where do vernacular forums fit in the South African legal order? This chapter expounds on the reasons behind interest in the topic of vernacular forums. First, people continue to use these forums despite the fact that existing legislation is out of step with how they actually operate and, second, controversial draft legislation, the Traditional Courts Bill, has been proposed to regulate the forums effectively to ensure access to justice for ordinary rural people. The chapter discusses how 'traditional courts' were contentiously regulated under colonialism and apartheid and what their legal status is today (particularly relative to other courts, especially Magistrates' Courts). It particularly describes the field site studied – and briefly also the methods used – in order to obtain the information presented in this book.

Following on from the methodology, Chapter 2 then turns to theoretical discussion on what vernacular dispute management is. The chapter defines the concept of 'dispute management', and why it is more suitable than 'dispute resolution'. The chapter also discusses forum-shopping: the ability to choose between multiple kinds of forums in order to effect a claim in the forum one judges to be most likely to produce one's desired outcome in one's present conflict circumstances. This chapter draws out key points in what has previously been written about how vernacular forums operate in South Africa,

83 Alkire (2003) at 13.

presenting this information as an initial indication of what might be found in practice in Msinga.

The second section of the book focuses on the institutional attributes of dispute management in Msinga. It opens with Chapter 3, which is concerned with the subject matter that the forums deal with and therefore asks what disputes are heard. The chapter sets out the kinds of matters (civil and criminal wrongs; personal, commercial, and public wrongs) that are brought to the attention of the vernacular dispute management forums. Chapter 3 also looks at which matters the forums hear and which matters they redirect, as well as the localised and personal considerations that inform these controversial decisions. In this respect, the chapter reveals that certain matters are clearly very sensitive and make the authorities nervous; however, the deciding considerations are not necessarily generalisable across local contexts or always easily predictable. Furthermore, Chapter 3 outlines the social implications of the matters that come before these forums and the forums' abilities to deal with them effectively.

The fourth chapter – on authority – closes the second section of the book by describing the forums that make up the landscape of vernacular dispute management forums in Msinga and their jurisdictional parameters. Distinguishing 'a case' from 'a plea/cry' (a petition), the chapter briefly discusses the processes that disputes follow in their dispute management in Msinga's vernacular forums. The chapter explains who constitutes the forums charged with these disputes and over what spheres the forums have and compete for authority ('personal', 'territorial', and 'subject matter'), while also detailing the roles that the constituent members play in their respective forums. The discussion is also historically contextualised.

The chapter concludes that the forums are typically informally constituted and their roles informally spread among their members in ways that depend on context and highly localised forum culture. Chapter 4 also explores the relationships between the forums, placing particular focus on the ways that the South African Police Service (SAPS) uneasily fits into the picture of vernacular dispute management. It includes consideration of the potential conflicts of interest that exist for certain authorities when charged with particular responsibilities.

Section 3 focuses on the (inter)personal attributes of dispute management in Msinga. It begins with Chapter 5, which asks the question, who is disputing with whom and why? In answer to this question, this chapter provides a sketch of who the disputants typically are and what relationships form the foundation of the tensions being brought before a forum. Given in what close proximity people live with their families and the extent of social and economic interaction that takes place between family and neighbours, often one finds that the relationships forming the background for disputes are intimate, even as the kinds of disputes between them range from private to public, and from minor to severe. Hence, there are often deep contradictions inherent in disputes that take place between parties whose relations are premised on social trust. These paradoxes are clearly illustrated by the history and context of witchcraft accusations and the interpersonal and group violence they can propagate in a context with a violent history, such as Msinga.

Gender and age form the centre of Chapter 6, which is concerned with the fears, vulnerabilities, and strengths that come with parties' profiles. The chapter identifies gender identity, sexuality and violence as key elements in the socio-legal space of disputing and the management thereof. Chapter 6 demonstrates that a loose typology can be crafted of the kinds of grievances and disputes that arise, depending on one's age and gender, and evaluates the influence of these personal attributes on the dispute management process.

These personal traits frame the kinds of fears and vulnerabilities that accompany living in Msinga for certain groups and the vulnerabilities and strengths that influence the prospects of certain dispute management outcomes. Whether affecting the likelihood that an offence will be a group or repeated offence or partly predicting what aggravating or mitigating circumstances may arise in a dispute, these personal characteristics are important to observe.

Section 3 concludes with Chapter 7, which focuses on what people really want when they bring their matters to dispute management forums. The chapter digs beneath the surface of what people request as relief in their disputes, to identify why people actually dispute. In other words, the chapter investigates what objectives people are actually pursuing by bringing disputes to vernacular forums for management.

Sometimes people say what they want (perhaps an apology or reconciliation), but at other times, the confounding desire beneath the expressed request must be discerned from a comprehensive reading of the situation and subsequent interviews with both parties. The reality of this tension is often consistent with the transformations that the initial issues in a contest might undergo in the course of management. Looking beyond articulated requests – a simple remedy of a guilty or not guilty verdict, declaratory order, an interdict, repossession, damages or compensation – Chapter 7 seeks to clarify what people really want to get out of the dispute management process. It then investigates with what degree of finality the desired outcomes are produced by the proceedings.

The fourth and final section of the book deals with the ways the Traditional Courts Bill's multiple iterations have misunderstand vernacular forums and presents conclusions that the empirical findings detailed in the book lead to in terms of understanding vernacular forums for the purposes of future regulation. Chapter 8 begins with a brief analysis of the problematic assumptions and content of the Traditional Courts Bills' various visions for vernacular forums relative to the book's findings on dispute management in Msinga. The chapter argues that the overall vision of vernacular forums offered in the Bills is inconsistent with how the forums actually operate and the functions that they serve in people's lives. Worse still, as I argue in this concluding chapter, even the 2017 Bill is unlikely to regulate the forums in such a manner as to ensure their effective provision of 'access to justice'. The primary reason for projecting this ineffectiveness is that the Bill has not fully taken into account the contexts in which people who use the 'courts' live, the security and justice needs to which their contexts and identities give rise, and the limitations that stand in the way of vernacular forums meeting these needs.

The bulk of Chapter 8 is devoted to the question of what is, in fact, needed by and from both the vernacular forums and other state organs in order to address the problems and conflicts faced by people in places like Msinga. I argue that some progress can be made toward this goal by the forums adopting less, rather than more, of a judicial approach. This requires that they develop and strengthen their mediation strategies and skills. I further contend that improving dispute management in places like Msinga can only be but a part of the solution to 'access to justice' needs in the context. Wider socio-economic interventions constitute what is ultimately needed – because, more than just 'access to justice' in the technical sense of 'access to court remedies', residents of Msinga need 'human security'. The chapter therefore advocates for systemic change that implements a collaborative governance model. To realise this model, I argue that rhetorically existing cooperative governance arrangements (including social services) need to be holistically reviewed and adapted to the particular conditions and needs of people who rely on vernacular forums such as those found in Msinga for justice and security.

Section I

Interpolating vernacular dispute management in South Africa

2 Contentious background

History and theory

What makes a headman's or chief's court?

In 1923, a case came on appeal before the Appellate Division (AD) of the Supreme Court of South Africa. In *George Makapan v Jan Khope*,[1] the 'native headman' of a recognised 'tribe' had summoned two people, David and Ephraim, to his 'court' for a case. A third party, by the name of Jan Khope, had apparently misbehaved and was insulting to the headman during the proceedings. The headman, Samuel Khope, took the matter to the chief, who heard the complaint and, after also suffering disrespect from Jan, found that Jan was in contempt of court. The chief fined Jan a head of cattle, which was subsequently seized from him when he failed to pay the fine. The ox was slaughtered and distributed by the members of the court (the chief and his councillors).

The matter had come to the AD on appeal after Jan sued the chief for the cost of the ox and the Magistrate found in favour of the chief. Unsatisfied, Jan took the matter on appeal and succeeded before the Supreme Court. Now, before the AD, several issues were up for debate. First, the AD needed to determine whether the headman had had jurisdiction to sit as a court. It turned out that the legislation at the time[2] did not recognise headmen as having jurisdiction to hear cases. It specifically provided that courts could be instituted by legally recognised chiefs.

The irony is that, as it did fancy footwork, the AD ambivalently held that the law that constituted chiefs' courts meant that they possess 'the same authority as other courts of justice in the Transvaal'[3] but the same law 'was not intended . . . to recognize native courts as judicial tribunals in the Republic.'[4]

1 1923 AD 551.

2 Law 4 of 1885 (Transvaal), which was later replaced by the Native Administration Act 38 of 1927, and had provisions that were basically the same.

3 1923 AD 551 at 556.

4 Ibid. at 554. Such was the court's interpretation of section 2 of Law 4 of 1885 which read: 'The laws, customs or usages, hitherto existing among the natives shall continue to remain in force in this Republic as long as they have not appeared to be inconsistent with the general principles of civilisation recognised throughout the civilised world.'

In the court's interpretation, this meant that the legitimacy of a headman's forum before the people who use the forum as a court was insufficient to give that forum legal standing; rather, it was the recognition in law that made the chief's forum legitimate.

This points to the second issue debated by the AD: the failure to recognise the headman's forum as a court was clearly in direct contradiction with the reality that his people recognised his forum as such. As the AD observed:

> Though Samuel, therefore, appears to have been recognized by members of the tribe as having authority to hear and decide disputes, nevertheless, inasmuch as he was not a chief, no legal recognition can be accorded to his so-called court or Lekgoatla [sic], nor would any judgment given by him be enforceable at law.[5]

Hence, while the norms of the community itself were that the headman was the dispute management forum preceding that of the chief's, this 'court' was not recognised, and was therefore illegitimate, according to the state law.

A third point is that the AD's finding on the illegitimacy of the headman's court meant that the violation on which Jan's presence before the chief was based had been legally artificial. The AD worked around this hurdle by foregrounding the fact that Jan had insulted the chief, who did have a legitimate place, and emphasised: 'To hold that, whenever a judicial tribunal is acting in excess of its jurisdiction, the judge on the bench can be insulted with impunity would be highly prejudicial to the dignity of the Court and to the proper administration of justice.'[6]

Finally, the AD had to deal with the fact that the chief had not sat in his court alone but with his councillors – something also not provided for in the law. While the judges acknowledged that Law 4 of 1885 (predecessor to the Black Administration Act of 1927), a law to 'provide for the better administration of justice among Blacks,'[7] couched authority to adjudicate disputes in only the chief, they nonetheless accepted the chief's acting in unison with councillors who formed part of the chief's court.

The court held that, since the legislation stipulated that the chief should proceed in accordance with 'native law and usage', the participation of councillors probably being such a usage, it was appropriate for the chief to adjudicate the matter with them.[8] One of the judges continued that it would be contrary to the spirit of the law to disallow

> for instance, a young chief [from] calling in the assistance of his more experienced counsellors, who, in the absence of all writing, would have

5 Ibid. at 555.
6 Ibid. at 556.
7 Section 31 of Law 4 of 1885 (Transvaal).
8 1923 AD 551 at 561.

> their knowledge of native law and custom engraved on the tablets of their memory. There can hardly be a more satisfactory mode of arriving at a just conclusion in regard to native law and custom. I think we should be careful not to discountenance such a practice, for otherwise we might be acting contrary to the intent of the Act, which desires that effect should be given to the administration of actual native law and custom.[9]

In short, acting on the assumption that the councillors were elders who were the repositories of 'native law and custom' and being evidently determined to find in favour of the chief as judge, the AD was receptive toward the more participatory model of dispute resolution used by the chief's court. Jan therefore lost the case with costs, and the AD restored the order originally given by the Magistrate.

Continuous contestation: are 'traditional courts' real courts?

Until February 2014, the South African government seemed adamant about passing the Traditional Courts Bill of 2008 (reintroduced in 2012) – a controversial piece of legislation that, based on largely personal testimonies, seems immensely disconnected from the realities of rural people and, particularly, the needs of women. Yet, little contemporary, empirically grounded research has existed to demonstrate where the Traditional Courts Bill (B15–2008/B1–2012) went wrong in its attempt to regulate 'traditional courts' in a manner that fully respected vernacular law within the limits set by the Bill of Rights and enunciated by the Constitutional Court.[10] Nevertheless, even as politics, uncertainty, and controversy around the Bill persisted – and the grossly inadequate Black Administration Act 38 of 1927 (BAA) continues to govern the dispute management space – poor rural people, of whom women make up the vast majority, have had to try to find access to justice and security somehow. And they do.

People in rural South Africa live subject to at least two distinct legal universes, and their respective dispute management forums: state law and vernacular law. This pluralism presents opportunities and challenges. The main opportunity might be that this dual system gives them options for escape when their ability to obtain justice locally is compromised – something that is conventionally known as 'forum-shopping'. However, perhaps the greatest limitation that comes with this

9 Ibid. at 562.

10 *Ex Parte Chairperson of the Constitutional Assembly: In Re Certification of the Constitution of the Republic of South Africa, 1996* 1996 (4) SA 744 (CC); *S v Makwanyane & Another* 1995 (3) SA 391 (CC); *Alexkor Ltd v the Richtersveld Community* 2004 (5) SA 460 (CC); *Bhe v Magistrate, Khayelitsha; Shibi v Sithole* 2005 (1) SA 580 (CC); *Shilubana v Nwamitwa* 2009 (2) SA 66 (CC); *Tongoane v National Minister for Agriculture and Land Affairs* 2010 (6) SA 214 (CC); *Mayelane v Ngwenyama and Another* 2013 (4) SA 415 (CC).

legal situation is the uncertainty of whether, in either forum, the people will obtain a form of justice that will give them the security or relief that they seek.

One of the aims of the Traditional Courts Bill (TCB) of 2008/2012 was to reduce the uncertainty of obtaining justice in the vernacular dispute management forums, especially for those many who will be able to turn only to these forums for redress. Yet, there were questions about the Bill's ability to accomplish this goal, given the framework and wording the Bill adopted.[11] The new Traditional Courts Bill (B1–2017) is much improved.[12] Yet, one thing that remains unaddressed – and is, in part, stifled – by the Bill is the equally potent need to increase effective access to the state courts for rural people for the kind of justice that is obtainable there. As this book ultimately suggests, access to justice for rural residents in vernacular forums may depend just as much (if not more) on effective access to state courts and other state resources as on the regulation and repair of vernacular forums themselves.

This book's primary institutional focus is on the headmen's and chiefs' 'courts'. However, the interplay between these forums and the many others (formal and informal) that compete with, complement, support, or undermine them, both locally and beyond community boundaries, make up an important part of the picture. The informal forums include family councils, neighbourhood councils, forums of men (who discipline other men), forums of older women (who conduct virginity testing on younger women), and paid vigilante groups that negotiate or coerce solutions in instances such as stock theft. The formal institutions are the state police, who are sometimes used as pawns in the vernacular system and sometimes as an independent means to justice, as well as the magistrate's court.

As part of the book's discussion of the diverse forms of dispute management forums in the vernacular setting, the book problematises the decision-making powers that traditional leaders are stereotypically thought to hold in light of what the empirical evidence suggests are powers that are rightly shared with ordinary people. Therefore, key to the book is a discussion of the nature of authority in its various guises in the context of vernacular dispute management.

The ways in which disputes are managed in the vernacular forums sometimes offer striking contrast to how they would either ideally or actually be managed in the formal courts. However, that difference in management is sometimes the very reason why a matter is brought to a vernacular forum instead of the state courts. This situation calls into question the very meaning of the 'justice'

11 Mnisi Weeks, Sindiso (Summer 2012) 'Regulating Vernacular Dispute Resolution Forums: Controversy Concerning the Process, Substance and Implications of South Africa's Traditional Courts Bill' *Oxford University Commonwealth Law Journal*, 12(1): 133–155.

12 Ubink, Janine and Sindiso Mnisi Weeks (December 2017) 'Courting Custom: Regulating Access to Justice in Rural South Africa and Malawi' *Law and Society Review*. Also see 'South Africa's Traditional Courts Bill 2.0: Improved but Still Flawed' *The Conversation (Africa)*, 29 March 2017 (accessible at https://theconversation.com/south-africas-traditional-courts-bill-2-0-improved-but-still-flawed-74997) (accessed on 29 March 2017).

to which the Traditional Courts Bill is intended to ensure access, because the assumed meaning of 'justice' in the state court system is not necessarily shared by its vernacular counterpart. Whereas the TCB-2008/2012 practically implied that 'traditional courts' would employ a more punitive form of justice, the TCB-2017 both explicitly and implicitly provides for 'the resolution of disputes, based on restorative justice and reconciliation'.[13] Yet how much restoration, reconciliation and harmony are the vernacular forums really able to produce? Furthermore, in a context in which personal insecurity is pervasive, the issue arises of whether the working notion of 'justice' takes adequate account of this element of people's experiences and their felt need for security as a priority.

These are all issues that date back to the days of *Makapan*, and even earlier, and that are of continued relevance in the regulatory debates of our time. This book takes the discussion of how 'traditional courts' are to be regulated out of the legislative arena and back to the empirical context in which these forums exist and operate. The book thereby returns the discussion to foundational, conceptual, and empirical questions that seem to have been omitted in the initial legislative process. The book starts by asking, what *are* 'traditional courts', what are the purposes they serve, and how do they function in practice?

The book is premised on the argument that good law-making begins with empirically-based research[14] and that regulating vernacular dispute management forums in order to ensure 'access to justice' for the millions of South Africans who depend on them requires comprehension of the complexity of the vernacular system's many parts. The book therefore seeks to provide in-depth understanding of the empirical realities of vernacular dispute management and, by extension, the dissonances between vernacular dispute management and the formal development of this system through proposed legislation.

The relevance of vernacular forums for study today

Between 16 million and 21 million[15] people live in the former homelands of South Africa: a large proportion of them in remote, deep rural areas which were systematically disenfranchised and deprived of resources by the apartheid government and thus left with only poorly funded traditional structures as their form of local government.[16]

13 Section 2.

14 Erlanger, Howard S., Bryant Garth, Jane E. Larson, Elizabeth Mertz, Victoria Nourse, and David B. Wilkins (2005) 'Is It Time for a New Legal Realism?' *Wisconsin Law Review*, 2: 335–363.

15 See Debbie Budlender as quoted in Claassens, Aninka and Sizani Ngubane (2008) 'Women, Land and Power: The Impact of the Communal Land Rights Act' in Aninka Claassens and Ben Cousins (eds.) *Land, Power & Custom: Controversies Generated by South Africa's Communal Land Rights Act.* Cape Town, Juta at 154–183 at 168 fn 22.

16 Oomen, Barbara (2005) *Chiefs in South Africa: Law, Power and Culture in the Post-Apartheid Era.* Oxford, James Currey Ltd at 37–86.

This approximately 42% of the South African population therefore has very limited access to the centres where state courts are to be found. While some of the men might still be migrant labourers and thus be mobile enough to participate in the formal economy, the majority of women (who make up 59% of the residents of these deep rural areas)[17] are not.[18] Without the economic activity that earns one the material resources to access and navigate the state courts, most rural people are unable to use them. Indeed, the state courts are beyond most rural people's plausibility structures.[19]

Vernacular dispute management forums therefore form the main and often even the exclusive institutional means of accessing justice in instances of rural people's disputes. They are by far the most accessible and are relatively economical. Yet, they are also riddled with problems ranging from inadequate resources right through to dysfunctionality, corruption, and abuse.[20] Neglected for decades by the apartheid government, these forums developed in regressive directions. This transformation occurred while the then government negatively intervened in traditional leadership, turning it into an unaccountable and even despotic form of rule, and similarly interfered with gender relations, emphasising the patriarchal over the matriarchal elements of traditional cultures.[21]

In many places, the forums lost their accountability to the communities they served and became quite brutal, especially toward women.[22] Even where they did not become brutal, they lost much of their effectiveness as they became less and less able to enforce their decisions against the parties – especially where parties were highly mobile and could simply go to alternative forums.

Part of the neglect these 'courts' suffered is evident in that the legislation regulating them today dates back to 1927. When passed, the BAA envisioned traditional courts as chiefs' courts. As *Makapan* suggests, this vision of the courts was a fiction invented by the colonial order[23] to fit their notions of despotic, barbaric chiefs.[24] Quite soon after the legislation was passed, the legislature recognised that the state had to at least also recognise headmen's courts.[25]

17 Budlender (above).
18 There are some exceptions – see Debbie Budlender, Sibongile Mgweba, Ketleetso Motsepe and Leilanie Williams (2011) *Women, Land and Customary Law*. South Africa, Community Agency for Social Enquiry.
19 There are some exceptions, such as the fact that in North West province, it seems that the only courts that are used by local people are the magistrates' courts.
20 See the case of Dalindyebo in Mnisi Weeks (above).
21 Mamdani, Mahmood (1996) *Citizen and Subject: Contemporary Africa and the Legacy of Late Colonialism*. Princeton, NJ, Princeton University Press.
22 Claassens, Aninka (2005) 'Women, Customary Law and Discrimination: The Impact of the Communal Land Rights Act' *Acta Juridica*, 42; Curren, Ericka and Elsje Bonthuys (2005) 'Customary Law and Domestic Violence in Rural South African Communities: Notes and Comments' *South African Journal on Human Rights*, 21(4): 607–635.
23 Chanock, Martin (2001) *The Making of South African Legal Culture, 1902–1936: Fear, Favour and Prejudice*. Cambridge, Cambridge University Press.
24 Mamdani (above).
25 Native Administration Act, 1927, Amendment Act 9 of 1929, section 6(1).

However, the state erroneously assumed that these lower level 'traditional courts' were structured much like British courts, with a judge who presided over the proceedings and made the decision at the end. In Chapter 4, I will go into detail on just how erroneous this conception has always been. For now, it should suffice to say that the state's attempt to regulate these forums did not fit with their actual functioning and served only to advance the state's own notion of authoritarian rulers accountable to no one but the government.

Since this outdated and ever-incorrect conception and legislation of traditional courts persists, it is important that contemporary information be acquired that might show how vernacular dispute management forums are in fact constituted and operate. Moreover, as the modern democratic government seeks to replace this 1927 Act with current legislation, the government should do so based on reliable information and not make the errors of its predecessor by reinventing the entities it seeks to recognise and regulate.

There is yet another set of reasons for paying attention to vernacular forums today: namely, for some ordinary rural people and in some legal matters not technically[26] supposed to be considered by state courts (such as witchcraft, *ukungena*[27] and post-death marriages),[28] vernacular forums are very important to managing people's disputes. Additionally, the Constitution observes the right to cultural recognition and respect of those who observe non-mainstream cultures.[29]

Hence, it is important that the government understand these cultures (including their ways of dealing with disputes) and give them due recognition in a manner consistent with their core values. At the same time, the government should also strive to bring them in line with the Bill of Rights so as to ensure that rural residents are adequately protected in law.

The invention of traditional courts

Building on the *Makapan* case and several others, it can be demonstrated that 'traditional courts' were invented by an authoritarian government that recognised that dispute resolution is a key dimension of government and control.

26 There is evidence that magistrate's courts often consider matters that they are not technically supposed to consider. See Mnisi Weeks, Sindiso (2010) *The Interface between Living Customary Law(s) of Succession and South African State Law*, unpublished DPhil thesis, University of Oxford.

27 The levirate: that is, the practice by which, when a man dies, his wife becomes the wife of his brother.

28 When a man has died without having completed his marriage process by paying the *lobolo* (bridewealth) in full and hence has not completed the marriage ceremony done after the *lobolo* has been settled in full, the outstanding amount of *lobolo* can be paid after his death and the marriage ceremony performed in his absence. This serves to legitimate the marriage fully – and recognise his wife fully – even after the husband's death, giving her access to all the rights and responsibilities of a widow.

29 Sections 30 and 31 of the Constitution of South Africa.

Vernacular forums in the South African justice system under colonialism and apartheid

Power over dispute resolution is widely recognised as a central aspect of governance.[30] The colonial and apartheid governments acted in accordance with this idea in establishing 'native' courts in vernacular groupings as a central part of colonial and apartheid strategy to assert effective authority over African people. In fact, the establishment of 'native courts' formed one of the three key components of 'indirect rule'. This colonial policy was articulated by Frederick Lugard to enable the minority settler population to achieve effective governance of the majority native population in Nigeria in the early 1800s.[31] The same policy was then adopted by Theophilus Shepstone in the Natal Colony later that century.[32]

These traditional courts continue to be regulated through legislation up to the present day. This is so despite the fact that the formally recognised traditional courts are not representative of the full spectrum of vernacular dispute management forums one finds in vernacular groupings (what are commonly referred to as customary communities). Furthermore, the rules that govern traditional courts are inconsistent with the ways in which vernacular forums operate in practice.

As previously mentioned, since 1927, traditional courts have been governed by the BAA. Following the model of its predecessor,[33] this legislation recognised and regulated traditional courts as forums primarily – if not exclusively – constituted by 'chiefs' (that is, senior traditional leaders). This description of traditional courts can be seen from the titles of the relevant sections of the BAA: namely, 'Settlement of civil disputes by native chiefs' (section 12) and 'Powers of chiefs to try certain offences' (section 20). In terms of the legislation, senior traditional leaders were made both legislators and adjudicators. Sections 12 and 20 were subsequently amended in 1929 to recognise headmen's courts as forums below the level of chief's courts.

30 Turner, Victor (1957) *Schism and Continuity in an African Society: A Study of Ndembu Village Life.* Manchester, Manchester University Press; Roberts, Simon (1994) 'Law and Dispute Processes' in T. Ingold (ed.) *Companion Encyclopaedia of Anthropology: Humanity, Culture and Social Life*, 962–982 at 972; Lund, Christian (2002) 'Negotiating Property Institutions: On the Symbiosis of Property and Authority in Africa' in K. Juul and C. Lund (eds.) *Negotiating Property in Africa*, 11–44.

31 For the articulation of this policy, refer to Lugard, Frederick J. D. (1922) *The Dual Mandate in British Tropical Africa.* Edinburgh, William Blackwood and Sons at 193–213.

32 Mamdani (above) at 67; Church, Joan (2005) 'The Place of Indigenous Law in a Mixed Legal System and a Society in Transformation: A South African Experience' *Australia and New Zealand Law and History E-Journal*, 94 at 98; Mcclendon, Thomas (2004) 'The Man Who Would Be Inkosi: Civilising Missions in Shepstone's Early Career' *Journal of Southern African Studies*, 30(2): 339–358.

33 Section 31 of Law 4 of 1885 (Transvaal).

In terms of the BAA, chiefs and headmen were empowered to settle disputes that arose in their jurisdictional areas – that is, within the territories over which they had state-sanctioned 'control'. The chiefs and headmen themselves had to satisfy two criteria: first, they had to be formally recognised or appointed by the state and, second, they had to acquire specific authorisation for deciding civil matters, with this permission having to be written in order for chiefs and headmen to legitimately hear criminal cases.[34]

Although traditional leaders' jurisdictions were largely defined on the basis of 'territorial' boundaries, these jurisdictions were also defined in 'personal' (specifically, racial) terms. In other words, with the requisite authorisation, traditional leaders could settle civil disputes only between black persons who resided within their jurisdictional areas, and leaders could only be empowered in writing to 'try and punish' black persons who had committed crimes within the leaders' areas of legal jurisdiction. This remains the case in law.

With regard to 'substantive' jurisdiction, traditional courts were allowed to hear any civil matters, with the exclusion of matters relating to issues of 'nullity, divorce or separation arising out of a marriage'.[35] Schedule 3 of the BAA excluded an extensive number of criminal matters from the jurisdiction of these courts. The exclusions were treason; *crimen laesae majestatis*;[36] public violence; sedition;[37] murder; culpable homicide; rape; robbery; assault with the intention to do grievous bodily harm; assault with the intention to commit murder, rape or robbery; indecent assault; arson; bigamy; *crimen injuria*;[38] abortion; abduction; offences in terms of any law relating to stock theft; sodomy; bestiality; breaking or entering any premises with the intention to commit an offence either under the common law or in terms of a statute; receiving any stolen property while knowing it to be stolen; fraud; forgery or uttering a forged document while knowing it is forged; any offence under any law relating to illicit possession of or dealings in any precious metals or precious stones; any offence under any law relating to conveyance, possession, or supply of habit-forming drugs or intoxicating liquor; any offence relating to coinage; perjury; pretended witchcraft; faction fighting; man stealing; incest; extortion; defeating or obstructing the course of justice; any conspiracy, incitement, or attempt to commit any of the above-mentioned offences.

This list shows how technically the 'traditional courts' were approached and how little their jurisdiction and purpose was grounded in the empirical reality of the needs of their communities. These limitations are only emphasised by the fact that the courts' jurisdictional parameters were and remain

34 Section 12(1) and 20(1) of the Black Administration Act.

35 Section 12(1).

36 Treason.

37 Effectively, rabble-rousing.

38 Wilful injury to one's dignity by using obscene or offensive language or gestures. Effectively, the criminal version of defamation and hate speech.

little observed because of how poorly they fit with real life as experienced by rural communities.

An important apartheid objective that was accomplished by the Act was that it introduced Native Commissioners' Courts and the Native Appeal Courts. In other words, the BAA formed a completely separate state court system for black people. Thus, when matters were not successfully settled in the headmen's and chief's courts, they could go to the commissioners for resolution. The functions of these courts were transferred to the Magistrates' Courts in 1988. Thus, section 12(4) of the Act presently provides for appeals to the Magistrates' Courts from the traditional courts.[39]

This section of the Act implies that, in civil matters, traditional courts do not possess exclusive jurisdiction over the people subject to their territorial jurisdiction. Thus, black people living in a traditional court jurisdiction could elect to launch their civil cases at the Magistrates' Courts instead. But one can also read from the section that, if a matter is first initiated in the traditional court, it can then go on appeal only to the magistrate's court.

In 1967, Chiefs' and Headmen's Civil Court Rules[40] were passed under section 12 of the BAA. Of these, rule 1 provided that the procedure to be followed in civil claims should be in accordance with 'the recognised customs and laws of the tribe'. As far as those rules relating to appeal processes were concerned, rule 6 required that quadruplicate records be kept of the proceedings: one was for the Commissioner, one was for the plaintiff/applicant, one for the defendant/respondent, and the last for the traditional court's own record. Under rule 7, the judgments recorded in terms of rule 6 had to be registered with the area Commissioner and hence one of the quadruplicate copies was to be furnished to him. Rules 9 and 10 provided for the appeal of decisions from the traditional courts to the Commissioner responsible for the relevant area (later replaced by the Magistrate). Where such appeal took place, rule 11 required that the chief furnish the Commissioner (or Magistrate) with reasons for the chief's judgment.

Rule 13 stipulated a detailed fee scale for payments that had to be made to the chief in the absence of a prescribed fee under the relevant 'tribe's' own customary law. Two rand was due to be paid in advance for the chief's hearing the case on the first day and giving judgment, with one rand extra to be paid for every subsequent day of hearings. Twenty-five cents was due him for providing a written record of the case and another twenty-five cents for his attending the Commissioner's Court in the event of an appeal, to provide reasons for his judgment as the court of first instance.

In the same event, an additional twenty-five cents per mile of the shortest route to the Commissioner's Court was due the chief for his travel to and fro. The messenger of the traditional court also received something for his travel,

39 A person can appeal a matter where the value is more than R10.

40 Government Notice R2082 of 29 December 1967 (repealed in KwaZulu in 1989).

when necessary, excluding his travel to deliver the written record to the Commissioner's Court. He was to receive 2.5 cents per mile of the shortest route for his troubles. For service, delivery, and execution of a message on behalf of the traditional court, the messenger was due twenty cents.

Under section 20(2) of the BAA, the procedure followed for trials and 'the punishment, the manner of execution of any sentence imposed and . . . the appropriation of fines' were to accord with customary law, except in so far as the Minister were to modify this procedure. The only ministerial modification that took place, in terms of the power to make regulations under subsection (9), was regarding notice of appeal.[41]

This discussion gives a detailed account of the traditional court system as it had been constructed by the government through legislation. As one can imagine, this system was hardly representative of the reality of dispute management in most vernacular groupings. Hence, it is worth taking a moment to look at what contestations were brought to the state courts against the government's manufactured idea of traditional justice. After all, the 'natives' were not silent during this time. (Much more detail will be presented on this counter-narrative later in the chapter, when empirical accounts of vernacular dispute management forums and their processes during this period are discussed.)

A study of the cases heard by state courts about the jurisdiction and powers of traditional courts demonstrates how contested the state imagination and invention of traditional courts was from the early 1910s onwards.[42] The same is true of the government's imagination and invention of traditional leaders as the only recognised actors constituting these courts. In this regard, several cases relate to the role of the chief in the judicial process, how much power he possesses, whether the chief should act unitarily or with others, and whether the chief is the only person in the community with the right to resolve disputes or if other members and structures (at different levels of social organisation) may do the same.

At a time when the government was inclined to ignore the lower level vernacular dispute management forums, several cases came forward that made reference to headmen playing a role in the judicial process. As discussed in the opening of this chapter, *Makapan v Khope*[43] overtly addressed this tension. The latter part of this chapter will demonstrate that this practice of drawing on councillors was not the exception but the rule and that, in principle, a core element of vernacular dispute management is that the chief does not make a decision on his own but decides according to the weight of advice he receives.

However, for the state courts, this finding was unconventional because the prevailing wisdom at the time said that the chief was a repository of vernacular

41 Proclamation R45 of 1961.

42 *Makapan v Khope*, *Mogale v Mogale* 1912 TPD 92, *Morake v Dubedube* 1928 TPD 625, etc.

43 1923 AD 551.

law and knowledge who acted solely in dispensing justice and, hence, did not need to consult. As argued vis-à-vis *Makapan*, the AD made its conclusion primarily because it wanted to preserve the notion that the chief's decision had some validity. It went to great lengths to come to this finding, even though *Makapan v Khope* had no basis as a case because the injury on which the whole case was based was that the headman's court had been insulted but, according to the state, headmen's courts were not courts and therefore could not suffer contempt. The AD also held that the chief could consult with his council, even as his authority persisted independently of the council. Consequently, even as the court accepted the council's participation, it did not completely deviate from the prevailing wisdom that chiefs are sole actors.

Despite the positive statements by the court in *Makapan* on the legislature's failure to formally recognise the headman's court on grounds that it was 'recognized by members of the tribe as having authority to hear and decide disputes',[44] this decision was also a precedent for the troubling conclusion that, in terms of section 4 of Law 4 of 1885, the body that is formed as 'a court of justice' in law is the chief 'alone'.[45] Furthermore, the court arbitrarily permitted a chief to find people in contempt of his court (and even to fine them), even when the case for which a person was called to the chief's court was outside of the chief's jurisdiction.[46] In this way, the court reverted to the prevailing idea that chiefs were despots of a sort whose authority and stature had to be protected with extensive statutory powers.

The court in *Mokhatle and Others v Union Government (Minister of Native Affairs)*[47] reinforced and relied upon the *obiter dictum* in *Makapan* that, in principle, the chief's power of dispute resolution permitted him to act alone. In *Mokhatle*, this power extended to the unilateral authority of a chief to expel members of the 'tribe'.

At issue in *Mokhatle* was the expulsion of nine members of the Bafokeng 'tribe' in the Transvaal province, for maintaining an unauthorised council and undermining the recognised tribal authorities. The expulsion had actually been effected by the Governor-General but his decision, as the 'Supreme Chief', to expel the men was rationalised through the lens that '[t]he Government to-day has the power the old chiefs exercised'.[48] This justification was given in terms of section 13 of Law 4 of 1887.[49] The question at issue then became whether the 'supreme chief' would, in terms of 'native law and custom', need the

44 *Makapan* (above) at 555.
45 Ibid. at 555, 561.
46 Ibid. at 556.
47 1926 AD 74.
48 Ibid. at 76.
49 Ibid. at 80: 'The Governor shall exercise and enjoy over all the chiefs and natives in the Colony all the power and authority which, according to the laws, customs and usages of natives are held and enjoyed by any supreme or paramount native chief.'

support of his councilmen and the permission of a court judgment in order to expel members of his 'tribe'.

In its decision, the court suggested that the 'native mind' was more suited to a less democratic process, wherein the chief had full discretion to determine such matters, and others did not need to be consulted.[50] The court therefore confirmed this decision of the Provincial Division:

> A paramount or supreme chief possesses the power to direct the removal, by means of expulsion from the tribal property, of any natives who have committed acts of insubordination and hostility to the duly constituted authority of the chief or any sub-chief under him.[51]

The court acknowledged that in the submitted evidence a difference of opinion was reflected among tribal members as to the extent to which a chief should consult others.[52] Regardless of this, the court ultimately ruled in favour of chiefly (and, ultimately, state)[53] hegemony.

A number of subsequent cases alluded or dedicated some discussion to the functioning of the traditional court as a collective exercise of chief and headmen, with headmen often playing a major role in the dispute resolution. In *Rex v Kumalo and Others*, the court spoke of the chief and members of his council as deciding upon the proper punishment for a man for contempt of court.[54]

Another case, *Rex v Ntwana*, gave effect to the notion that members of the chief's council are notable participants in the traditional dispute management process.[55] In this case, the respondent was punished not only for contempt of court before the chief, but also for disobeying his headmen.[56] *State v Mngadi* also noted that the headmen served as the investigators for the chief and were integrally involved in the processes of the court.[57]

On the slightly separate question of whether traditional courts existed at a level beyond the chief's court, the judgment in *Rex v Masembura* specifically stated that a headman had attempted to resolve a dispute of whether or not a

50 Ibid. at 79, also see 77. In *Mogale* (above), the court held that 'the magistrate has no jurisdiction to override the decision of the chief in regard to a dispute between native and native'. In *Morake* (above), the court, in its obiter dicta, stated that chiefs need not hear evidence in the form of witness testimony to prove native custom, but rather can rely on their own conceptions of communal tradition.

51 Ibid. at 77.

52 Ibid. at 75–77.

53 Because the Governor-General is said to have the powers of a paramount chief in terms of the legislation.

54 1952 (1) SA 381 (A).

55 1961 (3) SA 123 (E).

56 Ibid.

57 [1971] 2 All SA 394 (N).

boy had assaulted a girl, but because the headman was unable to resolve the issue, the controversy was then sent to the chief for resolution.[58]

It therefore came out clearly in this case that there existed a multileveled system of courts in vernacular groupings that the state courts would not ordinarily encounter because the disagreements presented in those lower forums would not often be appealed to the state courts. The vast majority of matters would be resolved there, within the communities, in forums at levels lower than that of the so-called chief's court.

The above sampling of cases gives credence to the notion that authority in traditional courts had not entirely rested with the chief as the sole arbiter of disputes. In many cases, the decision-making of the traditional court appeared to be of a collaborative nature between councilmen and chief. Also, in a number of cases it was made clear that this particular issue of who has power to resolve disputes in customary communities – whether it was the chief and chief alone – was a controversial one. The cases point to the fact that state legislation centralised the power of dispute resolution in the individual – that is, the chief. Furthermore, the cases contradicted the representation in the BAA that traditional courts existed only at a single level.

Vernacular forums in the South African justice system today

Many of the legislative terms and rules governing traditional courts under apartheid continue to prevail in today's order. Only three provisions of the Black Administration Act of 1927 remain in operation, and these are the provisions that deal with traditional courts.[59] Hence, these provisions currently govern vernacular forums at the senior traditional leader and headman level.

A number of pieces of legislation were passed by the former homelands and continue to apply to vernacular forums also.[60] This is in accordance with the transitional arrangements provided in item 16(1) of Schedule 6 of the Constitution, which says: 'Every court, including courts of traditional leaders existing

58 1937 SR 43.

59 Sections 12 and 20, and Schedule 3, listing the crimes excluded from traditional courts' jurisdiction.

60 Regional Authorities Courts Act 13 of 1982 (Transkei); KwaNdebele Traditional Hearings of Civil and Criminal Cases by the Lingwenyama, Amakhosi, Amakhosana and Linduna Act 8 of 1984; KwaZulu Amakhosi and Iziphakanyiswa Act 9 of 1990; Venda Traditional Leaders Administration Proclamation 29 of 1991; Bophuthatswana Traditional Courts Act 29 of 1979; Transkei Authorities Act 4 of 1965; Chiefs Courts Act 6 of 1983; Ciskei Administrative Authorities Act 37 of 1984; QwaQwa Administration Authorities Act 6 of 1983. These laws have been assigned to the Provinces under item 14 of Schedule 6 of the Constitution. In terms of item 2 of Schedule 6 of the Constitution, they continue to apply until repealed or replaced: '(1) All law that was in force when the new Constitution took effect, continues in force, subject to: (a) any amendment or repeal; and (b) consistency with the new Constitution'.

when the new Constitution took effect, continues to function and to exercise jurisdiction in terms of the legislation applicable'.

In the context of the uncertainty about whether traditional courts are rightly conceived of as courts or informal tribunals that mediate local people's disputes, the Constitutional Court weighed in early to rule that they are courts. In *Ex parte Chairperson of the Constitutional Assembly: In re Certification of the Constitution of the Republic of South Africa, 1996*,[61] the Constitutional Court held that customary courts fall under section 166(e) and are, thus, one category of 'any other court established or recognised in terms of an Act of Parliament, including any court of a status similar to either the High Courts or the Magistrates' Courts'.

The confusion that this finding caused in the context of drafting the terms of replacement legislation – notably, the TCB-2008/2012 – and deciding what powers these forums can rightly have and handle is immense. For present purposes, note that both the very different nature of these forums and their practical limitations, as this book will discuss, make it difficult to consider them courts in the sense described by section 166(e) of the Constitution and dispute resolution tribunals in terms of section 34 of the Bill of Rights.[62]

Some changes that are more in the spirit of the Bill of Rights have taken place to the legislative provisions formally regulating traditional courts. Mostly, these changes have taken the form of limitations on the powers of traditional leaders in their capacity as traditional courts.[63] First, traditional leaders are disallowed from punishing people by 'death, mutilation, grievous bodily harm or imprisonment'. Second, these leaders cannot impose a fine of a value higher than R100 or 'two head of large stock or ten head of small stock'. Third, they cannot impose corporal punishment.[64]

In terms of the detailed fee structure provided by the rules governing civil cases, it is difficult to discern how much the fee structure was ever realised in practice but scholars generally accept that it is not effective in current practice.[65] Empirical evidence suggests that the fee structure is no more than vaguely conformed to.[66] Hence, fees are usually charged by traditional courts for initiating a case with them. This fee can range anywhere between R30 and R100. Some courts require that only the applicant pay the fee for bringing the case

61 1996 (4) SA 744 (CC).

62 Mnisi Weeks (Summer 2012) at 147–149.

63 Section 20(2) of the Black Administration Act, amended by section 2 of Abolition of Corporal Punishment Act 33 of 1997.

64 Ibid.

65 South African Law Reform Commission (January 2003) *Report on Traditional Courts and the Judicial Function of Traditional Leaders, Project 90* at 25; Himonga, Chuma, Thandabantu Nhlapo, I. P. Maithufi, Sindiso Mnisi Weeks, Lesala Mofokeng and Dial Ndima (2014) *African Customary Law in South Africa: Post-Apartheid and Living Law Perspectives*. Southern Africa, Oxford University Press.

66 Ibid. Also see Mnisi (above) at 266, 281.

and be reimbursed by the respondent at the time of judgment if the case is successful. Other courts require that both parties pay the fee upfront.

In some places, an amount is paid at the end of the case to 'raise the court' which has been seated to hear the matter. This amount of possibly R50 is used to purchase food and drinks for the council members who sat to hear the case. In other areas, the fee payable is more substantial and might simply be the chief's due – for instance, the chief might charge an extra cow over and above the cow sought by the applicant from the respondent.[67]

It goes without saying that the maximum fine for criminal matters of two head of large livestock or ten head of small livestock is not valued at the R100 given in the alternative in the legislation. These maximum fines are therefore out of keeping with reality.[68] In practice, most traditional courts equate the value of a single head of large stock with about R1,500 in cash.[69]

Moreover, these fines are often not only applicable as criminal sanctions but also as civil ones too. Yet, in civil matters what is ultimately paid by the one who loses the case depends on local practice as well as what is requested by the complainant (based on the complainant's valuation of his/her loss and the compensation sought for it). Compensation is commonly also granted in criminal cases and varies similarly.[70] Compensation incorporates the damages suffered by the relevant party and can be punitive as well as restorative. These empirical findings will form part of the record of what this book describes of the Msinga dispute management system.

Some additional crimes have been excluded from the traditional courts' jurisdiction, notably crimes pertaining to corruption.[71] Two key things are striking, when one looks at the full list of criminal exclusions in the BAA. First is that most of the offences listed would not constitute offences under customary law (predominantly because many of the situations would not naturally occur in vernacular settings).

And second, some of those excluded offences that do arise in vernacular contexts are heard by traditional courts, notwithstanding their prohibition in law. *S v Dalindyebo*[72] is a case in point. In this case, the king of the Thembu

67 Ibid. The author has encountered all of the cited examples in different fieldsites in Mpumalanga and KwaZulu-Natal. Vast divergences in practice can be found even within a small area, where there might be two different traditional communities living adjacently.

68 The SALRC recommended raising the maximum for fines to R500.00, as in Small Claims Courts, or small stock. See South African Law Reform Commission (January 2003) *Report on Traditional Courts and the Judicial Function of Traditional Leaders, Project 90* at 25.

69 Mnisi (above) at 266–267.

70 Ibid.

71 Specifically, 'any offence referred to in Part 1 to 4, or section 17, 20 or 21 (in so far as it relates to the aforementioned offences) of Chapter 2 of the Prevention and Combating of Corrupt Activities Act, 2004'.

72 *S v Buyelekhaya Dalindyebo*, Eastern Cape High Court, Mthatha, Case No. 267/04, unreported.

people of the Eastern Cape was convicted of inhumane offences committed as punishments of his people who he had found guilty of crimes such as murder, rape, and robbery in his traditional court.[73]

In truth, however, many vernacular forums attempt to resist hearing cases concerning anything but petty offences. When they do try cases relating to serious offences, they do not tend to do so imagining that they have the legal jurisdiction to do so but the means of seeking to satisfy people's claims for compensation (which would normally be considered civil claims in the state system when they happen separately to the criminal case).

Hence, often the criminal matter that is at the root of the compensation claim that the vernacular forums might hear is in the process of being handled by the state police and courts, or it has been dropped by them. Again, these contradictions between the law in the books and that in practice are born out in Msinga, as will be described in subsequent chapters.

Really, the most interesting question about traditional courts and how they fit into the South African justice system today concerns the appeal system and the extent of harmonisation and communication between Magistrates' Courts and traditional courts. As earlier mentioned, initially the civil process rules for traditional courts (at least, chiefs' courts) required them to operate in close alliance with the Commissioners' Courts: that is, to record summaries of the proceedings and findings for the Commissioners' Courts, to formally register decisions with them, and to testify in appeals to them. When the Commissioners' Courts ceased to exist in the late 1980s and their dispute resolution functions were taken over by Magistrates' Courts, this close alliance did not transfer with the Commissioners' Courts' core function.

As a result, the formal means of communication between traditional courts and Magistrates Courts was never as strong as that between traditional courts and Commissioners' Courts. Consequently, appeals from traditional courts to Magistrates' Courts do not take the form of appeals but of new hearings. Magistrates may ask the appealing party what had happened in the traditional court but they have no way of really knowing.

In all honesty, it is difficult to know how much of a practical difference this really has made – namely, how much the Commissioners' Courts actually benefitted from records taken by relatively illiterate traditional court officials, how seriously Commissioners' Courts actually took the testimonies of traditional leaders when the traditional leaders gave evidence on the initial proceedings in the traditional courts, and how this evidence influenced what ensued in the Commissioners' Courts' proceedings and decisions. That is something for others to take up in future studies.

However, it is still meaningful that that information from the previous process undergone, and arguments put forward, in the traditional courts is simply not made available to the appeal court at all anymore. To be fair, Magistrates' Courts

73 See Mnisi Weeks (Summer 2012).

have many other responsibilities and struggle to keep up with the rest of their work, let alone the added demands of taking over the work of the Commissioners' Courts as well and trying to carry it out at their level of purported efficacy. Nonetheless, it makes an important difference that most magistrates are hearing customary law cases as probably a small part of their caseload while commissioners heard them exclusively and would thus have (presumably) developed some degree of understanding and sensitivity toward the subject matter.

In short, then, the reality is that traditional courts cannot be said to be a robust part of the South African justice system – not from the formal legal perspective. It is only from the empirical perspective (drawing on rural people's lived experiences) that we determine that they matter a great deal and ought to be better harmonised with state courts.

Msinga as the chosen field site

This book's empirical findings are based on research gathered in Msinga, KwaZulu-Natal, during the period of October 2009 and December 2014 (the most concentrated observation and interview period being March 2011 to February 2012). Msinga was chosen as the fieldsite for the study because it is a deeply rural area where people still observe a very traditional lifestyle and values. This meant that the vernacular dispute management forums in this area were likely to be vibrant and highly functional, with ordinary rural people using them for many of their disputes and, indeed, evincing the widest array of disputes likely to arise in a contemporary vernacular grouping.

This vibrancy and high functionality of the vernacular forums were a high priority because my organisation at the time, the Centre for Law and Society at the University of Cape Town, and I were interested in finding out how vernacular forums work when they work well. This information would hopefully prevent the creation of a strawman for any critique that might necessarily follow from the findings on the forums' limitations and failings. Moreover, people in Msinga are generally very poor and, hence, would not likely have much access to or extensive engagement with the state courts.

Msinga was also attractive because it had two adjacent 'tribes' (nations) that had distinct histories and politics, though similar structures, culture, language, and interrelations.[74] The distinctions between the two communities meant that the comparative picture that would emerge would be more nuanced than if I were studying a single, relatively isolated community.

Both communities that were studied in Msinga have a senior traditional leader (*inkosi*) at the helm. At the time of our data collection, the Nezikhathi

74 Cousins, Ben, Rauri Alcock, Ngididi Dladla, Donna Hornby, Mphethethi Masondo, Gugu Mbatha, Makhosi Mweli and Creina Alcock (2011) '*Imithetho yomhlaba yaseMsinga:* The Living Law of Land in Msinga District, KwaZulu-Natal'. PLAAS Research Report 43, Cape Town, The University of the Western Cape.

community of about 80,000 had a much beloved traditional leader whose well-regarded son (referred to as *Umntwana*, literally meaning 'child') had already taken over the running of the community, as his father was very elderly. The father has since passed away and the son has officially become the traditional leader of the community. The Nakudala community, numbering around 50,000, had a less esteemed traditional leader who died not very long after the research had ended. His less respected son,[75] who was also meant to be referred to as *Umntwana* while his father was alive but insisted on being called *Ndabezitha* (an address reserved for the official *Inkosi* or 'chief') before his father died, had also taken over the running of the community at the time, while his father was very ill.

Below the senior traditional leader, in each community, are a number of headmen (*izinduna*) who administer wards (called *izigodi*). Under each headman, are a small number of headmen's policemen (named *amaphoyisa*) who administer units called subwards (*imihlathi*). The Nezikhathi community has 34 headmen (including five chief headmen), while the Nakudala community has seven headmen of wards and one chief headman in the area (though the community claims to have a total of 35 headmen). In both communities, the chief headman, or *Ndunankulu*, is more senior than the rest (though he gives up the administration of a ward with his status) and serves as the *Inkosi*'s assistant. The headmen serve as the primary dispute management agents as individuals and are the site and core members of the main vernacular forums, giving the headmen's councils their name. The headmen also sit with *Inkosi* to form his council (*ibandla lenkosi*) in hearing disputes at the 'tribal' (or macro Traditional Community) level.

The research was carried out in six wards in the Msinga District. With the help of our organisational research partner, Mdukatshani Rural Development Trust (MRDT), three wards were chosen from each of the Nezikhathi and Nakudala communities, and local fieldworkers were identified (and trained) to record disputes in each ward over a period of 11 months, from March 2011 to January 2012. The purpose was to obtain information that would reflect the internal and local differences within communities as well as a holistic picture of each *isizwe* (or nation). These localised elements might be influenced by

75 I would possibly even go so far as to say that the legitimacy of the Nakudala traditional leader is more questionable – not his genealogical legitimacy but his socio-political legitimacy. For this concept of legitimacy, I draw upon the work of Lund, Christian (2006) 'Twilight Institutions: An Introduction' *Development and Change*, 37(4): 673–684 at 676–677: '[When] an institution authorizes, sanctions or validates certain rights, the respect or observance of these rights by people constitutes recognition of the authority of that particular institution. In order to understand how political power is exercised, we therefore need to have an eye for the processual aspects of the formation of public authority, and in particular how it takes place in day-to-day social encounters. Yet, legitimate authority is not necessarily legitimate authority for good but must be vindicated and legitimated through a broad array of political practices. In essence, such practices constitute the negotiation of public authority in a particular context.'

differences of personality, views, strengths, and political positioning of the various headmen, as well as location of and social conditions in the ward (as much as these might vary).

The data analysed for the findings in this book were principally collected through observation of primarily headmen's councils', some chiefs' councils', and some neighbourhood or subward dispute management proceedings during this time. A research assistant and I also conducted follow-up interviews with willing parties to the proceedings. Sometimes we were able to speak to parties more than once. Further material, which also informs the findings of this book, was obtained through daily interviews with the headmen overseeing the selected wards: in particular, the interviews revealed what disputes the headmen had had reported to them and/or managed outside of their councils' processes, as well as other work the headmen had been called upon to do that day. Finally, we conducted a series of focus groups at the start of the observation period and reportback sessions after analysis of the data was completed.[76]

During the focused observation period, we recorded 35 'cases'. As will quickly become apparent, the concept of 'cases' in Msinga requires specific definition, because some 'cases' are adjudications while others are more like mediations and/or arbitrations. These definitions will be provided in the theory discussion below, and their complex application is demonstrated in Chapter four. We also recorded 36 'mediatory meetings' in the same period. These are instances in which vernacular groupings hold meetings that seek to resolve – either prospectively, and thus anticipatorily, or retrospectively – conflicts in the relevant locality. When referred to jointly, I label the two categories of 'cases' and 'mediatory meetings' as 'disputes'.

We recorded a further 183 matters that were separate occurrences of people reporting conflict to their headman. I have simply called this category 'reports'. In some of these reports, no further action was recorded as having been taken; perhaps the parties that reported the disputes were instructed to resolve their disputes within their families. Yet, other reports were followed by records of the headmen's attempts to manage those problems by means of negotiation with, or mediation between, the parties. I refer to all three categories of reported and managed conflicts – generically or cumulatively – as 'matters' or 'conflicts'.

We were fortunate to have the local non-governmental organisation, MRDT, with which to partner for access and support with the research. And, since Msinga is a much-researched area (though only really in the areas of HIV/

76 For this study, focus groups were conducted in February and March 2011 with our non-profit partner organisation, Mdukatshani Rural Development Trust, two Traditional Councils, two groups of ordinary male members of the community (one in each Traditional Community), and two groups of ordinary women in Msinga (one in each Traditional Community). These focus groups were a complement to the preliminary interviews and observations conducted from October 2009 to February 2011, as well as follow-up interviews and report back sessions conducted from February 2012 to June 2015.

AIDS, beading, music, livestock and land), there was much background material to draw from – particularly of the historical and sociological kind. The most recent of these studies are twofold: first, the 1,000-household Survey on Women, Land and Customary Law conducted by the Community Agency for Social Enquiry[77] in 2010; and second, the research project on the living customary law of land in Msinga done by Ben Cousins of the Institute for Poverty, Land and Agrarian Studies (PLAAS), the MRDT, and the Learning and Action Project (LEAP).[78]

Because I sat on the reference group for the former study and have participated in several conversations with the primary author and other participants in the second study, these engagements form an important part of what informs the research and findings captured in this book. One of the key considerations that emerges from these studies is the differences that arise in Msinga between the 'tribal locations' which were under the administration of the traditional councils during apartheid ('tribal authorities' at the time) and the labour tenant farms which were formerly owned and managed by white farmers and therefore developed independent systems of land administration and local authority. Hence, one of the wards included in the study is such a site as the latter.

An important consequence of choosing Msinga as the fieldsite for this study is that it may render the findings less generalisable because the extent of interpersonal violence in Msinga is arguably unique. I qualify my statement of the uniqueness of violence in Msinga with 'arguably' because Msinga is not the most violent place in the country anymore – though it was popularly known to be so in the early 1990s – but it is still distinguished by the ready access to illegal firearms locally. As a consequence of these widely available firearms, in Msinga (maybe unlike anywhere else in South Africa), disputes escalate quite rapidly from a seemingly minor altercation to gun violence. A study of police dockets and formal pathways to justice in Msinga by my colleagues Dee Smythe and Diane Jefthas will shed greater light on this question.

Theory: what is vernacular dispute management?

When a single dispute takes on multiple forms

A woman I shall call MaMakhe accused her neighbour of being a witch. The conflict had been managed by a vernacular forum and litigated right up to the chief's council. The accuser had been found to be in the wrong, and the woman said to be a witch, innocent of this accusation. Nevertheless, MaMakhe's daughter

77 Report by Budlender et al. (above).

78 Cousins et al. (above). I am also grateful to Meintjes, Louise (2017) *Dust of the Zulu: Ngoma Aesthetics after Apartheid*. Durham, NC, Duke University Press for sharing her manuscript with me prior to its publication, as well as Creina Alcock for her supplementary research and historical resources shared from her personal archives.

then accused their same neighbour, MaMsolwa, of an act of witchcraft – namely, wanting to kill her mother – and thus the same family was being taken to task for making witchcraft accusations again.

The context in which MaMsolwa was accused of witchcraft is of some interest. MaMakhe's son reported to the headman's forum that he had been woken by the barking of the dog and, when he went out, he saw someone standing at the gate and woke his mother to alert her. He then realised that the person at the gate was MaMsolwa, who was speaking to another neighbour and seemed harmless, so he returned to sleep. However, his mother, sister, and brother were already up at this point and rushed to the gate. His sister testified that, at the gate, MaMsolwa had said to MaMakhe, 'If I die, I will have died at your home, MaMakhe'. MaMakhe's daughter had said, likewise, 'If my mother dies, she will have died at your hand'.

Naturally, this conflict was not taking place in a vacuum. When the headman asked MaMakhe's daughter why she had said what she did, she replied that it was because she knew that her mother did not like MaMsolwa. It took some probing to get to why MaMakhe and MaMsolwa did not like each other, and it turned out that, by rumour, MaMakhe had heard that when lightning struck the home of MaMsolwa, she had said that it had been sent by MaMakhe (the implication being that the lightning was sent by witchcraft).

The witchcraft accusation that was presently before the headman and his council had been made about six months later, after a cellphone had disappeared from the accuser's home and she alleged that it had been taken by her neighbour's children. Her neighbour, MaMsolwa, had permitted MaMakhe's children to search her home, but they had not found the cellphone.

At that moment, MaMsolwa said, MaMakhe's children had threatened to destroy her phone in place of finding theirs. MaMsolwa said that she had then shouted out for the neighbours' attention because she had heard, via rumour, that she was also accused of having been seen come to perform witchcraft at MaMakhe's home. It was at that point that she had elected to report the matter to the headman and ultimately take it right up to the chief's court. It seems, therefore, that MaMsolwa made the current report to the headman from a place of resentment over the unhealed wound that MaMakhe created by accusing her neighbour of witchcraft.

Yet, still, this wound was not healed, and had seemingly been reopened by MaMakhe's daughter. The headman's council ordered that MaMakhe's family cleanse her wrongly accused neighbour's home. He said that this would enable them to forgive each other, reconcile, and be true neighbours as before. He specifically said that they should make amends by the blood of an animal and not by money because this had not been a case but they were all just correcting each other.

Theorising disputing: management, not resolution

As discussed in the first chapter and demonstrated by MaMakhe and MaMsolwa's dispute, vernacular dispute management forums are important – particularly in remote rural contexts – mainly because they are accessible. This accessibility lies in how proximate, relatively cost-effective, speedy, and informal they are, as well as how they are conducted in local languages and in a relatively informal format.[79] Of course, these forums operate in a context distinct from that of state courts, wherein the forums' primary aim is to enable members of the vernacular groupings to live together as people who are mutually dependent for their security and survival. The term popularly used to describe this objective is 'maintain harmony'.

The consequence of this aim is that access to 'justice' in such a setting might sometimes mean something different than it does in the context of state courts. (In fact, one might even ask whether the question of access to justice is strictly relevant to these forums at all, in light of what they set out to accomplish.) Yet, it is important to note that, at different times, people might want and need the distinct kinds of 'justice' offered by both state courts and vernacular forums and may thus value that it is possible for individuals to choose between them according to their own needs at any point.

The primary subject matter of this book is most commonly referred to as 'dispute resolution'; however, I have forgone that label as an erroneous descriptor. Instead, I prefer to use the term 'dispute management'. The theory section of this chapter therefore begins with an explanation of the reasons for this choice as well as the choice to abandon the use of the legislative labels 'traditional community' and 'customary law', in favour of 'vernacular groupings' and 'vernacular law', respectively.

The second part of this theory section provides the reader with some theoretical context for the book's later explanation of patterns of disputing in Msinga, by briefly setting out some key theories of disputing. The third part of the theory section then discusses the phenomenon of forum-shopping. By 'forum-shopping', I refer to the movement of persons between different kinds of forums observing different legal systems, according to what individuals determine will yield the best outcome in their conflict at the time. The fourth part of the section provides an overview of ethnographic accounts of vernacular dispute management in twentieth century South Africa and argues that these accounts provide some indication of what can be expected of the dispute management system in Msinga.

The remainder of this chapter argues that the concept of dispute resolution as developed for the formal state system is different from vernacular dispute management in important ways that should be taken into account when attempting to regulate the vernacular dispute management system. As part of this argument, the chapter highlights a methodological approach that places emphasis on empirically informed law- and policy-making.

79 Ubink and Mnisi Weeks (above).

Vernacular dispute management defined

Vernacular law and groupings

While convention might dictate that I use the readily understood term 'customary law', I resist this temptation. 'Customary law' is too closely allied with colonial policy and is, as argued by Martin Chanock, in fact an invention of that regime.[80] Under the auspices of codifying indigenous norms, colonisers actually distorted them, imposing upon the indigenous norms conditions such as repugnancy clauses in service of the government's 'indirect rule' policy objectives. Colonisers therefore effectively brought a new legal system into being that more closely approximated their own ideals of indigenous norms and culture than the actual customs and ideas of the indigenous people.[81]

As a consequence, the term 'customary law' is tainted with either associations with state dictates or uncertainty around what it refers to – though some have attempted to clarify the term by distinguishing the 'official' from the 'living' form of this law.[82] Yet, even with these distinguishing attempts, 'customary law' remains saddled with negative associations of an outdated legal system deeply transformed and manipulated by colonial and apartheid governments and beholden to formal legal institutions (such as the Constitutional Court) even today.

By contrast, 'vernacular law' reflects more clearly that the normative order at issue is one owned and developed by the people who observe it through their use. This does not mean that the term is exclusive.[83] 'Vernacular law' integrates imposed and elective elements of other normative orders – sometimes consciously and at other times not. That too is captured by the adjective 'vernacular'. In the same way that language described as 'vernacular' is not stagnant but evolves with the people, vernacular *law* evolves with the legal needs of the people it serves and adapts to their changing uses.[84] Usage of this term to describe the normative order studied in this book also captures the emic approach adopted to understand the dispute management norms of the people in Msinga.

80 Chanock (above) at 4, 34–35.

81 Ibid.

82 See, for example, *Shilubana* (above); Himonga, Chuma and Craig Bosch (2000) 'The Application of African Customary Law under the Constitution of South Africa: Problems Solved or Just Beginning?' *South African Law Journal*, 117: 306; Bennett, Tom (2008) '"Official" vs "Living" Customary Law: Dilemmas of Description and Recognition' in Aninka Claassens and Ben Cousins (eds.) *Land, Power & Custom: Controversies Generated by South Africa's Communal Land Rights Act.* Cape Town, UCT Press, 138–153.

83 See discussion of 'vernacularisation' of human rights by Merry, Sally Engle (1996) 'Legal Vernacularization and Ka Ho'okolokolonui Kanaka Maoli, the People's International Tribunal, Hawai'i 1993' *POLAR: Political & Legal Anthropology Review*, 19: 67 at 68.

84 Merry, Sally Engle (2001) 'Changing Rights, Changing Culture' in Jane K. Cowan, Marie-Bâenâedicte Dembour and Richard Wilson (eds.) *Culture and Rights: Anthropological Perspectives.* Cambridge, Cambridge University Press 31 at 45.

Most importantly, such an approach incorporates what is championed by Sally Engle Merry as a 'concept of culture that allows for agency and contestation in situations with multiple and contradictory cultural logics and systems of meaning.'[85] This book owes part of its title to this concept.

In the same way that 'customary law' is jettisoned, the legislative term 'traditional communities' is eschewed, and 'vernacular' is attributed to the local groupings at different levels of social organisation in Msinga. This terminology accentuates the fact that the members of the groupings flexibly define the scale of association and social organisation that is relevant to them at any point in time. This choice also reflects a conscious rejection of the statutory prominence of macro-level ('tribal'), territorially defined boundaries fashioned by the apartheid government, which were adopted by the Traditional Leadership and Governance Framework Act 41 of 2003 and prevail even in the TCB-2017.[86]

Again, as part of this study's emic approach, I employ the scale of association that the relevant grouping's self-identified members perceive to be significant at any one point of the dispute management process, to define the applicable jurisdiction. This approach requires also embracing that people's self-identities are nested, layered,[87] and fluid and that the boundaries of their groupings are also nested and layered and thus change according to the situation.

Dispute management

The conception of what is described in this book as 'dispute management' rather than 'dispute resolution' enables the perception and accommodation of the social context in which disputes arise as distinct from the context that is assumed for state courts. As was noted in Chapter 1, in the rural context that forms the setting of this book, people's lives are very intertwined because the people rely on one another for their security and survival. Their relationships are also entangled, and their contact with one another is regular in a manner that renders repeated conflicts – varying from petty to severe – unavoidable.

Dispute resolution posits that disputes are terminated by the deliberation process. Arguably, this is not the case in any disputing situation – even those that follow the state court route. However, it is certainly not the case in a relatively contained society such as that in Msinga, where interactions and physical closeness must necessarily persist beyond the conclusion of the disputing process and hence the conflicts between the people also persist.[88]

85 Ibid.

86 Section 28(3) of Traditional Leadership and Governance Framework Act 41 of 2003.

87 Cousins, Ben (2008) 'Characterising "Communal" Tenure: Nested Systems and Flexible Boundaries' in Aninka Claassens and Ben Cousins (eds.) *Land, Power & Custom: Controversies Generated by South Africa's Communal Land Rights Act*. Cape Town, UCT Press, 109–137 at 129.

88 This is similar to what is described by Merry, Sally Engle (1979) 'Going to Court: Strategies of Dispute Management in an American Urban Neighborhood' *Law & Society*

A number of forums exist, variously constituted and varying in their formality, to meet the need that people residing in such close socio-economic relationships have for regular opportunities to deal with their evolving differences using a variety of methods. That way, they can have their matters considered by means of mediation, arbitration, and adjudication in the varying forums, quickly and with relatively little fuss.[89]

At the same time, given how regularly conflicts erupt and how intimately connected the parties are, their differences are 'settled' without too much conclusiveness. Disputes themselves evolve and are transformed by the process as they escalate or reappear as new iterations of earlier or extended conflicts, and these disagreements concern discernible but not necessarily stated tensions.[90]

In the rural context, avoiding the significant investment of emotions, energy, time, and money required by the state system would be quite important.[91] Furthermore, many of the seemingly petty issues or cases on subject matters like witchcraft are routinely considered by vernacular forums but might not be heard by state courts, which would typically consider them to be of a non-legal nature.

The fact that the state courts might consider many of these matters trivial does not render them insignificant in the social reality of the parties, and thus such conflicts require meaningful consideration by some dispute management forum to enable the parties to continue with life, together or apart. The time and costs involved in attempting to get matters considered and decided by state courts is mostly beyond the means of ordinary rural people, the vast majority of whom are living below the poverty line.[92]

Conventional remedies given by state courts in both minor cases and major cases like rape and murder may also not meet the expectations of the parties who come from a socio-legal setting that is distinct from that in which the state

---

Review, 13: 891 at 899–900. This can be contrasted with the situation described of the United States where 'there is no anticipated future relationship' by Galanter, Marc (1983) 'Reading the Landscape of Disputes: What We Know and Don't Know (and Think We Know) about Our Allegedly Contentious and Litigious Society' *UCLA Law Review*, 31: 4 at 24–25. As will be seen below, this expectation of continued relationships of some mutual dependency, is part of the reason why cases do not often go to the state courts which are viewed as more disruptive of such continuing relations. (See Merry (above) at 894–895, and Miller, Richard and Austin Sarat (1980) 'Grievances, Claims, and Disputes: Assessing the Adversary Culture' *Law and Society Review*, 15: 525 at 526).

89 Merry (above) at 894–895.

90 Felstiner, William, Richard Abel and Austin Sarat (1980) 'The Emergence and Transformation of Disputes: Naming, Blaming, Claiming . . .' *Law and Society Review*, 15: 631 at 639 argue that this is the case with all disputing processes, even those that make it to and result in a decision by a state court.

91 Ibid. at 654.

92 In 2015, the national poverty line was set at R779 per person per month (or R25.50 per day) while the poverty line for the province of KwaZulu-Natal was set at R757. This reassessment was based on 2011 poverty data, though at the time of the study, KwaZulu-Natal's poverty line was R354 per person per month.

courts developed. Therefore, one finds that even where state courts are turned to by local people from Msinga for assistance, the relief these courts provide does not necessarily conclude the matter. Rather, the party who feels wronged may simultaneously or subsequently present his or her grievance in a vernacular forum, appealing for a form of relief other than that issued by the state court.

Because of this fact, the 'extended case method' used by legal anthropologists is a preferred methodology for this research. The extended case method follows the dispute from its inception in the social context from which it originates through the process it follows in a number of forums that vary in formality and that may be either legal or social.[93] This method therefore provides a detailed understanding of the transformations that disputes undergo. These transformations necessitate the description of the disputing process as 'management' instead of 'resolution,' on the basis that the former is more empirically valid while the latter fetishises the decisions of formal courts despite their lack of true finality.[94]

What is perhaps most important in the choice of dispute 'management' over 'resolution' is that it allows me to consider a large array of motives that drive people to initiate cases[95] or introduce other intermediations into their long-standing conflicts. This choice is as an alternative to focusing on an individual decision issued at the conclusion of a process of adjudication by the highest court approached in a case.[96]

Consequently, I am not limited to looking only at a guilty or not guilty verdict, interdict, the restoration of property, payment of damages, or cost order. I can look at the myriad other forms of 'satisfaction' that people can seek to obtain by making a claim. These include publicity of the wrong they feel they have suffered, the other party's acknowledgment that they have wronged the complainant, or an apology.

The bringing of a claim can serve as a warning to the other, a way of shaming them into doing what is perceived to be owed, an attempt to prevent (further) victimisation or violence, a way to pursue a declaration by an external body that proves one right or affirms the complainant in his or her position or even compels the other to take financial responsibility. The vernacular dispute management forum can be asked to (re)unify the parties or help them find a way to continue co-existing in peace. A person might also bring a claim out of a simple desire that their vernacular grouping re-affirm or re-articulate what the person perceives to be essential and shared values.

Thus one sees that there is a wide range of objectives that may underlie the steps people take to bring a claim and the decision they might request and obtain from a dispute management forum of an interdict, a restoration of

93 Felstiner, Abel and Sarat (above) at 639.
94 Ibid.
95 Ibid. at 642–643.
96 Galanter (above) at 26.

property, damages, or compensation. Similarly, the offence at issue might itself have been committed with various objectives worth noting. As Felstiner, Abel and Sarat summarise, we cannot

> assume that the overt cause of the disagreement is the real matter that has to be negotiated. . . . A minor offence may be seized on in order to force the offender to come into the public arena where he may be confronted with a more serious matter which he is avoiding. A frustrated complainant may deliberately commit a petty offense in order to provoke his reluctant opponent to action. Once in the public arena, the real issue may be broached and defined.[97]

Dispute management in theory

To provide some necessary background, I begin with theories around disputing.[98] Disputes generally occur through a process that begins with a party feeling wronged – specifically perceiving and naming their experience as an injurious act and attributing blame for their injury to someone. This composite step constitutes the 'perceived injurious experience' (PIE).[99]

Once a PIE has taken place, the wronged party can approach the person by whom they feel wronged to claim a remedy from them.[100] The making of an external claim is determined by whether the person feels he or she was wronged by someone else – if the party feels personally at fault for the injury, he or she will not likely blame another or pursue redress from an external source.[101] Yet, their notion of whom the wrong is attributable to might change with the passing of time, consultations with or advice from others, and the response to or treatment of the grievance by an institution to which it is brought for management or adjudication.[102] The party's own beliefs and the scope of conflict that the forum approached for management will take into account also can affect the transformation of a PIE from stage to stage, by (re)framing the conflict in certain ways.[103]

97 Felstiner, Abel and Sarat (above) at 676.

98 For more, see Mnisi Weeks, Sindiso (2015–2016) 'Access to Justice?: Dispute Management Processes in Msinga, KwaZulu-Natal, South Africa' *New York Law School Law Review*, 60(1): 227–249; Mnisi Weeks, Sindiso (2016) 'Women Seeking Justice at the Intersections between Vernacular and State Laws and Courts in Rural KwaZulu-Natal, South Africa' in Heinz Klug and Sally Engle Merry (eds.) *The New Legal Realism, Vol. 2: Studying Law Globally*. Cambridge, Cambridge University Press at 113–142.

99 Felstiner, Abel and Sarat (above) at 635–636.

100 Ibid.

101 Ibid. at 641.

102 Ibid.

103 Ibid.

What is described here in the form of the transformation of a PIE into a claim is also known as the escalation of a conflict from a mere grievance (unarticulated) to a claim (articulated and brought to the attention of the other party) to a dispute at full scale (to be managed by some formal forum).[104] It is worth noting here that, as I use the term, a conflict exists where one or more parties feel aggrieved, whether or not they express this publicly or explicitly. One often finds that two parties feel aggrieved but do not expressly declare their grievance. They may nonetheless demonstrate the tensions that exist between them in subtle ways or implicitly.

As Richard Miller and Austin Sarat write, 'A dispute exists when a claim based on a grievance is rejected either in whole or in part.'[105] Thus, empirically, we find that it is most common that PIEs – and hence low-level conflicts – do not escalate to become outright disputes, especially not disputes brought to a public forum for management. For example, when a grievance arises within a family, it is most likely that people will try to avoid confrontation and rather 'keep the problem quiet'.[106]

A number of studies have demonstrated that people adopt various means to deal with their grievances and secure a remedy.[107] Self-help is the most widespread. Here, the party feeling wronged produces his or her own remedy by perhaps avoiding the one who wronged them,[108] enduring the situation that is causing unhappiness or even harm, threatening the other with violence, or even committing a violent act against the perceived wrongdoer.[109] Sorcery or witchcraft can be categorised as self-help remedies.[110]

104 Miller and Sarat (above) at 527.

105 Ibid.

106 Ibid. at 531.

107 Merry (1979) (above) at 894; Nader, Laura (2002) *The Life of the Law: Anthropological Projects*. Berkeley, CA, University of California Press at 150; Prinsloo, Johan (1999) 'Conflict Resolution Amongst Traditionally African Cultures' in Irene Sagel-Grande (ed.) *Models of Conflict Resolution* at 19–20. Norgren, Jill and Serena Nanda (1996) *American Cultural Pluralism and the Law*. Greenwood Publishing Group at 285: 'pluralism expresses itself not only in the different issues brought to courts for resolution, but also in decisions not to use courts at all. Even when courts are called upon in dispute resolution situations, it may not be for their traditional, and legitimate dispute resolution functions. Courts do cast a shadow; but it is often distorted . . . they may serve . . . as institutions to be manipulated in intracommunity and interpersonal struggles.' Also see classic studies such as Bohannan, Paul (1957) *Justice and Judgment among the Tiv*. London, Oxford University Press; Gluckman, Max (1955) *The Judicial Process among the Barotse of Northern Rhodesia*. Manchester, Manchester University Press; Schapera, Isaac (1955) *A Handbook of Tswana Law and Custom*. London and New York, Oxford University Press.

108 Merry (1979) (above) at 894, 903, where she helpfully distinguishes avoidance and endurance.

109 Miller and Sarat (above) at 531–532, 539; Merry (1979)(above) at 900–901.

110 Prinsloo (above) at 19; Ashforth, Adam (2005) *Witchcraft, Violence, and Democracy in South Africa*. Chicago, University of Chicago Press.

An alternative to self-help solutions is negotiation.[111] In such an instance, the party perceiving him- or herself to be injured would approach the other party to request what the injured party feels he or she is owed.[112] Once a party resorts to negotiation, a dispute exists because the PIE (and the conflict that exists because of it) has been vocalised in a manner inviting a mutually agreed remedy, such as reconciliation, and at least partially rejected. That is, negotiation is itself a mark of a dispute. The result of the negotiation could be a compromise offer, but this is, in fact, a partial rejection of the claim made and therefore a dispute, regardless of its brevity.[113] If a mutually satisfactory agreement cannot be reached, the matter may then escalate further.

The next stages of escalation of a dispute are mediation or arbitration. At this point, the disputing parties bring in a third party to either assist the parties in their discussions to reach a healthy compromise (mediation)[114] or deliver a finding on who is right between the parties, a decision that will bind them both and be enforceable in law (arbitration). The final stage, which is infrequently reached, is that of adjudication of a formally lodged case before a court of law.[115]

In this book, the number of councils that make up the vernacular dispute management system are equated with courts of law in so far as they are the ultimate forums to which matters can escalate within the vernacular system. This approach is also consistent with the fact that local people conceive of vernacular councils as courts, as well as with the fact that these councils exist on a permanent basis to manage disputes, are empowered with punitive powers, and can deliver pronouncements that are ostensibly final and enforceable.

Nevertheless, aligning with the categories described above is a valuable distinction worth noting about these forums: namely, they can play different roles at different times.[116] At times, the councils sit in a mediatory, instead of adjudicatory, capacity. Local people therefore distinguish between 'a case' and a process by which parties are 'just being reconciled'. The formations of the forums change accordingly. These permutations will be further detailed in Chapter 4.

111 Galanter (above) at 16–17, 28.
112 Merry (1979) (above) at 919.
113 Miller and Sarat (above) at 527.
114 Ajayi, Adeyinka Theresa and Lateef Oluwafemi Buhari (April 2014) 'Methods of Conflict Resolution in African Traditional Society' *African Research Review*, 14(2): 138–157 at 149–150; see also Woodman, Gordon R. (2011) 'A Survey of Customary Laws in Africa in Search of Lessons for the Future' *The Future of African Customary Law*, 9: 14 (Jean-marie Fenrich et al. eds.).
115 See Mnisi *London School of Economics Monographs* (2015–2016) for more.
116 Of course, with the growing movement towards restorative justice, state courts are providing more and more mediation also. Thus, this is not such a fundamental distinction. Yet, state courts are still mostly associated with adjudication whereas, as I will argue in this book, vernacular forums are actually more associated with (and better suited to) mediation and limited arbitration.

The value of forum-shopping and shopping forums

In her insightful article on forum-shopping, Keebet Von Benda Beckmann describes the multilayered and nested levels that form the Minangkabau village social organisation and dispute management. I draw from this work principles that apply to South African vernacular groupings also, on the basis that strong similarities exist between the *adat* manner of dispute management and forum-shopping found in the Minangkabau village and vernacular systems and practices in South Africa.

Firstly, in terms of the *adat* procedure, forums can be formed of a single lineage or neighbourhood, or of different lineages combined, or be a 'higher forum at the more inclusive level' (that is, at the macro level) of vernacular grouping.[117] Thus, Von Benda-Beckmann notes that '[s]olutions for problems must be found at the lowest level of authority, and if no solution is found the case must be taken higher up, step by step, until a solution is found.'[118] In other words, significant authority to resolve disputes is situated at the lower levels of organisation, and the authority of the higher levels depends on the failure of lower-level courts to settle matters.

Indeed, as Von Benda-Beckmann describes it, '[h]igher *adat* institutions have only as much authority as has been conceded by the lineages and is necessary to sustain a common government'.[119] She observes too that the lineages (lower levels of social organisation) try to remain autonomous and that this autonomy is secured by their having their own property,[120] which they manage.

My suggestion here is that much of the same can be said to be true of South African vernacular groupings, as will be seen below and in subsequent chapters. Because the lineage authorities were in competition with the colonial government and its newly introduced institutions, as Von Benda-Beckmann notes, '[d]ealing with disputes . . . became an important instrument in the struggle for power at local level.'[121] In that context, the principle of 'joint deliberation' was also important.[122] In other words, the participatory nature of dealing with disputes, which was inclusive of lineage members, was an important feature of the forums' attempt to preserve their authority in competition with the state. It even provided a tool by which the local authorities maintained their legitimacy through their discourse in the context of how they discussed disputes in seeking to resolve them.

117 Von Benda-Beckmann, Keebet (1981) 'Forum Shopping and Shopping Forums: Dispute Processing in a Minangkabau Village in West Sumatra' *Journal of Legal Pluralism*, 19: 117–160 at 137.

118 Ibid.

119 Ibid. at 138.

120 Ibid.

121 Ibid. at 139.

122 Ibid. at 137–138.

The key point is this: this emphasis on an inclusive deliberation process occurred at least partly because the *adat* (as local-level forums) were engaged in the exercise of 'shopping'[123] – that is, they were 'negotiating' legitimacy in their subjects' eyes.[124] Though external forums may have presented a threat to vernacular groups, in this particular instance, the external forums also helped to keep the internal forums accountable, because external forums made respecting the 'joint deliberation' principle and other rules or values important for the internal forums as a bid to maintain *adat* authority over local people's cases.

Below, I argue that the South African situation also suggests that the availability (and viability) of multiple dispute management forums can be a useful tool for keeping intra-community dispute management forums accountable. This benefit potentially outweighs the risk of external courts undermining the continued functioning of the vernacular forums. I will also demonstrate the centrality of inclusive participation in dispute management in South African vernacular groupings.

Belgian scholar Filip Reyntjens has contended that informal dispute settlement is the most important judicial setting, asserting, '[i]n Africa, the introduction of modern judicial institutions has resulted in a marked reduction of access to justice for most people. Accessibility declines in proportion to the increase of professionalisation and westernisation of the court system.'[125] I partly disagree with him in that, as I argue below, modern courts as alternative forums have come to serve as important options for people, and a means by which they can try to hold vernacular forums accountable. However, I also go on to agree with Reyntjens's point that professionalisation of vernacular forums themselves holds negative consequences for their accessibility to their users.

Vernacular dispute management in the twentieth century

David Hammond-Tooke notes that despite 'the establishment of magistracies, the informal moot courts and courts of headmen still function'.[126] He was writing about the then-Transkei (from the late nineteenth century until the 1970s), but numerous other scholars researching communities throughout Southern Africa (from the early 1900s) reiterate his point.

123 Ibid. at 138–139.

124 See discussion of these negotiations that take place in Mnisi Weeks, Sindiso (2011) 'Securing Women's Property Inheritance in the Context of Plurality: Negotiations of Law and Authority in Mbuzini Customary Courts and Beyond' *Acta Juridica*, 140–173.

125 Reyntjens, Filip (1993) 'The Future of Customary Law in Africa' in Joan Church (ed.) *The Future of Indigenous Law in Southern Africa: A Collection of Papers and Comments Presented at a Conference Held under the Auspices of the Centre for Indigenous Law, UNISA and Vista University at UNISA on 21–22 October 1991*. Pretoria, Centre for Indigenous Law, UNISA, 3–23 at 15.

126 Hammond-Tooke, William David (1975) *Command or Consensus: The Development of Transkeian Local Government*. Cape Town, D. Phillip at 3.

Colonialism and apartheid, and their policies, did not manage to do away with vernacular forums. These forums continued to exist, and scholars who studied them help us to understand what they looked like and how they functioned – both independently of and in conversation with the imposed regimes. Consequently, ethnographic research on vernacular forms of law and dispute management has provided extensive evidence to say that vernacular dispute management forums display three major characteristics that are immediately relevant.

First, vernacular dispute management forums in South Africa are shown to have multiple levels and to place the greatest emphasis, responsibility, and expectation to resolve disputes on lower-level forums. Monica Wilson wrote in 1952, about the area of Keiskammahoek (in the then-Ciskei), that social convention dictated that disputes were to be solved within the family, and only if they were unable to be settled there did they proceed to the highest local forum.

She refers to the 'lineage remnant' council (which comprises the adult male kinsmen of that lineage remnant) as the family dispute management mechanism wherein private family matters are discussed and resolved. Civil wrongs are primarily considered to be family or inter-family matters and are thus to be resolved either by the lineage remnant council of the family or the combined councils of both families involved in a dispute. Agnates (other male relatives) and friends may attend these meetings by invitation. If this level of management fails, the parties might go to the local village section council, which comprises the men of the area and the subheadman. The parties may then appeal to the headman's court.[127]

Observing the Pedi, H.O. Mönnig noted in 1967 that there the internal hierarchy of the courts was very strictly observed. It began with family and proceeded up through two levels to the chief's court, which was the final forum of appeal within the community.[128] Resolution in subordinate forums had to be sought before litigants could proceed to the chief's court, and (since the court's duty was to reconcile the parties) it was not unusual for a forum to send a case back to the families involved to have it resolved by them.[129] The suggestion here seems that the settlement of disputes by lower vernacular forums was preferred. In fact, according to Hammond-Tooke, although in theory appeals from lower forums could go to chief's courts in the Transkei, 'it seems this was rare in practice.'[130] He goes on to quote a regent named Isaac Matiwane as saying, 'Subjects of the *isiduna* were allowed to take their cases on appeal to the chief's court if they were not satisfied with the *isiduna's* verdict. But such cases were very rare. In fact this was not encouraged'.

Regarding the Swati, Hilda Kuper agrees with other writers on vernacular forums in other areas and says that there is a multileveled court system. She

127 Wilson, Monica, Selma Kaplan, Theresa Maki and Edith M. Walton (1952) *Keiskammahoek Rural Survey, Vol. 3: Social Structure*. Pietermaritzburg, Shuter and Shooter at 31–32.

128 Mönnig, H. O. (1967) *The Pedi*. Pretoria, Van Schaik.

129 Ibid. at 308.

130 Hammond-Tooke (above) at 64.

adds that there is an informal dispute management forum which involved the neighbours informally banding together to resolve an issue arising in their area. They will often identify a respected, neutral third party to oversee the solving of their disagreements.[131]

Also, the Swati King and Queen both had a court – the Queen's court being the second-highest in the land, after that of her son.[132] As it happens, among the Pedi, women had their own system of dispute management, whereby, if they had disputes with other women, they could bring their cases to the superior wife of the headman or the principal wife of the chief. These forums were strictly mediatory and depended on the parties' agreement, as they had no powers of enforcement.[133]

Second, vernacular forums are shown to most often be the first ports of call in the case of a disagreement, though people do also go to the state courts if the parties are not satisfied. Monica Wilson observes that it was widely practiced that the matters in dispute should go to the village authorities first. If there were delays in appealing to the headman's court or dissatisfaction with the traditional law solutions, people might take their matters directly to the Native Commissioner's Court as the court of first instance.[134]

Mönnig also reflects on the impact of the Black Administration Act of 1927 and says that in the Pedi area few people took cases to the Native Commissioner of their own accord, and only chiefs appointed by the central government actually referred cases to them.[135] Hammond-Tooke observes that in his area of study, appeals went directly from the courts of headmen 'to that of the Resident Magistrate (later styled Native Commissioner)'.[136] Thus people could actually 'by-pass the chiefs' courts entirely'.[137]

D.H. Reader, who wrote on the Makhanya of Southern Natal in 1966, also observed a multilayered court system that culminated in the chief's court hearing an appeal. He observed that when the chief's verdict failed to express the opinions of those present at the court, the matter must simply be taken to the Native Commissioner.[138]

131 Kuper, Hilda (1947) *An African Aristocracy: Rank among the Swazi of Bechuanaland.* London and New York, International African Institute, Oxford University Press at 65.
132 Ibid. at 54–55.
133 Mönnig (above).
134 Wilson (above) at 32.
135 Mönnig (above) at 313.
136 Hammond-Tooke (above) at 78.
137 Ibid.
138 Reader, Desmond H. (1966) *Zulu Tribe in Transition: The Makhanya of Southern Natal.* Manchester, Manchester University Press at 259–260. His fieldwork having been done pre-1951, Reader observes that 'in no aspect of Makhanya life has the South African Administration intervened more decisively than in the judicial sphere'. He says that the legal system there is a complex of European and tribal judicial institutions which have gradually come together over a period of more than 100 years. Giving consideration to the Black Authorities Act and Natal Code, this can scarcely be denied.

As one sees here, defection was an important check on the power of traditional leaders in the South African context.[139] This means of accountability was only partly disrupted by apartheid legislation that forced limiting boundaries on people. Even with the existence of imposed jurisdictional boundaries for 'tribes' and their 'traditional courts' (so that people could no longer secede), the alternative system of courts made available to them – namely, the state court system – served as an important alternate accountability mechanism.

The possibility of electing to avoid 'traditional courts' when they were unjust served an important function, particularly for women.[140] This function is especially important because of the colonial and apartheid governments' entrenching of patriarchy in 'traditional communities'. As demonstrated in cases like *Makapan* and *Mokhatle*, above, people would turn to a state court to defend them against – or simply allow them to avoid – unjust rulers' actions, laws, and judgments.[141] In other words, the introduction of state courts alongside vernacular forums served a valuable function in a manner like that described by Von Benda-Beckmann. In a modest but important way, this forced co-existence caused the vernacular forums to remain in part dependent on their accountability to their people for their legitimacy, relevance, and use.

Interestingly, in 1970 Isaac Schapera considered the impact of British interventions and laws on vernacular forum systems and laws in Botswana. He noted that the law imposed major changes in the hierarchy of the courts around 1934–35: namely, the lower ward courts were no longer recognised, despite the fact that they did most of the work. However, he observed that these lower forums continued to operate without legal recognition, and in practice, most parties accepted the lower ward courts' decisions.[142]

Finally, vernacular forums are shown generally to be inclusive of the general members of the vernacular grouping, and traditional leaders' powers in dispute management are circumscribed by customary law and tradition. In other words, chiefs and headmen are not powers unto themselves.[143] Hammond-Tooke references this point in a remarkable claim that the 'chiefship is sacred and, as such, must be above criticism or reproach. This is achieved by effectively withdrawing

139 Claassens (above) at 71–72.

140 Chanock (above) at 262; McClendon, Thomas (1995) 'Tradition and Domestic Struggle in the Courtroom: Customary Law and the Control of Women in Segregation-Era Natal' *International Journal of African Historical Studies*, 28(3): 527–561; Roberts, Richard (2005) *Litigants and Households: African Disputes and Colonial Courts in the French Soudan, 1895–1912*. Portsmouth, NH, Heinemann at 18–20.

141 Reader (above).

142 Schapera, Isaac (1970) 'Tribal Innovators: Tswana Chiefs and Social Change, 1795–1940' *London School of Economics Monographs on Social Anthropology no 43*. London, Athlone Press at 92.

143 Of course, women were generally excluded, but the vernacular grouping was otherwise included in the courts' processes of hearing and deciding the case; these structures were not elite institutions nor ones centralised to an individual in power.

the chief from the decision-making process.'[144] Thus, decisions are made by the 'community-in-council'.[145] Indeed, as an informant told Hammond-Tooke, law-making was deeply consultative and '"[a] chief who dared to go against the wishes of his people ran the risk of losing their support, and perhaps his chieftainship." . . . Consensus was all important.'[146]

This is not dissimilar to the comment, above, by Reader vis-à-vis the Zulu that if ever the chief handed down a decision that deviated from the views articulated by those present at the hearing, the matter had to be appealed to the Native Commissioner.[147] Peter Alan Wilson Cook writes of the Bomvana in 1931 that, when matters went to the chief, the decision he would make would have to be based on the traditions of the 'tribe', the decisions of the old chiefs, and the general opinion of the men gathered at court.[148] Mönnig repeatedly notes that among Bapedi, any initiated man was expected to attend the forums at various levels as often as they could.[149] One should also note the similar claims of Major E.A.T. Dutton regarding the Basotho headmen's forums:

> Anyone can ask questions and there is no unseemly hurry; . . . the smaller fry among the men of the lekhotla give their opinion, the more important people next, and finally the headman gives his decision, which is generally the summing up of the views of the majority. In theory, he can give any decision he likes, but in practice, . . . the final verdict is really the general opinion of all present.[150]

In summary, the weight of research on South African vernacular groupings from the last century confirms that vernacular forums are essentially multilayered and inclusive of multiple voices in dispute management processes, rather than unilevelled and uni-vocal (that is, centralised).

Concluding remarks

Even after the introduction of colonial and apartheid interference that directed otherwise, the vernacular forums proved remarkably resilient and thus largely

144 Hammond-Tooke (above) at 68.
145 Ibid. at 74 fn 13.
146 Ibid. at 67, 68. At 74 fn 13: 'by "consensus" I do not mean unanimity or absence of conflict, but merely legitimation of commands by the majority decision of a broad-based body . . . [a] 'community-in-council (Kuper (above) at 14)'.
147 Reader (above) at 259–260.
148 Cook, Peter Alan Wilson (1931) *Social Organisation and Ceremonial Institutions of the Bomvana*. Cape Town and Johannesburg, Juta & Co. Ltd at 146. This is not dissimilar to the observations of Comaroff, John and Simon Roberts (1981) *Rules and Processes: The Cultural Logic of Dispute in an African Context*. Chicago and London, University of Chicago at 80–83 concerning the parameters of Tswana chiefs' law-making power.
149 Mönnig (above) at 309.
150 Dutton, Major E. A. T. (1923) *The Basuto of Basutoland*. London, Jonathan Cape at 59–60.

retained the multileveled and participatory form described, though more strongly at lower levels of social organisation than in the chiefs' courts. Vernacular forums remained the primary spaces for dispute management but met with some competition in the existence of an alternative court system. The latter system afforded people a tool by which to try to hold the vernacular forums accountable by avoiding them if they did not perform in the manner desired.

The listed attributes of the system of vernacular dispute management observed by mid-twentieth century scholars remain largely apposite. There is evidence of the relevance of these attributes regarding the Tswana[151] and Zulu.[152] Recent studies that I have conducted among Swati-speaking communities in Mpumalanga[153] also confirm them. Moreover, in consultation meetings held on the Traditional Courts Bill in multiple provinces of South Africa, participants have referred to these aspects of vernacular dispute management.[154]

The representation of the Msinga system in subsequent chapters will largely resonate with this scholarship. However, it will also reveal that, while the system has proven remarkably resilient to the social, economic and political inequalities of colonialism and apartheid, nevertheless, it has suffered some harm in the process and continues to face tremendous challenges. The Msinga system will therefore show that vernacular systems are even more nuanced than what I have reported from the mid-century scholarship on other areas, thus making the task of legislating to regulate these forums in a way that guarantees all ordinary rural people access to justice even more challenging.

151 Comaroff and Roberts (above); Oomen (above).

152 Alcock, Rauri and Donna Hornby (March 2004) 'Traditional Land Matters: A Look into Land Administration in Tribal Areas in KwaZulu-Natal', Pietermaritzburg, Legal Entity Assessment Project (accessible at www.mdukatshani.com/resources/traditional%20land%20matters%202004.pdf).

153 Mnisi (above).

154 Claassens, Aninka and Sindiso Mnisi (2009) 'Rural Women Redefining Land Rights in the Context of Living Customary Law' *South African Journal on Human Rights*, 25(3): 491–516.

Section II

Institutional attributes of dispute management in Msinga

3 Controversial subject matter

What disputes are heard?

When ordinary assault could lead to war

Vakashile was making a late evening trip through one of the subwards in Msinga when Yaziwa told him to hand over his jacket. Vakashile claims that when he refused, Yaziwa jumped him and, in short order, was joined by his four friends. Vakashile said that they took his sandals, phone, and cap. Besides that, they gave him a solid beating.

After this incident, Vakashile and his family made a complaint to the headman of the subward where the assault had taken place. Thereafter, the families of the alleged assailants had gone to Vakashile's family to return his goods – including a new phone to replace the one of which he had been dispossessed. They thought that the matter was settled but soon learned that Vakashile's family did not share this view.

Before the joint council, composed of the Msinga ward's headman and the headman of Vakashile's ward, which was part of a different *isizwe* (nation), Vakashile's family brought a case for damages, specifically for the beating that Vakashile had suffered. Vakashile testified that he did not know any of the young men who had assaulted him. He said that he had heard Yaziwa referred to by name during the attack. In his testimony, Yaziwa said that he did not know Vakashile but was familiar with him because Yaziwa had seen Vakashile as he walked by Yaziwa's home. Yaziwa had not known the complainant's name before the present conflict.

Yaziwa placed initial blame for the assault on another young man, Mshaye, who was not present for the hearing. Yaziwa said that he and another neighbour had joined the fray only in order to stop Mshaye from hurting Vakashile. Yaziwa then said he had been at that particular place where the assault occurred because he had been asked by a friend to accompany him to another friend's home. The group of alleged assailants included Chuku, who, Yaziwa said, was known for bothering people when he encountered them on the road. Yaziwa testified that Chuku had joined in the assault against Vakashile. Yaziwa gave the names of the five young men who had been there when the assault occurred – the other young men were not present for the hearing, though some of their parents were in attendance.

In the latter part of the hearing, testimony was given that contradicted Yaziwa's representation. One of the men in the community, Laka, who had arrived late for the hearing, suggested that the young men accused of the assault smoked marijuana and then blocked people in the road and caused mischief. He thought that the young men ought to be corporally punished right there in order to deter others from the same behaviour. Laka thought that the money asked in damages was too little. He expressed his view in disagreement with Yaziwa's father. Laka's idea for alternative punishment was not carried forward.

In pleading for the damages requested to be lowered from R1,500 (and then further still from the reduced R500) per assailant, Yaziwa's father had mentioned that people did not have much money and their sons did not work. In light of this fact, in one sense, this case was just a matter of a handful of young men who did not have much to do seeing an easy target from whom they could get some desirable material possessions. They may also have just seen an opportunity to give a tough time to a young man who was courting a young woman who they viewed, possessively, as their own.

Yet, the matter can be seen more expansively than that. I would argue that most matters that present in Msinga hold the potential to turn very violent. The fact that this dispute traversed borders between not just two wards but also two nations makes it one that could easily have escalated into an intertribal conflict. Certainly, if Vakashile had been killed in the assault (and this possibility was angrily raised by his kin when they defended their demand for damages in the case), the fatality may have given rise to cycles of retaliation. In other words, it could have led to feuding between the wards and/or nations. Thus, though the matter superficially presented as just an ordinary dispute, it held potential to quickly become much more than that. And, as I have shown in previous chapters, this is true of many disputes that occur in Msinga.

'Mere disagreements'

During my research, informants described the vernacular forums' dispute management authority only in vague terms. When I enquired about subject-matter jurisdiction – specifically, what kinds of matters the vernacular forums have the authority to formally manage or do in fact manage – the typically summative response I received was '*imibango nje*' (just disagreements or mere altercations). Even when asked to give specific examples of what kinds of matters the vernacular forums heard, respondents who provided examples would still typically conclude their modest lists with, '*imibango nje*'. The implication was always that these forums deal only with minor disputes (really, squabbles), such as petty disagreements between neighbours.

This is not so. As the most accessible forums in Msinga, vernacular forums are the first port of call when matters arise within the vernacular grouping. Since, as I will describe in Chapter 5, most matters do not escalate either to the highest forums within the vernacular system or to the state courts, the lowest and mid-level vernacular forums hear the bulk of matters that arise locally.

Even when these matters present as being minor, they often actually have serious implications for the parties involved – for instance, a seemingly simple marriage dispute can be a matter of life and death to one of the parties who stands to lose her livelihood if the matter is not agreeably resolved. The disputes may even be potentially violent in terms of their immediate cause or long-term risks or consequences. A dispute surrounding a false witchcraft accusation is technically only a matter of defamation but holds the potential to get someone killed, for example.

Furthermore, since local people are often concerned that matters brought to state authorities will not lead to the outcomes that the complainants wish, they often choose to bring even matters that ought legally to be taken to the state courts to the vernacular forums instead. For instance, the family of a victim of statutory rape might be disincentivised by the likelihood in their minds of the teenage perpetrator's long-term incarceration under state law. The family might also prefer the probability that the vernacular dispute management process will yield compensation to them as the victim's family. It is therefore not surprising that the matters heard by vernacular forums extend from relatively superficial civil matters to profoundly criminal ones.

Yet, the state's proscription of the hearing of severe criminal matters other than by state courts has had an effect in Msinga. As discussed in Chapter 2 under the history of state regulation of traditional courts, the criminal matters that could be heard by vernacular forums were significantly circumscribed. Indeed, they were limited to relatively minor criminal offences such as assault and stock theft. The evidence from Msinga shows that this ban has had some effect – at least, in terms of framing how the local vernacular groupings perceive the nature of offences (for example, distinguishing between civil and criminal matters).

More significantly, this regulatory prohibition has had an effect on what the vernacular forums consider matters that they are at liberty to hear. As mentioned, when I asked what matters vernacular forums hear, the most common response I received was '*imibango, nje*' (again, 'minor disagreements'). It turns out that this response aligns with what matters the vernacular forums know are the only ones that they are supposed to hear. Nonetheless, the category of matters heard by the forums, in fact, extends beyond what is permitted by state law. Moreover, even when the vernacular forums do not hear prohibited matters, the reasons for their compliance are usually more complex than simply that the state has forbidden it.

For these reasons, this chapter is not simply about subject-matter jurisdiction. That would be too limiting. The current chapter will instead discuss what kinds of issues empirically present themselves in the vernacular groupings of Msinga, whether the forums presented with these matters deal with them and, if not, the reasons for which the forums both say and, in fact, decide not to. The questions here are: which matters are the forums asked to hear, which do the forums actually hear, and which do they reject and/or redirect, and for what reasons? This chapter will focus on the *kinds* of conflicts the vernacular forums hear; the question regarding the *manner* in which dispute management is effected in these conflicts will be discussed in Chapter 4.[1]

The present chapter is ultimately concerned with the social implications of the matters that come before these forums – especially those that do so repeatedly – and the finite ability of the forums to deal with many of them effectively. However, the chapter stops short of fully satisfying that ultimate enquiry, because it deals in a rather technical manner with the subject-matter disputes that the forums confront. The broader question implied is revisited in Chapter 7, where I engage more substantively and evaluatively with the difficulty of what people really want when they approach the vernacular forums and the constraints on the forums to provide that for which people are, in essence, asking.

Nature of subject-matter

The kinds of matters that arise and are brought to the attention of the vernacular dispute management forums in Msinga are both civil and criminal, and range in nature between personal, commercial, and public concerns. Recognising that the terminology of state law would be inappropriate and overly constraining in the context of vernacular dispute management in Msinga, I rather refer to the matters using more general descriptors. Therefore, I categorise them as private, commercial, and public wrongs (all being a kind of civil offence), and criminal violations.

I conclude with a category of what I term 'uncertain offences', which are wrongs that are raised by the members of the vernacular grouping but are not strictly considered wrongs by the vernacular dispute management forums. This category includes acts that are individually or locally perceived as wrongs but that defy strict categorisation as private, commercial, and public wrongs or criminal violations. Sometimes how these offences are perceived locally contradicts how they are portrayed by the state. Evaluative judgments aside, it is important to recognise these differences between vernacular groupings' and state perceptions. More than that, it is important to observe the internal tensions around some of these differences in perception within the vernacular groupings themselves.

A key caveat is that the categorisations I ascribe here to the matters that are presented to the vernacular forums are not primarily those used by participants in the vernacular dispute management system. Rather, these categorisations are analytical references assigned by me, based on how I understand the participants in the system to perceive the nature and seriousness of the disputes that they bring to the relevant forums. Thus, though the labels are informed by participants' perceptions, I have assigned these categories to facilitate the reader's understanding of the subject matters that come before the vernacular forums.

1 For a more detailed discussion, see Mnisi Weeks, Sindiso (2015–2016) 'Access to Justice?: Dispute Management Processes in Msinga, KwaZulu-Natal, South Africa' *New York Law School Law Review*, 60(1): 227–249.

The categories are therefore not definitive. This fluidity of categories is in keeping with the flexible approach taken by vernacular forums in contrast to that of the state system, as well as in keeping with the approach that I am taking in this book in my attempt to highlight the systemic differences between the vernacular and state forms.

Private wrongs

In Msinga, the family is the primary subject. Therefore, when matters appear before the vernacular forums, they are most often presented as being conflicts between families even if the acts that gave rise to the disputes were actually perpetrated by and between individuals. We should keep in mind, therefore, that though in a western court many of the kinds of wrongs described below would present as matters between individuals, in Msinga they are typically presented as being between families.

The first and perhaps primary kind of private wrong is the marital dispute. Under this category falls conflict between wives of a polygynous marriage and the objection raised by a wife in a polygynous arrangement that the husband shows preference of one wife over another. A wife's eviction by her husband or his family also falls in this category of wrong, and her request to return to her marital home would also be categorised as a private wrong. A related matter is the birth family's 'repossessing' a wife (their daughter) as leverage for outstanding *lobolo* (bridewealth), or the counterclaim of a husband's demand for the return of his wife by her birth family. Finally, in this category of claims are matters pertaining to separation and divorce. Predictably in such a context, marital disputes often present a mix of these different claims simultaneously.

The second large set of wrongs between private persons is non-marital disputes that are internal to the family. These might end in rifts and break-ups and maybe include insults, arguments (sometimes leading to or including physical fighting), intimidation, and physical separation or eviction. In one conflict that we learned about while in the field, two young male cousins (Mzala and Mfowethu) got into an argument at a bar, and one called the other a witch, which lead to an assault. The family chose to discuss the matter in private, and the only report we received, from an extended family member who had been in attendance of the discussion, was that the family had successfully resolved the conflict.

Another important category of private disputes involves children. As in the state courts, matters commonly arise to do with paternity and illegitimacy, maintenance and custody. Yet, a significant difference is that these matters as they present in the vernacular forums often largely have to do with whether the child can bear the father's surname. It is on this question that legitimacy or payment of damages has primary bearing. The paternity and illegitimacy issue, however, usually arises simultaneously with a maintenance claim, because the young man's family typically does not want to pay damages to the young woman's family or maintenance for the child, at least not until they are satisfied that the child is 'theirs'.

That said, it is worth noting that, at least in one matter we recorded, the boy's family did not deny paternity or try to shirk responsibility for maintenance. In this matter, the young woman's family reported that the young man's family had not made any contribution toward the raising of a daughter, Wamkelwe, who was born outside of marriage. The young man's family confirmed that the child in question was their son's but said that the young man had nothing to contribute at the time. He had gone to Johannesburg for work.

Custody can be tied into these conflicts but is most often raised in the context of women leaving their husbands. In those situations, if a husband is unsuccessful at getting his wife back (or if he does not want his wife to return to the marital home), the husband and his family will claim that the wife cannot take the children with her. In such disputes, the children are almost inevitably considered to belong to the husband's family.

Disputes related to death form another category of private wrongs. They include disputes over the body of the deceased and who gets to bury the deceased, in what location or when. In an illustrative daily report, a headman divulged that the family of one deceased man, Shonile, had set the date for his burial on a day – namely, a Saturday – that his surviving wife could not attend for religious reasons. To her objections, the husband's family members said that she was the one who attended the church that observed the Sabbath on a Saturday, and they wanted to return to work in Johannesburg and other locales.

In a matter that was heard by one of the headmen's councils, the natal family of a married woman, MaSishiyile, brought a case against the woman's marital family on the basis that the natal family had not been informed when she died. The marital family had just buried her, and thus none of her natal family had been able to attend her funeral – even though, her natal family said, she was their daughter and not that of the marital family.

What follows a person's death – namely, matters of succession – is an important area of private wrongs. The eviction of a deceased's wife and children, and property-grabbing by members of the deceased family can also give rise to conflict. Finally, in this category of private disputes pertaining to death, contention over *ukungena* (the levirate) can also manifest.

A further category of private disputes includes matters to do with reputation. These disputes typically arise out of 'bad' gossip (often among neighbours, most commonly but not exclusively among women), or as a result of an insult, insolence, and defamation. In terms of defamation, common parties are neighbours, though matters sometimes arise between schoolchildren or are a function of concerns about children disrespecting local adults. Sometimes parties are local youth challenged for disrespecting local authorities such as a tribal policeman, headman, or chief. For instance, one young man, Biziwe, was summoned to the Nezikhathi chief's homestead because he had been heard insulting the chief as the chief drove by.

These matters of reputation very often relate to further disputes over other issues. For example, they commonly occur in relation to witchcraft allegations or accusations of stock theft – both of which are, in essence, about some unexplained loss that has been suffered by the accuser and the belief that the accused is a traitor or simply cannot be trusted. Examples include one neighbour, Sihluphi, accusing another of stock theft, and another person alleging that his or her neighbour performs witchcraft, by which means she or he killed the accuser's wife[2] or child.[3]

I relate accusations that one is a snitch or sellout to witchcraft allegations because of the similarity of the consequences of such a reputation, whether founded in reality or merely due to aspersions being cast. I would also argue, in the case of MaThembile, that a witchcraft accusation was made indirectly, the allegation being implied in the accusation that she had poisoned other people's animals.

If there is tangible suspicion of witchcraft, this accusation can require disproving by consulting a seer. As explained in Chapter 1, if the person rumoured to be a witch, snitch, or animal poisoner asserts that the accusation is unfounded, they are required to dispel this rumour through public process and obtain an apology from the person who made it, because of the threat the accusation presents to the accused individual's life.

In a whistle-blowing matter, a man, Soliwe, was accused of being a snitch to the police about members of his ward being in possession of illegal firearms. He denied the allegations but other members of the ward testified against him and said he had done it before. He was cautioned and told that he was putting his life in danger, putting himself at the risk of people killing him. This caution is linked to how the assault on one's reputation is sometimes complemented by an assault on one's body: the verbal assault escalates to a physical assault. I will return to physical assaults later in this chapter, under the section on criminal violations.

Verbal assaults – especially concerning young women as they relate to young men – often imply doubt about a girl's virginity or implications of a girl's hypersexuality. The latter takes the form of either sexual overtures made to the young women, though these are perpetrated by men who perceive the girls as ripe for them, or sexual innuendo about them, which can be verbalised in the form of accusations by other girls as well as men. In a Nakudala matter, for example, a dispute was appealed right up to the chief's council and then to *isikebhe*, a vigilante society, because one young woman, Mthuki, had called another 'a wife', thus implying that Ntombi was no longer a virgin.

These kinds of assaults on reputation can be related to seduction matters or disputes to do with *ukuqoma* (entering into a relationship with a boy or man). In one example, a girl, Nqabile, had rejected a young man, Soka, who was pursuing her, but she found herself being pressured into the relationship by the girlfriend of Soka's friend. For Nqabile, not being in a romantic relationship was a matter of principle and the underhanded tactics used by Soka's

2 MaSitolo.
3 Yedwa.

friend's girlfriend, Zifakile, in order to give the impression that Nqabile had entered into such a relationship stood to tarnish Nqabile's reputation. These tactics included stealing Nqabile's clothes and placing them at Soka's home.

Two final categories of private wrongs are worth mentioning. One is between neighbours when they disagree about the boundary between their properties. As MaSitolo's case demonstrates, a long-standing yet unresolved dispute over a boundary can lead to ongoing tensions that later emerge as insult-related disputes. In this matter, MaSitolo's brother was called a witch and stock thief after he had contested the boundary move.

Another category of private wrong is between ordinary individuals and the traditional authority responsible for hearing their disputes, when people feel that the leader in charge of the vernacular forum has shown bias, unfairness, or injustice in exercising his dispute management or administrative authority. Bias on the part of the headman was implied by a young male defendant's family in the matter of their son, Ngetshe, being accused of grievously assaulting a young woman with stones and thereby knocking her teeth out. The young woman's mother, who had initiated the original complaint of assault, also claimed that there had been corruption in the case and she explicitly said that she knew her headman to be susceptible to being bought off with alcohol.

Commercial wrongs

Because people in Msinga are so poor and their land relatively unproductive, commercial activity makes up a limited basis for people's interactions and thus forms only a minor proportion of disputes that arise in the area. Moreover, the main disputes that arise from commercial relationships are relatively minor and involve relatively small sums or items of little financial value. That does not mean, however, that the matters are insignificant. The amounts and values involved in the disputes are of great significance to the people concerned.

The primary commercial wrongs that occur in Msinga are contractual disputes. These disputes mainly concern breach of contract, largely pertaining to conflicts over cattle or money. These matters typically relate to debts, such as outstanding *lobolo* payments, unsettled loans, or non-delivery of objects agreed for exchange. For example, a man, Bolekile, had been loaned R200 fourteen years before and had still not replaced it with the goat he had promised. In a similar matter, a man, Msebenzi, who had borrowed a cow in order to host a celebration had not replaced it with another cow, as had been agreed at the time of the loan.

Some contractual disputes relate to sales, such as a car sale gone wrong (perhaps because the car turned out to have been a stolen vehicle belonging to someone other than the purported seller), or non-payment of the sale price agreed upon. Such a dispute arose between two relations, Babazala and Mthengi, when Babazala had sold his son-in-law a car and an outstanding sum of R2,000 had yet to be paid. In keeping with the laden nature of relationships and hence disputing in Msinga, this claim was brought after the woman they had in common (one of the men being her husband and the other her father) had died. When the son-in-law was summoned to a hearing by the headman, he said he did not want to see his father-in-law and would pay the amount to the headman in four installments.

In an extended sense, these kinds of breach of contract disputes also regularly relate to non-payment of damages for another kind of wrong. What the subordinate wrong often entails is a private wrong, such as impregnating a girl outside of marriage or compensation for a criminal violation that had been previously managed, whether negotiated, mediated, arbitrated or adjudicated. For instance, a man, Mbambeni, murdered a young schoolgirl. He was subsequently convicted and was serving jail time when the girl's family brought a R9,000 claim against the family of the convicted perpetrator, for compensation for their loss. Mbambeni's family agreed to pay the sum in small installments. Commercial disputes may also include eviction or repossession as an attempt to settle the first wrong.[4]

As in the case of private wrongs, commercial wrongs may principally occur between individuals, but they will often ultimately be managed as disputes between the families to which the individuals belong. This is particularly so when the matters involve members of the same extended family, for instance, when a wife, MaLwimi, accused her two uncles-in-law of witchcraft.

Families get involved in individual disputes, particularly, when the disputes involve women – such as in the dispute mentioned above between Mthuki and Ntombi, over Ntombi's virginity. Family involvement was also seen when Mtshali, the owner of a garden plot that had been rented from him by a woman, challenged her for stealing his irrigation pipes when she left the plot on termination of their agreement. Though the suspected woman, MaMqashi, largely spoke for herself in the proceedings before the headman's council, her husband was part of the dispute management and was, at least notionally, representing her.

Public wrongs

The line between private and public wrongs is not a clear one. For instance, while boundary disputes occur between neighbours, they can escalate to disputes between subwards, wards, or even nations. At that scale, they obviously cease to be private wrongs and become public ones. Of course, boundary disputes do not all originate in the private sphere. Often enough, they arise from unfinalised historic disputes between vernacular groupings at whatever scale is apposite. For example, a long-standing boundary and land dispute between the labour tenant occupiers and ward (*isigodi*) members in one of the 'traditional communities' is the most direct instance of such group conflict that arose in the data we collected. New disputes can also spring up almost spontaneously.

4 Ndodakazi.

As suggested above, the same murkiness between public and private appears in offences such as whistle-blowing (snitching) and witchcraft. Typically, the allegation that one is a snitch or witch emerges in the instance of an accusation by one individual against another – but usually in a private or semi-public setting.

For example, as already mentioned, despite vehemently denying the accusation of whistle-blowing, Soliwe was cautioned that he was putting his life in danger, because people would wish to silence him. This warning was issued in a public forum: a gathering of the men in Soliwe's (sub)ward. Likewise, one member of a vernacular grouping might accuse an individual of witchcraft, but the accused individual is then seen as a threat to, and thus enemy of, the whole grouping.[5]

One other kind of wrong sometimes included among public wrongs is stock theft. For instance, a man by the name of Mdlinzo was suspected of cow theft, and the ward discussed the matter at the headman's tree. Communally, the ward members wanted to know who was responsible for cattle disappearing and wanted that individual stopped. In this sense, this individual offence of stealing a ward member's cows took on the form of an offence against the vernacular grouping as a whole.

Another way of conceptualising public wrongs is as taboos, that is, attitudes and practices that offend the vernacular grouping's sensibilities and notions of what is socially or religiously acceptable – what is 'done' or 'not done'. These taboos engender public mistrust and suspicion, and thus might even lead members of the vernacular grouping to dissociate themselves from the person accused of those offensive beliefs and behaviours.

Not participating in public life and ceremony can be viewed as such a taboo and lead to the suspicion that the suspect practices other taboos and to the negative reactions that commonly accompany taboos. This suspicion was seen in the MaThembile matter, in which it was revealed that she had had approximately nine goats die on her property. It later emerged – after she had been shot in an attempt on her life made by an unidentified person – that she had lived in a manner that was socially isolated, and people therefore suspected her of having deliberately poisoned their livestock.

An interesting public offence is one against nature – that is, trees or other resources. This offence is interesting because of its history.[6] Of course, the

5 Notably, witchcraft was specifically listed among chiefs' and headmen's jurisdiction (among activities they are required to prevent) in Proclamation 110 of 1957 in Government Gazette of 18 April 1957, Regulations Prescribing the Duties, Powers, Privileges and Conditions of Service of Chiefs and Headmen, clause 12.

6 Proclamation 110 of 1957 in Government Gazette of 18 April 1957, Regulations Prescribing the Duties, Powers, Privileges and Conditions of Service of Chiefs and Headmen – clause 9 says, '[An appointed chief or headman] shall ensure the enforcement within his area of laws and all orders, instructions or requirements of the Government relating to the administration control of the Natives in his area in general and to the following matters in particular: – . . . (f) the occupation or cultivation of land and the use of commonages; . . . (l) the preservation of flora and fauna and of water supplies; . .'.

regulation of natural resources makes sense in a vernacular grouping that shares them and depends upon them for its survival. However, the fixation on the power of traditional authorities – particularly at the most local level and thus, namely, headmen – to police the use of these resources in a very particular manner arises out of the peculiar regulation of their role by the apartheid government.

It is interesting how seriously some headmen take the task of policing people's cutting down of fresh trees. One must take into account that young brides are socially expected to cut down fresh trees and use them to build a structure in their back yard. This loosely woven mound dries over time and becomes a sign of pride for the wife and, by extension, her marital kin. Hence, cutting down living trees despite regulations against doing so is an expression of cultural expectations and is almost exclusively perpetrated by young brides. The diligence with which some headmen exercise their role of ensuring that the offence is not committed sets up an interesting social dynamic and raises questions about the headmen's motivations. For instance, one could be forgiven for thinking that, feeling disempowered and at great risk in the exercise of much of their role of maintaining law and order, some headmen take solace in this simpler task often carried out against less threatening perpetrators.[7]

In addition to social taboos, land is a frequent and often significant object of conflict. At the highest level and largest scale, tensions can arise over land claims that the vernacular grouping – or segments of it – makes to the government. These claims can give rise to conflict between different subwards, wards, or nations and/or their members.

These conflicts do not tend to end simply because a decision has been made by the government – for instance, a land application by *isizwe* (the nation) has failed or one made by a 'communal property association' has succeeded. Instead, often the decision by the government to grant the claim of a segment of *isizwe* or recognise the land claimed as belonging to *isizwe* at large – and thus as land

7 Also see Cousins, Ben, Rauri Alcock, Ngididi Dladla, Dladla Hornby, Mphethethi Masondo, Gugu Mbatha, Makhosi Mweli and Creina Alcock (2011) '*Imithetho yomhlaba yaseMsinga:* The Living Law of Land in Msinga District, KwaZulu-Natal'. PLAAS Research Report 43, Cape Town, The University of the Western Cape at 39: 'In relation to trees, some informants say that the *izinduna* of each *isigodi* are supposed to prevent people from cutting down living trees or green wood, but others say the *amaphoyisa* are supposed to police such resource use. Many people say that policing has broken down, in part because there is a shortage of wood, in part because the authority of the *izinduna* is no longer respected as much as it used to be.' On the other hand, Cousins et al. also observe at 82: 'In relation to use of natural resources, the key problem that many informants focused on was the erosion of the regulatory authority of *izinduna*. Examples included . . . non-enforcement of the rule that green trees should never be cut. One common reason offered for the waning authority of the *Induna* in relation to these rules is that many men now own firearms and threaten the *Induna* if he tries to enforce the rules.' As my findings show, while enforcement 'of the rule that green trees should never be cut' is not universal, by any means, it cannot be said (as Cousins' informants seem to believe) that there is total non-enforcement.

to be administered by the chief and his council – gives rise to outward and express conflict or exacerbates latent conflict. The boundary and land conflict in one of the wards of the Nezikhathi area exemplifies just this effect. The ward headman presumed to place people to set up homes on a part of the land 'returned' to *isizwe* that former labour tenants saw as theirs to administer. The Wesizwe faction of the Yisithupha ward argued that the land was to be administered by the headman as an ordinary part of *isizwe* (the Nezikhathi nation), while the Wabantu faction of residents of the former labour tenant farm disagreed.

Land issues also arise at a lower level and on a narrower scale. One category of these issues includes matters pertaining to land applications – particularly for use of and access to land for grazing, farming, schools, clinics, and other community projects. The conflicts over such applications are usually raised in the form of discussions of group matters (to resolve questions of local importance) in vernacular grouping meetings and do not necessarily involve particular individuals but a subset of the relevant vernacular grouping. These conflicts do sometimes have to do with a subset of people's behavioural choices, though.

In one exemplifying conflict, an adult man who was a ward councillor elected as part of local government representation for the area was helping to lead a vernacular grouping effort to get the government to build a clinic in the ward. The ward councilor, Khansela, stated that there had been a lengthy process to get government approval, a process in which he believed the young chief of his 'traditional community' had interfered midway through in order to get the clinic built in a part of the ward that he preferred. Khansela's argument was that the location preferred by the young chief was nowhere near as ideal for the bulk of the ward members and, furthermore, was not the location that had been agreed upon by the ward members who had had the initiative to apply for the clinic. Other than simply a land use dispute, this conflict was also an expression of an authority dispute between the chief (a traditional authority) and the ward councillor (a local government authority).

In the other traditional community that I researched, Nezikhathi, I sat in on a traditional council discussion of a complaint that had been brought by one of the headmen about certain people in his ward defying his authority and building in an area that he had deemed dangerous due to the risk of flooding. Likewise, this disagreement had embedded within it some degree of conflict over authority.[8] This leads me to a related class of public wrongs that give rise to disputes.

This form of public conflict is a result of tension between customary authorities and ward councillors, local cooperatives, government bodies, outside funders, or community members. These matters mainly concern governance and the uncertainty or competition over a sphere of authority – subject, territory, and/or persons – and scarce government resources in a context of desperate material need.

8 This harkens back to the observation made by Cousins' informants that the authority of the headmen has been eroded but the contest is ongoing as the headmen seek to maintain and strengthen their authority in circumstances that challenge it.

Another source of conflict within a vernacular grouping at any level of social organisation can be a request to contribute to a cause for which money is being collected, or the failure to contribute. This cause may be a rite, feast, or festival initiated by the chief, for instance, or a tangible project such as a grazing or farming project and its administration. The failure to contribute can be read as an expression of disagreement with or refusal to submit to and respect a particular authority.[9] However, in the poverty that is common throughout Msinga, this refusal could just as much be a matter of a person's having no disposable income from which to draw resources.[10]

A final source of public conflict is succession. In this case, I do not mean inheritance within a family but inheritance of title and position of authority at the public level – such as by a chief's son or headman. Such contestation was occurring in the Nakudala traditional community at the time of our data collection. Because the old chief of the traditional community was very sickly and his son had taken over the chief's role, there were some murmurs in the community over the son's suitability. He had formerly been a policeman and had a spectre of corruption and criminal allegations hanging over him. Indeed, people alleged that he was tied in with the hijacking racket in Msinga and the criminals that ran it. Moreover, he insisted on being called '*Ndabezitha*' (Your Highness) rather than '*Mtwana*' (the chief's child who is in line to inherit), when the form of address, *Ndabezitha*, should not have been used while his father was still alive and technically still chief.

In summary, public wrongs are generally disputes of vernacular grouping-wide implication or small-scale issues that are at high risk of becoming widespread problems. In rare cases, these wrongs are against the chieftaincy directly. These disputes are managed by one of the low-level authorities, though they can escalate right up to the chief.

Criminal violations

In the vernacular language, criminal matters are referred to as *izindaba zegazi*, which literally means, 'blood matters'. This description evokes how such crimes are typically matters relating to some physical violence and harm. Of course,

9 In one example that was raised while we were doing research, the Nakudala chief had gotten married to a bride who had not been selected by his *isizwe* and wanted his headmen to collect money from the vernacular group members to contribute to the wedding. In what informants described as a subtle move of protest, the headmen said that they could not and said the chief should ask the people for the contributions himself as the people would listen to him. The chief never made the request. The informants saw this as a victory of the traditional safeguards activated by the headmen against unpopular chiefly action.

10 For more on the controversy surrounding tribal levies, see Claassens, Aninka (2011) 'Resurgence of Tribal Levies: Double Taxation for the Poor' *South African Crime Quarterly*, 35: 11.

they are not exclusively so. What is striking here is the way people's ideas about criminal violations in the vernacular context have been substantially shaped by the interactions between the state and vernacular systems of law.

Interviewees' first reference point in determining the criminal jurisdiction of vernacular forums is the types of matters the state law does and does not permit these forums to hear. Only when pressed will people concede that the state law does not necessarily determine vernacular forums' jurisdictional conduct. Yet still, in the end, people summarise the subject-matter jurisdiction of vernacular forums as '*imibango nje*' (minor disagreements) though, this is far from the case. In actual fact, while the statutes most dramatically curtail vernacular forums' criminal jurisdiction by limiting it to mainly minor offences and stock theft, these forums exercise broader criminal jurisdiction in reality.

The most extreme criminal wrongs that vernacular forums in Msinga come into contact with are murder, attempted murder and culpable homicide.[11] The means by which these wrongs are committed include shootings, stabbings, severe beatings, and witchcraft or sorcery. The first – that is, gunfire – is by far the most common proximate (by which I mean 'immediately traceable') cause of death in Msinga. Just as important are ultimate causes, yet these causes are more complex to identify. Sometimes the offence is committed in the course of vigilante 'justice' or 'dispute resolution'.

Assaults – both 'common' ones and those perpetrated with the intent to inflict grievous bodily harm (assault GBH) – are the most regular criminal occurrence in Msinga[12] and are routinely brought to the vernacular forums. Assaults occur in locations that range from drinking places, weddings, *imicimbi* (parties), or *imemulo* (growing up celebrations).[13] They happen both in the course of planned fighting – such as ceremonial stick fights between men at a community celebration – and in unplanned conflicts. Take, for example, the Mosha incident in which an intoxicated man shot at someone at the end of *umemulo* (a party to celebrate a girl's becoming a young woman). This shooting was addressed by the headman's council.

11 In 2011, the Police recorded 47 murder cases, 31 attempts and eight cases of culpable homicide. In 2012, they recorded 29 cases of murder, 40 of attempt and 15 culpable homicides. See Crime Stats Simplified (n.d.) for the full police statistics for 2005 to 2016 (accessible at www.crimestatssa.com/precinct.php?id=560).

12 In the data collection years of 2011 and 2012, the Msinga police district reported 313 and 317 total cases of assault, respectively (122 common and 191 grievous in 2011, and then 112 common and 205 grievous in 2012) among a total population of 177,577 in 2011. While crimes are under-reported to the Msinga police, their statistics give some sense of the prevalence of the offence – especially, that in most years the police report assault GBH as the highest incidence crime in Msinga. See Lehohla, Pali (Statistician-General) (2012) *Census 2011 Municipal Report – KwaZulu-Natal.* Statistics South Africa Report No. 03-01-53 at 65 for census data of 2011 and Crime Stats Simplified (above).

13 These are the Zulu equivalent of bat mitzvahs.

In contrast, consider the assault perpetrated by a man whose mentally disabled teenage daughter, Sphiwo, was raped by her distant 'uncle', the man's cousin.[14] When Sphiwo's father confronted the uncle, they had gotten into a fight. The knock Sphiwo's father gave his distant cousin turned out to be serious, and the cousin later died. The Magistrate's Court convicted Sphiwo's father, Buhlungu, for the offence.

A subcategory of assault is domestic violence[15] – namely, spousal abuse, mostly perpetrated by husbands against their wives, and the abuse of children. This subcategory takes the form of physical abuse, sometimes even resulting in death, and sexual abuse. While verbal and psychological abuse – particularly in the form of sexual harassment, though this is often accompanied by physical abuse – are common in Msinga, they are rarely considered offences or reported. I will therefore return to discuss sexual harassment as a subcategory of 'uncertain offences' below.

In the matter of Ngeniwe that was reported but not heard in an official forum, a woman who had lost her husband and entered into an *ukungena* (levirate) union with one of her husband's kin claimed that her new *ngena* husband was intimidating her and effectively subjecting her to domestic violence. The headman did not hear the matter but referred it directly to the chief's council, but no one attended the set date of the hearing and the chief's council did not follow up.

In Balekile's case, a woman was being abused by her husband and ran away to the home of one of her sisters. Her husband, Myeni, went to one of her sisters' homes and, when he did not find his wife there, assaulted the sister. He went to a second sister's home and fought with that sister's family. There, his wife's brothers jumped him. They then took the matter to the headman. Because Myeni was disrespectful of the headman's council, the headman referred the matter to the chief's council, where the matter was never finalised. The reason given for the matter not being finalised was that the wife had returned to her husband.

Another violation, illegal gun possession, is rife in Msinga[16] and is a factor in most criminal violations, especially the most severe ones. If the illegal

14 In many South African cultures, distant relatives or even people who share only the same name or approximate age of your blood relations are referred to in familial terms such as *baba* (father), *mama* (mother), *bhuti* (brother), *sisi* (sister), *mkhulu* (grandfather), *gogo* (grandmother), *malume* (mother's brother), and *mzala* (cousin).

15 The police do not collect or report data on this subcategory separately.

16 The police reported 115 cases of 'illegal possession of firearms and ammunition' in 2011 and 64 in 2012. There is evidence to suggest that the fluctuation of the incidence of this offence is more to do with the extent to which the police focus their energies on policing it (especially through search and seizure operations). In police records, this crime is listed among 'crimes detected as a result of police action'. In fact, because illegal possession is in some ways the easiest to enforce in a context of potentially overwhelming forms and levels of crime, the police may default to its enforcement whenever they need to strengthen their performance numbers. There is also a logical case to be made for the police efforts

possession of a firearm is reported or otherwise discovered by the police, this discovery is often associated with police brutality. That is, according to all focus group reports, violence is the means used by the police to compel disclosure and release of illegal firearms. And if someone in the vernacular grouping is known to have blown or is suspected of blowing the whistle, this 'snitching' can give rise to a dispute or to punitive, vigilante violence. The whistle-blowing case of Soliwe illustrates these potential consequences. Another dispute demonstrates it even better.

In this matter, a man named Sabiswa approached the headman and his council to ask them to help him and another person resolve their differences – in other words, to mediate the conflict. In requesting mediation Sabiswa alleged that men who said that they had a problem with him because he blew the whistle on the respondent's gun had twice followed him when he was walking in a certain local area. Sabiswa said that others had also told him that the respondent, Qhuma, wanted to kill him. Asked by the council if he had ever seen anything on which he could blow the whistle, the complainant said he had once seen people at the door of his home who, he believed, had come to attack the home. He had told his grandmother about that the next morning. He said he was not sure if that was what they wanted to kill him for.

Qhuma asked the council to ask Sabiswa to identify who had said Qhuma wanted to kill him. The council said that Sabiswa at least needed to reveal the names of the people who he had seen at the door coming to attack his home, which he refused to do. Though he said he knew them, he also said that they were not present at the hearing and that he would not be able to reveal their names. The council would not entertain the discussion without this information, so the mediation did not proceed any further.

Illegal gun possession also factors into the perpetration of burglary and robbery and may lead to people being harmed.[17] Burglaries happen on private and commercial properties[18] – in the form of housebreaking and break-ins at local shops and businesses. In one instance, a small group of young men burgled the

---

into eradicating illegal gun possession. Namely, while assault GBH is the highest incidence criminal violation that takes place (or is reported to the police) in Msinga, it could be argued that the prevalence of this offence is significantly tied to the wide availability of firearms, among other factors discussed in Chapter 1. Hence, eradicating illegal guns would presumably reduce the severity and rate of escalation of local conflicts to violence. Nevertheless, this intervention would not necessarily address the 'intent' aspect that enables the crime of assault GBH to flourish. See Chapter 7 for further discussion.

17 In 2011, 13 instances of 'common robbery' were reported by the police and 30 cases of 'robbery with aggravating circumstances', among which were seven cases of 'robbery at residential premises' and six 'at non-residential premises'. For 2012, the police reported nine complaints of 'common robbery' and 22 instances of 'aggravated robbery', which included four residential robberies and seven non-residential.

18 For 2011, 95 cases of 'burglary at residential premises' were reported and 40 'at non-residential premises'. In 2012, the police recorded 81 cases of residential burglaries, as well as 30 non-residential.

shop of one of their kin, Gqekezelwe, who then brought the dispute to a vernacular forum. In addition, though we did not observe any instances of hijacking,[19] we were told by a 'tribal policeman' who is in charge of an area where many such crimes occur[20] that guns also feature in the car hijackings happening in the vicinity, crimes often related to the taxi industry in Msinga.

However, guns were not always specifically implicated in house burglaries. For instance, in one ward, a pair of young men, Uyeba and Nonya, were repeatedly brought to task before the headman for breaking into local homes and stealing their contents. The two men were arrested when they also burgled a local school and stole its computers. Likewise, in a dispute from a different ward, two young men, Gangile and Mngani, burgled and looted from local women's homes. They got away with radios, clothes, blankets and even meat out of the freezer. They sold the household goods and barbequed and ate the meat. No firearms were mentioned in either of these instances but perhaps only because they did not 'need' to be used because no people were present when the offences occurred.

Another very serious category of criminal offence that occurs in Msinga is sexual violence. Unfortunately, rape is not an irregular occurrence.[21] It can be committed by a single perpetrator or by a number (hence, gang rape). It can happen anywhere, sometimes even in the home, and it can happen to women of any age, even young girls. As an example, one of the headmen reported[22] that one of the women in his community had come to tell him that two young men had raped her daughter, Buyekhaya, and her friend. She said that Kubi and a young man who is unknown to the family had purported to give the two young women a car ride home after dark but then took them to the home of Kubi's family, locked them inside, and sexually assaulted them there.

One important distinction to make is that in Msinga rape is typically considered to be a wrong against the family, not necessarily against the individual whose body was violated. This belief is grounded in social emphasis on family honour and the links between sexual purity of a girl and that honour, in contrast to the western emphasis on physical integrity and personal freedom. Yet, given that in the context of the prevailing culture in Msinga girls' extramarital sexual relationships are frowned upon and 'dangerous' allegations can be used as accusatory insults, rape can also be used against men in ways that

19 This is the illegal and forceful seizure of vehicles in transit from those in legal possession – a subcategory of 'aggravated robbery'. According to police records, four cases of hijacking were reported to them in 2011 and three in 2012 (two 'carjackings' and one 'truck hijacking').

20 This was not one of the wards that we were closely monitoring. As compared to the testimony of the 'tribal policeman' interviewed, the number of instances cited suggests gross underreporting of this offence to the police.

21 The police recorded 54 sexual offences in 2011 and 82 in 2012. It is clear from our study's findings that many sexual offences go unreported to the police, hence placing the police statistics in some doubt. See further, Smythe, Dee (2015) *Rape Unresolved: Policing Sexual Offences In South Africa*. Cape Town, University of Cape Town Press.

22 Headmen's Daily Reports: 1 May 2011.

may approximate how witchcraft accusations are sometimes used against women. In these instances, an illegitimate accusation of rape might essentially used as a tool of intimidation against a young man or his family. This is implied in the instance of MaMsukelani in which a mother accuses a young man of raping her daughter and during discussions between the families it allegedly emerges that the mother had falsely accused the young man.

As also demonstrated by Kubi and Buyekhaya's matter, other forms of violence that mostly happen to young girls are kidnapping and abduction – particularly, *ukuthwala* (forced marriage).[23] Although I learned that forced marriage does happen, even if rarely, in Msinga, we did not observe or record any hearings of such by the vernacular forums during the research period. According to the report we received of the Malunde conflict,[24] it could be said that a kind of *ukuthwala* may have occurred (that is, if we consider a form of statutory rape a category of *ukuthwala*). In this dispute, the family of a girl, Malunde, objected to her having slept at the home of a young man much older than she was. The young man said Malunde was his girlfriend, but Malunde's family denied this.

While another incident was not completely managed by a vernacular forum, we did record an instance of outright *ukuthwala* that was reported to one of the headmen[25] and in which he played a role, if only by giving advice. In the Mthwele matter, the mother of a girl who had allegedly been abducted (the mother said not for the first time) asked for the counsel of the headman of the ward in which the young man accused of abducting the girl resided. The headman advised that the mother take the matter to the police because such an abduction of a schoolgirl by an 'older young man' (that is, someone not in school) was tantamount to rape. The mother returned to the headman a month later to ask for further guidance as the young man's family had approached her family for forgiveness.

The same headman later reported[26] that he had settled an *ukuthwala* dispute in which a young woman, Ntshontshiwe, had been abducted by an ex-boyfriend and made to be his wife. Ntshontshiwe's family took her back and sought compensation in the form of two cows, two goats and R5,000. Xolo, the young man's father, approached the headman to ask him to mediate the conflict. As the one responsible for paying the damages, Xolo was seeking clemency because he said he had not known that his children were going to abduct a girl. The headman managed negotiations between these two families that reside in his ward. He pointed out that the damages sought by Ntshontshiwe's family are tantamount to *lobolo* and therefore seem to be excessive because the family had taken their daughter back, and Ntshontshiwe still wants to be with her existing

23 See generally, Thornberry, Elizabeth (2016) '*Ukuthwala*, Forced Marriage, and the Idea of Custom in South Africa's Eastern Cape' in Annie Bunting, Benjamin Lawrance and Richard Roberts (eds.) *Marriage by Force?: Contestation over Consent and Coercion in Africa*. Athens, Ohio University Press, at 137–158.

24 Headmen's Daily Reports: 3 June 2011.

25 Headmen's Daily Reports: 25 July and 28 August 2011.

26 Headmen's Daily Reports: 25 January 2012.

boyfriend. With the headman's assistance, the families agreed to compensation of a cow (to be paid in R4,000 cash) and further damages of R4,000. The former amount was paid on the spot and the parties would come to the headman's home to settle the remainder.

Arson is another criminal violation that occurs in Msinga. While the police statistics seem to suggest that it is a low incidence offence, the number of times that it appeared in our data suggests that it may occur rather frequently.[27] This offence takes the form of the burning of huts or houses on targets' properties and can cause immense damage due to the highly flammable nature of thatch roofs, which are a common feature on the Msinga landscape. A headman might hear such matters if the harmed parties bring it to him and if no one died in the attack. In one of the headmen's daily reports,[28] he disclosed that an old woman's hut (where MaNakekela slept with some children) had been burnt at about 11 p.m. Fortunately, MaNakekela had been awake still, and so she shouted for her neighbours to come to her aid. The perpetrators' faces were not seen, though those present were sure that the arsonists were male. The matter was placed under community investigation.

At a different time, the same headman shared[29] that someone had told him that the homes of a certain family within his ward had been burnt. The Dubulile home, in which the mother and daughter died, was the residence of young men who, the headman said, had shot at another home resulting in the death of the mother and a daughter. Those who had whispered this news to the headman also revealed who was suspected of having burnt the homes, suggesting that the arson was done in retaliation. At the time of our research, the matter had not yet been officially reported to the headman by the family of the burnt homes, but this matter would necessarily go to the police because of the two deaths to which it had led. Yet this would not prevent the headman from managing any compensation claim that might arise.

There were numerous other instances in which arson appeared often as a subordinate complaint in reports to the headmen, for instance, as cause for relocating,[30] as a form of self-help,[31] and as a threat used as leverage to secure something else.[32]

27 The Msinga police recorded 12 counts of arson in 2011 and 23 in 2012.

28 Headmen's Daily Reports: 28 January 2012.

29 Headmen's Daily Reports: 26 December 2011.

30 Headmen's Daily Reports: 25 July 2011. A man, Mfomdala, said his sister had twice had her home in the Nakudala area set on fire and had subsequently been shot at, and had her windows broken by people throwing rocks at her home. After trying to persevere, she had since relocated to her birth family's home. Mfomdala was reporting this to the headman so that the headman would know that she was back under his watch.

31 Headmen's Daily Reports: n.d. 2011. Here, arson was threatened as a form of self-help in a dispute between neighbours, Makhelwane and Omunye. The headman's council was asked to mediate.

32 Headmen's Daily Reports: 25 August 2011. One headman related that someone had reported being threatened with arson and asked the headman to keep an eye out. Mastende,

Another criminal violation is theft. It is no surprise that theft is common in Msinga. This is true of both petty theft[33] (especially of cellphones and money) and stock theft.[34] Both are matters heard by the vernacular forums. But stock theft, especially, is treated as very serious and is also attended by *isikebhe*, a vigilante society, the involvement of which may result in the perpetrator's death. (*Isikebhe* will be discussed in more detail in the next chapter.)

When money was stolen in the matters that we encountered, the theft involved substantial sums – such as when a young man, Webile, and his friend stole R50,000 out of a neighbour's house. When stock was stolen, it was mostly cows and goats, but it was once alleged that donkeys had been stolen too. In one serious instance of stock theft – as mentioned under 'Public Wrongs' above – the ward gathered together to accuse Dlinzela, whom they suspected of systematically stealing their cows.

During our research period, the forums heard numerous instances of disputes over cellphone theft. In two recorded instances,[35] there was traceable evidence that the stolen cellphone had been sold to a known person and then sold again to another. In both of these matters, the headman was able to find out in the end who had stolen the cellphone and who they had sold it to. And in the matter between Kweba, Fonofono and Mthengi, the buyer of the stolen phone brought it to the hearing and agreed to return it to the true owner. The thief was to refund the buyer his money.[36] In the other instance, the headman's council was not as successful at getting the cellphone back.[37]

Even other conflicts, such as disputes over a witchcraft accusation,[38] were sometimes linked back to a cellphone theft. In another matter, two young men, Sihlobo and Mndeni, who were cousins assaulted each other over the allegation

---

the complainant, also said that if anything happened to his home, the offence would be by a previously identified perpetrator. That is, Mastende was involved in a dispute over wages with Nkinga whom he had formerly employed to watch his house while he worked in Johannesburg. The former employee, Nkinga, was threatening Mastende with arson if Mastende did not pay him the money that he was demanding. It seemed that Nkinga was using this arson threat to extort money from Mastende.

33 Rates of theft in Msinga in 2011 and 2012 were as follows: six and five instances of 'theft of motor vehicle or motorcycles'; 24 and 16 cases of 'theft out of or from motor vehicle'; and 79 and 98 incidents of 'all theft not mentioned elsewhere'.

34 93 and 98 cases were reported in 2011 and 2012 respectively.

35 In the one matter, Cingo was accused of stealing a cellphone and selling it on but the headman's council found that the phone had actually been stolen by Sela. The council went to Sela's house and his family agreed to compensate the loss. In the other, Kweba stole Fonofono's cellphone and sold it to Mthengi. Fonofono reported the matter to the headman.

36 Mthengi returned the phone to Fonofono; in turn, Kweba agreed to refund Mthengi.

37 After numerous attempts, it seems that the owner was never able to retrieve his phone from Sela; hence, Sela's family was required to pay compensation. The matter was also complicated by the fact that the owner worked in Johannesburg and, because he was often away, it was difficult for him to diligently pursue the resolution of the dispute.

38 For example, the conflict between MaMakhe and MaMsolwa.

that Sihlobo had stolen Mndeni's cellphone from Mndeni's home. This matter ended up being mediated by the lower vernacular forums.

Uncertain offences

The wrongs in this category – though also mentioned in the previous categories – are wrongs in so far as members of the vernacular grouping see these acts as injurious. That people bring them to the forums for dispute management implies that these acts are perceived as 'wrongs'. However, what makes them 'uncertain' (or tentative and unclear) is the perception differences that disputes pertaining to them embody. While some members of the vernacular grouping may perceive these acts as injurious experiences and thus violations of one sort or another (private, commercial, public or criminal), the vernacular forums do not necessarily regard them as such. The categorisation of 'uncertain' is therefore based on how the forums treat disputes pertaining to these 'perceived injurious experiences', or PIEs.

The first of these is domestic violence. Vernacular forums demonstrate some ambivalence around domestic violence. Given the patriarchal nature of society in Msinga, there remain both underlying and overt assumptions that men can legitimately 'discipline' their women corporally. There is also a high level of tolerance for verbal abuse toward women in Msinga. Though the traditional authorities would say that marital sex should ideally be consensual, they would also consider marital sex to be a wife's – and less so, a husband's – duty. Thus, marital rape is not something that is considered an offence, as such.

In Msinga, sexual harassment is not widely accepted to be an offence. Some members of this society – especially men, who attend and contribute to dispute management in the vernacular forums – concede that some forms of sexually charged interaction, particularly those linked with intimidation, are unideal and maybe even inappropriate. Nonetheless, they would not typically consider sexual harassment to be very serious. Therefore, when it is reported – as it is, rarely – the vernacular forums do not treat it very seriously. Of course, women may not report such acts, because they themselves fail to perceive such conduct as a wrong, or because they know that they will not derive any benefit from reporting it to traditional authorities. Thus, largely gendered crimes in the form of both domestic violence and sexual harassment are rarely considered offences or reported to the vernacular forums.[39] This problem is particularly acute among older generations of women.

Yet this does not mean that these conflicts do not find public expression. One conflict finding its roots in sexual harassment came before a vernacular forum in the form of a severe assault on a teenage girl by the name of Moyizela

39 Since the police do not specifically report on these acts as independent categories, they probably appear in the police statistics only as assaults varying in severity or when they are as serious as to result in rape, murder or culpable homicide. Even so, they are not always reported.

with rocks, which knocked out her two front teeth.[40] In another complaint brought by a teenage girl, Hlukumezekile, the young man she had refused to date and his friends threatened her with what she believed to be a gun while she was walking back from school.

What about when another girl is a co-conspirator (perhaps even the protagonist) in trying to compel a young woman to enter into a relationship with a young man? This was the case when Zifakile actively partnered with her boyfriend and his friend, Sesheli, to try to persuade Nqabile to accept Sesheli as a boyfriend. The girl under duress, Nqabile, had already rejected the suitor being forced upon her.

Further still, doubt may be left at the end of the formal dispute management process as to whether the young woman involved is under duress or participating voluntarily in a relationship.[41] This happened in the Malunde matter referenced earlier, where the teenage girl concerned had spent the night at an older man's home. While this young man, Phendulile, insisted that she was his girlfriend, her family denied this. Though the headman requested Malunde's testimony, it was never heard because the families were said to have settled the matter by forgiving each other.

A related kind of violation that might be considered an uncertain offence is adultery. In Msinga, it is very certainly an offence for a woman to be unfaithful to her husband with another man, but it is nowhere near as clearly an offence when a man does likewise. The social expectation is that men will cheat.

The local saying is '*indoda iyinkinga*' (a man is a problem).[42] Women are therefore expected to be understanding and forgiving when their husbands stray. A woman is even expected to draw some comfort from her husband's being faithful – albeit to a number of women – in a polygynous marriage, which would be preferable to his having dalliances with women that he has not declared to his wife. (Defenders sometimes even describe polygynous marriage as a means of preventing the further spread of AIDS.)

Regardless of social expectations, however, there is a palpable sense of women in Msinga feeling wronged when their husbands are unfaithful. The example of Novalo – a middle-aged woman suffering domestic violence from her husband who was having an affair with another woman – demonstrates this perception of betrayal. The challenge for the women is that the vernacular forums do not necessarily treat husbands' adultery as a wrong, thus giving women little assistance in this sphere.

The final wrong falling into the category of uncertain offences is police brutality. The reader will recall that I defined 'uncertain offences' as PIEs from the

40 Moyizela/Ngetshe.

41 Smythe (above) at 69–80, 116–132, 187–201, provides rich context on this phenomenon.

42 Also see Alcock, Rauri and Donna Hornby (March 2004) 'Traditional Land Matters: A Look into Land Administration in Tribal Areas in KwaZulu-Natal', Legal Entity Assessment Project (accessible at www.mdukatshani.com/resources/traditional%20land%20matters%202004.pdf) at 9.

perspective of the victim that are not clearly treated as wrongs by the vernacular forums when managing them. While police brutality is unequivocally criminal, the failure of the justice system to prosecute and otherwise address this police conduct is what leads me to rather categorise it as an 'uncertain offence'. In the instance of police brutality, the authorities whose inaction is to be considered relevant extend beyond the vernacular forums.

As I mentioned in my discussion of criminal wrongs, focus groups revealed that police brutality is rife in Msinga. Such violence is largely linked with illegal gun possession and efforts by the police to find and allegedly destroy these illegal firearms. Focus group participants noted that the police use corporal punishment in the course of search and seizure operations as a way to elicit confessions that inhabitants have illegal guns or knowledge of where they are hidden. Focus group participants said that, usually, the police are at a home because a whistleblower has tipped them off; but sometimes the police conduct a random search just because they are hopeful that they might find something. This police behaviour helps us partly understand why whistleblowers – or 'snitches' – are so despised in Msinga. As one participant noted, '[W]hen they [the police] come, they hit anything and everything – woman, child, cat, dog'.

To my question about what remedy people could employ in the face of this kind of rights violation by these state authorities, people responded that they did not have one. They feel helpless.[43] One understands how this could be the case: the police are, in many ways, the highest public authority prevailing in the area. Despite the vernacular authorities contesting the status of the police in many modest ways, what secures the police their revered status is their agency on behalf of the juggernaut that is state government, which gives them the only legitimate claim on the use of force, a claim that is robust and seemingly unchallengeable.

The police are the primary face of government in the Msinga area and serve as (and are acknowledged as being) the ultimate authority. They are the ones typically brought in to use their force when all other more diplomatic means of ensuring social order and control have been applied and failed – including vernacular forums. If police use their force in directly abusive ways, the local people are left with no one else to turn to for assistance or relief. Or so it seems to the local people. This lack of recourse exacerbates the already ambivalent relationship(s) that vernacular groupings in Msinga have with the police.

Hearing certain disputes: safe versus 'dangerous' matters

An impression created by the data in hand is that there are some matters that the headmen, especially, feel comfortable hearing and others that they do not. It became apparent that the headmen would hear some cases with almost no

43 Also see Cousins et al. (above) at 82.

hesitation. But other types of cases the headmen only superficially hear, defer hearing or outright reject hearing.

As to which cases typically fall into which category, it depends on the severity of the matter, the personality and sense of security of the headman concerned, and the location and context of the headman, parties and matter. It is therefore difficult to predict which matters the headmen will hear and which they will refer on to another forum without hearing. However, as I will argue, the specific subject matter of the case presented to the headman plays a meaningful role in his decision.

The headmen are typically comfortable hearing matters that constitute minor or localised disagreements or altercations (that is, *imibango nje*) – even those leading to physical fighting. Most of the private and commercial matters discussed in this chapter would constitute *imibango nje*. Deviations from this norm might occur when at least one of the parties involved in a conflict is related to the headman. For instance, the headman of Kune explained that he referred one matter directly to the chief to avoid the appearance of favouritism or bias in favour of one of the parties, who was a distant relative of the headman.[44] He expressed the view that it is easy for people to jump to the conclusion that there is bias on the part of the headman, and he wanted to avoid any appearance of impropriety in this regard.

But this is by no means a consistent practice among the various headmen. In the case between Moyizela and Ngetshe, concerning assault with grievous harm, the headman of Kuthathu did not refer the matter in a similar way. Moyizela's mother (who said she was related to the headman, though she was not sure exactly how) claimed that the headman was biased in the case and might have been bribed by the other party. Moyizela's mother was unhappy with the way the matter had been resolved, ultimately feeling that the damages settled upon (which she said had been pushed by the council) were a pittance considering the fact that her daughter had lost her teeth for life and Ngetshe retained his.[45] On the other side of the dispute, Ngetshe's father did not accuse the headman of being biased in favour of the complainant's family but still said that they were unhappy with the way that matter was decided, as they did not feel that they had been given a proper hearing. The headman had not awaited

44 This was a conflict between neighbours, Hlobene and Sakhelene, who have a history of conflict, especially when they have consumed an alcoholic beverage.

45 Interestingly, she said that her family had considered taking the matter to the police but did not do so because her family members were confident that the police would ask them if they had tried to settle the matter at home between the respective families first. She said she knew for a fact that the police do this because she had a relative, Shayiwe, who had been assaulted by a neighbour; when Shayiwe's family took the matter to the police, the police asked if they had tried to settle it between the families first, saying they would only intervene if the families tried and failed at that level. The families had apparently tried then, and when they did not succeed, they had taken the matter to the headman. There, they had still failed so Shayiwe's family returned to the police. This time, the police had told them they would not 'resume' the matter.

the father of the boy for the matter to be heard in his presence and refused to reopen the matter after it had been decided, once the father of the boy had returned to Msinga from work.

One sensitive subject matter for a headman to possibly avoid is stock theft. For example, one dispute concerned the alleged theft by two young men of local people's cattle, and this matter had the headman of Kuthathu nervous. The family patriarch (the young men's uncle) had attempted to resolve the matter at home, but Ginsa and Bambisene had not been willing to listen to the family council. When the matter was brought to him, the headman had referred the matter directly *kwankosi* (to the chief's council). A major deciding factor in the headman's referral of this stock theft case was arguably the potential harm to him and the scale of the potential conflict that could result from this matter.

Potential conflict can also feature in land and boundary disputes. For instance, earlier in this chapter I mentioned an extended public conflict within the Yisithupha ward over which the headman had charge. The headman had made a good faith attempt to address the matter through diplomacy, but it became quickly apparent that this was a matter of large enough scale and severity that the chief had to be called in to mediate it.

While the dispute was purportedly between two subsections of the same ward, the traditional council's definition of being a ward (as requiring that land administration be done by the headman) was not embraced by all the parties involved. The Wabantu section of the relatively new ward strongly self-identified as a former labour tenancy and wanted to maintain its independent identity and structures, at least as far as land administration was concerned. This subsection was, however, willing to bring conflicts to the headman of the Yisithupha ward as expected by the traditional council. This land administration dispute (often described as a land conflict) held the potential to start a war.

Yet this principle of scale is not necessarily applied consistently, even by a single headman. For example, in the matter at the start of this chapter (between Vakashile and Yaziwa) wherein five young men had severely assaulted a young man from a different ward and traditional community while he was going to visit his girlfriend in the area, the headman of Kuthathu did not refer the matter directly on to the chief's council.

There is a way to read the distinction between this case and the earlier matter pertaining to stock theft other than to claim inconsistency on the part of the headman of Kuthathu or failure to apply the principle concerning potential scale of the conflict that could ensue. That is, because the conflict involved young men from different wards, it meant that the headman was not to hear the matter on his own. The headman of the ward from which the assaulted boy came was to form a forum with the headman of Kuthathu jointly. This joint forum provided the headman a greater measure of shelter and security than he would otherwise have in hearing such a matter alone.

Conversely, it is clear, from speaking with other headmen and knowledgeable members of the vernacular grouping, that it was, at best, an oddity for the headman not to have referred the matter to the chief and, at worst, a very unwise violation of due process. After all, the scale of fallout that could have resulted from this matter was tremendous. The conflict could have escalated into a feud between wards that form part of two different *izizwe* (nations). This particular headman's deviating from protocol in this way is ironic, given the fact that this headman is one of the more cautious of those involved in the study. Yet it was also perhaps justifiable in terms of his being the newest headman, and thus lacking the necessary knowledge and experience. As detailed in the next chapter, we had recorded him consulting with one of the older headmen on two matters.

Perhaps this is where the identity and personality of the relevant headman is most important – in making such highly discretionary decisions as when to hear matters and when to refer them on without first hearing them. Here, it is important that the headmen are subject to minimal oversight and do not have to report on their decisions on paper. They rarely have to justify them to anyone at all. A different headman – the headman of Kunye – exercised his discretion otherwise than did the headman of Kuthathu. At least during the time of our research, the headman of Kunye did not report much dispute management and, least of all, dispute management of minor matters. The two key matters that he did report having managed both dealt with extreme levels of violence.

In one matter, the headman of Kunye was dealing with gun violence that had escalated to engulf the whole Okunye subward. He described it as war. In another matter, between MaDlinzelwa and MaShonile, a conflict that had started off as an argument over an unpaid loan of money between the two women in a bar resulted in a feud involving multiple deaths and death threats – a feud spanning two or three wards. In both cases, the headman of Kunye reported playing a role in attempts to manage the situation. Other headmen reported that his ward was particularly litigious. It seemed, from various reports, that this ward might also have been among the most violent. Either way, the headman of Kunye did not shy away from being involved in resolving serious disputes. This strikes me as being consistent with the peculiarities of his personality,[46] as opposed to the less assuming personalities of the other headmen.

What this discussion points to is how difficult it is to know for certain whether a matter will be heard by the headmen or referred on. I have tried to show that subject matter is a key part of the headman's consideration. But it is by no means all. As suggested here, there is a normative ideal regarding when matters should be referred on. And when a matter is to be referred on, there is a hierarchy in place for where it should go. But the fulfilment of any ideal is

46 From watching him in the chief's council, this lack of conflict aversion was in keeping with his persona: he asked questions in a confrontational way – sometimes in a combative tone – and sermonised extensively. If one did not know otherwise, one would have thought that he was *umshushisi* (the prosecutor) – a role that informants usually ascribed to the chief headman. The chief headman was soft-spoken by comparison.

dependent on many contingencies, especially human contingencies. At the very least, a combination of dynamics – specifically, the geographical and social context within which matters arise, the likely scale to which a conflict might potentially escalate, and the temperament and confidence level of the headman – determine whether headmen hear a matter.

Concluding remarks

I began this chapter by pointing out the discrepancy between the common claim in Msinga that the vernacular forums only deal with minor matters ('*imibango nje*') and the reality that these forums deal with substantial concerns which they are often – at least, technically – legally forbidden from dealing with. Indeed, what we have seen so far is that the matters that the vernacular forums in Msinga are invited to resolve, because of their proximity and relative accessibility, are often very weighty.

Vernacular forums are approached with disputes concerning private wrongs between individuals, both related and unrelated. They are asked to intervene in commercial dealings that have gone wrong. Their mediation and arbitration is requested when wrongs occur that affect the public at large – whether at the level of neighbourhood, subward, ward, *isizwe* (nation) or across these territorial delineations. People attempt to enlist the full range of their assistance – mediation, arbitration and adjudication – when criminal wrongs take place.

The material situation in which these matters present is, as already highlighted, one of severe poverty and want and, as the cases used as examples in this chapter demonstrate, one of limited physical security. What has begun to emerge from the data presented in this chapter is therefore that the social circumstances in which the vernacular forums are called upon to intervene and manage disputes are such that the social fabric is worn and there are arguably quite low levels of social trust. Systemically, the police are only uneasily present and cannot be relied upon to effectively partner with the local authorities or necessarily advance the cause of justice even on their own. All of these tensions are borne out in the kinds of disputes that are presented to the vernacular forums.

With this background, it seems impossible to provisionally conclude anything other than that the vernacular forums deal with such subject matters largely because they cannot avoid them. Many of the disputes that come to them fall between the cracks of the criminal justice system as it is currently structured. They lie in the interstices between what the police are meant to deal with, can or cannot be trusted to deal with, and do or do not effectively deal with, on one hand, and what the vernacular forums are meant to deal with, can or cannot deal with, do or do not adequately deal with, and what they are nevertheless asked to help out with, on the other hand.

Of course, sometimes the vernacular forum authorities voluntarily exceed their legal authority because they themselves have an interest in making themselves seem indispensable. However, even then, in most cases it appears that these authorities take the steps they do at least partly because they feel an obligation drawn from moral and/or cultural authority, and because people with little other hope turn to these forums expectantly. Situated in their particular material, social and systemic context, these forums understandably, I would argue, exceed their legal authority sometimes and maybe even often – at least, at some level.

Nevertheless, the social implications of the matters that come before the vernacular forums appear to be very significant and may, in fact, extend beyond the competencies of the vernacular dispute management system as a whole. Big questions therefore arise in the face of these findings on what disputes are presented to vernacular forums.

Starting from the empirical baseline of what matters the vernacular forums are actually wrestling with, despite legal proscriptions, we should ask if these forums are the right ones to be trying to resolve such substantial issues. If not, how do we best intervene to try to dissuade and prevent the vernacular forums from continuing to manage some of these matters – and, in that case, which particular kinds of disputes ought they *not* to hear?

Then, revisiting the existing legal prohibitions, we need to ask, in which instances of the vernacular forums' defiance of the law should the law be maintained and vehemently enforced? Furthermore, are some of the kinds of disputes the forums are presently barred from trying to resolve inappropriately prohibited, and should these prohibitions therefore be reviewed and revised?

These are questions that are best left until the end of the book. First, it is necessary to develop a more complete picture of the jurisdictional authority vernacular forums do and do not claim to have, as well as how vernacular forums do in fact attempt to and, if at all, succeed at managing the disputes that are presented to them.

4 Competing authorities[1]

What forums exist over what jurisdictions and how do they manage disputes between them?

Being a headman is not easy and not safe

When I first met him in 2010, the headman, Nduna Nhliziyo had just been attending a case at the chief's court. A matter from his *umhlati* (subward) was being heard in the chief's council against Ginsa and Bambisene, two young men who were accused of stock theft. The family had brought the two young men to the chief's court in hopes that it would discipline them and stop them from stealing local people's cattle. This matter was not decided, however. Instead, it was referred back to the family council.

The chief and his headmen agreed that the matter should not have come to their forum but should have been settled by the family. The family patriarch, Baba Siphethe, complained that the young men refused to listen to him or allow him to attempt to resolve the matter at home. Ginsa and Bambisene were then fined a goat which was to be slaughtered and its blood used in a ritual to cleanse the family's home. The matter was otherwise returned to the family council.

The difficulty was that Ginsa and Bambisene had disrespected their patriarch and seemed to be resistant to his persuasion. Even now, Ginsa and Bambisene showed a hardness that made it hard to believe that the two young men would reform. When the chief's court adjourned for the day, my research assistant and I approached these young men, who had been the primary parties in the matter, to see if they would grant us an interview. At the time, they were waiting to go in to see the chief in his office after the matter; he had summoned them, presumably to chastise them. Other than grumbling about the goat they were required to tender for cleansing, they said they did not want to be interviewed.

Informants consulted about the peculiarity of this matter later told me that while the matter might seem innocuous to an outsider, it was not. In a matter of theft such as this, it was important for the family to correct the young men

1 See Lund, Christian (2006) 'Twilight Institutions: An Introduction' *Development & Change*, 37(4): 673; Lund, Christian (2006) 'Twilight Institutions: Public Authority and Local Politics in Africa' *Development & Change*, 37(4): 685.

before the wronged parties came after the suspects to kill them. Once the outsiders had killed the young men, the family would have to retaliate, which would initiate a feud. The only way to avoid a feud, if the young men would not hear the family's council, was for the family itself to kill them – or so the informants told me.

In other words, the chief's referral back to the family council was a kind of code to say that the family should resolve the issue amicably. If they could not, they would (indeed, they *should*) settle it by killing the young men, in keeping with the local honour code. In this instance, the family killing would serve to prevent a feud.

When Ginsa and Bambisene rejected our invitation to interview them, my research assistant, Moto, introduced me to Nduna Nhliziyo and asked if Nduna thought it would be possible for us to come and speak with him and Baba Siphethe, the patriarch of the family to which these young men belonged. Nduna Nhliziyo was very willing. At the appointed date and time, Moto and I drove to meet the headman.

In the heat of the lunchtime sun, Nduna Nhliziyo was waiting for us at the *spaza* (tuck) shop, which had a 'drinking area' (an informal bar) attached to it. I later learned that he had been drinking there, and often did, and that it was quite close to his home. He got into the back of our rental car and directed us to the family patriarch, Baba Siphethe, who was at work building a home for someone in the neighbourhood. Nduna Nhliziyo seemed really jumpy. He was speaking in hushed tones and kept looking around.

Nduna Nhliziyo explained that he was concerned for two reasons. First, this matter made the headman anxious because he knew *abafana* ('the boys') to be involved in a stock theft syndicate. He also knew that the syndicate, which terrorised his area, was dangerous – so much so that he no longer answered his phone at home at night in case someone was phoning just to see if he was home before *behlasela* (storming in) to kill him.[2] He was therefore somewhat worried about being seen speaking with us. It turned out that he had previously served as *igoso* (headman of the men) and so had inside knowledge to share with us.

Second, Nduna Nhliziyo was concerned for the old man that he was taking us to see. Baba Siphethe was at work, and – although he would not be taking the risk of meeting us at his home – he was taking time out of work to speak to us, and the headman worried that Baba Siphethe might run into problems with his boss.

I got to know Nduna Nhliziyo better over the subsequent two years. It turned out that there were two additional reasons for his jitteriness the day that I had first met him. For one thing, as he described it, he was new to the job of headman. From the way he said it, I got the impression that he had started only about a year earlier. A subsequent interview revealed that he had been appointed around

2 Even when the phone is not used for this specific purpose, nighttime calls typically bear bad news.

2001 – roughly nine years before our meeting. Moreover, he was of a more nervous disposition than most other headmen I had met in Msinga; in general, they seemed to be of a much quieter and calmer or otherwise bold and confident disposition. But that did not stop Nduna Nhliziyo from being very likable.

Nduna Nhliziyo took to what we had asked of him – recording his daily activities and the matters that he heard – with eagerness and dedication. He recommended a young woman, who lived nearby him and had completed high school but was unemployed, to work as his scribe. She herself was committed and fulfilled her task with diligence. He would let her know in advance when there would be a hearing at his home and telephone her whenever people arrived unexpectedly to report a matter they wanted him to mediate for them.

Their joint record keeping was consistent with the enthusiasm with which Nduna Nhliziyo carried out his job as headman. He would accompany members of his community when they went to the magistrate's court, either as defendants or as family of the defendant, for instance – something none of the other headmen reported doing. (Nevertheless, at least in one matter, Nduna Nhliziyo was accused, by one side, of being bribed with alcohol and, by the other side, of being biased. This kind of accusation is something all the headmen were sensitive to, and some spoke candidly of taking precautions, such as referring matters directly to the chief's council to prevent from being accused of bribery or bias themselves.) That said, virtually all of the headmen we interviewed in Msinga were very likable and showed commitment to a very challenging task, within the constraints of their individual circumstances – most notably the fact that they are all poor.

Nduna Nhliziyo is no different in that regard. Though he and his family live on a beautiful two-level site built into a ridge overlooking hills with colourful homesteads on them, they are very poor. In order to phone his community members, other headmen, the secretary of the chief's office, or his scribe, he admitted that he had to spend limited social grant money that was meant to be spent on raising the children he had with his two wives. Likewise, when he hosted us (as he always did generously, even when we were not paying to stay the night with his family), he bought Coca-Cola from the same limited source of funds. Other than this grant money, he and his family owned goats that roamed the property. Because of the devastating losses he had suffered due to drought, he had given up owning cattle.

The other people living with him and his wives, MaMdala and MaMzalele, were a son and daughter (both of whom are still in school), the young wife of his deceased older brother's son, as well as this nephew's illegitimate child from another woman. This nephew, Mshana, mainly lives and works as a minibus taxi driver in Johannesburg. Since his wife, MaKhuluma, had the most modern house,[3] furnishings, and tastes, she hosted us when we stayed at the headman's

3 The reader may recall that homesteads in Msinga are comprised of multiple huts and houses. Therefore, the daughter-in-law's house was one of several on the family plot.

home. We therefore learned a lot from her, including that she was a bit disgruntled with her situation. Part of MaKhuluma's discontentment had to do with not yet having a child – a rite of passage for any woman in Msinga. She resented her husband's illegitimate child joining the homestead – a source of conflict with her sisters-in-law that led to the police being called one night.

Most interesting was that, culturally, MaKhuluma was never allowed to set eyes on her father-in-law, or him on her. So if she were walking through the yard and Nduna Nhliziyo came out into the yard, she would run behind the nearest house. She could not then enter into her house until he had moved out of eyeshot of her door. In this respect, his informal dispute management forum was inconveniently situated.

The beautiful spot Nduna Nhliziyo and his family calls home is somewhat difficult to get to, but it is also vulnerable because, once one reaches it, it is not difficult to reach all the houses on the plot or escape into nearby bushes – despite the fact that it is near to neighbours. It is therefore not surprising that Nduna Nhliziyo should be concerned about being attacked at night, especially when we consider the fact that numerous headmen have died.[4]

Headman is a role that some had given up work in the city in order to take up in service of the chief, and at his call. Nduna Nhliziyo had himself once worked as a steelworker in Johannesburg. Now, he has a very tough job. It turns out that being a headman is a very vulnerable – indeed, life-threatening – calling with few rewards and little protection. Though we never learned if most of the headmen owned guns, one informant observed, 'Most of the *ndunas* have an enemy because of the cases'. One headman came out and said, 'You can't live without guns.'

Jurisdictional authority of Msinga's vernacular forums

This chapter focuses on authority as it presents in empirical terms – specifically describing the vernacular forums that exist in Msinga and the jurisdictions over which their authority extends. I begin by providing an overview of the numerous forums that make up the vernacular management system of Msinga, briefly noting who constitutes these forums and how they relate to one another within the system. These two elements form the focus of more detailed study later in the chapter; but before such a detailed discussion of the membership of the forums and the relationships between them, I will describe the territorial, personal, and subject-matter determinants of their jurisdictions.

4 Members of our NGO partner informed us of this fact. Then, after the period of our data collection, on 13 February 2016, one of the headmen who participated in our study, Nduna Mshushisi, was assassinated in broad daylight. According to our NGO partner's annual report, 'He was the third [Nakudala] induna to be killed in six months, a tally that makes it difficult to find a replacement for the job.' (See www.mdukatshani.com/resources/Annual%20report%20for%20Mrdp%202015%20final.pdf for a tribute to him).

In discussing the forums' membership, I will also describe the roles that are played by their members. Typically, the membership of the forums is loose and their roles mostly informally distributed among them according to a very localised forum culture. Positionality and circumstances of the people that constitute the forums are important elements to consider, as they sometimes give rise to conflicts of interest in the cases brought to the forums for consideration. Finally, while discussing the relationships between the forums, I will focus on the uneasy role of the state police and how the police relate to and are drawn upon by the forums.

Structure of vernacular dispute management system: an overview

As a means of orienting the reader, a brief overview of the vernacular dispute management system in Msinga as I was first introduced to it is fitting here.

Two forms of dispute management processes

In the initial focus groups that I conducted in Msinga, participants commonly told me that there are two kinds of dispute management processes available. The first is called '*icala*' (a case) while the second is referred to as '*isikhalo*' (a cry or plea).[5] The way in which informants described the difference between the two was that the first (*icala*) is a formal dispute, which is recognised by the fact that the initiating party pays money in order to launch the case with the relevant authority. (In one of the two nations that were the focus of my research, the respondent also put down a sum.)[6]

Informants said that the second kind of process (*isikhalo*) is initiated, without any payment of money, by the complainant coming to the chief to declare a complaint against another party. The informants emphasised that it was important to them that I understand that this procedure is different from a case. In fact, it was often described, first and foremost, in the negative: 'it is not a case, . . . it is a plea/cry'.

In the case of *icala*, the forum – typically, the headman and his council or, on appeal, the chief and his council of headmen – then hears the matter and hands down a decision of guilt along with a remedy the forum deems appropriate. Some informants mentioned that the remedy is open to some degree of negotiation or argument in mitigation, which is taken into account in the final order made by the relevant forum.

In the case of *isikhalo*, the complainant approaches the forum – typically, the chief (though some said that the headman provided a similar service) – on a

5 These are also discussed in Mnisi Weeks, Sindiso (2015–2016). 'Access to Justice?: Dispute Management Processes in Msinga, KwaZulu-Natal, South Africa' *New York Law School Law Review* 60(1): 227–249.

6 The relevant sum is R15 in Nezikhathi area and R30 in Nakudala area.

morning of the week when the authority hears such requests. After the complainant presents his/her account of his/her differences with the other person, who is typically absent, the chief writes a letter for the complainant to deliver to the other party, summoning them to the next session. At the next session, the other party has the opportunity to explain his or her side of the story. The chief then makes a decision that is aimed at reconciling the parties in a meaningful way.

Usually, the chief asks the party that is in the wrong to apologise and the wronged party to forgive. If the wrong is a continuous act, he asks the appropriate party to desist from his/her problematic conduct. If this attempt to reconcile the parties does not succeed, the parties can return and the chief might ask the party that is in the wrong why s/he insists on disrespecting him (the chief) in this way. A request from the chief, and especially one in such stern terms, is said to commonly cause the party that is in the wrong to conform. If all such attempts at resolving the issue fail, whomever of the parties feels wronged is free to initiate 'a case' to see if they could resolve the dispute by those means.

In rare instances, informants mentioned processes available through other forums. These included '*igoso*',[7] the headman[8] of the (young) men,[9] and

7 Some authors refer to this office as *igoso*. See Carton, Benedict and Robert Morell (1 March 2012) 'Zulu Masculinities, Warrior Culture and Stick Fighting: Reassessing Male Violence and Virtue in South Africa' *Journal of Southern African Studies*, 38(1): 31–53; Budlender, Debbie, Sibongile Mgweba, Ketleetso Motsepe and Leilanie Williams (2011) *Women, Land and Customary Law*. South Africa, Community Agency for Social Enquiry; Clegg, Johnny (1981) 'Ukubuyisa Isidumbu – "Bringing Back the Body": An Examination into the Ideology of Vengeance in the Msinga and Mpofana Rural Locations, 1882–1944' in Philip Bonner (ed.) *Working Papers in Southern African Studies, Vol. 2.* Johannesburg, African Studies Institute, University of the Witwatersrand at 164; Meintjes, Louise (2017) *Dust of the Zulu: Ngoma Aesthetics after Apartheid*. Durham, Duke University Press. Others use the name *igosa*. See Gibbs, Timothy (2017) 'Inkatha's Young Militants: Reconsidering Political Violence in South Africa' (accessible at http://discovery.ucl.ac.uk/1522091/1/Gibbs_Msinga%20youth_UCL%20open.pdf); Alcock, Rauri and Donna Hornby (March 2004) 'Traditional Land Matters: A Look into Land Administration in Tribal Areas in KwaZulu-Natal', Legal Entity Assessment Project (accessible at www.mdukatshani.com/resources/traditional%20land%20matters%202004.pdf); Cousins, Ben, Rauri Alcock, Ngididi Dladla, Donna Hornby, Mphethethi Masondo, Gugu Mbatha, Makhosi Mweli and Creina Alcock (2011) '*Imithetho yomhlaba yaseMsinga:* The Living Law of Land in Msinga District, KwaZulu-Natal'. PLAAS Research Report 43, Cape Town, The University of the Western Cape. I use *igoso* because that is how my fieldworkers, who are local residents, described the office in their notes.

8 Carton and Morell (above) at 49 describe this role as 'war captain' or, otherwise, at 43 as *umphathi wezinsizwa* (which I would translate as 'leader/manager of young men'). They distinguish this role somewhat from what they call *induna yezinsizwa* (headman of young men). Budlender et al. (above) refer to this role, at 16, as *igoso lezinsizwa* (captain of young men) and define it as 'steward'. Meintjes (above) at 14, translates *igoso* to 'captain'. Gibbs (above) translates *igosa* to 'young leader'.

9 The oft-used qualifier, 'young men', might mislead audiences that do not share Msinga's culture. The term might be more easily understood if it were expressed as 'men who do not qualify as children or the elderly' – that is, men who are part of a regiment because

'*isikebhe*',[10] the 'private security' or vigilante group.[11] Though the processes adopted by these forums seemed less defined than chiefs' or headmen's forums,[12] the informants divulged that *igoso* and *isikebhe* use a combination of mediation, shaming, intimidation, corporal punishment, and sometimes even worse forms of violence.

Local informants told me that, in essence, *igoso* convenes meetings where the men congregate to agree beforehand how they should conduct themselves at a public ceremony or ritual celebration.[13] If a member of the male regiment deviates from agreed practice (such as by bringing a weapon when he is not supposed to or by assaulting another man outside of the confines of jousting or duelling), he is chastised by the group in accordance with the means decided upon in dispute management proceedings over which *igoso*, as the headman of the men, presides.

This account is consistent with what other studies have found before me. As Rauri Alcock and Donna Hornby write:

---

they are not too young to go to war and are still able to fight on behalf of their vernacular grouping. According to this categorisation, at the age of 61, Nduna Nhliziyo would be *insizwa* (a young man) under the disciplinary jurisdiction of *igoso*. This same categorisation is related to Nduna Nhliziyo's choice of language in referring to Ginsa and Bambisene – who, being in their late twenties or early thirties, western audiences might more easily recognise as 'young men' – as *abafana* (boys).

10 Since we collected our qualitative data, *isikebhe* (literally meaning, 'sailboat') has been replaced in the area by a similar organisation named *umkhumbi* (literally meaning, 'ship or oceanliner'). I have so far been unable to find out why these organisations have been given the names of sea vessels.

11 For detailed discussion of vigilantism in democratic South Africa, see Buur, Lars (2008) 'Democracy and Its Discontents: Vigilantism, Sovereignty and Human Rights in South Africa' *Review of African Political Economy*, 35(118): 571–584; Buur, Lars and Steffen Jensen (2004) 'Introduction: Vigilantism and the Policing of Everyday Life in South Africa' *African Studies*, 63(2): 139–152; Oomen, Barbara (2004) 'Vigilantism or Alternative Citizenship? The Rise of Mapogo a Mathamaga' *African Studies*, 63(2): 153–171; Posel, Deborah (2004) 'Afterword: Vigilantism and the Burden of Rights – Reflections on the Paradoxes of Freedom in Post-Apartheid South Africa' *African Studies*, 63(2): 231–236; Smith, Nicholas Rush (2015) 'Rejecting Rights: Vigilantism and Violence in Post-Apartheid South Africa' *African Affairs*, 114(456): 341–360.

12 Alcock and Hornby (above) also speak to their relative appointments at 9, emphasising that: 'The current [*igoso*] calls together *izinsizwa* (young men) in his jurisdictional area and announces that he wishes to retire [then] calls for nominations for people who are trustworthy and honest ("*indoda ehlonip[h]ekile othembekile*"). When an *nduna* is appointed, the current holder of the position calls the *ibandla* to choose a new appointee. The *ibandla* together with the current holder of the position then report to the *inkosi* that a new *nduna* has been agreed to.'

13 I am indebted to Creina Alcock for sharing an archived simultaneous transcription and translation of an interview she conducted with a Nakudala Chief Headman at the time, while he was in hiding to avoid assassination in 1987. His descriptions are consistent with the summary provided by Alcock and Hornby (above) at 11, 13–14.

> the *igosa*, who operates in the same geographical unit as the *nduna*, namely the ward or *isigodi*, is primarily responsible for the behaviour of young men. The *igosa* and the *nduna* each has his own tree where meetings are convened and they govern men on distinct issues. You have to lead the dancing at ceremonial functions and keep the men in line. When there are disputes or fights, it is your job to stop them and to fine the wrongdoers. The *igosa* also fines men who take out another man's girlfriend and presides at trials involving men's issues inside the *isigodi*.[14]

While Alcock and Hornby place emphasis here on fines as the primary remedy used by *igoso*, the reality is that intervening to stop wrongdoers may require that *igoso* use force. Informants understood that, under state law, the forum is not allowed to use physical force; however, some informants admitted that they had sometimes seen it done (though some of the people we interviewed said it was only in other areas, not in their own *isizwe*).

Hierarchy of vernacular forums

At the lowest level of the vernacular dispute management system one finds the family councils and the neighbourhood councils, which are typically used as forums of first instance in different kinds of disputes. Above these are mainly the headmen's councils, followed then by the chief's council.[15] Each of the steps in the system is designed to provide an opportunity for the dispute to be settled as soon as possible and within the most immediate relational circle of the individual as possible.[16]

It is difficult to describe the system without using illustrations. What makes it especially difficult is the distinction between the functions of the family and neighbourhood councils, as well as the possibility of intermediate forums and different iterations of some existing forums. One illustration is a marital dispute, which will typically first be discussed by the man's family, into which the woman has married. If the husband's family fails to resolve the problem, then the woman's family may be brought into the discussions. At this stage, the two families would form a single family council for the purpose of resolving the specific marital dispute. Should this joint family council fail to reconcile the parties, the families might[17] approach the headman's policeman in their subward (if he is a policeman who hears cases) or go directly to the headman.

14 Ibid. at 11.

15 Also see Ibid. at 7–9.

16 Von Benda-Beckmann, Keebet (1981) 'Forum Shopping and Shopping Forums: Dispute Processing in a Minangkabau Village in West Sumatra' *Journal of Legal Pluralism*, 19: 117–160; Wilson, Monica, Selma Kaplan, Theresa Maki and Edith M. Walton (1952) *Keiskammahoek Rural Survey, Vol. 3: Social Structure*. Pietermaritzburg, Shuter and Shooter say the same of the forums they describe in different contexts.

17 There are slight variations to this pattern from one vernacular grouping to another.

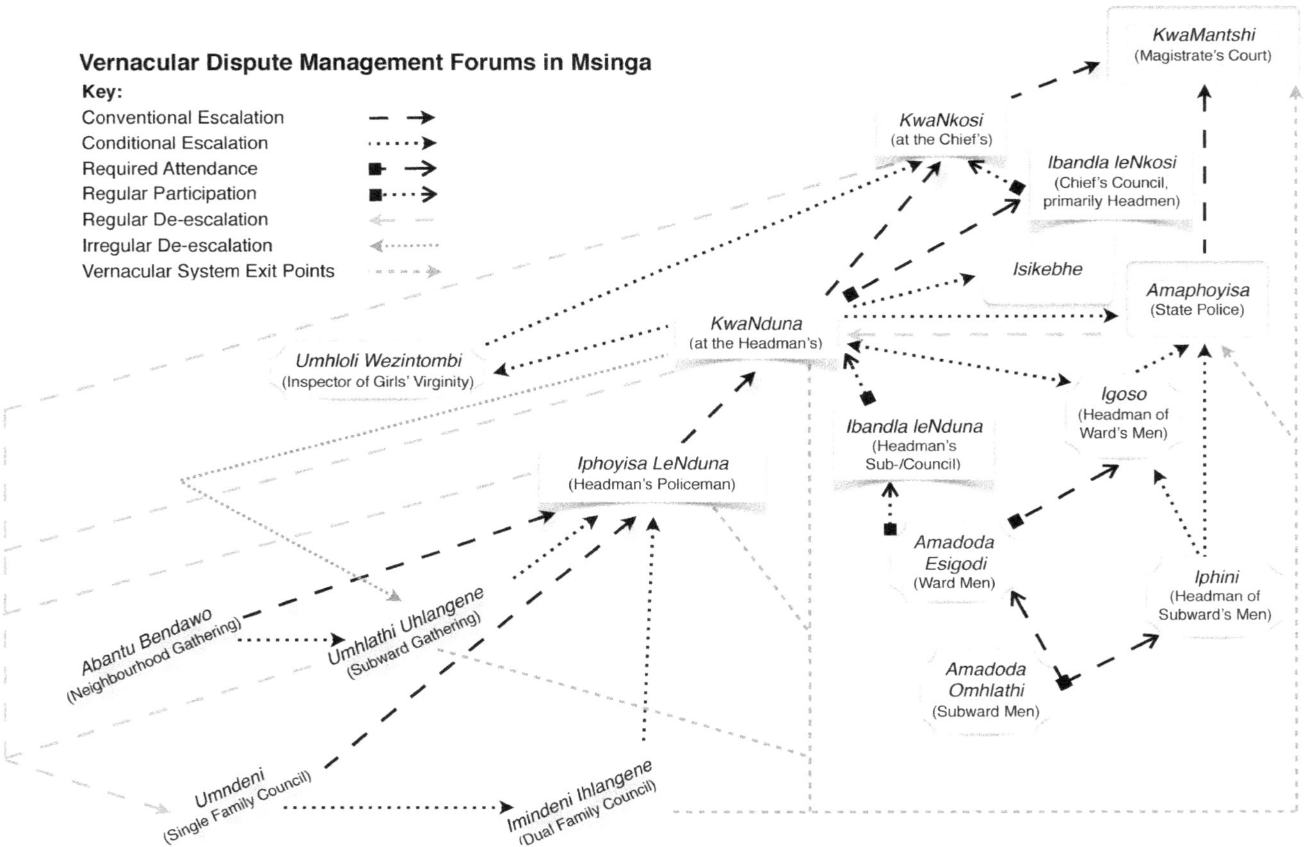

Figure 4.1 Vernacular Dispute Management Forums In Msinga

At this stage, the parties can either approach the headman informally, for him to mediate their discussions, or initiate a case. A case is indicated by the parties' payment of the prescribed sum of money to the headman. For an informal mediation, the headman may sit in on the matter alone or, especially if it is discussed under his tree – the same place where he resolves formal disputes – he may be joined by some of the men of the area. These men can be any from the ward under the headman's care who are able to attend on that occasion, and together they constitute the ward (or headman's) council. If the parties have brought the matter as a case, the headman will invariably hear the matter with his council, *ibandla lenduna*.

If the headman and council are unable to reach a satisfactory outcome or if the parties are unsatisfied and wish to appeal, the matter will be escalated to the chief's council. At the chief's council, the complaint may also come as an informal plea for the chief to hear alone: this hearing is not considered a case. Alternatively, the dispute may come as a formal appeal heard with the headmen (in some cases joined by the Traditional Council). This appeal would form a case and would be indicated as such by the payment of money to the chief's secretary. All in attendance may actively participate in the consideration of a dispute in the context of a case, and in the context of a mediation before the headman.

Another illustration of vernacular dispute management is a dispute between neighbours. This kind of conflict generally undergoes the same process except that instead of starting in the family, it starts in the local neighbourhood. That is, if the aggrieved neighbour has attempted to reason with the perpetrating neighbour and failed, s/he will then call together the other neighbours immediately surrounding them to assist the parties in reaching a satisfactory result. If this attempt fails, the aggrieved party might gather together the wider circle of neighbours – that is, the people in the subward within which the neighbourhood is situated. Should this attempt also prove unsuccessful in bringing about a satisfactory solution between the parties, the aggrieved party will then escalate the matter through the system, appealing next to the more formal dispute management officers and forums outlined above.

These examples illustrate the scaffolding of the system: that is, its core forums and the normative ideal of how the system works. However, there is much more to the vernacular system. For instance, sometimes additional dispute management officers and forums are available. These are responsible for very particular concerns, such as the disorderliness among and fights between men.

I have already mentioned those officials who deal with differences specifically between men at ward level (*amagoso* or 'headmen for the men'). These officials have, subordinate to them, the 'headmen for the men' at subward level (*amaphini*).[18]

18 In describing the structure of Msinga, at 7, Alcock and Hornby (above) observe:

'The governance structure then extends downwards into geographically defined wards (*izigodi*) in which *izinduna* (headmen) administer land issues with the assistance of a

Each of these are responsible for dispute management among the men, when they fight in ways that are against the regulations that bind them, which are partly negotiated by the men themselves. Alcock and Hornby note a man making overtures to another man's girlfriend as an example of a violation of regulations. Like *induna* and *igoso*, *iphini* also has his own tree under which he sits to hear disputes with the assistance of the men of the subward, as appropriate.

Informants said that matters did not, in practice, escalate from *igoso* to the headman, because *igoso* – and the council of all local men, with which he sits under his tree – always resolves matters successfully. Some expounded that *iphini* and *igoso*, between them, never fail to resolve their disputes within this subsystem, notwithstanding the fact that appeals between them (from the subward to the ward level) sometimes prove necessary. In this case, then, the normative ideal is that *igoso* is able to resolve all disputes between men that come before him.

Alcock and Hornby describe this expectation thus:

> [B]ecause the *igosa* is the head of a system of peer regulation, he is not obliged to report to either the *nduna* or the *inkosi*. The governance of young men is basically an "in-house" matter and is necessary because "*indoda iyinkinga*" (men are trouble-makers) and is only referred to the *nduna* or *inkosi* if women or older/younger people are affected or the *igosa* is unable to keep control of a particular man.[19]

This points to the overlap of personal, territorial and subject matter as bases for the jurisdiction of *igoso*. This overlap is visited in greater detail below.

Despite the normative ideal of keeping appeals strictly between *iphini* and *igoso*, as Alcock and Hornby also observe, these 'men's headmen' might sometimes appeal to the headman for intervention and, most rarely, even to the chief. Appeals to the chief occur mostly when the conflicts cross ward or nation boundaries and might require that the headmen of two wards sit together to resolve a matter, for instance, or that the chiefs of two nations resolve a matter. However, as the instance in which a gun had gone off at a celebration suggests,[20] the headman can sometimes elect to deal with an issue of male discipline without

---

functionary, *ip[h]oyisa* (tribal police officer), and *amagosa* (leaders of the men) and their female equivalents, *amaqhik[i]za,* regulate the behaviour of men and women respectively, particularly at cultural ceremonies. During times of war, the *nduna* subsides in prominence while the *igosa* becomes the primary *isigodi* leader. Below the wards are *imihlathi* (sub wards), where the behaviour of young men is regulated by *amap[h]ini* (*igosa*'s deputy).'

Meintjes (above) at 14 observes the mirror structure among *ngoma* dance teams of '[a]n elected *igoso* or *ukaputeni* (captain) and *iphini* (vice captain) are responsible for the training, discipline, song selection, choreography, and leadership of the team.'

19 Ibid. at 9.

20 See the dispute concerning Mosha. Likewise, in the matter concerning Gangile and Mngani (discussed below).

it having to be addressed by *iphini* or *igoso* first – because the headman has the authority to call ward-wide disciplinary meetings and because just men attend many of these meetings. There are many other deviations from the normative ideal, which I will delve into in much greater detail below.

Jurisdictional definition

In 1901, John W. Walsh argued 'that jurisdiction is the "right to hear and determine a cause."'[21] Accepting this basic definition, the forums in the vernacular dispute management system possess jurisdiction as defined in terms of geographic territory, personal affiliation with a party or the subject matter of a dispute. These various forms of jurisdiction can also overlap, and often do in practice. Each jurisdictional form is detailed below.

Territorial jurisdiction

The core forums in the vernacular dispute management system typically have their jurisdiction primarily defined by territory.[22] To have a matter heard by the forum, a party must reside in the particular geographical area over which the forum has jurisdiction. Thus, the chief's council deals with pleas and appeals from the entire *isizwe* (Traditional Community). The headman's council deals with those from his *isigodi* (ward). And the headman's policeman and council deals with disputes from *umhlathi* (subward) – particularly when the headman is far away from the subward in question. Similarly, the neighbourhood gathering can resolve only the matters of neighbours within the locale, and the (sub)ward gathering that might be appealed to would have to restrain itself from hearing matters of two persons living in other (sub)wards.

Nevertheless, while the jurisdiction of some of the other forums in the system is predominantly defined by the subject matter with which they are designed to deal, this jurisdiction is also curtailed by territory. Hence, *igoso* and his council of men are confined to dealing with disputes pertaining to men's fighting and misbehaviour when the men concerned are within his particular ward. Likewise, *iphini* and his council can only deal with such men's matters when the men involved reside in his particular subward. As mentioned above, if a matter concerns men from two subwards or more, *iphini* would meet with *iphini* from the other subward whose men are implicated in the matter and together form

21 Walsh, John W. (June 1901) 'The True Meaning of the Term "Jurisdiction"' *The American Law Register (1898–1907)*, Vol. 40 New Series, 49(6): 346–356 at 355. In this, he agreed with the United States courts in *Windsor v. McVeigh*, 93 United States, 274 and *Munday v. Vail*, 34 New Jersey Law, 418 ('jurisdiction may be defined to be the right to adjudicate concerning the subject-matter in the given case').

22 See Lund, Christian (2002) 'Negotiating Property Institutions: On the Symbiosis of Property and Authority in Africa' in K. Juul and C. Lund (eds.) *Negotiating Property in Africa*, 11–44 at 32.

a single forum – or the matter would have to be escalated to *igoso*, who has the jurisdiction to hear the matters of both subwards falling under his ward.

Exceptions are rife, however. For example, a matter could come before the ward gathering that concerns one party from their own ward and another from a different locale. Such a matter came up when Hlukumezekile, a girl from a different ward, came to one of the subwards of Kuhlanu, to complain about Songela, a boy who lived in that subward who had sexually harassed her and allegedly threatened her with a gun if she did not agree to date him. Hlukumezekile approached the subward to request that they chastise Songela and thereby prevent him from dealing with her in such a manner again. Hlukumezekile believed that the subward was the forum that offered her the best chance of achieving what she wanted: Songela's future restraint. This example raises interesting points about jurisdiction and how it can be based on territory or personal relationships, or some combination of the two.

Personal jurisdiction

There is evidently significant overlap between territorial and personal jurisdiction. By personal jurisdiction, I mean that which is based on interpersonal connections – one's membership in a certain identity group. As demonstrated by Hlukumezekile and Songela, what I have described as territorial jurisdiction can often equally – or sometimes even more aptly – be described as personal jurisdiction. Songela's residence in the territorial jurisdiction of the subward's council makes him a member of the subward's identity group because the connections (and obligations) between residents are not primarily understood as territorial but relational.[23]

One should recall here that territorial boundary definitions were given precedence, and often specifically imposed, by the colonial order. Before then, it is well documented that vernacular groupings principally defined themselves in terms of personal allegiances and relationships.[24] It was the personal allegiance

23 Plenty has been written about the formation of identity and the nature and development of 'in group' preference and even bias. See, for example, Geertz, Clifford (1973) *The Interpretation of Cultures: Selected Essays.* New York, Basic Books at 28, where he observes that culture is substantiated by 'the pattern of social relationships' that comprises one's milieu. Also see Dovidio, John, Samuel Gaertner and Tamar Saguy (February 2009) 'Commonality and the Complexity of "We": Social Attitudes and Social Change' *Personality and Social Psychology Review*, 13(1): 3–20 at 14, where they note: 'The psychological power of creating common identity, a sense of "we," is impressive. Categorizing others as members of one's group has a profound impact. Spontaneously, people think more deeply about and feel closer to and more positively about members of their own group (the ingroup) than about members of other groups (the outgroups).'

24 Delius, Peter (2008) 'Contested Terrain: Land Rights and Chiefly Power in Historical Perspective' in Aninka Claassens and Ben Cousins (eds.) *Land, Power & Custom: Controversies Generated by South Africa's Communal Land Rights Act.* Cape Town, UCT Press, 211–235; Guy, Jeff (October 1987) 'Analysing Pre-Capitalist Societies in Southern Africa'

to a leader that made a family, which was the essential unit of social organisation, a part of the leader's vernacular grouping. The primary significance of this fact is that the family could withdraw its allegiance at any time if it were not satisfied with the leadership (the leader to whom it had pledged allegiance) or the governance of the vernacular grouping. Thus, this ability to withdraw support gave the family a strong accountability check on the leader.

However, I want to suggest that there are two kinds of personal jurisdiction: *conditional* personal jurisdiction and *essential* personal jurisdiction. In the case of conditional personal jurisdiction, the personal nature of the jurisdiction is intimately connected with the territory and is, at least partly, conditional upon it. In the case of essential personal jurisdiction, the jurisdiction is in no way dependent on a territorial basis.[25]

In terms of essential personal jurisdiction in the pre-colonial context, withdrawal of allegiance could take the form of mere dissociation – that is, no longer bringing offerings, attending ceremonies, or bringing disputes to that authority.[26] Withdrawal of allegiance could also take the form of revolt, which assumes the form of banding together with other families in order to reject the leadership of the existing authority and perhaps to support that of another. The public show of no longer personally allying oneself with the leader was a statement of withdrawing oneself from his jurisdiction and, if done at large scale, effectively deposing him from power.[27] The personal relationship between the leader and his grouping was the pre-eminent and basically decisive basis on which he had jurisdiction over them.[28]

Alternatively, if a family had moved to the area from some place else and obtained the land on which it resided through that process of personal allegiance,

---

Journal of Southern African Studies, 14(1): 18–37 at 26–29; Peires, Jeffrey (1981) *The House of Phalo: A History of the Xhosa People in the Days of Their Independence*. Berkley, University of California Press at 31–41.

25 Here, personal jurisdiction can be likened with universal jurisdiction in international law, which allows a state or international organisation to prosecute a person accused of a crime no matter where the crime took place. Conditional personal jurisdiction then is akin to conditional (universal) jurisdiction whereby the individual must be present in the accusing state for prosecution to take place. Similarly, essential personal jurisdiction is much like absolute (universal) jurisdiction, which allows prosecution to occur regardless of the accused's physical location. My version of universal jurisdiction varies from the international law principle in that, in its strictest form, (absolute) universal jurisdiction in international law does not even require the accused to be a national of or have any relationship with the prosecuting state whereas in my conception some prior personal relationship (on the basis of which jurisdiction is claimed) is assumed and necessary. See Cassese, Antonio (2003) *International Criminal Law*. Oxford, Oxford University Press at 284–291; O'Keefe, Roger (2004) 'Universal Jurisdiction: Clarifying the Basic Concept' *Journal of International Criminal Justice*, 2: 735–760.

26 See Delius, Guy and Peires (above).

27 Ibid.

28 As Delius, Guy and Peires (above) all discuss, this personal relationship was expressed in material terms through cattle, labour and other forms of production.

the family could withdraw its allegiance by choosing to relocate to another area.[29] The family could then go and be on its own or submit to (and place itself under the protection of) another authority and its vernacular grouping.[30] Although the territoriality would be incidental to the personal foundation of the relationship, territoriality would be a partial basis of that relationship. Hence, the physical movement of the family would be a part of unequivocally showing that the personal jurisdiction over them had ceased. This type of relationship is therefore an instance of conditional personal jurisdiction because the personal jurisdiction is entwined with territoriality.

A much stronger manifestation of the conditional form of personal jurisdiction can be seen in the example of Songela, the boy who threatened a girl he wanted to date. The personal jurisdiction of the subward over Songela – to chastise him regardless of where he has threatened Hlukumezekile – is conditional upon his being a resident of that territorial sphere. If ever he and his family were to move, that personal jurisdiction would cease to be, along with the subward's territorial jurisdiction over him.

In another instance in which the close relationship between the personal and territorial jurisdiction of subward gatherings was demonstrated, a headman who had been approached with a matter instructed the council of the subward from which one of the individuals concerned came to hear the matter. The dispute concerned the assault and resultant loss of possessions that had been incurred by two young men, Gangile and Mngani, the latter of whom was a member of the Yesihlanu subward. Though the assault had taken place in a taxi transporting Gangile and Mngani from a different subward to their homes, the young men who assaulted Gangile and Mngani in the taxi were members of Yesihlanu along with Mngani.

The matter was de-escalated from the headman. The basis on which the Yesihlanu subward would hear the matter was only partly territorial: specifically, one of the young men who had been assaulted came from Yesihlanu and the young men accused of the assault were members of the same subward. The Yesihlanu council was therefore being invited to hear the young men's complaint about being assaulted; the headman was anticipating that the subward council would have to chastise the group of local 'boys' who had committed the assault.[31]

The fact that this was not a case but a mere discussion – the assaulted young men had approached the forum to seek guidance on how to proceed – made the disciplinary objective the only really attainable purpose. Put differently, advice and a reprimand of the ones who perpetrated the assault were the only real

29 In the words of both Delius and Peires, this was at a time when land was abundant and people in short supply.

30 See Delius, Guy and Peires (above).

31 Subsequently, the same subward council would have to try to discipline the two who had been assaulted and had themselves now also committed criminal acts.

remedies that the forum could give Gangile and Mngani. Hence, the personal dimension of the Yesihlanu council's jurisdiction over the matter was stronger than the territorial but was still dependent on there being a territorial connection with the young men. The personal strength of the jurisdiction was based in the subward's interest in disciplining its own sons and in one of its sons' request to the subward to protect him. This exemplifies conditional personal jurisdiction.

One final portrayal of conditional personal jurisdiction in Msinga can be seen in the now mostly historical practice of men who belong to a local (sub)ward returning from the cities, where they work, to be disciplined by the men in their local (sub)ward for actions taken in their workplaces or hostels.[32] This practice is clearly a matter of the men's urban residences being considered an extension of the local, vernacular territorial jurisdictional area. The basis for this practice is simply that the people carry with them *personally* the jurisdiction of the *territorially defined* vernacular grouping of which they are part in Msinga. In other words, a man from a Msinga subward can be disciplined by men from that same subward when he physically returns to that subward. His act of violating their shared code *outside* of the subward's geographical territory does not detract from his being one of their own or prevent him from being accountable to the men of his subward.

The second category of personal jurisdiction, which I have named 'essential personal jurisdiction' is 'essential' because it goes with the person no matter where s/he may reside and because the identity group to which it is linked is not at all dependent on a geographical location. Today, personal jurisdiction is most pronounced – and is essential – in the case of the family. The family council has authority to hear matters of its members, regardless of where the individual members may reside or where the anchoring family homestead may be located. This authority is recognised and respected – and sometimes even deferred to – by superior forums. Thus, as shown in the system diagram above (Figure 4.1), a matter can be referred back to the family from any of the high-level forums in the vernacular system.

This essentially personal jurisdiction has been demonstrated in numerous cases. In the case of Ginsa and Bambisene, the young men who had stolen livestock, the matter came to the Nakudala chief's council. The council heard the matter – begrudgingly, it seemed – but repeatedly noted, through different members' voices, that the matter should have been resolved at home and should never have come to the chief's council. In another case, Mdala, the patriarch of a family went to the Nezikhathi chief's council to report that his nephew, Mshana,

32 The strong links between men's identities and conduct in their urban workplaces and hostels and their rural homes is well documented. See, for example, Clegg (above); Beinart, William (September 1992) 'Introduction: Political and Collective Violence in Southern African Historiography' *Journal of Southern African Studies*, 18(3): 455–486; Campbell, Catherine (1992) 'Learning to Kill? Masculinity, the Family and Violence in Natal' *Journal of Southern African Studies* (Special Issue Political Violence in Southern Africa), 18(3): 614–628 at 622; Meintjes (above) at 8, 37–41, 129, 143–144.

had repeatedly threatened to kill him and was terrorising him with threatening phone calls. Despite Mdala's objections to the council's findings (because he said he did not trust the young man and felt terribly unsafe), the chief's council held that the matter should be resolved by the family sitting together.

The family's personal jurisdiction over its members is foundational and, at times, even treated as sacrosanct – with mixed results for the members themselves. This is seen in several cases where the headmen referred cases back to the family for them to resolve. In one example, Msukele sexually harassed a married woman, Walile. It seemed Msukele might have wanted to rape Walile, but Walile escaped from him before he could actually try. Walile's family (her husband's brother and other relatives) brought the matter to the headman. The perpetrator admitted his fault. When the headman asked Msukele what they should do about his wrong – suggesting that they might call the police – Msukele asked that '*balikhulume isikhaya*' (they discuss the matter 'home-style', meaning between the families). The headman and Walile's in-laws agreed.

A striking fact of this case is that the personal jurisdiction was such that the woman's in-laws handled the matter; her birth family was not called into the discussions. Once married, a woman comes under the authority of her marital kin and a wrong against her (and, here, her honour) is a wrong against her marital family. Her birth family would be called upon only if she had a dispute with her spouse that her in-laws could not settle or if she had a dispute with her marital kin as a group.

Subject-matter jurisdiction

As I have previously noted, several forums have jurisdiction that is primarily defined by subject matter. I have already highlighted in the 'Territorial Jurisdiction' section of this chapter the forums designed to deal with men's disciplinary issues, particularly around public fighting, especially in contravention of agreed protocol at celebrations. As mentioned, their jurisdiction is secondarily confined by territory.

Another forum that is similar in this regard is the Community Policing Forum (CPF). A state creation,[33] this forum exists on a ward-by-ward basis to assist in keeping law and order in the locale, with a particular focus on crime. It is intended as a partnership between the South African Police Service and local community to solve safety problems by preventing and eliminating crime as well as improving police services and police accountability to the community. Members of the CPFs, as they are called, have a precarious place in some parts because people assume them to be police 'snitches'. (As noted in the previous chapter, being thought a 'snitch' is typically very risky to one's life.) However, in some areas, as in Kuyisithupha, it seems that the CPF makes a concerted effort to

33 Section 19 of the South African Police Services Act 68 of 1995 requires that all provincial commissioners establish these 'forums at police stations in the province [to] be broadly representative of the local community'. Sub-forums may also be established.

regularly communicate and thus effectively partner with the community in preventing and solving crimes. This effort may put the lives of the CPFs less at risk.

There are other forums whose jurisdiction is defined by subject-matter and either not confined by territory or who operate at the macro-level of the vernacular grouping (the level of *isizwe*). The first of these, fitting squarely under the vernacular system, is '*umhloli wezintombi*'. This forum is lead by the woman who, with her committee of adult female assistants, inspects young women to establish their virginity. One might be tempted to conclude that she is not part of the dispute management system because her role is so particular to virginity testing. However, her subject-matter jurisdiction makes her the exclusive authority on disputes around the state of a woman's virginity, on which matters of reputation decidedly hinge. And this exclusive authority is jealously guarded by her. Nduna Nhliziyo reported a conversation he had with *umhloli* in which she had informed him that some of the young women in his ward were going to an *umhloli* in a different *isizwe*. She said she would provide him a list of their names and requested that the headman inform them and their families that this was improper.

The case of Mthuki and Ntombi makes a fitting illustration here. When, Mthuki, the young woman from the Nakudala Traditional Community indirectly accused another young woman, Ntombi, of being 'a wife' (that is, not a virgin), the accusation was treated not just as an affront to the girl herself but also to her family, which was the entity that brought the claim to their local headman. The headman heard the matter but could only get so far because of the need for evidence in order to settle the dispute. The matter was therefore referred to *umhloli* so that she could inspect the state of the allegedly maligned young woman's virginity. After a couple of delays, the inspection was done, and *umhloli* and her assistants found that Ntombi was still a virgin and ordered that Mthuki's family pay damages to the complainant's family for the wrong.

When *umhloli* and her assistants announced their finding, Mthuki started insulting them. *Umhloli* and her assistants therefore brought the matter of these insults to the chief's council, alongside the appeal brought by the maligned girl's family for damages as a result of her reputation being unfairly tarnished. At these proceedings the headman and *umhloli* met each other, and *umhloli* told the headman that he had been wrong to hear the matter between these girls in the first place, saying '*ungidlela umsebenzi*' (you are 'eating' my job). He was encroaching on her jurisdiction.

The remaining two dispute management forums that I will mention whose jurisdiction is based on subject-matter are not formally a part of the vernacular system. However, they are important to mention because of the role that they play within the universe of dispute management possibilities in Msinga. The first of these forums is *isikebhe* and the second are the state police.

Isikebhe is a self-described community forum or community crime-fighting association that is not unique to Msinga.[34] It is probably more appropriately described as a vigilante society. It was initially established for the protection of

34 Mapogo a Mathamaga is a widespread vigilante organisation that exists in parts of KwaZulu-Natal as well, as is described by Smith (above). Also see Oomen (above).

livestock but, toward the end of this research project, I discovered that *isikebhe* also hears matters that are unrelated to livestock – even civil matters. In its primary function, people with livestock pay fees to *isikebhe* (in the region of R2,000) in order to become members. If members' livestock is stolen, they report it to the group, and *isikebhe* investigates and retrieves the livestock. In the event of its failure to do so, *isikebhe* serves as insurance, because it will reimburse the member for his[35] loss.

While I cannot say with certainty what this vigilante security organisation's success rate is at retrieval, anecdotal evidence suggests that it is high. The means that *isikebhe* uses for effecting its 'justice' – a form of justice arguably recognisable to local residents – surely plays no small part in its allegedly high rate of success at stock retrieval. One of the most well-known facts about *isikebhe* is that it uses corporal punishment – and even violence – liberally. Discovered perpetrators are beaten or tortured,[36] both to extract evidence or confessions and to inflict punishment. Sometimes the suspected perpetrators of the stock theft are eliminated in the process.

Members of the South African Police Service are the only ones authorised by state law to use force, 'as may be reasonably necessary and proportional in the circumstances'.[37] But they themselves often exceed that mandate by using excessive force and unauthorised violence in managing disputes. I have given the example

35 I use the male form deliberately because Msinga is a patriarchal society and livestock ownership is highly gendered, resulting in men being the primary owners of (or people responsible for) livestock. See Carton and Morell (above) at 45.

36 See, for instance, Radebe, Mlondi 'MEC Mchunu Told of Stock Theft and Torture in Pomeroy Area' *The Witness*, 29 August 2012 (accessible at www.news24.com/Archives/Witness/MEC-Mchunu-told-of-stock-theft-and-torture-in-Pomeroy-area-20150430), where it is reported that a man *isikebhe* suspected of stealing cattle was 'tortured on his private parts with pliers'.

37 Section 13(3)(b) of the South African Police Service Act 68 of 1995 says: 'Where a member who performs an official duty is authorised by law to use force, he or she may use only the minimum force which is reasonable in the circumstances.' Such authoristion by law includes section 49(2) of the Criminal Procedure Act 51 of 1977 – as substituted by section 7 of the Judicial Matters Second Amendment Act 122 of 1998 and by section 1 of the Criminal Procedure Amendment Act 9 of 2012 – which says:

> 'If any arrestor attempts to arrest a suspect and the suspect resists the attempt, or flees, or resists the attempt and flees, when it is clear that an attempt to arrest him or her is being made, and the suspect cannot be arrested without the use of force, the arrestor may, in order to effect the arrest, use such force as may be reasonably necessary and proportional in the circumstances to overcome the resistance or to prevent the suspect from fleeing, but, in addition to the requirement that the force must be reasonably necessary and proportional in the circumstances, the arrestor may use deadly force only if-
>
> (a) the suspect poses a threat of serious violence to the arrestor or any other person; or
>
> (b) the suspect is suspected on reasonable grounds of having committed a crime involving the infliction or threatened infliction of serious bodily harm and there are no other reasonable means of effecting the arrest, whether at that time or later.'

of the police assaulting members of households during search and seizure operations. The police also often use unauthorised 'mediation' (referring some matters that come to them back to the vernacular forums), in order to manage disputes. For example, this occurred when Mndeni assaulted his cousin, Sihlobo, over the alleged theft of a cellphone. The mother of the injured Sihlobo (who was suspected of the cellphone theft) reported the matter to the police, and they told her that because the parties were family, she should rather try to resolve it through the vernacular forum. She then took the matter to the headman's council.

The police are called in, typically, when a crime occurs that people feel cannot be solved internally. An obvious example is a death by means that are obviously not natural. In such an instance, there is not usually a way to hide or get rid of the body without being found out, so the police enter the picture. Obviously, subject-matter (and territorial) jurisdiction of the police overlaps significantly with that of the headmen. This overlapping especially pertains to low-level crime. But it also occurs in higher-level crimes because the headmen are more proximate and are consequently often the first authorities at the scene of a crime or the first ones called when a crime takes place. The police's subject-matter (and territorial) jurisdiction also overlaps with that of *isikebhe* – particularly as concerns stock theft. Of course, sometimes *isikebhe* are perpetrators of crimes that the police would have the authority to investigate.

I will return to the relationship between *isikebhe* and the headmen – and thus how *isikebhe* fits into the vernacular dispute management system – as well as the relationship between *isikebhe* and the state police later in this chapter. But, first, it is necessary to provide historical context on the relationship between masculinity and (restraint from) violence, as well as the social value of cattle, in places like Msinga.

Pre-eminence and self-restraint: male responsibility and the vernacular forums

The constitution of vernacular forums and the manner in which the headmen approach their role – with a significant amount of restraint – can be fully understood only against a particular historical background regarding roles men have traditionally taken on in their communities. It is trite to say that pre-colonial Zulu society was patriarchal.[38] Egodi Uchendu observes, 'Zulu society was highly hierarchical, and men enjoyed positions of power in the home and in the wider

38 Carton and Morell (above) at 45: 'Since at least the sixteenth century, these homesteads (*imizi*) were the focal point of production, with one patriarch regulating a domestic hierarchy that subordinated women to men and juniors to seniors. Raising livestock (mainly goats and cows) was largely the domain of males, while crop cultivation was mostly the responsibility of females. Boys watched over the herds, passing the time by sparring with sticks.'

society. Maleness was superior; hence, men were served first and exclusively at all meals before women and children.'[39] Yet a hierarchy also existed among men – primarily on the basis of age with older men being entitled to greater respect than those younger than them.[40]

Thus, there were a multitude of masculinities given expression in historic Zulu society and these were partly dependent on performance.[41] As Uchendu writes:

> But the preferred masculinity by Zulu standards, combined martial prowess with honesty; high morality, as shown in the absence of pre-marital penetrative sexual interaction with a female subject even though intimate encounters were allowed; loyalty; aggressions; a sense of responsibility; courage; self-control; athleticism; alertness; endurance; and absence of emotion.[42]

Benedict Carton and Robert Morell reaffirm the emphasis on patriarchal honour and morality. In particular, Carton and Morell observe that 'household honour' entailed 'patience, sobriety and wisdom' and a duty to relatives and peers because the survival and health of Zulu society depended on mutual support between agricultural households.[43] The scholars elaborate this point by noting that pre-existing 'guiding idioms of the Zulu kingdom promoted subsistence – not "man slaying" – with one particular metaphor, *isbuko sikababa*, inspiring herd boys (the proto-stick fighters) "to mirror" the "gravitas" of their fathers who oversaw homestead production.'[44] As Carton and Morell conclude, 'Thus all people, young and old, were expected first to uphold life affirming heroic and householder traditions that preserved domestic security.'[45] Carton and Morell highlight the confined position of male 'man slaying' in historic notions of Zulu masculinity in order to contextualise the prevalence that this expression of masculinity has since taken in places much like Msinga.

Mark Hunter echoes this sentiment and provides some explanation for this shift in emphasis toward a much more belligerent Zulu masculinity. He writes:

> Zulu society emerged from a period of military warfare at the turn of the twentieth century and bravery and fighting skills were important attributes

39 Uchendu, Egodi (2008) 'Are African Males Men? Sketching African Masculinities' in Egodi Uchedu (ed.) *Masculinities in Contemporary Africa*. Dakar, Codesria at 8, referencing Bryant 1949 and Roberts 1974.

40 Carton and Morell (above).

41 Uchendu (above) at 8.

42 Ibid. Also see Mark, Hunter (July–August 2005) 'Cultural Politics and Masculinities: Multiple-Partners in Historical Perspective in KwaZulu-Natal' *Culture, Health and Sexuality* 7(3): 389–403 at 391–392.

43 Carton and Morell (above) at 41–42.

44 Ibid.

45 Ibid.

> associated with manliness. The central economic focus for *isiZulu* speakers, however, was *umuzi* (the homestead) and, in turn, the physical and symbolical centre of the institution was *isibaya* (cattle kraal). Big men accumulated many cattle, took several wives, and thus built a successful homestead.[46]

At this point in time, though men's ability to fight had become more important, the home and the man's ability to provide for his family and keep his family and home intact remained a key Zulu value, and marriage a valued institution.

Evidently, Zulu masculinity has changed over time as a result of various influences that I have described previously and further detail in subsequent chapters.[47] Specifically, with changing times, two dynamics occurred almost simultaneously. On one hand, the colonial state co-opted African men into tightening control over women and their sexuality.[48] On the other, the changes in the economy and forced migration for labour purposes made it increasingly difficult for men to realise their traditional role of maintaining a strong household.[49]

While men's circumstantially imposed twentieth century engagement in urbanisation did not displace traditional conceptions of manhood that being married and building a home are of central importance,[50] it contributed to the development of practices of masculinity that contested traditional ideas. Zulu people therefore saw urbanisation as a corrupting process that led to increased social and moral decay[51] and thus placed stress on traditional notions and arrangements. Indeed, the difficulty created by not being able to live with their families who were confined to the rural areas and not being able to fully support them financially made performing the preserved ideal of traditional masculinity barely possible. In short, therefore, masculine identity hit a period of crisis.

It is against this historical background that the restraint with which the headmen approach their role must be understood. The traditional values described undergirded Zulu society until the mid-twentieth century and the headmen constantly hearken back to them. All of them having been born and raised in the area in a different time and having come of age before the worst of the crisis hit in the 1980s, the headmen approach their role as one of safeguarding the legacy they inherited from their grandfathers.

46 Hunter (above) at 391–392.

47 Also see Mchunu, Mxolisi (2007) 'Cultural Change, Zulu Masculinity and Intergenerational Conflict in the Context of Civil War in Pietermaritzburg (1987–1991)' in T. Shefer (ed.) *From Boys to Men: Social Construction of Masculinity in Contemporary Society*. Lansdowne, University of Cape Town Press, 225–240; Hunter (above) at 395.

48 Hunter (above) at 394.

49 Carton and Morell (above) at 32.

50 Hunter (above) at 397; Campbell (above) at 619 refers to this as a mythical desirability of 'economic dominance' that is undermined by 'unemployment and low wages'.

51 Ibid.

The difficulty is that the social context in which they must operate today is vastly different from that in which their grandfathers existed. Yet the headmen conduct themselves as though they can take for granted that those who they are corralling more than rhetorically share their beliefs of what Zulu gender (especially male) identity is and their historical vision of where Msinga should be going. Likewise, they perform their task as though the methods that are familiar to them will achieve success. Studies show these assumptions by the headmen are not necessarily the case, and that this tension is reflective of a difference between the headmen and their sons' generation.

Catherine Campbell's research, for example, focuses on such dynamics within townships. I cite her work here because it bears many similarities to what took place in rural areas, particularly *after* the end of apartheid. In addition, Campbell's research is relevant to rural areas because of rural men's forced labour migration between rural and urban areas – albeit that, under apartheid itself, men from Msinga typically lived separately (though often according to their wards) in 'hostels' in the townships.[52]

In particular, the politically related dynamics that played out in the townships were dominated by the African National Congress (ANC),[53] and hence the struggle there was youth-led. These dynamics are only modestly applicable to Msinga. In Msinga (and in the Zulu men's 'hostels' in the cities), the Inkatha Freedom Party (IFP) dominated politics.[54] And, as Campbell observes of the IFP and other 'state-linked vigilante groups' in the Natal townships, they mostly comprised older men: '[t]heir agenda was perhaps not only to undermine progressive political forces, but also to put down the cheeky upstart youth who dared to think they could challenge the power of older men.'[55] She states that the same pattern continued into the 1990s, as IFP affiliated groups that were mostly composed of older men battled ANC-affiliated groups that were largely made up of young people.[56]

The point as it relates to Msinga is that in deep rural areas, the contest between older and young men did not really emerge in the way that Campbell describes until the 1990s. Yet, it did emerge – and, despite the delay, it manifested much as it had in the townships. Campbell's finding that, approximately in the 1975–1990 period, severe tensions had arisen between the generations, especially between fathers and their sons is therefore relevant in Msinga also.[57]

52 Campbell (above) at 622: 'Inkatha's power base lies not only in the support of large numbers of older men but also hostel dwellers with close rural ties and a deep commitment to the old-fashioned, rural-based "Zulu traditions".' Also see Meintjes (above) at 8, 39–41.

53 Campbell (above) at 621–622 calls the youth-led ANC affiliate in the township the Mass Democratic Movement – the ANC was still banned at the time, in the 1980s.

54 Meintjes (above) at 107–108 and 133–134.

55 Campbell (above) at 621–622.

56 Ibid.

57 Ibid. at 620.

In fact, as canvassed in detail in Chapter 7, the evidence base of this current study affirms the existence of such a tension between fathers and sons today. It shows that the fathers are largely committed to the old ways (and are especially committed to tradition and governance institutions related to it) but also feel emasculated by unemployment and poverty and thus, for comfort, have turned to alcohol, and sometimes to multiple sexual partners and violence. Illegitimate sons or sons separately raised by their mothers – though not as invested in tradition – are likewise demoralised by unemployment and lack of hope. They are widely engaged in extramarital sex, alcohol abuse, crime, and violence. Despite shared experiences of alienation, older and young men are in tension, as older men feel they have little, if any, control over the seemingly undisciplined younger generation.

The headmen are, in a sense, at the centre of the division between young and old men because they symbolise the old way as well as attempts by the older generation to control the younger generation.[58] Older men in the township resigned themselves to being helpless both against social dynamics that undermined their power and against their children, who rejected their fathers' traditional wisdom.[59] I would argue that those men who maintained strong links with the rural areas could still turn to these areas for some affirmation, because traditional roles had not been as significantly upset there. Indeed, in Msinga today, older men's authority has not been upset to the same degree as it has been in the townships. But, again, it has been upset – and to a notable degree, at that.

Many older Msinga men feel concern that their wisdom and influence no longer carry as much clout as did their own fathers' and grandfathers'. This is largely the position of the headmen, as they carry out their role according to the ill-fitting old rules set by their forefathers. And when young men assassinate a headman – one of the perpetrators uttering the words, 'Babulaleni bonke, bayizinja!' ('Kill them all, they are dogs!') – the symbolism of the generational division the headmen stand in the midst of is striking.[60] Obviously, other factors also count toward which headmen are placed at greatest risk by this tension; for instance, a more authoritarian style and jurisdiction over a more conflicted territorial area. These were all factors in the assassination of Nduna Mshushisi in broad daylight while he was in the company of other contemporaries, drinking at the 'spaza' shop, on their return from a meeting. The young men allegedly stole his legal firearm.

58 In 1987, the Nakudala Chief Headman (quoted above) said the following about being *induna* and situated in the midst of generational tensions and shifts: 'There's a time when the young men start calling each other and going off on their own and are strictly apart and start saying: "You old men are always trying to stop us doing things." Nobody is ever told openly who is the young leader. Not even the *gosa*. It's done so when the *gosa* is called to the chief, the magistrate or police to be asked who is in charge of fighting, he can truthfully say he doesn't know.' (Interview by Creina Alcock.)

59 Campbell (above).

60 Communication by NGO Partner per above, n 4.

Forum members and their roles

There are two main things to note about the membership of the bulk of the forums making up the vernacular dispute management system. The first is that the membership is made up of mainly ordinary members of the vernacular grouping concerned: whether family, neighbourhood, subward, or ward. While the membership of the forums is ordinary members of the vernacular grouping, it is also predominantly made up of male residents in that personal and/or territorial sphere. Young male participation is routinely lower than older male participation. And, unless young men are post-adolescence (which is also generally understood to imply married status), they are typically not invited.

Hence, in the family, membership includes mostly older male members of the family, though older female members of the male line (the father's sisters, for example) play a role also. In the neighbourhood, women are more likely to be present in discussions and, while not very likely to speak up much (except as witnesses), their attendance is welcome and often invited. In the subward, the same principles apply – though men are more likely to be present than women and play a more prominent role than women do. In the ward, typically, women will attend only as witnesses to particular matters, not as participants in the discussions or even observers.

The second thing to note is that each of the forums has some figure who chairs the proceedings and, in some instances, holds more sway in the process of decision-making; but the decision is not singly made by that individual. In the family forum, this figure is the patriarch: the eldest male member of the extended family unit. In the neighbourhood forum, the person chairing the proceedings may be an informally elected chairman. In the subward, it may be an informally elected chair, or it might be the headman's policeman.

In the ward, it is the headman, and he may or may not have a close circle of men who form a kind of mini-council that he asks to accompany him to mediations or whose opinion he gives greater weight in ordinary proceedings. These men also show greater confidence in proceedings and will often be the main ones asking questions of the parties and witnesses.

For example, the headman of Kuhlanu called upon two men to accompany him to a mediation, and one of them served as the acting headman in the headman's absence over several days. The headman of Kuthathu asked three other men to accompany him to hear a matter at the home of a family that had brought a legal complaint to him. The headman of Kunye seemed always to have at least two to three men with him when dealing with a matter. This was the case even when he called two young men to his home to chastise them for threatening gun violence.[61] There is no evidence of such councillor support being consistently drawn on in this particular way by the other three headmen who partnered with us in the research.

61 See Akezwa and Zwakakhulu.

One can see the value in having a small sub-council to support the headman in his work. The reason of the headman in Kuhlanu for having a sub-council seemed to be his rather more modern governance style. This modernity was expressed in other ways also, when he seemed quite willing to entrust others to do some of the dispute management work: for instance, he is the headman who referred the matter of the young assaulted men, Gangile and Mngani, to the subward council. He repeatedly showed confidence in delegation and de-escalation to subward gatherings. He also networked with forums like the local clinic's advisory council.

The reasoning of the headmen in Kuthathu and Kunye is likely different. These headmen perhaps had the most reason for hesitating to act alone. They had violent wards, and perhaps the sub-councils served as witnesses and some form of protection for the headmen themselves. Even though the headman of Kunye, Nduna Mshushisi, projected a very confident persona and was regarded as being very authoritative by other headmen, who consulted him on their own matters at times, his ultimate fate proves that he was not invulnerable. As previously discussed, the headmen of Kuthathu, Nduna Nhliziyo, was relatively new to his position and was of a much more nervous disposition.

This issue of positionality of the headmen relates to an important concern about the potential conflicts of interest that certain authorities face when they are charged with particular dispute management responsibilities. For instance, you may recall that we recorded that the Kune headman referred a matter on to a higher forum without hearing it, for fear of being accused of bias.[62]

In some instances, the potential conflict of interest was evident even though the authority did not identify the risk thereof or do anything to try to prevent it. For instance, in the matter concerning grievous assault committed by Ngetshe against Moyizela, when interviewed, both sides of the complaint expressed unhappiness about how the headman of Kuthathu resolved the matter. They each alluded to the headman's failure as the cause of their discontent. The complainant pointedly accused the headman of being open to persuasion by someone purchasing alcohol for him. The complainant claimed to be very familiar with the headman and his dealings; she suggested that she was related to him. The respondent side also accused the headman of showing unfair preference for the complainant and even violating protocol in the process followed in the dispute management of the matter.

In another example, the Nakudala chief was charged with hearing a land title dispute in which he was, in fact, a party and accused of making an unfair (indeed, corrupt) decision in the matter. The discontented party, Mhlupheki, said that some headmen had been present for the hearing and were thus accomplices to this alleged injustice against the complainant. He believed that the prejudice he felt he had suffered in this matter was a consequence of the other party's having influenced the chief by financial means.

Aside from whether the headmen use a sub-council, the headmen's councils (that is, their councils-at-large) also vary in terms of the centralisation of their process when it comes to questioning and opining. While in most of the

62 Hlobene/Sakhelene.

headmen's councils there was broad participation from local men, in the Kunye headman's council there was not the same degree of participation from ordinary members of the ward. This headman was verbose and spoke loudly in a voice and tone that made it clear that he would not tolerate disagreement. Even when he spoke in the chief's council, his commanding tone and lengthy diatribes mostly silenced participation, even that of the other headmen, a number of whom were relatively soft-spoken or not as confident.

By contrast, while the headman of Kune could speak strongly, he could also be contradicted. For example, in the matter between MaSitolo and Thunukala the Kune headman got angry with the way a respondent behaved in the vernacular forum and proposed that the matter be escalated to the chief's council but the headman was essentially overruled by the council. Thunukala was the male respondent to a claim that he had accused MaSitolo and her brother of killing his wife using witchcraft. When Nduna Hlekile said that the matter should be taken to the chief's council because of Thunukala's recalcitrance, others who made up the forum decided that the matter should end at the headman's council. Nduna Hlekile accepted this decision but fined the respondent R100 for the effective equivalent of 'contempt of court'. This fine was in addition to the R300 to be paid as damages to the complainant and her brother for calling them witches and also for calling MaSitolo's brother a stock thief.

The chief's council is in many ways distinct from the other core vernacular forums. (See Figure 4.2 below.) Because the forum is a hybrid between a vernacular and legislated forum, it bears a mix of attributes from both the vernacular and state systems. In both the Nakudala and Nezikhathi Traditional Communities, the forums bear some resemblance to the local Magistrate Court. For instance, the chief sits alone up front, facing the 'audience' – in one case, in the Nezikhathi area, on an elevated platform. The chief headman is deemed a kind of prosecutor – this was the term used by the Nezikhathi chief headman in describing his role – who questions the parties with some degree of intimidation (though other headmen and even people in the audience are allowed to also pose questions). The parties to the case sit directly opposite the chief, unable to see the bulk of the people in attendance behind them. Though the forums have been given witness boxes, the forums do not seem to make use of these.

This format is different from the informal context in which the lower forums operate (pictured on the book cover). In the headman's council, for instance, people gather under a tree in a loosely formed circle. In many instances, one has difficulty making out the parties to the matter from where they sit, so intermingled are they with the rest of those in attendance. Often someone who did not already know the headman might even have difficulty knowing for sure who was chairing the proceedings. Certainly, the headmen do not typically adopt an intimidating tone or posture typical of a supposed prosecutor or judge that distinguishes them. And, because the gathering sits in what is basically a spherical shape, everyone can mostly see everyone else. The family, neighbourhood, and subward gatherings are smaller-scaled versions of the same format. (See Figures 4.3, 4.4 and 4.5 below.) When women are present in a forum, the seating arrangement is divided along gender lines.

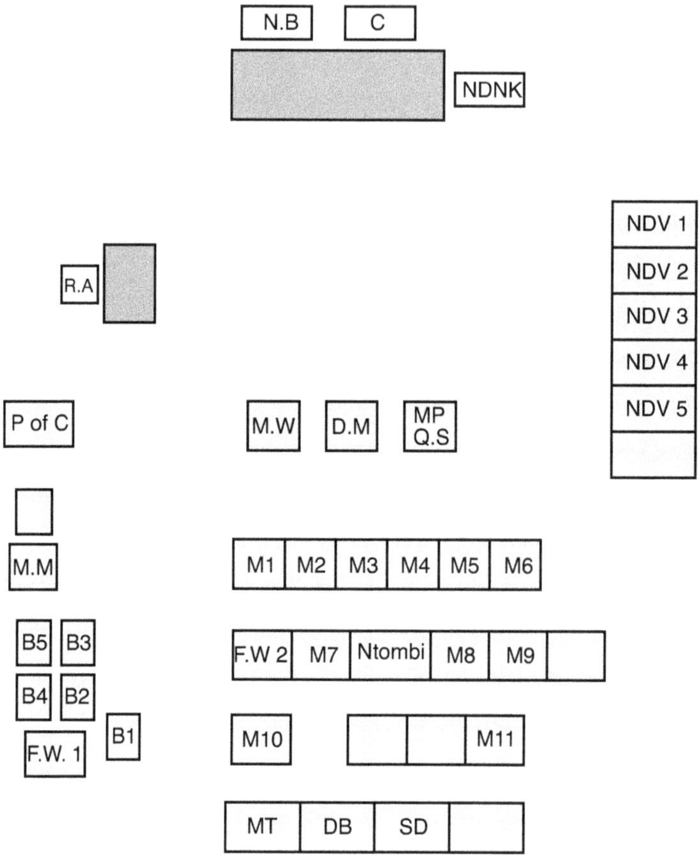

C = Ndabezitha (Chief)

N.B = Unobhala Wenkosi (Traditional Council secretary)

NDNK = Ndunankulu (Chief Headman)

R.A = Research Assistant

P of C = Iphoyisa lenkosi (Chief's security)

NDV 1 – 5 = Izinduna (headmen)

M.W = Umhloli Wezintombi (chair, virginity inspection committee)

B1 – 5 = Obaba (men)

M1 – 11 = Omama (women)

M.M = Mama Mhloli (member, virginity inspection committee)

F.W 1 = Fieldworker 1

F.W 2 = Fieldworker 2

Ntombi = Complainant

Figure 4.2 Diagram of a Case Before Nakudala Chief's Council

At the table at the top of the diagram (representing the innermost part of the long room), **C** is the Chief, **N.B** is the chief's council secretary, and **NDNK** stands for *Ndunankulu* (the chief headman). Sitting in a row going down part of the right side of the diagram are the headmen present for the hearing. The men present are depicted as **B1**, **B2,** etc., and are situated on the left of the diagram. **M1**, **M2,** etc., represent the women in the audience. In front of the women, basically in the middle of the room, are *umhloli wezintombi* (the woman who does the virginity testing) and her assistants. On the left hand side of the diagram – across from the authoritative women – is the **PofC,** who is the chief's policeman or bodyguard. The young women concerned in the matter are at the back of the room.

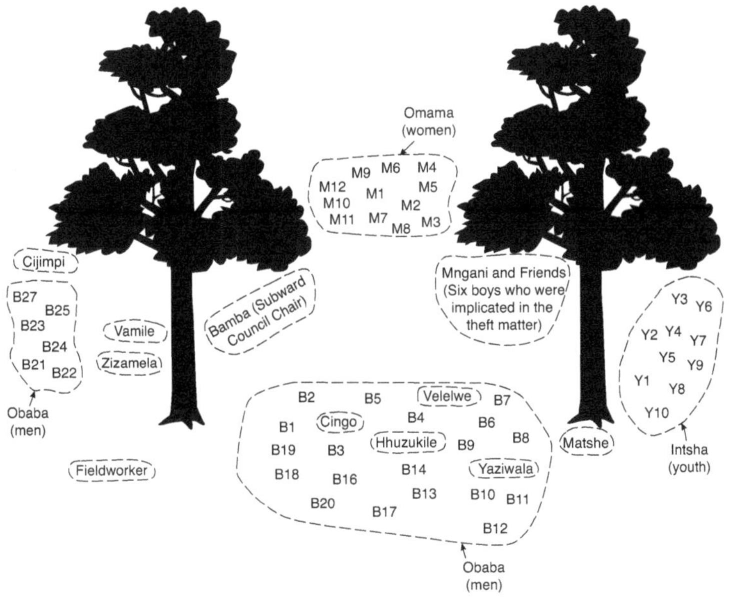

Figure 4.3 Diagram of a Mediation Before Kuhlanu Subward Gathering

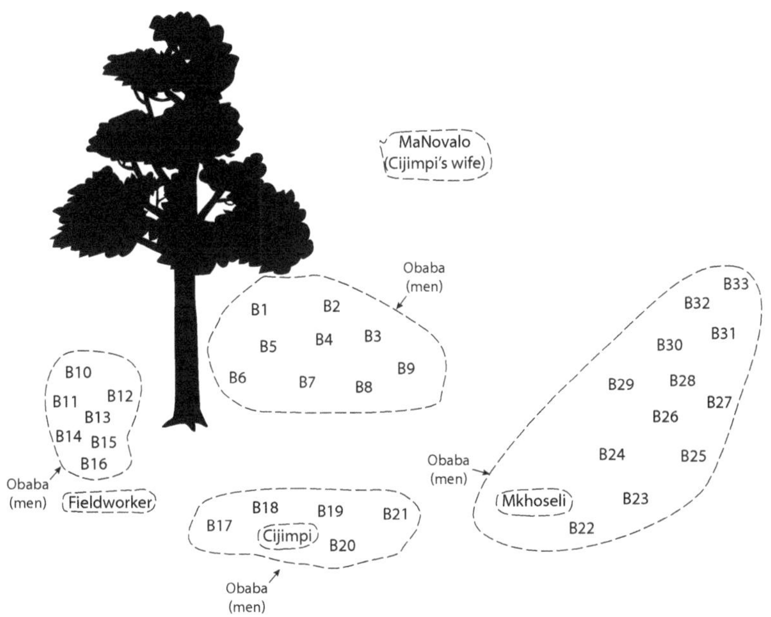

Figure 4.4 Diagram of Case Before Kuhlanu Headman's Council

In the above two diagrams, **B** represents *obaba* (men), **M** *omama* (women), and **Y** *intsha* (youth). The names spelled out in full are those of the parties.

In the first of the two diagrams, **Bamba** is the man charged with chairing the subward council and thus this matter that the council is hearing. Behind him are two notables in the subward who form the sub-council with him, **Vamile** and **Zizamela**. There is also a grouping of six young men (near the group of young people attending the hearing as observers) who are involved in the matter.

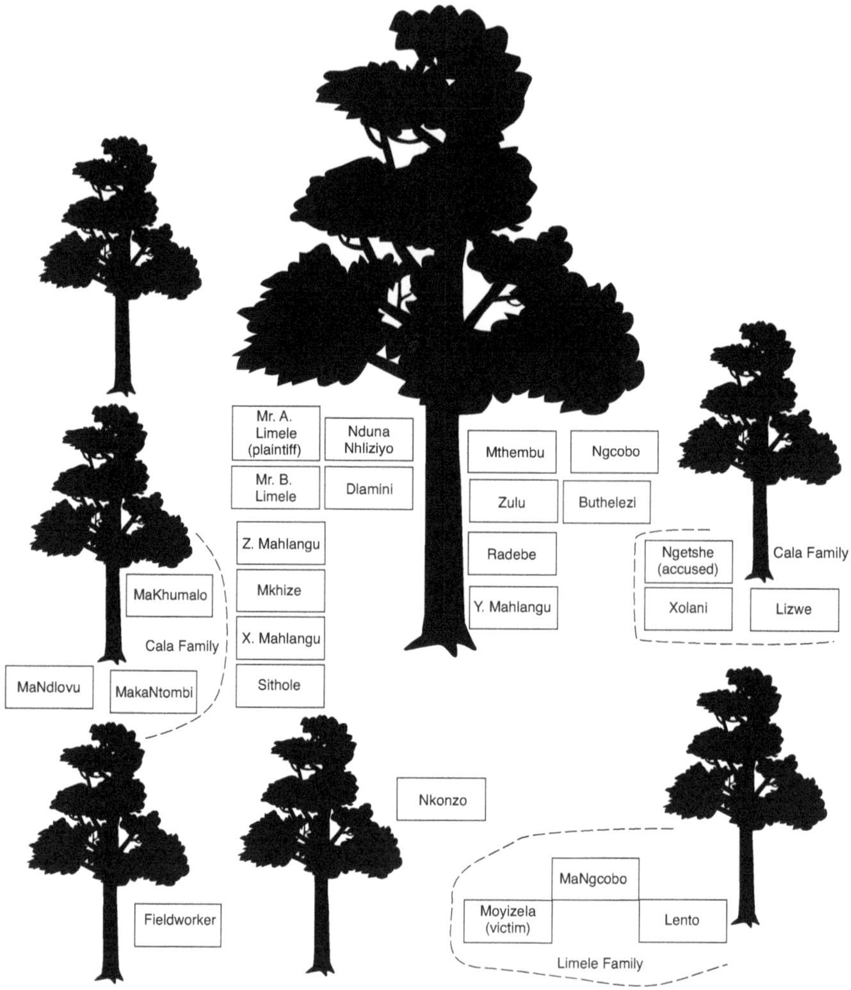

Figure 4.5 Diagram of Case Before Kuthathu Headman's Council

This diagram very much resembles the one that precedes it. It is only different in that women are present because they are witnesses or because they partly represent their children in this matter, though the children (that is, families at large) are technically represented by the men. Therefore, there is a small group of **Limele** women in the bottom right-hand corner of the image under one little tree – among them is the teenage girl who was injured in the assault. There is also another small group of women related to or accompanying the **Cala** family in the top left-hand corner under another little tree.

What, in the chief's council, bears any relationship to the other vernacular forums? Members of *isizwe* are welcome to attend and participate in the proceedings, but few dare. Those who attend are generally those with cases before the forum, those accompanying or witnessing for those with cases before the forum, or those with close relationships with the institution, such as members of the Traditional Council[63] or sometimes even headmen's policemen.

In the case concerning MaThembile, which opened this book and which I observed in the chief's council, the chief was mostly silent through the proceedings. Questioning in this case was primarily done by the chief headman and another one of the seven headmen of *isizwe*. Some questions and opinions on what was 'the truth of the matter' also came from the floor: from a member of the Traditional Council and from an older man in attendance.

The attendees were mainly men who were somehow associated with the other case being heard that day; only a few were attending merely out of interest. Also in attendance was the headman's policeman of the subward from which the accused woman, MaThembile, came. He was also questioned – sometimes accusingly – about the case's first hearing, for which he had been responsible. The questioning seemed to imply that he had failed to give the matter a proper hearing.

Regardless of how the form of the chief's council resembles that of other vernacular forums, the institution of the chief's council has an aura of intimidation and respect. This atmosphere is evident in the relatively few participants who speak freely and in the stiff air in the chief council's proceedings, as well as the limited attendance by ordinary people who are not compelled to be present. Yet, in all fairness, even assuming that the public were interested in participating in this forum, one of the main obstacles to wider public participation would be finances: most local people do not have the financial means to travel vast distances to the chief's council even when they have to. Furthermore, the intense physical demands of people's lifestyle do not permit the luxury of prioritising participation in dispute management at the chief's council. At least, such participation appears to be a luxury, given a context in which more basic needs for subsistence – rearing livestock, raising crops, fetching firewood and water, or migrant labour – are not conveniently attained.

Physical proximity, more palpable social expectation (because one is more likely to be seen by one's neighbours or local authority and questioned if one were absent), and more felt social need (to ensure harmony and security in one's immediate surrounds) make prioritisation of forum attendance more feasible at lower levels of social organisation. But even the lower forums often complain that people – especially men, for they are the ones expected to participate consistently – are 'not attending meetings anymore'.

It is true that some men are prevented from attending the forums by work. Yet, as previously explained, employment rates in Msinga are low. It is arguable that the decrease in turnout reflects relatively low investment and confidence in the core forums (an issue I discuss in great detail in Chapter 8) that is also consistent with the generational decline in commitment to traditional values

63 The legislative-administrative body constituted in terms of sections 3 and 28(4) of the Traditional Leadership and Governance Framework Act 41 of 2003.

discussed above. Certainly, this difference in rates of participation shows an increase in formalisation and a diminishing role for ordinary members of the vernacular grouping the higher one goes up the forum system. While some have said that this phenomenon is to be expected as a result of the evolution of any legal order,[64] formalism and less participation of ordinary people were deliberately engineered in the vernacular system: it is in the higher levels of the system that the state interfered in order to formalise and centralise authority.[65] Initially, this interference was intended to centralise authority in the person of the chief, in the chief's council, but later attempts were made to do likewise in the headmen's councils and centralise authority in the headman. Of course, much less of this centralisation was achieved in the headmen's councils, because of the substantially greater number of headmen's councils, as well as the state's limited means and reach.

While rates of participation present an issue for the core forums in the vernacular system, they are not as much of an issue for the forums focused on men's disputes – hence, reinforcing the point that increased formalisation of a forum affects rates of participation. This chapter has already pointed out that *igoso* and *iphini* perform their role with the support of the men of their respective areas of jurisdiction. Thus, though *iphini* is the primary authority over men's misconduct in the subward, he does not carry out his function alone. In fact, he must carry out his disciplinary role in the presence of and with the support of the men of the subward. The same is true of *igoso* as the primary authority with personal jurisdiction over the men of the ward. Thus, the men of the subward or ward play an important role in asking questions, giving counsel and disciplining one another (corporally, if it comes to that).

For example, a young man by the name of Chuku had gotten drunk and then entered one of his friends' home, where a number of men were gathered, and threatened them with a firearm. The matter was first discussed by the neighbours. The conclusion of the discussion, in which a number of local men spoke – asking questions, testifying to what happened, and critiquing the wrongdoer's conduct – was that the young man should bring his firearm to the men of his subward for confiscation. This decision was reached after the accused's brother (who represented the young man in his absence because the accused

64 So suggests Hart, H. L. A. (1961) *The Concept of Law*. Oxford, Clarendon Press. Cf. Cheyette, Frederic (1970) 'Suum Cuique Tribuere' *French Historical Studies*, 6(3): 287 at 290 who argues, based on the experience in France, that formalism is an adapted preference: 'There is no reason to believe that individuals . . . prefer objective neutrality to partiality in their own favor. . . . Neutral, objective order is very much a learned value.'

65 Lord Hailey *Native Administration in the British African Territories* (1950–1953) Vol. IV 36, as cited in Reyntjens, Filip (1993) 'The Future of Customary Law in Africa' in Joan Church (ed.) *The Future of Indigenous Law in Southern Africa: A Collection of Papers and Comments Presented at a Conference Held under the Auspices of the Centre for Indigenous Law, UNISA and Vista University at UNISA on 21–22 October 1991*. Pretoria, Centre for Indigenous Law, UNISA, 3–23 at 9.

himself was said to be afraid) requested that the group not take the matter to the police, to avoid the accused's arrest. This appeal implied that the firearm was illegal. Since those concerned were from the subward, the matter was then taken to the tree of *iphini*, where it was used as a teachable moment for all the men in the subward.

Forum relationships

One of the things that I have attempted to capture in Figure 4.1 is how the forums relate to one another in terms of passing matters from one to another. What is more difficult for the reader to know from simply looking at the diagram and reading an overview is how the forums relate to one another in subtler ways: how the forums actually manage individual disputes – that is, by what internal processes, in the vernacular forums, and by what external processes, in escalating the matters from forum to forum.

Because the superior forums refer matters back to the family councils, one can say that there is great respect for these family forums. Even where the family council has proven ineffectual at dealing with a situation, faith in their being the best forum for dealing with internal family disputes endures. We have already seen this faith above, in the case of Mdala, the patriarch who was appealing to the Nezikhathi chief's council for protective intervention. This patriarch was effectively saying that he was unable to discipline Mshana, the young man who would not submit to the patriarch's authority as chair of that forum and was instead threatening his life. Of course, what was also going on in this matter was an abdication of responsibility. This abdication was accompanied by a somewhat disguised admission by the chief's council that it was powerless to address the problem, which one of the headmen participating in the study openly divulged.

In the study, three headmen emerged as having good relations with four forums, respectively. First, the headman of Kuyisithupha had a good relationship with the CPF because he, himself, was one. Jakoob, a white farmer in the area, came to the headman to inform him that the repeated theft on his property was causing him great distress. Jakoob asked the headman to assist him in curbing the crime on his farm. The headman responded that, in his capacity as headman, he could not do anything to help the farmer; however, in his capacity as a CPF, he would bring this to the attention of the other CPFs and they would discuss how they could assist.

Second, in Kubili, the headman would refer matters to *iphini* and, as shown in the matter pertaining to Chuku and his gun, Nduna Thulile was invited by *iphini* to attend (something a headman would not ordinarily do)[66] and publicly

66 In 1987, the Nakudala Chief Headman (quoted above) said the following about being *induna* versus *igoso* (and, by extension, *iphini*): 'A *gosa* is a more popular man. An *induna* is respected. A *gosa* calls men for popular things like parties. An *induna* calls us for cases. . . .

clarify the rules relating to such a violation as Chuku's. Third, the headman of Kuhlanu had good relationships with the subward in which he was resident. He seemed to have great regard for its disciplinary and crime-solving role and often referred matters to the subward council. He also had at least some collaborative relationship with *isikebhe*. We recorded that he partnered with it to investigate and settle a livestock theft on one occasion when *isikebhe* came to him to tell him of a goat that they were looking for. Nduna Nyanga accompanied the representatives of *isikebhe* to the suspected perpetrator's home, where they did not find the alleged offender but left a message. They later returned to the home together and found the offender, Mbuzihambile, and agreed with him that he would pay for the replacement of the illicit goods.

I have previously suggested that there are strong relationships between some of the headmen too. For instance, we recorded a couple of instances in which the headman of Kuthathu telephoned the headman of Kunye for advice on questions relating to fulfilment of the administrative side of his job. It is worth noting again that personality may have been a significant contributor to this relationship. Conceiving of himself as relatively new to the job and sometimes even jittery, Nduna Nhliziyo was much more open and consultative by nature, whereas Nduna Mshushisi was rather dominant and headstrong, and generally exuded confidence and thus somehow commanded deference from at least some of the other headmen.

The relationship between the headmen's councils and the chiefs' councils differs between the Traditional Communities (*izizwe*) and wards. In *isizwe* of Nakudala, all seven headmen are expected to attend hearings at the chief's council weekly (or whenever they take place). By contrast, the headmen – numbering over 30 – in the Nezikhathi vernacular grouping do not always

---

An *induna* does not attend meetings with the *gosa* at the *insizwa* [young man] tree. He may go if he tells the *gosa*: "I'm coming as myself". Or the *gosa* will say: "Come, but not as *induna*." When you come you announce this. When they are almost ready to finish you will leave early because people can't say their things while you are around. You allow them privacy. . . . The chief knows who is the *gosa* from the *induna*, who has been told by the young men. The chief can't call the *gosa*. The chief can't give the *gosa* instructions. At the chief's *bandla* [council] he is respected.' This may be the principle (the normative ideal) but practice may vary and it is clear that the headman can be turned to when *igoso* must be held accountable or replaced – hence, he does not necessarily only find out who *igoso* is from the young men whispering it to him. In Kuthathu, for instance, the headman held a meeting with the men in his jurisdiction in which the matter of the ward no longer having *igoso* came up. The headman was part of the discussion on why *igoso* had effectively resigned (*igoso* allegedly said that when he calls meetings people do not come); the headman said they had to properly interview him and, after he had been fined for not performing his duty, they could appoint a new *igoso*. The men were looking to the headman to give them a date to meet when they would all appoint a new *igoso*. In a different ward, the headman was approached to mediate between *igoso* and the men, who accused him of being uncooperative: e.g. when they tell *igoso* about meetings or celebrations, he does not attend then alleges that the meetings were 'in the bush'. The headman called a meeting and sent a letter to *igoso* for him to attend.

attend hearings and are too geographically spread out to do so. For instance, the Nezikhathi headman of Kuyisithupha would have to travel at a cost of R75 each way for over an hour to get to the chief's council. However, the headmen feel a responsibility to regularly report to the chief or, if he cannot be reached, to his secretary about what is going on in their respective wards. The headman of Kuhlanu could do so regularly because he lived quite close to the traditional council offices where the chief officially sits. The headman of Kune also could do so often because the chief's home was in his ward.

The most interesting relationship is that between the state police and the forums constituting the vernacular system. Though officers in the vernacular system – especially headmen – commonly bemoan the inadequate respect shown by the state and its officials for vernacular officers and their contributions to the administration of justice and maintenance of order, vernacular officers also sometimes talk of a partnership existing between the institutions. What this patently unequal partnership looks like varies.

Many of the headmen will call the police or advise local people to call the police when a crime that has occurred and been reported to them is severe. When a crime that headmen understand to be more minor is reported to them, the police can be used as a stick (threat) and the vernacular system the carrot (a gentler alternative). This approach was exemplified in Kuthathu when Msukele attempted to rape Walile, who was someone's young wife. He was given the choice between calling the police and discussing the matter between the families and thereby coming to a mutually satisfactory agreement on compensation instead of facing jail time. Of course, what constitutes a minor crime according to the headmen may not be what the police or reader would consider minor.

One sees that the police can also sometimes be used to support the function of the headmen. For instance, I spoke with one headman's policeman who had a valid gun license and who was responsible for a subward where hijackings happened frequently. He said these crimes were usually committed by a group of jobless young men in the area, and he would sometimes call subward meetings or meetings with the young men in particular to discourage the crime, warn them of punishment, or sniff out the perpetrators. He claimed that he was very good at sniffing out the perpetrators and said, with some pride, that the locals knew that when he called the police, the police would come. Hence, he conceived of his close relationship with the police as a show of his strength and used this relationship as muscle for his own local authority.

In a similar vein, the headman of Kunye was responsible for the management of a war in Okunye, one of the subwards in his jurisdiction. As part of his management, he called a subward meeting to which he invited the police, asking them to simply be present but not try to make any arrests. This meeting was meant to be a safe space for people to discuss the problem and come to a resolution about stopping the war.

The police came, supposedly to help mediate the war on the agreed terms. This attendance by the police bolstered the headman's authority by giving the outward impression of a robust partnership between them: the headman calls the police and they come in support of his dispute management initiative. However, a few days after the meeting, the headman learned that the police were raiding homes, demanding illegal firearms. The headman phoned the police to ask them to stop and to allow some time for the headman and the police, together as authorities, to see if the meeting had had any success in stopping the war.

In this example, the headman fancied himself an equal partner with the police, even to the extent of thinking he could tell them what to do and expect them to honour their agreement. However, the police evidently were not of the same view and continued with their primary priority in the area, which was to confiscate illegal firearms. They had partnered with the headman only to advance their own objectives. The headman persisted in his attempt to partner effectively with the police by trying to negotiate with them that they allow time to see if the vernacular attempt at a solution would work. In essence, the partnership was definitely not equal: the police saw the headman as needing them more than they needed him and, likewise, they saw their mandate as superior to his.

Was the headman deluded in thinking that there should be a more effective partnership between the police and his office? No. Periodically, the police hold meetings between themselves and vernacular groupings or their headmen, to encourage effective cooperation. During the period of data collection, these meetings were recorded as having taken place in Kuyisithupha and Mpunga and having been attended by the headman of Kuyisithupha and some of the Nakudala headmen. However, clearly what is expressed as a goal is difficult for the police to realise in practice. The police seem to be in an ambivalent position: seeking to partner with the headmen is good rhetoric, but the police seem to ultimately believe that they do not need the headmen as much as the headmen need them.[67] This idea is contrary to the view of the headmen, who see their role as indispensable.

Nevertheless, the relationship between the police and the headmen is arguably stronger in the Kuyisithupha area than in Msinga's main site (where the nearby town and police station is Tugela Ferry), based on instances of the police referring matters to the headmen's councils, the degree to which the headmen seemed to feel that they could request police cooperation, and whether the police responded to the headmen in keeping with their requests. The stronger relationship in Kuyisithupha may partly be explained because the police there have a smaller burden of cases and Traditional Communities to deal with.

In the Moni incident, a goat was discovered locked in a house in Kuyisithupha. Since goats should ordinarily roam free, this raised suspicion that the goat

67 This relationship has important historical roots whereby the police were previously the enforcement arm of government in the area to maintain law and order among the 'natives' (later 'bantus' and then 'blacks'), and were therefore definitively superior to the traditional authorities. See Alcock, Creina in Cousins et al. (above).

must have been stolen. The ward council met to discuss this situation, and then the headman's council went to report the matter to the police, who in turn accompanied the council to the scene, broke down the door of the home, and retrieved the stolen goat. The theft matter was then managed by the headman's council, which decided to banish the guilty party, who was also suspected of other misdemeanours.

In another instance reflecting the relationship between the police and vernacular system in Kuyisithupha, the police referred a matter back to the headman's council. In this matter, a young man, Sihlobo, was severely beaten by his cousin, Mndeni, over a cellphone that his cousin and aunt (Mndeni's mother) accused Sihlobo of stealing. The injured Sihlobo's mother brought the matter to the headman, who said that because it 'involved blood', she should rather report it to the police. The police, however, said that because the matter was between family members, they should discuss the matter at home between them as kin; if that did not work, she should refer the matter to the headman and, if that did not work, she could return to the police.

Of course, this relationship between police and vernacular forums can have negative consequences for the person who might thus feel trapped between two systems, both of which refer him/her to the other, and neither of which will take responsibility for giving the person legal assistance. But not always. For instance, it was not so in the matter of Sheliwe, a young woman whose family's property had been damaged by another young woman. Sicabha had caused the damage when she sought to assault Sheliwe, claiming that Sheliwe was having a relationship with her boyfriend (Sicabha's child's father). The police had been called at the time of the incident but had counselled the complainant to pursue vernacular management. Sheliwe and her family were advised that this was best because they said they were related to the accused: Sheliwe's and Sicabha's mothers shared the same surname. The complainant did turn to the vernacular management forum and obtained the bulk of the remedy she and her family had wanted.

As a final example, the headman of Kuthathu was playing a unique role vis-à-vis his interaction with the police. He was accompanying locals accused of crimes to the police when their hearings came up.[68] It did not surface that he was doing anything significant in those matters but to assist in representing the people before the police and subsequently to be present for the hearings as a support or, when needed, a character witness. But he would also follow up on matters referred to the police, to see how they ended.

Conversely, the headman of Kunye did not seem to play this kind of role in interpersonal disputes. For instance, he was presented with a situation in which two young men, Uyeba and Nonya, were accused of breaking into a house and stealing its contents. They were arrested before he was able to hear that matter,

68 For example, Shisile asked the headman to accompany him to the Magistrate's Court for his arson trial. The headman obliged and Shisile paid for the headman's transport.

because they had broken into the local school and stolen its computers, and the head of the school had reported this matter to the police. When a second person reported to the headman that his house had also been broken into by the same young men, the headman told him and the first complainant to go to the police. He did not accompany the two complainants or Uyeba and Nonya in reporting or observing the case.

Concluding remarks

It is evident that the popular conception of the vernacular dispute management system as being composed of only headmen's and chiefs' councils is an impoverished idea. Many other forums that exist in Msinga – single-family councils, dual/joint family councils, neighbourhood gatherings, subward gatherings, headmen's policemen, *amaphini* (the men's sub-headmen) and *amagoso* (the men's headmen), *umhloli wezintombi* (the virginity tester) and *isikebhe* (the vigilante/insurance organisation) – all constitute and inform the vernacular management system. Additionally, the state-created institutions of Community Policing Forums and the South African Police Service play an important role as well.

Similarly impoverished is the popular idea that the known forums simply have territorially defined jurisdiction. As I have discussed in this chapter, there is a profound interrelationship between the territorial and personal parameters of the jurisdiction of the core forums in the system. What is often described as territorial jurisdiction can often more appropriately be called personal jurisdiction (mainly in the instance of conditional, as opposed to essential, personal jurisdiction).

Therefore, while it is true that the chief's council deals with matters of *isizwe* (the Traditional Community at large) and the headman's council deals with matters of *isigodi* (the ward), it is even truer that both *isizwe* and *isigodi* are personally affiliated groups that live on shared territory. The councils have jurisdiction over the people in their areas, but the people in their areas are there because they opt into and affiliate with the relevant group over which the chief and/or headman is a recognised and legitimate authority. The language people use to describe themselves is a clear marker of this fact. This means that imposing jurisdiction of an authority just because people live in that territory offends the underlying value of voluntary affiliation and recognition of the legitimacy of the relevant authority.

Particularly when it comes to the jurisdiction of *igoso*, who is limited to dealing with men's disorderliness in the ward, and *iphini*, who deals with the same but only in the subward, the territorial confines of the forums are subordinate to the subject-matter of disputes, which is the primary determinant of their jurisdiction. Subject-matter jurisdiction is also possessed by *umhloli wezintombi*, as well as CPFs, *isikebhe*, and the state police. The consequence of there being these various forums with subject-matter jurisdiction is that sometimes conflict arises among the various forums about who has jurisdiction. Conflict occurs because several forums may share territorial jurisdiction or even share subject-matter jurisdiction in the same territory, and compete for the authority to decide a matter. Conflict also occurs partly because, as Keebet Von Benda-Beckmann observed in a different context, '[d]ealing with disputes . . . became an important instrument in the struggle for power at local level.'[69]

Two significant points should be taken from my discussion of the membership and characteristics of vernacular forums. First, their membership is mainly made up of ordinary male members of the vernacular grouping concerned at whatever level of social organisation that applies, and each forum is chaired by a man who is the key authority figure for the social unit that the forum serves. In this sense, the patriarchal nature of these forums remains. Second, there is much variation in practice between the forums in terms of allowing increasing levels of female participation.

Typically less formally constituted and observing a less formal procedure than the higher forums, lower forums allow for more independent female involvement. Moreover, the horizontal variation among forums at the same level of social organisation means that forum cultures are partly localised as well as context-dependent and personality-driven. Women's participation and other elements of dispute management are affected by this variation. While the authority figure at each level chairs the forum at his respective level, decision-making remains a task to be exercised by the ordinary members of the relevant vernacular grouping sitting in council. Women's substantial exclusion from this process means that their voices are not well represented in the development of local norms.[70] This is a matter of such significance as probably ought not to be left to individual personalities – in the form of the authorities chairing particular dispute management councils – to decide. The significance of gender disparities in disputing is something I return to in Chapters 5 and 6, which focus on the relational aspects of dispute management in Msinga.

The historically shaped internal cultural differences between the headmen and the populations they serve suggest the need for the headmen to reconsider their

69 Von Benda-Beckmann (above) at 139. See Roberts, Simon (1994) 'Law and Dispute Processes' in T. Ingold (ed.) *Companion Encyclopaedia of Anthropology: Humanity, Culture and Social Life*. London, Routledge, 962–982 at 972, who draws on Turner to observe: 'claims about "wrongdoing" are closely interwoven with struggles for political ascendancy and competition for resources.' Also see Burris, Scott, Michael Kempa and Clifford Shearing (2008) 'Changes in Governance: A Cross-Disciplinary Review of Current Scholarship' *Akron Law Review*, 41: 1 at 3: 'Governance is about how people exercise power to achieve the ends they desire, so disputes about ends are tied inextricably to assessments of governance means.'

70 In 1987, the Nakudala Chief Headman (quoted above) said the following about training to be a headman who adjudicates justly: 'No one teaches you. Men tell you when you make a decision: "No, *nduna*, that's not how it's done." They won't say that in front of you. They'll say: "*Hawu, nduna*. This is a hard case. Let's postpone it."' He goes on to describe perhaps getting an idea in a conversation at a 'beerdrink' and maybe raising the matter in discussions with the chief who can refer to law books. All of the interactions that the chief headman describes as informing his informal training are with men.

catering to their 'ideal' of what gender identities should look like in Msinga. This reconsideration would and should shape even their own roles vis-à-vis how they carry out leading dispute management in the area.

Among the forums making up the vernacular system or playing a role within it, it is evident that family councils still hold an important place in the system, given the extent to which matters pertaining to their membership are referred back to them. As seen, referrals back to the family councils occurred at all levels of the vernacular system and even sometimes from the state police. These referrals constitute deviations from the normative ideal. Likewise, the different relationships between the headmen's councils and the chiefs' councils – shown in this chapter to differ between the wards and nations – form part of the discussion of divergence from the normative ideal.

As discussed, the degree of partnership between the headmen and forums like the CPFs, *iphini*, subward gatherings, *isikebhe*, and the police varied among headmen. With regard to the police in particular, it is evident that police support for and partnership with the headmen and headmen's policemen are important factors in the vernacular forum authorities' constitution and defence of their own power through competitive behaviours. The extent of cooperation (as opposed to competition)[71] is judged on the basis of recorded instances of matters being referred from the police to the headmen's councils, the extent to which the headmen felt that they could make requests of the police and the responsiveness of the police to the headmen in a manner according with their requests. Concern with cooperation between the forums involved in the management of disputes in Msinga is of vital importance in so far as it affects the ability of each forum to successfully resolve disputes brought to it by leveraging the resources of and partnering with other existing forums.

So far, it seems clear that the relationship between the headmen and the police presents many tensions and, though the police play an indispensible role in vernacular dispute management, their fit in the vernacular system is uneasy. One of the ways in which this manifests is in relation to the back and forth (or even 'passing of the buck') that sometimes takes place between vernacular forums and the police over matters 'involving blood'. Evidently, here too, there is deviation from the normative ideal that the police alone deal with such matters.[72] All of these dimensions of dispute management signal the importance of interpersonal and professional relationships premised on social trust to the system's weaknesses and strengths. Hence, I turn to discussion of relationships in the next chapter.

71 Von Benda-Beckmann (above).

72 For more on deviation from the normative ideal – especially in the vernacular dispute management system – see Mnisi Weeks (above).

Section III

Interpersonal attributes of dispute management in Msinga

5 Contradictory social relations

Who is disputing with whom and why?

It is in the family

A complaint against MaLwimi was brought to Nduna Hlekile on the grounds that she had called her in-laws witches and said that they were bewitching her husband. The husband's two paternal uncles – Babomkhulu and Babomncane – who brought the case against their niece-in-law had heard her insult the family. They were her neighbours and she had not said it very softly.

MaLwimi initially denied that she had accused her in-laws of witchcraft, but her husband provided testimony supporting his uncles. One of the accused uncles' wife, MaFakazi, also testified to say MaLwimi had first said that the family had refused to give her a chicken and later said that they perform witchcraft. It seemed, therefore, that MaLwimi's resentment of her in-laws' prior failure to give her a chicken had prompted her to accuse them of performing witchcraft against her husband, Bekekithi, specifically when he was going to his uncles to borrow an animal for a ceremony.

MaLwimi was required to pay R2,000 (the amount demanded by Babomkhulu and Babomncane). When she asked for them to reduce the damages, the uncles refused on the basis that this was not the first time their niece-in-law had made this malicious accusation against their family. She indicated that she would pay the required damages in two instalments, out of her social grant money, which was in fact intended to support her children.

In a different ward, a rapidly escalating conflict ensued. A bar fight between two women, MaDlinzelwe and MaShonile, over an unpaid loan between them inexplicably led to MaShonile dying. The deceased woman's husband attributed her death to witchcraft on the part of MaDlinzelwe, who was reported to have fatally struck MaShonile during their fisticuffs. MaShonile's family said that MaDlinzelwe must have struck Mashonile with something that was *muthi*, a kind of potion.

At his wife's funeral, MaShonile's husband was heard saying that, before the sun set on his wife's funeral, there would be 'crying/weeping' (*ukukhala*, the same word as for 'mourning') at MaDlinzelwe's house. When, in short order MaDlinzelwe was murdered, MaShonile's husband was suspected of arranging the killing of the presumed witch.

On MaDlinzelwe's death, MaShonile's husband hired Mthuthisi to promptly move him and his belongings out of the Msinga area. It was not known whether he wanted to escape because he was guilty or because he knew he would be *thought* guilty, but public opinion declared it to be the former. Mthuthisi – who was a resident of a different ward – was then killed. Rumour had it that he was killed for moving MaShonile's husband – and, indeed, all local observers presumed it to be so.

At this stage, a rumour developed that the family of Mangele, the secretary of the Nakudala Traditional Council, had harboured those who had killed the mover. All of the regular residents of the secretary's family home were women – her mother, Mangele herself, and her daughter, who was born outside of marriage. Mangele's father was away frequently because he worked in Johannesburg. According to the rumours, if the family had hidden Mthuthisi's murderers, the women must have hired – or even assisted or supported – the murderers in the task of killing Mthuthisi.

Mangele and her family were afraid that they were next in the wave of revenge killings and requested the intervention of the chief and his council of headmen. In this matter, the vernacular authorities were asked to stop the violence, in part by establishing what exactly had happened and who the culprits were. By intervening promptly and publicly, holding a community meeting to discuss the conflict across the two wards, the headmen were able to stem the tide of retaliations. But, two years later, Mangele said that she and her family were still afraid that something might happen to them.

'Disputing with' and 'listening with'

This chapter provides a sketch of people who are typically disputing in Msinga and the relationships that form the foundation of the tensions between them. The reader no doubt has noticed by now that most disputes in Msinga are between people who know each other well. Typically, given in what close proximity people live with their family and the extent of social and economic interaction that takes place between family and neighbours, one finds that the relationships forming the background for disputes are often intimate.

This relational proximity between your average disputing parties persists even though the kinds of disputes that present range from private to public, and from minor to very serious. In other words, this relational proximity holds despite the fact that the kinds of wrongs committed against kith and kin can be fatal, and sometimes even deliberately so. As seen in Chapter 3, the nature of disputes that are brought to the vernacular forums are reflective of the history and existing social and economic conditions. This tension between relational intimacy and persistent potential for conflict demands extended examination, especially as relatives not only may have been involved in harming one another but also are required to be involved in the repair that might come through the dispute management process.

In that role of assisting in dispute management, the particular relations who play a role in proceedings are sometimes contrary to parties' and authorities' expectations – certainly, they are not always consistent with the normative ideal. For example, women play a more significant role in party representation in vernacular forums than conventional wisdom would say that they do. This phenomenon, again, is linked to the socio-economic changes that are occurring on the ground.

Goods commonly fought over include relationships, land, goats, homes or their content, and work or its yield (even from illegal activity such as marijuana production). Most of the conflicts occur between people who are related to one another – people who are in some ways kin. For historical and socio-economic reasons later canvassed in this chapter, the largest proportion of conflicts involve men and, commonly, alcohol – sales and use (or, more often, abuse) – as well as guns. Theft is a common occurrence, and if not that, then outstanding payment on a debt. Suspicion – whether of stealing something tangible or practicing dark arts in the realm of the supernatural – and accusations are also repeated occurrences that undermine social trust.[1]

Women appear in many of the recorded disputes, though often as witnesses. Sometimes this is simply because they have been involved in spreading the news of something, and they are then required to give account for what they said and where they saw what they talked about or whom they heard it from. In a handful of disputes, women were called to testify to something they had said about a threat to kill someone or an actual attempt made on someone's life. More will be said on this below and in the next chapter.

If they are disputants, women tend to be involved as such in mostly non-violent cases – sometimes as the objects of contention, for instance in marriage disputes in which the petition is for the bride to return to her in-laws. In family and neighbour conflicts, mothers make the most appearances, distantly followed by daughters-in-law and then daughters. Yet a distinction must be drawn here between mothers' participation, mostly but not exclusively, as supports – that is, representatives and witnesses – compared to daughters-in-law and daughters as parties to the disputes.

1 Social trust is a subset of social capital that – along with social networks, reciprocity and other norms – enables the 'coordination' and 'cooperation' (collective action) necessary for mutual benefit at the relevant level of social organisation. See van Deth, Jan W. and Sonja Zmerli (2009) 'Introduction: Civicness, Equality, and Democracy: A "Dark Side" of Social Capital?' *American Behavioral Scientist*, 53(5): 631–639 at 633. Also see Gittell, Ross and Avis Vidal (1998) *Community Organizing: Building Social Capital as a Development Strategy*. Thousand Oaks, CA, Sage; Putnam, Robert D. (1995) 'Bowling Alone: America's Declining Social Capital' *Journal of Democracy*, 6(1): 65–78; Putnam, Robert D., Robert Leonardi and Raffaella Y. Nonetti (1993) *Making Democracy Work: Civic Traditions in Modern Italy*. Princeton, NJ, Princeton University Press; Schuller, Tom (2007) 'Reflections on the Use of Social Capital' *Review of Social Economy*, 65(1), 11–28.

To illustrate, in the matter between Kanankinga and Landula, Kanankinga's mother was accused of insulting his girlfriend and saying that Landula is lying when she claims that the child she had outside of marriage is Kanankinga's. The son did not support his mother in her claim and said that he knew the child to be his, thus standing by his girlfriend in the paternity dispute. Yet, more typically, the mother of the young woman, Phikile, who was accused of stealing an older man's employment benefits using his government-issued identity number brought a case against the older man, Dakiwe, because he shouted this insult against her daughter in the mother's yard. The case superficially presents as one between Phikile's mother and Dakiwe but it is actually more a conflict between Phikile (who is represented by her mother) and Dakiwe.

In both of these cases, among others, the fathers were absent from the picture. This situation is different from several other cases in which the father was not physically present but was nonetheless a moral presence in the dispute. An example is the case of Ntombi, who was accused of no longer being a virgin. Though Ntombi attended the case, even in the chief's council, with her mother, grandmother and sister, at every stage of the case's escalation (from the headman to *isikebhe*), she described the impetus behind pursuit of the case as being her father's say-so. A similar dynamic is seen in the case in which Ngetshe assaulted Moyizela and knocked her teeth out.

When women are involved in violent disputes, they are involved mostly as victims and, as discussed below, they are in many such cases actually silent in the dispute management process itself. An example is the matter in which Ntombazane was gang raped, and her family discussed and decided what would be done – whether charges would be laid against the young men or the matter would be discussed between the families at home. Ntombazane had not been consulted in the making of the decision and said she would probably have decided differently than her family had. (Of course, men can be victims too. Indeed, much male violence is directed at other men.)

Like women, children can be embroiled in conflict because of things they say (especially when insulting older people) and their involvement in relatively petty offences,[2] as well as their often being objects of contention, especially in the midst of marriage and paternity disputes.[3] In some instances, children are the perpetrators of very serious acts or the victims of such – especially children at the cusp of becoming young men.[4]

When close relationships sow deep divides

The question of who is involved in conflicts – mostly people who are closely related – requires that we try to understand what it is about the circumstances

2 For instance, at school, Chukuluza accuses Deleliwe's brother of practicing witchcraft.

3 See Kanakinga/Landula; Zama/Nkani.

4 Matshe/Hhuzukile; Toho/Semncane; Abafana; Webile.

in which people in Msinga find themselves that precipitates profound interpersonal conflict. Part of the explanation can be found in the study of witchcraft accusations and the worldview that informs them. Empirical and historical studies of South African vernacular groupings in the last century and more have reflected on the fact that witchcraft has held significant purchase for members of those groupings, and played a noteworthy socio-political role.[5] Note that the family as a primary site in which identity crises are played out is highlighted in studies of witchcraft.[6]

Witchcraft accusations typically occur between people who know each other well. Walter van Berek refers to them as 'the terror of closeness'.[7] He notes that '[i]n a society where close relationships should provide shelter against an oppressive outer world, witchcraft accusations form the reverse of this model of close relations. The alleged witch is the enemy within the gates, a situation sometimes shared with spirits in the invisible world.'[8]

Further explanation is provided by other scholars who argue that the primary reasons for witchcraft accusations occurring in contexts of relational proximity are that witches have to be close enough to their intended victims to develop a motive against them.[9] They should also be close enough to know their victims' areas of weakness and be able to get hold of 'bodily dirt, nail clippings or hair samples in order to carry out the deed. These relics contain the person's *moya* (soul). Fellow villagers, neighbours, and household members are therefore the most common victims and perpetrators of witchcraft.'[10] The people accused of performing witchcraft are said to cause illness or death by poisoning food,

5 Ashforth, Adam (2005) *Witchcraft, Violence, and Democracy in South Africa*. Chicago, University of Chicago Press; Ellis, Stephen and Gerrie Ter Haar (September 2007) 'Religion and Politics: Taking African Epistemologies Seriously' *The Journal of Modern African Studies*, 45(3): 385–401; Ellis, Stephen and Gerrie Ter Haar (1998) 'Religion and Politics in Sub- Saharan Africa' *The Journal of Modern African Studies*, 36(2): 175–201.

6 Redding, Sean (September 2004) 'Death in the Family: Domestic Violence, Witchcraft Accusations and Political Militancy in Transkei, South Africa, 1904–1965' *Journal of South African Studies*, 30(3): 519–537.

7 Van Beek, Walter E. A. (2006) 'The Escalation of Witchcraft Accusations' in Gerrie Ter Haar (ed.) *Imagining Evil: Witchcraft and Accusations in Contemporary Africa*. Trenton, New Jersey, Africa World Press 293–316 at 302.

8 Van Beek (above) at 302. Also see Hammond-Tooke, David (1989) *Rituals and Medicines: Indigenous Healing in South Africa*. Johannesburg, Ad. Donker at 81: 'Witches as a category are veritable fifth column within society. As such, they must be identified and eradicated as soon as possible.'

9 Standler, Jonathan (1996) 'Witches and Witch Hunters: Witchcraft, Generational Relations and the Life Cycle in a Lowveld Village' *Africa Studies*, 55(1 & 2) at 93. Van Beek (above) at 301: 'Accusations are motivated by envy, jealousy, greed, hatred, rivalry, vengeance, misunderstanding or a lack of information, feelings and factors that are usually easily recognised by the people themselves, or at least by bystanders, neighbours and kinsmen.'

10 Standler (above) at 93.

sending disease, causing severe accidents,[11] or directing lightning toward an intended victim, all in order to do harm to someone who is within social reach.[12]

Westerners who read about witchcraft are often perplexed by the significance it seems to hold for members of vernacular groupings.[13] These westerners hold a worldview different enough from the vernacular groupings that subscribe to beliefs about witchcraft and so misunderstand this practice's actual meaning and significance for those who believe in it. As Sean Redding explains:

> The accusations of witchcraft that sometimes accompanied episodes of familial violence were part of a pervasive belief that the malevolent use of supernatural powers was a real and valid explanation for misfortunes suffered. The term "witchcraft" was not usually a metaphor for the people speaking of it; rather, it was a real force in the world that was often associated with power and wealth and not just with social marginality.[14]

Put differently, witchcraft was believed to be real, and not just a proxy or manner of speaking about something else that is (more) real – which makes understanding it merely functionally inappropriate.[15] This power to manipulate or control spiritual forces and natural elements[16] in order to affect other people's lives, usually to cause harm, was wholly embraced by the accusers as one of several legitimate elucidations of the ills that people experienced.[17] It remains so.

It is central to valuing the dignity of the groupings firmly subscribing to beliefs that witchcraft is real that we appreciate their lived experience and perceptions as Redding does. Yet, I think that trying to understand the contextual factors that may breed a larger number of witchcraft accusations and motivate severe social responses to them is similarly important to our appreciating these groupings' humanity. The latter, functional type of explanation might be given to witchcraft accusations as Selaelo Thias Kgatla does:

> Witchcraft accusations in South Africa are caused by many factors. They flourish where people experience mysterious natural phenomena or live

11 Harnischfeger, Johannes (2000) 'Witchcraft and the State in South Africa' in John Hund (ed.) *Witchcraft Violence and the Law in South Africa*. Pretoria, Protea Book House at 47.

12 Standler (above) at 90, 92; Kgatla, Selaelo Thias (2006) 'Containment of Witchcraft in South Africa: A Search for a Transformational Approach to Curb the Problem' in Gerrie Ter Haar (ed.) *Imagining Evil: Witchcraft and Accusations in Contemporary Africa*. Trenton, New Jersey, Africa World Press at 270.

13 Ashforth (above); Ellis and Ter Haar (2007).

14 Redding (above) at 521.

15 Ibid. Also see Hammond-Tooke (above) at 84.

16 Standler (above) at 92.

17 Redding (above) at 521: '"Witchcraft" . . . might better be replaced with the unwieldy phrase "the cause of harm through supernatural powers" [and] was one of many possible causes for any given event."' Also see Ashforth (above); Ellis and Ter Haar (2007); Ellis and Ter Haar (1998).

> through a social crisis. Enabling conditions include soured relationships, poverty, political uncertainty, psychological needs and social anxiety . . . Having no say in matters affecting them directly, poor people fall victim to the circumstances and tend to rely on mystical forces for their protection and prediction of the future . . . . Unemployment and lack of economic activity lead to idleness and rumour-making.[18]

In Kgatla's view, these systemically adverse socio-political conditions favour the continuation of witchcraft accusations and their destructive effects in poor African communities. Johannes Harnischfeger agrees, saying that it is true in many African countries: 'the increase of witchcraft accusations is a modern phenomenon, closely related to the decline of the moral economy and the widening gulf between rich and poor.'[19]

David Hammond-Tooke agrees with this argument that 'competition for scarce resources' drives witchcraft accusations.[20] Yet, as Hammond-Tooke explains, the envy and rivalries out of which witchcraft accusations emerge are deeply human and therefore timeless.[21] Staying with the functional approach, van Berek observes that:

> There is no problem so new that it cannot be interpreted in witchcraft terms. It can be used to contain the ambitious upstart or to condemn the non-conformist types in society, it may blame the weak in society or form a handy tool to eliminate competitors and rivals, or be a way to keep claims of poorer kinsmen at bay.[22]

Indeed, Kgatla summarises that accusations can be used to try to restrain those who are socio-economically successful – dissuading them from realising their full potential. That is, the poor and weak may use such accusations to limit the prosperous and powerful from creating greater inequality and thus leaving them too far behind.[23]

18 Kgatla (above) at 285–286. Also see Comaroff, Jean and John Comaroff, eds. (1993) *Modernity and Its Malcontents: Ritual and Power in Postcolonial Africa*. Chicago, IL, Chicago University Press.

19 Harnischfeger (above) at 48–49. Also see Ellis and Ter Haar (2007).

20 Hammond-Tooke (above) at 84.

21 Ibid. at 81: 'It is obvious that harmonious social life is fundamentally threatened by negative emotions such as envy, jealousy and pride, which are present in every community and the people themselves often explain witchcraft in these terms. These universal features of human psyche feed on rivalry and competition, and are found in even the most apparent tranquil community.'

22 Van Beek (above) at 300.

23 Kgatla (above) at 270. Also see Harnischfeger (above) at 48–49, who emphasises that witchcraft is used by both rich and poor against each other.

In particular, being accused of performing witchcraft can have grave consequences and even be injurious to the one so accused who can lose their reputation, be banished from their family and home or be subject to violence or harm.[24] Such violence could include arson, murder or assault.[25] Responses to suspecting someone of witchcraft may, however, vary from place to place.[26]

In keeping with the current discussion of the relational proximity between the parties typically involved in disputes, however, Redding emphasises having found in the Eastern Cape, 'remarkable [historical] evidence . . . of the intimate nature of most witchcraft accusations and the relationship of such accusations to familial violence.'[27] Women tended to be the focal point of such tensions within the family, which I will explore more fully below and in the next chapter.

Redding provides a helpful, historical account of the reasons for women's particular susceptibility to witchcraft accusations in South Africa. While, as set out before, Zulu vernacular groupings were historically patriarchal, Redding sets out the context of witchcraft accusations by first noting that African societies have historically understood women as being powerful and potentially violent.[28] Hence, there has always existed an inherent ambivalence surrounding women, which largely turns on the heightened capacity for witchcraft that they are believed to have.

Some of the mistrust of women was due to the fact that, as wives, they are (in Monica Wilson's words) 'always something of an outsider'.[29] However, we should not forget that, as Hammond-Tooke reminds us, co-wives would commonly accuse one another in polygynous Nguni families where there was often competition and rivalry 'between houses for status and scarce resources.'[30] Yet, as Redding states, women's power and danger was seen as derived from their ability to call on their own ancestors or their having access to magic potions.[31]

> Witchcraft accusations could thus divide a family, and turn violence inward towards close family members. They also, typically, highlighted both the spiritual assets and liabilities of being a woman. A woman's ancestors

24 Redding (above) at 529.
25 Ibid. at 522, 527.
26 Van Beek (above) at 295–296. Also see Hammond-Tooke (above) at 81: 'In the past the reaction to discovered witches was violent. They were put to death [by what] was in essence a *public execution*. Among South African peoples witchcraft and the killing of the chief's messenger were in fact the only capital crimes.'
27 Redding (above) at 522.
28 Ibid. at 519.
29 Wilson, *Reaction to Conquest* at 43, as quoted in Ibid. at 524.
30 Hammond-Tooke (above) at 87. He concludes: 'Wives are ever on the watch for husbandly favouritism for either another wife or her children.'
31 Redding (above) at 531. Also see Hammond-Tooke (above) at 74: 'Witchcraft is believed to be inherited, thus running in families, and the witch-child is carefully trained in the techniques of her trade.'

> protected her even when she was married, but her ancestors were a real danger to her husband's family. People assumed that women had access to supernatural powers; the real question was whether they used them for good or ill.[32]

A paradox therefore existed for women who were wives or widows, especially, because society acknowledged that they needed the protection of their ancestors (from their birth families) but feared that these would bring harm to their marital families.[33]

The key irony in women's being so fundamentally distrusted, of course, was that women were simultaneously indispensible to the establishment and perpetuation of the primary social institution that is the homestead. They gave birth to and reared children and often looked after the animals and did the cultivation[34] – especially when men were in the cities as migrant labourers.[35] In the latter case, men had little choice but to leave the rural home, thus giving women a significant degree of autonomy. This, of course, did not usually stop them from blaming women whenever things went wrong.[36]

Rather crucially, Redding highlights the need to be aware that women had some powers available to them, including that of perpetrating violence.[37] This was so even within the context (emphasised by scholars cited above) of gender roles being in flux.[38] In fact, Redding notes that this instability of gender roles could itself have potentially caused violence within the family.[39] In other words, in the same way that I have noted that men exercised some agency within the confines of their declining authority during uncertain times, it is important to similarly observe that women had some avenues for exercising agency also, no matter how modest.

Recognising women's agency is particularly important in the context of discussions (like that which will follow later in this chapter) of violence as something that men predominantly perpetrate.[40] It is wrong, as Redding points out, to 'suggest that men have been the only ones capable of violence, or that it is only men's violence that has been socially significant.'[41] Women are not always

32 Redding (above) at 531.

33 Hammond-Tooke (above) at 74.

34 Guy, Jeff (1990) 'Gender Oppression in Southern Africa's Precapitalist Societies' in Cheryl Walker (ed.) *Women and Gender in Southern Africa to 1945*. Cape Town, David Philip, 33–47.

35 Redding (above) at 519.

36 Ibid. at 525.

37 Ibid. at 520.

38 Ibid.

39 Ibid: 'Understanding the powers available to women, including the power to be violent themselves, reveals the flux in gender roles which may in itself have become a cause of violence among family members.'

40 Redding (above) at 520.

41 Ibid.

victims. Indeed, in matters pertaining to witchcraft, women are often themselves the accusers of other women, and men, and are sometimes the initiators or perpetrators of violence.[42] It is similarly problematic for studies that focus on violence to ignore, as they all too often do, 'tensions *within* the family as basic causes of the violence, and the ways in which certain beliefs may have affected the outcome' in such conflicts.[43] Further still, it is wrong to ignore the reality of external factors that made it virtually impossible for black people to build healthy families under the political and economic arrangements established during colonialism and apartheid, which I discussed in Chapter 1.[44]

That said, there is precedent for men being accused of witchcraft and being accusers. There is some scholarship that suggests that men can also be the prime targets of witchcraft accusations under certain – mostly material – conditions. Jonathan Standler notes: 'While the anthropological literature on both Southern Africa and more especially European witchcraft indicates a tendency for women to be accused, in Timbavati this trend was reversed [because] the notion of envy has assumed conspicuously generational dimensions.'[45]

Witchcraft in Msinga relationships

The principles set out above significantly apply to witchcraft and accusations in Msinga. The accusations largely occur in the family or vernacular grouping, most notably the neighbourhood, and are typically mobilised in the context of socio-economic tensions or relationships under stress. In a context and time of severe material want – and, much less so, inequality locally – jealousies and resentments are rife and find expression in a number of ways, one of which is most certainly witchcraft accusations.

Witchcraft accusations therefore occur both as independent expressions of tension (and thus initiate overt conflict)[46] or as complements to (and thus as

42 Ibid. at 535.

43 Ibid. at 520.

44 Redding (above) at 536–537 herself briefly points to these difficult political and economic conditions. She observes that 'people acted violently according to their own assessment of their problems and their causes. The principal problems that people tried to resolve through witchcraft accusations and violence often stemmed from broader social issues that they then analysed in very intimate terms. Many rural people needed an explanation for why they were unable to establish a minimum viable homestead.'

45 Standler (above) at 95. What Standler describes at 93 is not as true of Msinga: 'Elders are regarded as especially prone to feeling envious of the success of the relative affluence of younger men and women [who] are expected to support their aged parents, but . . . often renege on these obligations. Older people who complain of this are suspected of resorting to witchcraft in order to re-impose their power over juniors.'

46 In one instance, while drunk, one cousin seemingly spontaneously accused the other of witchcraft – both were young men. The matter was discussed within the family and the family did not want us to record their discussions and did not share its outcome with us. We were therefore unable to fully investigate the roots of this conflict.

transformations of) existing conflict. At least ten of the 35 'cases' we recorded expressly involved witchcraft accusations; there were others that did so implicitly. In the latter instance, we recorded accusations that, for example, followed on a boundary dispute,[47] a witchcraft dispute that had already been managed by a vernacular forum previously and turned out to have originated with the disappearance of one party's cellphone[48] and three accusations that followed on the pain over the inexplicable death of a family member.[49] After we had formally ended our data collection, I learned that one of the people I had interviewed in relation to a case[50] was fatally struck by lightening while visiting the home of a party to another dispute we had previously recorded.[51] Rumour had it that her mysterious death was caused by witchcraft.[52]

The disputes used as examples at the beginning of this chapter illustrate the ways in which witchcraft, as a symbolic threat with significant explanatory power, and accusations of witchcraft, as instruments of violence, hold tremendous purchase.[53] The first conflict was a repeated occurrence within a family, between MaLwimi and her uncles-in-law, toward whom MaLwimi seemed to feel resentment that her husband was too beholden to his uncles. The second was a conflict between two women over a monetary debt, in which the death of MaShonile was explained in terms of MaDlinzelwe's having used witchcraft and, through the spoken word and rumour, the conflict escalated to fold several people (some of whom died) across ward boundaries into it. In this sense, it is reminiscent of MaThembile's case in Chapter 1, though MaThembile was not explicitly accused of witchcraft.

Women – especially elderly women who live alone or sometimes with children – are the most common people toward whom these accusations are pointed in Msinga,[54] but only by a narrow margin according to the evidence we collected. In these cases, it would seem that witchcraft accusations are substantially linked

47 Thunukala/Thango (MaSitolo's brother).

48 MaMakhe/MaMsolwa.

49 In one matter, one woman, Solekile, accused another, Shonelwe, of saying Solekile had killed Shonelwe's child with witchcraft. Solekile said she had been told by her brother-in-law, Sbali, that Shonelwe had said this. Also see Yedwa; MaSitolo/Thunukala.

50 Ngetshe/Moyizela.

51 Mthuki/Ntombi.

52 Kgatla (above) at 48–49 argues that 'the capacity of the powerful to keep the community in a state of stagnation and submissiveness thrives where fear of the supernatural is great.' For instance, Africans mostly believe that witches can use the lightening in thunderstorms to strike people, and '[i]t is primarily the poor and vulnerable that are affected by thunderstorms, and every year several people in the rural areas are killed by lightning.' Instead of insisting that the material conditions and injustices be addressed, poor people can therefore just attribute their misfortune to witchcraft, allowing the wealthy and powerful to take advantage of such (mis)attribution of fault. And, as observed by Redding (above) at 522, 527, witchcraft as justification of ill fortune can lead to material and physical violence, which would be perceived by the perpetrator as equally justified.

53 Ashforth (above); Ellis and Ter Haar (2007); Ellis and Ter Haar (1998).

54 E.g. MaFukuza; MaThembile.

with social marginality. However, they are not exclusively so. Indeed, in some recorded instances of witchcraft accusations – especially against adult or older men – it seemed to be because of their relative means compared to those who accused them. MaLwimi's case pertains as her husband's need to continually borrow from his uncles, who had means, seems to have partly fuelled the repeated accusation.

The potential relevance of relative means was also evident in the case where an adult man, Thunukala, levelled an accusation against MaSitolo, the adult woman who owned the shop from which he was going to buy beer. Though he did so in her absence but in the presence of her child and mother, he accused MaSitolo of killing his wife and said he wanted to know why. He simultaneously accused her brother of being a livestock thief – another crime the accusation of which can put the accused person's life at risk.

Though it ultimately emerged that the dispute had originated when the woman's brother, Thango, had complained at his neighbour's moving his border onto his land, in this case also, I suspect that economic considerations might have factored into the conflict. Thango (who had complained about the border) had a job and MaSitolo had a shop. This made them people of some means as compared to Thunukala who was going to buy beer in the middle of the day because he had nothing else with which to pass his time.

Yet, whoever is the target of the accusation, whether male or female, suspicion and accusation can rapidly escalate to condemnation and violence. In other words, the notion of being innocent until proven guilty is very feeble in the context of witchcraft accusations. People are therefore very wary of them.

While context matters, everyone recognises witchcraft accusations as dangerous.[55] Yet, the response seems to depend on relational proximity. Hence, if the accusation is made among close family, it will probably be handled with more leniency and less urgency, whereas if it occurs between more distant relations, friends or neighbours, it will be treated with greater seriousness and pursued right up to the chief's council, if (deemed) necessary. In the latter instance, one finds an example of a chief's council hearing about the allegation by one woman that another woman who lives in her area is a witch who killed the accuser's child.[56]

In several witchcraft matters, when the parties presented their concerns to the vernacular forum of their election, they stated that 'witchcraft [accusations] kill'. Indeed, such accusations – or the mere belief by parties who have suffered some ill that an identifiable party has caused that ill – can lead to deaths. This was demonstrated at its worst in the matter shared at the opening of this chapter, in which MaShonile inexplicably died after a bar fight with MaDlinzelwe over

55 In Mdala/Mshana, the nephew expressed the belief to his uncle, Mdala, that the mourning clothes of his grandmother had been bewitched by the same uncle. Mshana therefore threatened to kill Mdala, which Mshana expressed to his uncle every time they saw each other.

56 Solekile/Shonelwe.

the fact that one had not repaid the other a loan made. MaDlinzelwe then died under the suspicion that she had used some potion to kill MaShonile when striking her.

Male and female, Msinga residents are therefore highly sensitive to such accusations. When people are publicly accused – even if this happens in the context of a private conversation between third parties and the accused only catches wind of it by rumour or as a matter of hearsay – the one accused of witchcraft will promptly bring it to a public forum for deliberation. It is insufficient to defend oneself by merely approaching the person who issued the accusation and denying the assertion directly to them. It is therefore an almost universally used tactic to employ publicity as a defence against such an accusation – that is, bring the accusation to a vernacular forum to be disproved.

It will suffice if the vernacular forum only concludes that, because the accuser cannot prove that the accused practices witchcraft, it must not be true and thus orders that the accuser cleanse the home of the accused with incense or the blood of a slaughtered animal.[57] Yet, it can take multiple forums to effectively persuade the accuser that they were wrong about the accused or compel them to accept that they cannot prove it and, hence, it must not be true.

In most of the cases we recorded, the accuser denied having made the accusation outright or claimed ignorance of it, perhaps because they were intoxicated at the time. We did not record any instances in which a diviner was approached to 'smell out' an offender. It is therefore interesting that vernacular forums – despite subscribing to supernatural beliefs – would choose to rely on a formalistic and materialistic test (whether there is a witness or material evidence in support of the accusation) to determine guilt regarding a spiritual matter. I would argue that this is yet another manifestation of the longer-term effects of the state's intervention in attempting to manage violent vernacular grouping responses (termed, vigilante justice) to witchcraft accusations.[58]

Until the accuser accepts the penalty imposed by the forum (ideally, also apologising for casting aspersions on the accused's name), it behoves the accused to pursue the matter to the highest forum necessary. This, as I will discuss in greater detail in Chapter 7, is most important for those accused who are socially marginalised. It shows seriousness to the objection as well as the more important appeal to the vernacular grouping for support, which in turn repositions one who may have been at the margins of the grouping closer to the centre.

Foundations of interpersonal and mass social violence

A key point to pay attention to with respect to the nature of witchcraft accusations is the close linkage between violence at the intrafamilial and social

57 MaFukuza/Siqhwaga; MaMakhe/MaMsolwa.

58 See, for example, Harnischfeger (above); Redding (above) on the state's handling of 'witch killings'.

levels – that is, between interpersonal and public violence. This is the subject that I will canvass in the remainder of this chapter and further develop in the following. In my discussion on violence, I draw a distinction between public or social violence and interpersonal violence, particularly within the family. With respect to public violence, I set out the very particular history of attitudes and relationships to violence that developed in Msinga. I start by contextualising pubic violence in this chapter and argue, with other scholars, that this history is critical to understanding the 'ideology of vengeance' (or, at the very least, a worldview that renders violence a legitimate form of dispute management alongside formal attempts at conciliation) that forms the foundation for much of the violence in Msinga. In the next chapter, I make the argument that this historically-formed ideology enables significant intra-familial and other interpersonal violence.

As briefly shown in Chapter 4, for a long time ideal Zulu masculinity was defined by honour shown largely through restraint. The ideal changed radically, gravitating toward the expression of masculinity through martial prowess, under the force of social pressures since the mid-1800s. Benedict Carton and Robert Morell tell us, 'At the turn of the twentieth century, martial activities amongst older boys took on a greater significance, as male circumcision was phased out by chiefs like Shaka who enrolled cadets and their commanders, *izingqwele* (respected young men with stick fighting expertise) in the *amabutho* system.'[59] The *amabutho* system refers to the structure formed by men being conscripted into generational divisions for the purpose of fighting on behalf of their *isizwe* (nation or 'tribe'). This is one way in which stick fighting became highly militarised and thus virtually inextricable from violent conflict. There is yet another way that is particular to Msinga.

In Johnny Clegg's paper on stick fighting in the Msinga area in 1882–1944,[60] he describes how, historically, in Zulu culture stick fighting was used as a form of play and performance (with strict etiquette) at weddings and other celebrations.[61] This etiquette was consistent with values of rhetoric, honour, defence,

59 Carton, Benedict and Robert Morell (2012) 'Zulu Masculinities, Warrior Culture and Stick Fighting: Reassessing Male Violence and Virtue in South Africa' *Journal of Southern African Studies*, 38(1) at 45.

60 Clegg, Johnny (1981) 'Ukubuyisa Isidumbu – "Bringing Back the Body": An Examination into the Ideology of Vengeance in the Msinga and Mpofana Rural Locations, 1882–1944' in Philip Bonner (ed.) *Working Papers in Southern African Studies, Vol. 2*, Johannesburg: African Studies Institute, University of the Witwatersrandat 164.

61 Meintjes, Louise (2017) *Dust of the Zulu: Ngoma Aesthetics after Apartheid.* Durham, NC, Duke University Press draws connections between 'ngoma' music and dancing, on one hand, and stick fighting culture, on the other. Specifically, at 97, Meintjes comments on the connection of both with violence: 'Multiple reminders point to the fact that ngoma is not real violence, but in part an artful representation of the possibility for violence, tied to other artful representations of that possibility.' She later continues at 128: 'While multiple factors remind one that ngoma is not real violence, it is by force of circumstance implicated in processes of violence. National politics, waged violently during South Africa's transitional

deference and self-control that were strongly identified with ideal masculinity.[62] Carton and Morell observe that 'valorous stick fighters were expected first to protect themselves and pull back if an opponent lay defenceless, for instance, if a contestant could not compete and so reverted to his primary identity as a non-combatant whose labour and fealty were essential to family and community'.[63]

The idea of men 'playing' provided the key frame for stick fighting, and in parts of Zulu society, this idea persists even today. As Clegg states:

> Although it is admitted that serious injuries can be inflicted with sticks and that in some instances people are killed this does not alter the fact that men were "playing". The death is an unfortunate event but that does not invalidate the "play" nature of stick fighting.[64]

This key framing idea supports the fighting that happens within *isizwe*, between its wards[65] (what Clegg calls inter-district fighting). This, *umgamela*, was seen as necessary to allow the warrior men of that nation to determine, grow and come to trust each other's martial abilities. In the absence of a nation's wards having opposed one another, the nation was said to be unable to be(come) powerful.[66] In Clegg's words, 'So long as the expression of the district opposition assumes a "play mode", it is quite acceptable'.[67] Despite the structural justification given for this fighting internally, in reality a further justification

years through noisy mobile bodies, and ngoma performance, expressing in motion and sound the experiences and perspectives of its practitioners, were at once intricately and loosely connected.' Meintjes also discusses counter-narratives, embodied in music, which declare gun violence as futile 'cannibalism' and call Zulu men back to the origins of stick fighting.

62 Carton and Morell (above) at 32.

63 Ibid. at 33.

64 Clegg (above) at 18. Also see Carton and Morell (above) at 42: 'The sport was potentially hazardous'.

65 According to Creina Alcock, formally speaking, wards (or the term) only came into existence as such after a 1949 commission recommended them so as to 'confer criminal jurisdiction on the chiefs . . . [and make it so that] it will no longer be possible for headmen (indunas) to evade their responsibilities by pleading that the area under their control is not occupied by members of their tribe'. See Alcock in Cousins, Ben, Rauri Alcock, Ngididi Dladla, Donna Hornby, Mphethethi Masondo, Gugu Mbatha, Makhosi Mweli and Creina Alcock (2011) '*Imithetho yomhlaba yaseMsinga:* The Living Law of Land in Msinga District, KwaZulu-Natal'. PLAAS Research Report 43, Cape Town, The University of the Western Cape at 24.

66 Clegg (above) at 18.

67 Ibid. Carton and Morell (above) at 41–42: 'Stick fighting tested and preserved the body by reinforcing norms of *inkuliso*. Moreover, integral rules of the sport underscored the vitality of kinship, not the destruction of it. When stick fighters competed, they were "playing with others", *ukudlalisa izinduku*, on a sanctioned pitch that elevated champions and shamed losers.' Ngoma, then, is a form of such "play" – see Meintjes (above) at 105–107, 135–140.

existed for it: namely, that it allowed tensions to be aired within strict normative constraints.

However, Clegg argues that this kind of 'play' stick fighting evolved over time in Msinga. He attributes its evolution to historical factors particular to the locality – especially, the substantial relocation of people to the reservations under the colonial policies of that time and the inter-tribal fighting over land that took place in the area as a result of consequent land shortages.[68] Wards of Msinga wanted to preserve their autonomy and independence, and protect their grazing land from the influx of outsiders, and their desire came with the inherent threat of violent confrontations.[69] The members of the wards emphasised their unitary identities as districts. By doing this, they 'generated a powerful idea of territorial affiliation which played down and over-rode kinship consideration in the feud.'[70] They also appointed 'war captains' (*abaphathi bezinsizwa* – literally, the leaders/managers of the young men) as military coordinators to ensure protection of the land held by their districts.

Others do not accept Clegg's explanation as conclusive. As Creina Alcock says, 'Poor environmental conditions may be a necessary, but not a sufficient condition for the incidence of feuds'.[71] Such scholars argue that comparative research – which is sorely missing – would be needed to confirm the thesis.[72] Whatever the reasons for this normative evolution, Clegg observes that, in Msinga, stick fighting was called '*udede*' (which refers to a 'no holds barred clash' between wards) and acquired an importance that, though still structurally justified, rendered the stick fighting itself in no way playful in its traditional sense.[73] He argues that while stick fighting was a game, it could not retain its playful quality in a context in which genuine conflict existed at scale and required some sort of expression. Moreover, the ramifications of losing or winning in clashes between wards in the circumstances were just too great – with parties seeking to defend their territory, and hence their livelihoods, from one another – for any fighting to be just a game for participants.[74]

Clegg summarises, 'While a structural need to express district opposition was present, the means to do so (play fight) was not.'[75] To qualify Clegg's initial articulation: the means for expressing opposition was still available. After all, stick fighting still remains in Msinga and continues to be described (and, really,

68 Clegg (above) at 18.
69 Ibid. at 18–19.
70 Ibid. at 22. Cf. Carton and Morell (above) at 41–42 who describe the importance of fidelity to family for preserving the values of male honour and restraint, even in the context of fighting.
71 Alcock in Cousins et al. (above) at 24, quotes Prof. W. J. Argyle's April 1987 conference paper, 'Faction Fights and Problems of Explanation in Social Anthropology' (delivered at conference on 'Faction Fights in Modern Times').
72 Ibid.
73 Clegg (above) at 18–19.
74 Ibid.
75 Ibid. at 19.

in some cases, disguised) using the framing idea of it being a constrained form of 'play'. What no longer accompanied stick fighting was its management by the strict normative constraints that were previously perceived to be inherent to this particular form of expressing conflict.[76]

This qualification is evident in Clegg's expansion on his summative sentence:

> No matter how much a fight was called playing, the 'play' aspect of it had been overlaid by a whole new set of connotations. Losing a 'play' stick fight with another district immediately reflected on your ability to defend and protect your district's estate. This added a very serious element to the 'play' fight. This was compounded by the fact that when a man was killed in such a clash, the dead man's district had to avenge his death, for to neglect to do so would give the killer's district the impression that the dead man's district was incapable of standing together as a corporate group to protect its estate. If vengeance is not exacted it will be said that the people of such and such district 'have not built their homesteads firmly', and reflects on the district's firmness (*ukuqina kwesigodi*)[77]

Thus, stick fighting became largely unconstrained, and there was no readily or culturally available way to control it. In fact, the manner in which it manifested leant itself to rapid escalation of group violence.

The level of conflict that Clegg describes could not be limited to fighting between wards alone. Subwards started to compete between themselves for land held by the 'tribe' at large for grazing and farming. In some instances, this inter-subward conflict (that is, intra-ward conflict) was limited by the need to hold together at the ward level in order to protect the ward's land. But other wards buckled under the weight of inter-subward conflict and divided.[78] These were bloody conflicts, in which many died ('neighbour killing neighbour')[79] and, even once peace was reached, the tensions continued to bubble – mostly beneath the surface but sometimes even overtly.[80]

Of these kinds of internal divisions, Clegg concludes, 'The phenomenon of "breaking inside" of districts is considered to be a terrible aberration (*umkhokha*) by the Msinga people but once it starts there is no mechanism which can bring the hostilities to an end.'[81] He goes on to illustrate the spread of fighting between wards, in some cases fuelled by purported solutions given by

76 Again, see Carton and Morell (above) at 32.
77 Clegg (above) at 19.
78 Ibid.
79 Ibid.
80 Ibid.
81 Ibid. Alcock disagrees that there is no mechanism to end social hostilities.

government officials (Native Commissioners) to existing boundary disputes.[82] Alcock supports this observation in her introduction to Ben Cousins' study of living customary land laws in Msinga today.[83]

Cousins provides a specific example of bloody inter-ward conflict:

> Conflicts between Mathintha and Nqumantaba have been on-going for many decades. In 1981 their men went to war over guns, and nine died. In 1987 more such violence led to the South African Defence Force moving into Msinga, setting up roadblocks at Mathintha and Nqumantaba. A war between the two *amahlati* [subwards] in 1989 saw twenty seven men dying.[84]

This is only one example. For a sense of scale, one need only consider that such occurrences were not infrequent in Msinga's past, and remember the large size of Msinga's 'tribes'. According to Alcock, in 1933 the Mthembu taxpayers numbered 8,275; and Mchunu taxpayers, 9,054.[85] This made them the largest 'tribes' in Natal at the time.[86] They remain very large, at populations between 50,000 and 80,000.

The discourse surrounding feuding, as Clegg describes it, is important. The need for revenge is described as a blood 'debt' (*isikwelete*), and the 'act of feuding' is called *ukukhokhisa* (literally, 'to enforce payment', to make one pay) or *ukubuyisa isidumbu* ('to bring back the body', because a body from the killer's area is taken in payment of the dead person in your own).[87] If the perpetrator cannot be found because he has gone into hiding, a substitute from his area is killed instead.[88] The proverb used to explain this vengeance is that 'a thorn is removed by means of another thorn'.[89]

What happens when such a narrative meets with the wide availability of guns? Of this, Alcock writes, 'If landscape is a key to understanding the conflicts, so is the character of the 'tribes': big refugee 'tribes', jittery about attack and ready to invest in guns. As early as 1851, the magistrate of the Mzinyathi Location, George Ringler Thompson, was asking "How am I to act with regard to Natives possessed of guns?"'[90] In January 1851, Theophilus Shepstone said that Africans who seemed 'determined to purchase firearms' had been sold these 'in hundreds by unprincipled Europeans'.[91] Alcock also reports that, in 1868, men who had

82 Ibid.
83 Alcock in Cousins et al. (above) at 20–24.
84 Ibid. at 42 fn 81.
85 Ibid. at 24.
86 Ibid.
87 Clegg (above) at 20.
88 Ibid. at 20–21.
89 Ibid. at 20.
90 Alcock in Cousins et al. (above) at 24.
91 Ibid.

walked over 600 kilometres to work as diamond miners in Kimberley earned guns as part of their wages: 'The guns were accumulated against a background of rumours that the Zulus had thousands of guns in their possession.'[92] She further reports that by 1932, '[g]uns were replacing spears in fights, and bullet wounds were becoming common.'[93]

Alcock goes on to note that '[i]n 1957 Msinga's Active Native Commissioner, J.H. Reibeling, reported that "The increasing use of firearms is causing concern. Faction fighting is developing into gun battles. This is everywhere in the District". Msinga had become the centre of the gun trade in South Africa'.[94] Despite the presence of a fulltime Firearm Squad for 45 years since then, '[t]he Squad had little impact on the incidence of fights.'[95] In 1973, things had gotten so bad that the KwaZulu Government saw fit to pass special legislation to attempt to curtail the fighting in the district. This legislation[96] allowed the 90-day detention of persons suspected of any involvement in a crime of violence.[97] It was in the wake of this determination by the government that one of the Msinga chiefs was banished.[98]

With respect to the surrounding 'jitteriness about attack' mentioned by Alcock, Bhekuyise Mthembu describes how there were several 'tribal' conflicts taking place between 1874 and 1906 all over the Msinga area.[99] He mentions wars between aMabaso and abaThembu, partly attributing the faction fighting between the two 'tribes' to the fact that abaThembu surrounded aMabaso, and the latter therefore felt vulnerable and threatened. He also portrays tensions between the Sithole 'tribe' and aMaqamu, as well as between aMaqamu and amaBomvu.[100] He concludes by mentioning 'devastating wars between abaThembu and amaChunu in 1922 and 1944.'[101] Alcock observes that, although 'tribal' conflicts were originally a tremendous obstacle and threat, the latter conflicts between abaThembu and amaChunu were moderated by intermarriage between the two nations, as this allowed for informal communication and conflict management.[102]

92 Ibid. at 25.
93 Ibid.
94 Ibid.
95 Ibid.
96 Proclamation 103 of 1973.
97 Alcock in Cousins et al. (above) at 25.
98 See Ibid; Saleem Badat (2013) *The Forgotten People: Political Banishment Under Apartheid*, Leiden, Brill.
99 Mthembu, Bhekuyise Isaac (October 1994) *Faction Fighting in Msinga District from 1874 to 1906* – A Dissertation submitted to the Faculty of Arts in the fulfillment of the requirements for the degree of Master of Arts in the Department of History at the University of Zululand Kwa-Dlangezwa. (Supervisor: Prof. S. J. Maphalala) at vi–vii.
100 Ibid.
101 Ibid.
102 Alcock in Cousins (above) at 27.

Clegg recounts how direct confrontation between the wards' men had originally been the way these group conflicts occurred. He then goes on to explain how the need for many men to be in the cities for work, and the difficulty these men had in returning home for days at a time in order to participate in these 'wars', had necessitated a different way of fighting. Thus, because those who had survived clashes did not want to lose their jobs due to abrupt absences from work, 'assassination squads' were created instead.[103] These squads fulfilled the task of revenge killings. Of the 'assassination squads', Clegg writes:

> These squads are also powerful forces within their own district by virtue of the fact that they are very well armed and hold the lives of the district's members in their hands as they try to ensure that the other district's "assassination squad" is not effective. Although the scale of the fighting has been reduced by the squads they kill more people than would have been killed in a big confrontation because they are highly mobile, small and ruthless.[104]

With guns in hand, these 'assassination squads' are, indeed, very well armed and highly effective at their task.

From this discussion, one might assume that 'assassination squads' displaced ordinary faction fighting, especially in the form of stick fighting. More reason for suspecting this is given by the accounts of older men who bemoan this way of fighting since they say that, before the invention of the squads, the 'battle would become a major aspect of the district's history because it was a *social* act and the deaths took on an air of legitimacy and appropriateness'. As Clegg puts it, '[E]ach and every fighter . . . was able to defend himself and the clash would therefore reveal the true mettle of each district's men. It was more "fair" and acceptable than an anonymous assassins [*sic*] bullet in the night. After the big regimental confrontation it was said that those involved became "satisfied".'[105]

While the older men's recollection of the past was somewhat idealised, it cannot be said to have been ideal in reality. In fact, Clegg reminds us that the 'satisfaction' described by the older men as deriving from face-to-face combat was only temporary – even in the old days of feuding. He reports, 'The feud would die down until the generation of youngsters began to *bodla* (bellow, come of age). They would tell the other district's men that: "You beat our fathers, but we were not there". And the scene would be set for another big regimental confrontation.'[106] This phenomenon may partly explain the cyclical nature of violent group conflict in Msinga.

103 Clegg (above) at 21.
104 Ibid. at 19.
105 Ibid.
106 Ibid.

In reality, of course, the existence of 'assassination squads' has not led to the displacement of faction fighting in its traditional form. In Mthembu's account,[107] the communal faction fighting – and the disruption that is a consequence of it – persists alongside 'assassination squads'. He therefore writes of the late 1980s and early 1990s:

> The main significance of faction fighting is that it affects all aspects of life of the people involved. It is still very difficult to develop these victims economically and even educationally . . . . When a faction fight breaks out, schools are usually disturbed because boys are bound to join their ward male members. They remain in hiding, preparing for attack or counter-attack, until fighting is over. Should fighting intensify, schools stop functioning altogether. Many boys leave school in such circumstances.[108]

Nevertheless, the existence of 'assassination squads' may indeed have taken something away from the traditional way of feuding in Msinga, but what has been taken away is not necessarily what the older men described as 'satisfaction'.

Perhaps what the invention of 'assassination squads' has detracted from is twofold: first, a degree of containment of conflict to a narrow time and locale, where conflict takes place publicly and by agreement in advance, and, second, a portion of the shared motivation for wars to come to an end (even if only temporarily, for a single generation). The older men may therefore be correct that the long-term perpetuation of hostilities may be exacerbated by the existence of the 'assassination squads', because the latter are paid to fight and are thus incentivised to ensure that the war does not end. This motivation persists regardless of whether perpetuation of hostilities takes place through the prevention of 'satisfaction' of one generation or through a new generation of young men 'bellowing'. I would therefore say that the older men interviewed by Clegg correctly recognised that 'it is not in [the assassins'] interest to allow hostilities to cease'.[109]

More than that, I think it is true that with 'assassination squads' conflict can be chronic and can occur at any time and place (privately, and without warning). As a consequence, this form of fighting has all but eliminated temporal and geographical spaces where one can be truly safe in Msinga. It has also made available a group of people who can be hired to kill, not only in the context of group conflict, for which they were originally designed, but in other more interpersonal conflicts as well.

This situation has important implications for modes of dispute management used locally, in both the vernacular forums and the other informal forums that

107 Published in 1994 whereas Clegg's was published in 1981.
108 Mthembu (above).
109 Clegg (above) at 19.

exist around them. In the vernacular forums, violent tendencies might be expressed in the course of mediation or arbitration attempts, hence sabotaging the process. Furthermore, as I have shown in Chapter 4, the vernacular forums exercise their role under the spectre (and thus constant threat) of groups and individuals simply defying the law by resorting to vigilante action.

Clegg concludes his article by pointing out that 'the general land squeeze both in and outside the reserve generated inter-tribal wars which developed into a tradition of self-help.'[110] This point is an important one in light of the tradition of 'self-help' that I argue in Chapter 7 is prevalent in Msinga. He adds,

> The struggle over land gave rise to strategies like hut burning where each tribe/district/[subward] as the case may be tried to force the boundary back into its opponent's territory. . . . The colonial government gave the reserve an external boundary but left the people in the reserve to sort out their own internal boundaries, paving the way for the emergence of an "ideology of vengeance."[111]

This notion of an 'ideology of vengeance' puts words to something that, as I will show in this and the remaining chapters, stands out in the data as being highly present in Msinga: the ease with which a seemingly minor conflict can escalate to multiple killings.[112] However, I would rather refer to the basis of this ease as the plausibility of violence as a tool for managing conflict.[113]

Again, as Alcock emphasises, the resource-focused explanation of the development of anything like an 'ideology of vengeance' in Msinga is inconclusive. But, regardless of the state's periodic and mostly unhelpful interventions in the issues of boundary establishment and dispute management, it is not contested that the internal community and its subsets were largely left to resolve their own tensions.[114] This situation was only exacerbated by the reality of large proportions of subjects of the 'tribes' of Msinga actually residing on white-owned farms.[115] In Alcock's words,

> [t]he farms made life difficult for the chiefs. They had limited jurisdiction – but were expected to keep control. They couldn't allocate fields, stop

110 Ibid.
111 Ibid.
112 The conflict of MaShonile/MaDlinzelwe refers.
113 In sociology (especially that of religion), a 'plausibility structure' is the socio-cultural context that forms and informs one's system of meaning, within which the meaning one makes of life events is considered plausible, and therefore makes sense. (See Berger, Peter (1967) *The Sacred Canopy: Elements of a Sociological Theory of Religion*. New York, Anchor Books at 45, 192.) My argument here is that, within the plausibility structure that prevails in Msinga, violence makes sense – or so parties in conflict perceive it – to varying degrees.
114 Alcock in Cousins et al. (above) at 24.
115 Ibid.

> evictions, or summon a farm worker to a tribal court. They were instructed to appoint tribal headmen, the *izinduna*, who had all the duties of tribal police. In an "excellent system . . . of legal obligation imposed on the native tribal officers" they had to report all crimes, offences, accidents, sudden deaths or looming trouble – while their areas of authority remained undefined.[116]

This kind of ambiguity and ambivalence pertaining to the role of traditional institutions in dispute management – relative to state institutions and particularly to land that notionally forms part of the 'tribe' but may fall outside its formal boundaries – continues to be a significant problem in Msinga.

I share Clegg's article – modified by Alcock's historical introduction – in so much detail because what he writes about Msinga's history of violence is extremely applicable today. As the reader will learn, the show of honour through fighting[117] and revenge killings retain some pertinence in Msinga today, along with the heightened seriousness of consequences that Clegg begins to unpack in his writing on land disputes at the turn of the century. Moreover, the importance of land and related resources – and their ability to incite widespread violence – as well as the clashes that take place between subwards or wards persists in Msinga's conflict landscape today. This is true in the context of both public and private disputes.

Also still highly relevant to conflict in Msinga today are the widespread impact of so many guns; the cyclical and generational nature of conflict; the existence of paid (and payable) killers, especially in bad economic times and circumstances;[118] and the use of hut burning as a technique for 'resolving' disputes. The weakening of kinship and broader social ties is similarly relevant in the contemporary context. Yet, it is worth acknowledging, as Alcock suggests, that there are ways in which intergroup conflict is sometimes settled.[119] Moreover, when I reported

116 Ibid.

117 See Carton and Morell (above) at 32.

118 Meintjes (above) at 107–108.

119 Alcock provided the example of the former chief headman of Nakudala who had gone into hiding when an attack took place with the intention of killing him in August 1987. The men of two wards had a 'beerdrink' six months later to celebrate the end of a nine month war between them at which some young men from the other ward placed ten beers before the chief headman and said it was to apologise for that night when they had tried to kill him. They had not known that he was not there; instead, they would have killed the woman who owns the home. Alcock observes that it is believed to be bad luck to kill a woman and if there was revenge after each killing, then there would be several revenge killings, and thus feuds, in Msinga. She therefore argues that it is the mechanisms for preventing blood feuds that we ought to be examining. I agree that these mechanisms need to be investigated. However, a longitudinal study beyond the scope of this one would be needed to effectively answer the question. (Cf. the discussion on the Okunye war in Chapter 4 and the matter relating to MaDlinzelwe/MaShonile, as well as the management of tensions between the Wesizwe and Wabantu factions in the Yisithupha land administration dispute. These examples provide some insight into how local forums try to manage conflicts of such scale.)

back on the findings of this study to the headmen in both the Nakudala and Nezikhathi chiefs' councils, separately, they wanted to assure me that, though there are certainly problems still, things are better than they were. The headmen were particularly keen that I not make Msinga sound as 'barbaric' as it has been portrayed previously. Indeed, my understanding is that the scale of intergroup conflict in Msinga has decreased since the political conflicts of the early 1990s.

Nevertheless, the manner in which the government really provides only outer boundaries and does not effectively help sort out the internal problems that those exterior limits and surrounding socio-economic conditions very often create is evident in the disputing that occurs in Msinga. The latter leads me to argue, in Chapter 7, that the people in Msinga are partly led to a culture of 'self-help' by the sense – substantially informed by reality[120] – of being left to resolve their problems all on their own.

Concluding remarks

I have made the case that, because of the paradoxical essentiality of social trust that results from the combination of the very close proximity in which people in Msinga live in their families and neighbourhoods as well as the socio-economic volatility of their condition, disputes usually take place between people who know each other intimately. In many cases, the disputes are therefore grounded in a meaningful conflict history. In fact, the acts that give rise to disputes take place in spaces of relating – that is, spaces in which, according to cultural beliefs and values, relationships ought to be strengthened. These are also mostly spaces where in an unbroken context people should be secure from violence. These spaces primarily include people's homes, shared celebrations, drinking places, schools, and thoroughfares. More discussion on this tension surrounding spaces that should be safe is provided in the next chapter.

The expectation is that disputants will be assisted and supported by their families in disputes. When the disputes occur within families, real rifts can appear, parties being forced to take sides and publicly support or disagree with members of their kin: a son testifying against his mother on his alleged child's paternity[121] or a husband testifying against his wife on her accusing his family of witchcraft,[122] as seen above. This testimony can, however, just be the public expression of conflicts the parties have been aware for a long time.

Masculinities – and femininities – are evidently in flux in Msinga, especially, given the shifts that are occurring with respect to men's and women's economic means

120 Note, for example, how woefully under-resourced Msinga's police station is: it has 105,67 police per population of 100,000, compared with 1948,18 in the capital city of Pietermaritzburg and 1388,37 in the economic hub of Durban Central. Ranking at 160 among the 185 stations in KwaZulu-Natal, Msinga is one of the least resourced stations in the province. (This data is courtesty of criminal justice statistics expert, Jean Redpath.)

121 Kanankinga/Landula.

122 MaLwimi.

and their consequent ability to live up to cultural ideals and roles. As a consequence, women's roles in providing representation and support for family members in disputes are growing. Yet, men still dominate in the sphere of dispute management. In both the case of men's and women's roles, there is a substantial divide between young people and the older generation. This is even more pronounced in the context of the kinds of disputes in which people of particular identities find themselves embroiled and how their conflicts are resolved – all of which forms the subject of the following chapter.

One challenge to the expansion of women's participation in disputing – undermining men's and women's confidence in women's participation – is prevailing and seemingly entrenched attitudes about women's predispositions. Women continue to be perceived as not fit for such roles, and (as several focus group participants observed) household responsibilities also keep them from having the time for socially participating in these ways. Yet, with small changes in young women's attitudes and women's increased participation in 'mediatory meetings', there seems to be hope for transformation in this regard.

Witchcraft accusations remain a significant threat to the lives of people in Msinga and, more extensively, to social stability. Their strong link to violence and more common use against people fitting certain profiles make them additionally worrisome. However, the fact that the evidence on witchcraft accusations enables us to predict to some degree the kinds of people they might be used against may help us to prevent their systematic use against certain groups of people and the severe harm caused by such accusations in a context in which violence as a form of conflict management is a highly plausible resort. Vernacular forum authorities possessing awareness of the vulnerabilities of people in a certain demographic may be able to take special precautions in managing these delicate types of disputes. With this goal in mind, in the following chapter, I develop a kind of typology for further understanding the profiles of people who are vulnerable to different kinds of offences (particularly violence), as well as those who are particularly prone to commit them, and why.

6 Conflicting identities

Fears, vulnerabilities and strengths accompanying gender and age

When staying married is your (only) means of keeping marital property

MaNovalo, an older adult woman in middle age, was the victim of severe and repeated domestic violence by her husband, Cijimpi, who wielded a gun and tormented her whenever he was drunk, which was often. The matter had come before the headman's council for management only because Cijimpi had attempted to shoot a neighbour, accusing him of harbouring his wife – who had fled to the neighbour's house because her husband was yet again threatening to shoot her. When interviewed, the tormented wife told us why she had not left her husband.

MaNovalo said that she was aware that her husband was having an affair and that he was terrorising her in order to get her out of the house. In MaNovalo's estimation, her husband would always threaten her with his firearm when he returned from being with his other woman. MaNovalo was sure he wanted to get her out of the house so that the other woman would come and take her place. It emerged that, no matter the cost (namely, her own well-being and the mental disturbance suffered by her daughter), MaNovalo was not prepared to leave the home, because she said she had built it. In tears, she said that she was prepared to die if she had to do so in order to hold on to her home.

In its attempt to mediate the matter, the neighbourhood council was unable to effectively manage the dispute. Cijimpi had admitted to the conflicts between his wife and him over his mistress. The council told him he should have gathered the family council; when asked, he could not provide a reason for failing to do this. The council members then suggested that Cijimpi should rather move MaNovalo back to her birth home, instead of shooting at her. They petitioned him to stop harassing his wife and instructed her to be respectful and patient toward him and his affair.

In a different dispute, MaZimele, another older adult woman – nominated by the Nezikhathi traditional leadership to serve on its legislative-administrative council – was chased away from her marital home by her husband because she refused to conceal a firearm at his request. MaZimele took the matter to the chief as *isikhalo* (a cry or plea). There, her husband said he could not be with a wife (one of three) who 'refused to listen to him'.

Unable to reconcile the parties, the old chief found in MaZimele's favour, and she moved back from her brothers' home to her marital home. She moved there because, she said, she did not want to leave her children. Her husband, Gwajisa, and his older wife, MaMdala, then moved out of the home; the third wife already lived in town. Remaining alone at the home, MaZimele made improvements to it.

Gwajisa then brought a charge against MaZimele for damaging existing property. In order to make improvements, she said, she had removed the rubble of houses belonging to the older wife, which MaMdala had destroyed before moving. Gwajisa accused her of doing this damage to 'his land' without his approval. MaZimele maintained that she would have moved to other land if her husband had given her some or helped her to obtain it by asking for land on her behalf. (At the time, women were still unable to obtain land independently of men.)[1]

MaZimele reported that it was obvious that her husband wanted to kill her. Unfortunately, the chief seemed unable to provide her with help beyond his order, as he had already found in her favour in this matter. He recommended to her that she report the matter to the police. Meanwhile, Gwajisa refused to return to the chief's forum, despite being summoned to further dialogue there. He obviously knew that he would not win there. Instead, he had initiated civil proceedings against his wife through a lawyer. She said she did not have the means to defend herself against such a lawsuit.

The social politics of gender and age

I have previously introduced the importance of identity characteristics for understanding the extent and roles particular individuals play in disputes and their management. This chapter builds on this introduction by discussing gender and age as key elements in the socio-legal space of disputing and its management. The chapter demonstrates that, to a meaningful extent, a typology can be crafted of the kinds of grievances and disputes that arise in Msinga relative to one's age and gender, as well as the influence that these personal attributes will most likely have on the dispute management process. These personal traits frame the kinds of fears and vulnerabilities that accompany living in Msinga for people in certain identity groups and the vulnerabilities and strengths that influence the prospects of certain dispute management outcomes. Whether because they affect the likelihood that an offence will be a group or repeated offence or because they might partly predict what aggravating or mitigating circumstances may arise in the matter, these personal characteristics are important to observe.

Much scholarship has been produced on masculinities and the themes of violence, gender and sexuality in Zulu culture.[2] This wide-ranging scholarship

1 MaZimele also wanted to stay under her husband's socio-legal covering for the sake of staying with her children.

2 See Campbell, Catherine (1992) 'Learning to Kill? Masculinity, the Family and Violence in Natal' *Journal of Southern African Studies* (Special Issue Political Violence in Southern

has focused on Zulu masculinity in the family and in society at large, and on the crisis of masculinity that has faced men in the last century. The literature emphasises the generational differences between older (especially married) men and younger (unmarried) men that I introduced in Chapter 4. The scholarship connects these socio-cultural shifts to patterns of violence, as I began to do in Chapter 5.

This literature puts little emphasis on femininity, except as it relates to men's performance of their masculinity or their crisis over it. Yet some important observations can still be drawn from the literature as it relates to the social pressures and risks with which young women are faced. Again, a strong emphasis is placed in this literature – and, likewise, in my findings – on overwhelming overall socio-economic insecurity that faces nearly all people in Msinga. In Chapter 7, I will link this with a discussion of the geographical, physical and socio-political isolation that also contributes to a kind of helplessness in people's attempts at addressing their socio-economic and legal problems in Msinga.

Men and women, sex and violence

The changes in stereotypical male and female roles – specifically, how gendered identity is to be performed in relation to sex and violence – gives us important perspective on the highly gendered nature of common disputes in Msinga.

Evolution of masculinity: on sexuality

Against the historical backdrop of the pattern of dejection undergone by Zulu men outlined in Chapters 1 and 4, Mark Hunter describes this pattern's perpetuation in the contemporary situation (post 2000). In particular, he observes what the current state of unemployment and low incomes has done to exacerbate the paradox that faces Zulu men. In the wake of relentless social commitment to the traditional ideal of *umnumzan*' (a gentleman, sir/mister – a label attributed to the master of his own homestead), men's regular and high levels of

---

Africa), 18(3): 614–628; Carton, Benedict and Robert Morell (2012) 'Zulu Masculinities, Warrior Culture and Stick Fighting: Reassessing Male Violence and Virtue in South Africa' *Journal of Southern African Studies*, 38(1) at 41–42, 45; Hunter, Mark (July–August 2005) 'Cultural Politics and Masculinities: Multiple-Partners in Historical Perspective in KwaZulu-Natal' *Culture, Health and Sexuality*, 7(4): 389–403 at 397; Uchendu, Egodi (2008) 'Are African Males Men? Sketching African Masculinities' in Egodi Uchedu (ed.) *Masculinities in Contemporary Africa*. Dakar, Codesria at 8. Also see mention made of this subject by Meintjes, Louise (2017) *Dust of the Zulu: Ngoma Aesthetics after Apartheid*. Durham, NC, Duke University Press at 23–24; Beinart, William (September 1992) 'Introduction: Political and Collective Violence in Southern African Historiography' *Journal of Southern African Studies*, 18(3): 455–486 at 474. For pre-colonial perspective on Zulu gender relations, see Guy, Jeff (1990) 'Gender Oppression in Southern Africa's Precapitalist Societies' in Cheryl Walker (ed.) *Women and Gender in Southern Africa to 1945*. Cape Town, David Philip, 33–47.

unemployment and low wages have been incredibly demoralising.[3] Men's inability to arrive at the prized 'status through work, marriage and fulfilling a "provider" role is the context in which expressions of manliness that celebrate numerous sexual conquests must be understood.'[4]

Scholars have found that, prior to the impact of colonialism and apartheid policies, when it came to sexuality in particular, Zulu society considered it inappropriate for a man to engage in sexual behaviour to the extent of deflowering a girl to whom he was not formally betrothed or married.[5] In keeping with the value of self-control and morality previously examined,[6] and the need to control and limit procreation to the expansion of a (married) household and its production,[7] a man was to restrain himself from such behaviour. Failure in this regard attracted public shame and financial loss for him and his family, as his father's cattle might be confiscated and he might be disinherited, banished, or even killed.[8] This norm has transformed significantly.

Prompted by the limited powers given to them by the colonial government for this purpose, African men (and older women) tightened control over women and their sexuality such that having multiple quasi-sexual partners became much more frowned upon for women than it had been previously.[9] At the same time, male sexuality has become less constrained so that sexual restraint is no longer widely practiced or even expected of young men and the man's family is only called upon to pay damages if the woman with whom he had premarital or extramarital relations bears a child after it.

Hunter notes that, in parts of Africa, men have sought to bolster their self-esteem by having relationships with multiple partners and perpetrating violence against women.[10] Reshma Sathiparsad affirms the idealisation of this kind of masculinity in her study in which she reports that young Zulu men in the rural area that she studied associated masculine identity with insatiable sexual appetite and thus the need for several female partners.[11] She states, 'For many of the young men in the focus group having many girlfriends meant that "*I'm lucky, this man has wisdom*" and "*he is a Casanova because some males cannot even get*

3 Hunter (above) at 397.
4 Ibid. See also Meintjes (above) at 39–41.
5 Hunter (above) at 392.
6 See Carton and Morell (above) at 32.
7 Hunter (above) at 392; Guy (above).
8 Uchendu (above) at 8.
9 Hunter (above) at 394: 'A persistent theme in writings on colonial Africa is how African men and the colonial state looked towards customary law to solidify patriarchal traditions. The control of women, and women's sexuality, was especially paramount given the expansion of opportunities for women in towns.'
10 Ibid. at 397.
11 Sathiparsad, Reshma (2007) 'Masculinities in the Era of HIV/AIDS: The Perspective of Rural Zulu Youth' in T. Shefer (ed.) *From Boys to Men: Social Construction of Masculinity in Contemporary Society*. Lansdowne, University of Cape Town Press 181–194 at 187.

one girlfriend."'[12] The Zulu term for such a man – a 'Casanova' or 'lady killer' – is '*isoka*'.

As Hunter observes, while men who have multiple partners are celebrated, women who are perceived to do the same meet with social disapproval and are sometimes even completely shunned.[13] Simultaneously, men are allowed, and even encouraged, to have multiple girlfriends, but girls are forcefully kept from the same – whether by social coercion (such as shaming) or, as I discuss below, by interpersonal violence.[14] As Nicholas Smith shows, rather than cultivating empathy, 'rights' can be viewed as compounding the problem of immorality by being too permissive.[15] Men (and their female allies) can therefore see themselves as tasked with disciplining the women corrupted by rights.

What drives the socially coercive perception of any particular woman as being promiscuous is a matter of interest, especially in how it relates to the crisis men face around their own masculinity.

> Women seeking education and other opportunities have long been scorned *izifebe* (loose women) and today the disciplining of rebellious women as loose still serves to bolster male power . . . The insult of *isifebe* [in its worst usage, meaning 'bitch' or 'whore'] hovers over women who challenge gendered roles in the home and elsewhere.[16]

The combination of the new masculine ideal as one of sexual prowess and the feminine ideal as one of subjection to male authority in the home and society serves to reinforce men's social power, undermine women who challenge it, and shore up men's threatened confidence. As Hunter notes, 'The binary categories [of *isoka/isifebe*] also, of course, help to reiterate the normativity of heterosexual masculinities.'[17]

Naturally, the preservation of the *status quo* cannot be wholly attributed to men. Both men and women contribute to this kind of patriarchal normativity. Women can, and often do, defend prevailing notions of masculinity or fail (even refuse) to challenge them.[18] Catherine Campbell highlights the important role the family plays in constructing a masculinity that allows the link between male identity and violence to persist and even hold a 'socially sanctioned place'.[19] In fact, Campbell observes that women themselves are so heavily socialised into subscribing to the existing power relations that they do not see challenging

12 Ibid. Italics in original text.
13 Hunter (above) at 398.
14 Also see Campbell (above) at 626–627.
15 Smith, Nicholas Rush (2015) 'Rejecting Rights: Vigilantism and Violence in Post-Apartheid South Africa' *African Affairs*, 114(456): 341–360.
16 Hunter (above) at 398.
17 Ibid.
18 Ibid.
19 Campbell (above) at 617.

them as an option. Instead, her female respondents saw avoidance and tolerance as their only choices: 'None of them mentioned redefining gender relations.'[20]

Hunter correctly reports, also, that '[w]omen's efforts to secure livelihoods in harsh socio-economic circumstances can also serve to reproduce dominant masculinities.'[21] Through their participation in – and hence perpetuation of – male dominance, in their attempts to ensure their own material security, women sometimes contribute to making women (as a group) sexually and physically vulnerable.

Agreeing with what is found by Campbell and Hunter, Sathiparsad shows how dominant views on masculinity are encouraging the spread of HIV/AIDS in rural communities, as women's voices are silenced when it comes to sexual issues.[22] She notes that, due to gender inequality, 'physical violence, the threat of violence and the fear of abandonment prevent women from negotiating condom usage or leaving relationships that are physically unsafe.'[23] She found that many women felt powerless and voiceless – particularly feeling that they lacked the ability to realise their choices to reduce behaviour with their partners that puts them at risk.[24] The risk of men returning from their city jobs to their rural wives and infecting them is very high because these women hold little power in their relationships and therefore usually cannot ask their husbands to use condoms.[25]

Yet HIV/AIDS is also having contradictory effects on masculinity. Hunter refers to the form of masculinity that glorifies multiple partners as '*isoka* masculinity' and argues that HIV/AIDS is 'bearing heavily down on' it.[26]

> HIV/AIDS related illnesses transform some of the most virile and popular bodies into barely living skeletons, shunned by friends and neighbours. Outwardly confident about being *isoka*, at times men betray their inner doubt. The contradictions of being *isoka* in the era of HIV/AIDS are perhaps most tragically played out at the many funerals in the area; previous players are buried by their friends who were once envious of their ability to attract women. Consequently, men and masculinities are under huge scrutiny and critique, even if women are still commonly blamed for promiscuity and AIDS.[27]

Thus, though society glorifies men who are successful at seducing women in a serial fashion, the brutality of HIV/AIDS – and especially the indignity with

20 Ibid. at 625.
21 Hunter (above) at 398.
22 Sathiparsad (above) at 181.
23 Ibid.
24 Ibid. at 182.
25 Ibid.
26 Hunter (above) at 397. Also see Meintjes (above) at 184–185.
27 Hunter (above) at 397.

which those who have it typically die – calls into severe question the desirability of that kind of performance of masculinity.

Masculinities and interpersonal violence: linking mass social violence to violence against women

As we have seen, for a long time ideal Zulu masculinity was defined by honour shown largely through restraint. Under the force of social pressures in the last century-and-a-half, this ideal changed radically with respect to men's identities as they relate to both sexual restraint and martial prowess. In the literature on the evolution of stick fighting covered in the previous chapter, Clegg and Alcock speak only to large-scale expressions of conflict through violence.[28] As the reader will observe in the latter half of this chapter, my contribution is primarily concerned with how violent conflict plays out in smaller-scale ways, in Msinga – especially in a gendered pattern.

Mxolisi Mchunu links the mass violence described by Clegg and Alcock back to the crisis over male identity. He notes: 'Like Campbell I have also found that men who have been unable to meet their role of breadwinner feel disempowered. Their frustration then results in desperate measures to institute discipline, as in "kangaroo courts" so as to forcibly retain their position as men.'[29] One can extend this argument to interpersonal violence between and among men in drinking places, at celebrations, in the street and at home. For instance, in Sathiparsad's study done in a different Zulu-speaking area, she found that most of her focus group participants accepted and even approved of the prevailing idea of masculinity as male dominance over women and the perpetration of violence by men against women.[30] Is the same true in Msinga? Based on focus groups done separately with men and women in Msinga, whose findings are detailed below, I would argue that it is so to a meaningful degree.

Not only that, but such a prevailing set of notions of masculinity is very much embedded in the broader social and cultural currents that I have already set out in this book. That is, the changes that have taken place in gendered relations within the family relative to the broader political economy in South Africa at large, and in Zulu society specifically, have significantly affected male identity and its formation. As Campbell reasons:

28 The 'ideology of vengeance' that Clegg describes, whether truly leading to endless feuding or simply the pervasive sense that 'violence happens' provides important context for understanding what I refer to as the plausibility of violence as a conflict management strategy in Msinga.

29 Mchunu, Mxolisi (2007) 'Cultural Change, Zulu Masculinity and Intergenerational Conflict in the Context of Civil War in Pietermaritzburg (1987–1991)' in T. Shefer (ed.) *From Boys to Men: Social Construction of Masculinity in Contemporary Society*. Landowne, University of Cape Town Press 225–240 at 234.

30 Sathiparsad (above) at 189.

> The crisis or undermining of masculinity is one of the intricately interlocking contextual factors that cannot be ignored in attempting to understand the upsurge of violence in working-class communities. In a community where the opportunities for assertion of masculine power are limited, violence is a manifestation of the structural forces of patriarchy reasserting themselves at a time when race and class oppression had dealt the status of adult men a particularly severe blow.[31]

Shula Marks demonstrates how these very dynamics drove the deepening of patriarchy among African men as early as the 1930s.[32] Likewise, I essentially argue that the factors that have contributed to the development of the plausibility of violence as conflict management in Msinga in particular[33] have greatly impacted the framing and performance of male identity in the area.

To the extent that social norms in Msinga embrace and even encourage violence, and especially that against women, we must try to understand why.[34] The question must thus be asked (and has been by other scholars), how do the contemporary forms and levels of interpersonal violence in Msinga – particularly as these relate to violence against women – connect to the background of stick fighting and the warrior culture that has since evolved to be at least one prevalent performance of Zulu masculinity? Carton and Morell explore this as it pertains to Zulu culture in general.

Their conclusion is equivocal. On one hand, they find that

> [t]he association between a proper *isoka* and a proper sportsman illuminates the importance that female admiration held for stick fighters hoping to impress, with prowess and restraint, their watching sweethearts. Here the role of older girls and young women should not be underestimated. To a certain extent they legitimised the sport by actively attending bouts and bestowing attention on their favourite contestants. Yet female agency had its limits in martial play that motioned more ominous intentions, as when a stick fighter's desire to lash out extended to the adolescent girl who declined his amorous overtures.[35]

31 Campbell (above) at 624.

32 Marks, Shula (1989) 'Patriotism, Patriarchy and Purity: Natal and the Politics of Zulu Ethnic Consciousness' in L. Vail (ed.) *The Creation of Tribalism in Southern Africa*. Berkeley, CA: University of California Press, 215–240 at 219–221.

33 Msinga is obviously not the only place in South Africa where violence is such a highly plausible conflict management tool. See, for example, Smith (above).

34 I have shown the inconsistency between the normative ideal and reality in other spheres. The same is arguably evident as regards the principle, pointed to by Creina Alcock, that it is bad luck to kill a woman.

35 Carton and Morell (above) at 42.

Hence, Carton and Morrell seem to conclude that there may be some link between men's participation in the socially glorified art of stick fighting and their redirecting their fighting passions to the girls who were the objects of their unrequited affections.

Yet, on the other hand, Carton and Morrell then go on to say that we should not assume that feuding culture necessarily led to male violence. Again, their statement is ambivalent:

> Yet stick fighting was and is predicated on degrees of belligerence. Even more so, the sport embodied past military exploits particularly those of the *amabutho*. It also could be unpredictable, when rules of engagement failed to thwart eruptive energies that placed vulnerable people at risk before and after a bout. Yet these factors should not lead to the conclusion that the formative experiences of stick fighting drove Zulu men into bloodletting.[36]

On reading this, one is left wondering how a practice based on aggression is not to be understood to form men into (at least, potentially) violent actors. Seeming to restrict themselves to the history of stick fighting, Carton and Morell argue that stick fighting emphasises 'honourable restraint' and 'cemented bonds between men because it valorised robust masculinity'.[37] Even if their observations are true for other Zulu communities, I have demonstrated through Clegg's and Alcock's work that they do not really apply to Msinga, where feuding moved very far away from its original form of highly rule-governed 'play'.

Yet, even Carton and Morell acknowledge the spill-over of aggression that sometimes occurred from stick fighting into ordinary interactions with young women – especially when a young woman declined the stick fighter's romantic advances.[38] As I will illustrate below, in Msinga, young women who resist or show themselves independent of the need for men in their lives are subject to violence – arguably as a form of protest against these young women's alternative version of femininity and the perceived emasculation of men.

I will agree with Carton and Morell that we should not simply *assume* that stick fighting '*invariably* stoked aggressive masculinity and violent criminality in South Africa'.[39] Indeed, my argument is not that stick fighting *alone* did this in Msinga, but that a number of troubling factors – among which is the development of a culture deeming violence a plausible means of dispute management – achieved this.

Here, I also return to Campbell's work, in which she argues that there are numerous ways that masculinity may attempt to reassert itself whenever it is in

36 Ibid. at 52.
37 Ibid.
38 Ibid. at 42.
39 Ibid. at 52. Emphasis added.

crisis, such as men's withdrawing from their families by drinking heavily and philandering.[40] A key way is tyranny and violence, particularly perpetrated within the family.[41] Campbell contends that this is the alternative that Zulu men appear to have taken to deal with the crisis surrounding their masculinity.

Readers will recall the contest that developed between older men committed to the traditional ideal of the 'father', 'provider', repository of knowledge and councillor to the community, on the one hand, and young men who led the resistance against apartheid in the townships, on the other. As a product of this period, Campbell argues that 'violence and masculinity are closely intertwined in the macho culture of resistance.'[42] This link explains the ideal masculinity that primarily prevails among young men – though, as I argued in Chapter 4, in Msinga, it does not find its origins in young men's resistance to apartheid but to the factors I have set out drawing on Clegg. Namely, the culture of stick fighting and feuding within and across sub/ward boundaries and the plausibility of violence that results in conflicts always being ripe for taking a violent turn or being reignited once they have died. In summary, and with greater nuance, Loiuse Meintjes describes this context out of which violent expressions of masculinity perpetually erupt as 'Msinga's history as a long-standing zone of conflict'.[43] She aptly includes in this description the susceptibility Msinga has experienced to violence and conflict perpetrated or cultivated by the colonial (and apartheid) state.[44]

Drawing from Hunter's and Campbell's work, I would argue that women take part in maintaining such a notion of masculinity. Indeed, the family plays an important role in constructing a masculinity linked to violence that holds a 'socially sanctioned place'.[45] By collaborating in this way, women in fact perpetuate their own and other women's physical insecurity. In this vein, Mchunu says that he 'found that mothers tacitly "spoil" their sons, many of whom are illegitimate, encouraging their masculine assertion, which could be termed indiscipline by traditional standards'.[46] Recalling to mind the metaphor that Carton and Morell described as the traditional ideal for young men, that they be *isibuko sikababa* (the father's mirror)[47] and demonstrate responsibility and restraint in all areas of their lives, Mchunu further avers that:

> in regard to the "sons" using African concepts of discipline to rationalise their behaviour, one reads in sociological studies about male children who do not have role models in their fathers, who then overcompensate by

40 Campbell (above) at 623.
41 Ibid.
42 Ibid. at 624.
43 Meintjes (above) at 3.
44 Ibid.
45 Campbell (above) at 617.
46 Mchunu (above) at 234.
47 Carton and Morell (above) at 41–42.

> becoming extremely "masculine" in an ill-perceived notion of what this means, and who may "act out" as violent hooligans.[48]

Perhaps this observation bears some truth for those young men raised without fathers.

Regardless, there is evidence to support the point that, as Campbell further argues, young men learn violence from seeing fathers beat mothers in order to secure their 'obedience' – this includes beating the young men's mothers even for things like gossiping. Young men also learn violence from seeing their older brothers supposedly 'guarding' their sisters by violent coercion.[49] Indeed, as Campbell describes in her findings:

> The ability of men to control women, or to keep them in line, and the use of violence to ensure this control, is one area where the power of working-class men has not been threatened by a racial capitalist society. Male respondents laid tremendous emphasis on the importance of being seen to have an obedient, faithful and home-bound girlfriend, who did not have too many friends since "friends tend to confuse a girl and serve as a bad influence".[50]

Men use violence, sometimes even fatally, in order to control women's movements and associations.[51] They use it to force women, often their girlfriends, into sex. They also use it against men who threaten their sexual relationships.[52] All of this is played out in the cases recorded in Msinga.[53]

The situation for young men is also worsened by the easy availability of guns 'even in the absence of a faction fight' and the fact that, as Bhekuyise Mthembu avers, a man without a gun is looked down upon and 'derogatorily referred to as a woman'.[54] In all the conflicts we recorded in six wards over eleven months, I can identify only one reference to knives and two to stones. Virtually all violence was perpetrated with a gun. Moreover, young men perpetrate much of the interpersonal violence. Even if they are in school, they are vulnerable to getting drawn into mischief or violence. The material conditions in which these

48 Mchunu (above) at 235.
49 Campbell (above) at 625–627.
50 Ibid. at 625.
51 Ibid. at 626.
52 Ibid. Readers might also recall that one of *igoso*'s responsibilities is to keep the man who pursues another man's girlfriend in check.
53 These cases and more are enumerated in the discussion that follows below: Moyizela/Ngetshe; Hlukumezekile/Songela; Buyekhaya/Kubi; MaNovalo/Cijimpi; Ngeniwe; Balekile/Myeni.
54 Mthembu, Bhekuyise Isaac (October 1994) *Faction Fighting in Msinga District from 1874 to 1906* – A Dissertation submitted to the Faculty of Arts in the fulfillment of the requirements for the degree of Master of Arts in the Department of History at the University of Zululand Kwa-Dlangezwa. (Supervisor: Prof. S. J. Maphalala) at vi–vii.

young men exist are dire, and they are presented with little prospect of escaping them. Theft is hence also rather common among them. A machismo culture, and careless bravado, has developed as the predominant version of young masculinity. Families and headmen largely agree that they do not know what to do to save these young men.

Notwithstanding this rather grim picture, Sathiparsad also argues that dominant Zulu masculine views are beginning to change, as some youths begin to consider it necessary that women should be able to make decisions regarding their sex lives. In fact, she writes:

> The fact that some participants contested hegemonic masculinities and demonstrated support for more equitable relationships with girls suggests that alternative forms of masculinity were operating around and within dominant forms. . . . [I]n fact one young man viewed a girl's refusal to have sex as a display of strength against male dominance, providing evidence of an emerging gender consciousness within a context where dominant patterns of masculinity can begin to be renegotiated.[55]

As previously mentioned, Sathiparsad's research was done in a different field site. But I would argue that it offers some hope for Msinga, and I can point to very modest indications of such change occurring there as well.

Specific findings on vulnerability and proclivity in Msinga disputing and management

I now turn to discuss the data on the susceptibility of people fitting certain profiles in Msinga to either experiencing particular violations against them or perpetrating specific violations against others. While some of the discussion will look at non-violent offences, the bulk will focus on violent offences, including potentially violent conflicts. This approach is based on the concern raised by the data and interviews with informants around violence and the threat that it poses in Msinga, as well as the difficulties that the vernacular forums are having with managing it. Finally, the history of the region discussed so far confirms that violence is an important theme in Msinga.

As catalogued below, it is evident from the data that young men tend to be the most often involved in criminal activity – especially as perpetrators in violent or potentially violent matters. Young women were involved in these matters, typically as victims but they did rarely get involved in violent behavior themselves too.[56] Young men were also most often involved in theft or material loss.[57]

55 Sathiparsad (above) at 189–190.
56 See, for example, Sicabha/Sheliwe.
57 Gqekezelwe; Toho/Semncane; Webile etc.

What is further striking about the conflict patterns in Msinga is that a number of considerations repeatedly appear to aggravate local conflicts. These considerations include the existence of conflict history. In other words, often disputes erupt out of a past conflict between the parties or those to whom they are in close relationship in some form. Another element is that conduct that gives rise to disputes is sometimes repeated. Hence, a conflict reoccurs because the behaviour performed previously, having given rise to conflict the first time, is performed again by the party who was perceived by the other as being in the wrong in the first place. Sometimes the conduct is performed even after a penalty has been imposed through a prior dispute management process. Alcohol appears repeatedly – both as contributing to the occurrence of new conflict and as a meaningful contributor to the repetition of offences. Very rarely, drugs feature too.[58]

The goods most often fought over include family/kin and relationships – among them, men, women, and children – as well as elements already mentioned as common causes of aggravation, such as alcohol and guns. The widespread role played by – and social concern over – guns is worth illustrating here. A number of matters stand out – none of them 'cases'. One is a matter in which some boys threatened a girl, Hlukumezekile, who did not want to date one of the young men, Songela. In this matter, the chair of the dispute management forum attempting to mediate the dispute asked where the teenage boys got the gun. The boys denied knowledge of a gun, denying using it to threaten the girl. The chair warned the young men, saying to them that they knew the police would beat them until they produced the gun.

As another example, a gun was mentioned in a ward meeting concerning local criminality, where it was said that *abafana* (some teenage boys) used a gun that they claimed had no bullets to rob people who harvested marijuana. *Abafana* were accused of then drying the marijuana to sell it, and they confessed to this act. These boys had stolen the gun from the school guard. The matter in which a young man named Soliwe was accused of being a police snitch revolved around his allegedly reporting to the police who in his community was in possession of an illegal firearm so that the police could raid the people's homes, confiscate the guns, and assault and arrest the guilty parties. This young man was threatened with being in danger – implicitly, also, of being injured or killed with a gun. Incidentally, in another ward, the elected CPF, Zikhali, was not trusted because people in the ward thought that he would report their illegal gun possession to the police.

As seen in the opening of this chapter, a gun was (repeatedly) used by Cijimpi to perpetrate domestic violence against his wife and daughter – alcohol was also involved in this matter. Drunk again, the same man used the same gun to threaten his neighbour after insulting him. Having already attempted to shoot

58 Drugs were more likely to be discussed as income generation (marijuana growing) than a use and abuse problem (in which context they were raised only once).

his wife, Cijimpi fired his gun over his neighbour's home while accusing his neighbour of harbouring his wife. A different gun was used by a different man, Zwilakhe, in terrorising his community by firing his gun at night. Yet another man's bullet went over his neighbour's home while the neighbour's kids played in the yard.[59] Guns were used in threats,[60] including the use of a gun as a threat amidst a fight over beer. In this latter matter, the older men threatened then assaulted the young man because he was disrespecting them while drunk.[61]

As mentioned in the previous chapter's conclusion, the relational proximity of parties is important because of the relationship it also bears to the typical locations of offences within Msinga. The sites of offences are mostly people's homes, ceremonies or rites, school, and the veld or bush (in other words, thoroughfares and other in-between spaces). Quite a bit happens in Johannesburg also, and in other cities to which Msinga people (mostly men) go to work or to search for work. Indeed, work was mentioned as a reason for postponing proceedings at least twice.

Below, I will also draw attention to the ways in which identity can impact the dispute management process. In a few cases, it emerges quite clearly that the relief that parties get from the vernacular forums – or the failed delivery of the requested relief – is affected, if not entirely determined, by the parties' relative identities. In keeping with the discussion in the previous chapter, the identities of those to whom a disputant is related (whether or not they are present to support or represent the disputant) can heavily impact the treatment the disputant gets in the dispute management system and the decision that is ultimately made.

Young men (15–25 years old)

In most matters concerning break-ins and robberies, it was young men who were the accused. I have already mentioned the numerous instances in which young men had stolen people's cellphones. In fact, cellphone theft or loss was recorded in five disputes.[62] In all of these, young men were involved as the alleged wrongdoers or both the wrongdoer and the wronged. In a couple of instances, assaults also took place between the parties – such as in the Sihlobo/Mndeni case brought by one sister against another when the son of one assaulted that of the other over the alleged theft of a cellphone.

One adult woman, MaBazene, brought a claim against a young man who had come into one of the houses on her property while she was in the kitchen and stolen a television set along with a cellphone. Her child had seen the thief

59 Zihlalele/Phutha.

60 MaNovalo/Cijimpi; Soliwe; Sabiswa/Qhuma.

61 Chuku.

62 Out of 71 disputes: in two cases (MaMakhe/MaMsolwa; Sihlobo/Mndeni) and three informal dispute management discussions (Cingo/Sela; Fonofono/Mthengi/Kweba; MaBazene/Wonile).

and fought with the young man over the television. When MaBazene heard the commotion and came out to see what was happening, the thief dropped the television and ran away with the cellphone. The child who had seen him said that it was his teenage uncle, Wonile, who was still in school and known to have a history of stealing. The young uncle denied the allegation. During the proceedings, the complainant's husband, who was the accused's brother, testified that there was no point in asking for compensation because Wonile had no money. The matter therefore did not come to a meaningful resolution.

In a separate dispute, a young man, Bhala, had stolen and then sold a wheelbarrow. In yet another matter, a young man named Buyisimbuzi was brought to the vernacular forum under the accusation that he stole local ward people's goats. What is evident in this example and several others is that the young men were often repeat offenders. In this matter, it surfaced that Buyisimbuzi had previously been imprisoned for arson. This was one of several instances of young men being accused of stealing people's livestock[63] – and even marijuana[64] – to sell.

Further instances of young men's involvement in theft include a matter in which Gangile and Mngani were accused of breaking into a house and stealing its contents.[65] At the same time, in a different ward, Uyeba and Nonya had broken in and stolen goods from the Bekezela's house. The headman referred Bekezela to the chief's court where the matter was postponed because of a death in the Bekezela family. In the meantime, Uyeba and Nonya had broken into a local school and stolen its computers. The principal of the school had reported the matter to the police, and thus the boys had been arrested and were in custody for this offence. When Tshontshelwe reported that the same young men had also broken into his house, the headman recommended that this new complainant and Bekezela also go to the police.

While these opening examples focus on young men's involvement in non-violent offences, we also observed that young men were the group most often involved as offenders in violent or potentially violent disputes. As seen in the matters used as illustrations of gun violence, most of these violent or potentially violent matters implicating young men involved firearms, all of which were illegally possessed. That said, rocks were used in a young man's murder of his wife[66] and infant in a matter that arose during our data collection period but which we did not specifically record, because it went to the police rather than through the vernacular system and occurred in a ward that we were not monitoring.

Of course, young men can also be on the receiving end of violent and potentially violent offences. In one instance, Semncane, was accused of stealing

63 E.g. Mdlinzo; Ginsa and Bambisene.

64 Toho/Semncane; Abafana.

65 Gangile and Mngani, and MaZizamela. Mngani was also a witness in the matter concerning the theft of MaMalinga's windows; the mystery of this theft remained unsolved.

66 Moshile/Limele.

someone's marijuana overnight. Toho, the adult man who attributed the loss to the young man, threatened him, saying he would get hurt if he did not stop. The matter came to the vernacular forum at the initiative of Toho's father, who feared that his son was genuinely going to get hurt if the matter was not resolved. As it happens, the warning from the wronged man was all that Toho's father would get, as the headman told them that they should resolve the matter among themselves because he should not hear disputes over marijuana (because marijuana cultivation is illegal).

Arguably, the most violent offences performed by young men are done in groups. For instance, the single burglary of a business that we recorded was a group offence in which the aggrieved business owner said the perpetrators were kin.[67] Another example is the grievous assault of Vakashile by five young men. A final example is the gang rape of a 16-year-old girl by five young men, allegedly including her boyfriend as an accomplice.[68] A couple of the gun-related examples above are also group offences.[69]

What is interesting in a number of disputes concerning young men – and is linked to the fact that the young men usually appear as the accused – is that the matters concerning them are typically brought by someone else, often by the concerned family or vernacular grouping surrounding them. At least two matters were heard at the request of the young men's fathers.[70]

In other disputes, subward or ward members who believed they had been wronged by young men in their locale brought the matters to the attention of their vernacular grouping for aid. For instance, MaZizamela, who had had two local young men steal food, mostly meat, from her refrigerator appealed to the subward gathering to mediate and get Gangile and Mngani to repay the stolen meat. She had received the rest of the wares that the young men had simultaneously stolen – namely, radio, blankets and clothes – when they had been arrested by the police. They were subsequently released and Gangile ran away to Pretoria, so he was not present for the mediation.

In these disputes, it was generally assumed that the young men were in the wrong. Indeed, there was often good evidence presented – the young men themselves often appeared to testify. Sometimes they denied being guilty; but often they confessed. The forums tried, seemingly feebly, to chastise the young men and encourage them to do better. There is no evidence that I can directly point to of this approach having worked. Rather, it seemed, from the accounts that we recorded of young men getting into trouble, that they had often gone from smaller to bigger wrongs, despite having been cautioned against such behaviour.[71]

67 Gqekezelwe.
68 Ntombazane/Ncolisile.
69 Abafana; Hlukumezekile/Songela.
70 Webile; Toho/Semncane.
71 See, for example, Webile; Uyeba and Nonya; Gangile and Mngani; Buyisimbuzi; MaBazene/Wonile.

Young women (15–25 years old)

In the evidence we collected, there are a number of matters in which young women were involved. In some, they are the offenders, while in many they were the ones against whom offences occurred. I have already pointed out that often the disputes in which young women are involved relate to their sexuality and relational status (which is, in turn, linked to social status) in some way.

Readers may recall that we recorded an illustrative matter in which a teenage girl, Malunde, slept at the home of a much older boy. Phendulile claimed that Malunde did so voluntarily while Malunde's family said she did not. When the headman mediated this dispute with both the families, Phendulile reiterated that Malunde was his girlfriend and her family continued to deny the fact. In the end, the headman said that he managed to reconcile the families: he said that the families had forgiven each other. It is notable that Malunde's side was never heard from her lips in any of the mediation discussions.[72]

A more subtle example is the case that was brought against an older man, Dakiwe, by the mother of the young woman this man had insulted. As noted in Chapter 5, the case was presented as one of defamation. The older man, Dakiwe, had gone to the women's home – he later claimed that he had been intoxicated at the time – and accused the young woman, Phikile, of having stolen his government-issued identity document and then used it to steal his employment benefits. She had captured his identity number when she had worked for the census project almost a decade before. She said that she had promptly disposed of his details when she had concluded her employment. She speculated that his reason for accusing her was as revenge for her having vehemently rejected his recent overtures towards her. He explained that he had just been drunk and successfully negotiated a reduction of damages on the basis that he was unemployed.

In the matter of Ntombi and Mthuki the fetishisation of a young woman's relational status was obvious as Ntombi was allegedly insulted by Mthuki with the term 'wife', that is, 'non-virgin.' As readers will recall, the case came before the local headman, was adjudicated by the chief (with witness testimony from the women who conducted virginity testing), and was lastly heard and deliberated by *isikebhe*. In each of these attempts at the case's management, Mthuki – who claimed Ntombi was no longer a virgin – was found to be in the wrong.

Whether the forums' consistent finding was correct or not, what is most interesting in this matter is that the statuses of the young women seemed to matter meaningfully – both independently and, ultimately, relative to one another. The young woman who had issued the insult was a single woman with children out of wedlock. This was a blight on her own reputation and status, as she sought to put a similar blight on the reputation of her opponent. Mthuki also lived with her brothers, who were regarded as a criminal nuisance in the ward

72 See the similar dispute of MaMsolile.

in which they lived – the same ward as Ntombi's family. This was an additional blight on the accused's position. Indeed, the brothers' bad reputation was mentioned in the course of the hearing in the chief's council. These notorious brothers never attended the hearings, though multiple postponements were made for the purpose of requiring them to attend in support of their sister and represent her in the proceedings, especially in the chief's court.

Conversely, the girl who had been insulted still lived with her parents and had finished school only a year before. The case was initiated by her father, though he was not there in most of the hearings (certainly not in the headman's and chief's forums). Ntombi's mother was at every hearing, however, and it is worth noting that her mother was a councillor on the chief's legislative-administrative council. Though she never received special acknowledgment in the proceedings, it is my assessment that her relative position gave her daughter an air of respectability that Mthuki did not have. It did not help the accused Mthuki when the older women who had conducted the virginity testing testified that she was rude and defiant toward them while they did their job, allegedly going on to insult them when they told her that they found that the complainant was in fact still a virgin.[73]

I have already noted that a substantial number of disputes concerning young women are matters of paternity in which young women became pregnant outside of marriage – something that is frowned upon, though it is not an infrequent occurrence. In these matters,[74] the young women's families usually wanted two related things from the young men's families: that the young men acknowledge the children as their own and that their families pay damages for 'spoiling' the young women. It can be very difficult to get either or both of these forms of relief out of the young men's families.

I have also suggested that young women pay a high price for rejecting the overtures of young men. In my discussion of the use of guns, I shared the matter of Hlukumezekile, the teenage girl who was allegedly threatened with a firearm by the rejected suitor, Songela, and his friends when she was walking back from school alone in the late afternoon. As Hunter's discussion helps us understand,[75] the young men may have been particularly displeased by her rejection of the potential suitor being expressed in terms of her preferring to focus on her education.

Another instance of this riskiness in rejecting male propositions is seen in the Moyizela/Ngetshe case in which a teenage girl was grievously assaulted with rocks by a young man who, it also seems, may have been a rejected suitor. Moyizela and her sister had been walking from her mother's house to the home of her mother's family, carrying goods on their heads, when they came across

73 Three years after the case, after trying to access higher education or get a good job, Ntombi, who had been working at a bottle store, was pregnant yet she was still unmarried.

74 E.g. Wamkelwe; Kanankinga/Landula; Nhlamba/Yala; Sukela/Fanele.

75 Hunter (above) at 398.

Ngetshe and some of his friends, who were playing on some big boulders. Ngetshe asked Moyizela to shake his hand – an ambiguous gesture that can have sexual overtones. She refused. With the advantage of altitude over the two girls, the young man started throwing rocks at her. One of them struck her front teeth, dislodging them and causing much bleeding. The girls threw stones at the boys as they ran for cover and then ran back to their mother's home.

Several other matters arose that were linked to young women's sexuality.[76] Regrettably, as was shown in Sphiwo's experience,[77] disability does not immunise a young woman to such violation, even from a distant uncle. These instances of young women as victims of male perpetrators pursuing romantic and sexual relations are symbolically related to the following conflicts between two sets of young women that arose over young men and their attraction to certain young women as their (potential) girlfriends. In one instance, one young woman, Sicabha, accused the other, Sheliwe, of making moves on her boyfriend. Sicabha then went on to attack her perceived competitor's home with rocks, causing damage to the back door of the house. These girls lived in the same subward and were distant relations.

In the matter concerning Nqabile, one young woman, Zifakile, told another, Nqabile, that she wanted to set her up with her boyfriend's friend, Sesheli. In an effort to seal the deal against Nqabile's will, the matchmaker went to the extent of stealing the resistant Nqabile's clothes and took them to the imposed Sesheli's home. The matter reported was that Nqabile wanted her clothes returned and the record set straight that she was not interested in Sesheli and had not given permission for her clothes to be left at his home. Nqabile's desire was for her reputation not to be tarnished and for the issue to be publicly cleared.

Adult women (26–59 years old)

When involved in conflict, adult women tend to get embroiled mostly in conflicts over seeming jealousies and what they have said or what has been said about them.[78] In one instance, one adult woman accused another of sleeping with her husband. MaNyonyoba, whose name stood to be tarnished by the accusation, brought a claim against MaMsolelani, the wife who had made the allegedly false accusation. The headman's council concluded that MaNyonyoba, who had brought the matter to the council's attention as a defamation claim, was likely sleeping with MaMsolelani's husband.

A different conflict arose around defamation and insult between two neighbours where MaDliwe's goat was eaten by MaSinekasikho's dog. The matter heard by the headman revolved around not just the damages

76 E.g. Msukele/Walile; Ntombazane/Ncolisile; Buyekhaya and Kubi.
77 Buhlungu: in re Sphiwo.
78 E.g. MaMsolile.

of the dog's eating the goat but also the fact that MaDliwe perceived there to be an embedded insult against her when MaSinekasikho said that it had been the goat that had gone looking for the dog. Indeed, I have shared several different fact patterns in this book that bear this tendency of adult women to end up in conflicts concerning what was said between them,[79] even in relation to witchcraft accusations.[80]

As we saw in the previous chapter, verbal assaults are not always (or even typically) the seedbed of banal conflicts. Again, witchcraft accusations tend to raise real concern for the person accused and necessitate bringing these disputes to a public forum. For instance, MaFukuza took her matter through to the headman's council because she was concerned about letting the accusation stand without being firmly disproved. This middle-aged woman had been accused of witchcraft by her neighbour's son of 30-odd years while he was inebriated one night. Siqhwaga had shouted it for all the neighbours to hear. MaFukuza responded by first inviting Siqhwaga's parents to come and discuss the matter with her. She hoped to persuade them to ask their son to withdraw the accusation publicly and apologise. She further hoped that they might even offer to make amends. However, Siqhwaga's parents did not come to her to discuss the matter, so MaFukuza gathered the neighbourhood together to discuss it publicly. When the neighbourhood council was unable to get Siqhwaga to unequivocally withdraw his witchcraft accusation and apologise, though he admitted that he had never caught her in the act of witchcraft, MaFukuza escalated the matter to the headman's council. Returned from work at the time, her husband accompanied her to the headman's council hearing.

The headman's council concluded that the woman had been wronged and should have damages paid to her. She refused substantial damages and asked only that the accuser pay R10; the money would be used to buy incense and cleanse her home of this terrible wrong. She said that her intent with the formal dispute was just to have her name cleansed. She was especially concerned about her name because, she said, she was a believing woman (a Christian) and because she was a member of the chief's legislative-administrative council. The latter status may be of some relevance to the fact that her matter was so well resolved.

In terms of conventional externals, she was a middle-aged woman who lived with her four daughters (a couple of whom were in their late teens) while her husband spent most of his time working in Johannesburg. Living alone with her daughters made her somewhat vulnerable to such accusations as those of witchcraft. Yet, her status as a married woman – and, thus, her having a husband who did return from time to time to lend stature to the home – was a meaningful counter to that vulnerability.

Her further status as a councillor also lent her credibility that she might not otherwise have had. As I argued with respect to Ntombi (the young woman

79 E.g. Kanankinga/Landula.
80 E.g. MaMakhe/MaMsolwa.

who was called a non-virgin), the young woman's mother being a councillor made some difference to the treatment and outcome of the case. I would argue the same here. Yet I would emphasise that this contribution to one's status has to be read with other contributors to or detractions from it.

Compare this woman's situation to that of MaThembile (the woman who was accused of something symbolically equivalent to witchcraft: killing people's goats on her property with poison). That woman lived on her own with some young children. Significantly, she did not have a husband who returned periodically to lend her home stature, and when her matter went to a vernacular forum for management, it was her brother who represented her, and he was not even able to be at all of the hearings. Like MaFukuza (the Traditional councilwoman accused of witchcraft), MaThembile said she was a Christian, and yet she had less credibility. It would seem that her lower level of credibility may have at least partly resulted from her not having the stamp of authority and added status that comes with being a Traditional councillor or having a husband who is at least periodically present.

Yet we must add to the important differences between them the fact that MaFukuza was not socially marginalised. In fact, she referred to her opponent as someone who she considered her son, thus indicating a closeness with her neighbours. To state the obvious, she had also acted in accordance with this social inclusion by reporting the accusation to her neighbours when Siqhwaga's family did not discuss the matter with her privately. MaFukuza's social embeddedness had probably given her the local 'common sense' and confidence to act promptly in this way. In short, therefore, I would argue that adult women's status, relations, and social embeddedness matter for the purposes of determining their vulnerability to accusations of certain wrongs in Msinga. Indeed, these elements matter even for determining adult women's power – and, by extension, largely affect success or failure in dispute management processes.

Of course, adult women can also be disadvantaged by their relationships with men with bad reputations, which the example of Mthuki (who was disadvantaged by having brothers who were regarded as a nuisance in their ward) demonstrated is also true for young women. We came across at least two instances in which adult women stood in the line of fire – literally – because their husbands had been involved in some violence and had run away to escape retaliation. One woman named MaFihlile reported to her headman that she was feeling unsafe after someone had knocked on the door to her home at night and threatened to kill her. MaFihlile did not see the suspect (she thought, from his voice, he was a man), but she speculated that it must be the man who had been in a gunfight with her husband. MaFihlile's husband had since run away from home to hide.

In MaSenkingeni's instance, she brought a case against MaMbuze for the latter's spreading rumours that the complainant's husband hired people to kill the complainant's lover. MaSenkingeni's husband had long escaped to Johannesburg. When MaMbuze was asked where she had heard this rumour, she said that she had heard the alleged killers talking, but she refused to disclose their names. Because the women were from two different wards, the matter was first heard by their joint headmen's council but then had to go on to the chief's council. Though pleaded with in both forums, MaMbuze would not reveal the men's identities and was therefore fined.

A final kind of wrong that adult women are obviously particularly vulnerable to is related to their relative material insecurity. Here, the distinction between older adult women and younger adult women is worth making. I have previously written about the link between the social embeddedness of Msinga women's access to land and their vulnerability to or protection against eviction.[81] The interviews for that article were conducted with an older generation of married, divorced/separated, widowed, and unmarried adult women. The present dataset suggests that there may be some generational shifts taking place in this regard, particularly with respect to the decisions the women themselves make when faced with trouble in their marriages.[82]

One sees this shift evidenced by the difference between the two cases that opened this chapter[83] and the two case illustrations below. In short, in the cases of MaNovalo/Cijimpi and MaZimele/Gwajisa, you see two older adult women refusing to leave their marital homes for reasons of holding on to the property that is their home and livelihood (in which they have invested meaningful resources). They do this even at the real risk of their lives.

By contrast, the instances we came across of younger adult women who were faced with marital troubles were matters in which the women had left their marital homes. In Ndodakazi's matter, this woman had received assistance from her birth family in loading movable material belongings from her 'marital' home onto a rented truck and taking them back to her birth family with her. Ndodakazi was not completely married to the man but was living with him as one who was married to him;[84] they had also had children together. Her 'in-laws' laid a formal claim, before the headman's council, against her family for damaging the marital family's property and taking some property that was not theirs in the moving process, particularly the refrigerator.

Part of Ndodakazi's justification for leaving – and her father's reason for deliberately taking some of the husband's belongings – was that the 'husband', Silingo, was not maintaining their children. As it turned out, however, the

81 Mnisi Weeks, Sindiso (2013) 'Women's Eviction in Msinga: The Uncertainties of Seeking Justice' *Acta Juridica*, 118–142.

82 The responses given by women of different generations in the focus groups affirm this suggestion – e.g. some young women expressed dissatisfaction with rape matters being discussed at home rather than the perpetrators being prosecuted and incarcerated whereas older women were more circumspect, even when they had been victims of rape themselves.

83 MaNovalo/Cijimpi; MaZimele/Gwajisa.

84 *Ganile* is the term used for a woman who is 'incompletely' married. Some cows might have been paid for her *lobolo* (bridewealth) and she might live with her husband, but the marriage process – culminating in her dancing (thus making her '*gidile*') and stabbing her knife in the cattle enclosure (kraal) of her husband – has not been completed in its entirety.

refrigerator actually belonged to Silingo's senior wife. In the headman's council, agreement was reached between the parties that the refrigerator would be returned in exchange for two cows as damages and maintenance for the children the daughter had had with the man she had left.

In another matter, MaQhinga, just left her in-laws as though she were returning home only for the weekend and then never returned. On two attempts with the help of the headman's and chief's councils to have her return to her marital family, MaQhinga said before the forums that she would return. Yet she did not. The forums pleaded with her to, at least, tell them why she did not want to return, if indeed she did not. She would not say but told the forums that she would return. It later emerged that her husband, Shayene, was beating her. The headman in her area told me that they had ultimately managed to elicit a commitment from her husband that he would not beat her again. Yet the young wife did not return.

In the end, Shayene was harassing the headman of the ward in which MaQhinga's birth family lived, asking him what the headman was doing because this was the job of a headman. This comment annoyed the headman; he reported to us that he obviously could not make the girl return and he would not tell the man to go and retrieve his *lobolo* cattle. In the end, MaQhinga refused to return and did not tell anyone the final reason why. Her family agreed to return the cattle to the groom's family, which was a long way to drive the herd, because they lived in a distant ward in another nation.

In each of these cases relating to a younger adult woman's leaving her marital home, the birth and marital families together attempted to get the women to return but were unsuccessful. In the end, what was apparent was the inability of the families and vernacular forums to compel these younger adult women to return to their husbands. In the matter between Zama and Nkani,[85] Zama had left with her children and was refusing to return them to her husband's family, as culture seemed to demand. She was appealing to the civil court system to defend her, though she was not having much luck and believed that Nkani had bribed the court clerks.

Because these are not randomised controlled experiments, there is no denying that there are many variables in these disputes concerning older and younger adult women: the personalities of the parties involved, for one; the families' respective means, for another. However, in my observations, some weight must be given to the generational differences between the women involved and how much they feel they can step outside of conventional norms and expectations. The younger adult women seem to experience more freedom to leave their marital homes.

Interestingly, this is so in both the Nezikhathi and the Nakudala areas, though single women with children can obtain land independently of men only in the

85 Detailed in Mnisi Weeks, Sindiso (2015–2016) 'Access to Justice?: Dispute Management Processes in Msinga, KwaZulu-Natal, South Africa' *New York Law School Law Review*, 60(1): 227–249.

Nezikhathi area (since 2010). That change in Nezikhathi norms is attributable in part to older adult women like MaZimele, who served on the legislative-administrative council and, after her terrible experience with her husband, advocated for the change of norm so that women could obtain land on their own. Zama, on the other hand, was from the Nakudala area but had since moved out of the area to live in a nearby town. Surely, her having a job as a nurse and thus not being dependent on her husband allowed her to act more independently and be more resistant to conservative (and, in her case, oppressive) local norms.

It would seem also that the vernacular forums observe this greater freedom experienced by younger adult women with some degree of indulgence – really, resignation. It is as though the vernacular forum members regard younger women as lacking respect and discipline and being somewhat beyond the control of the forums. With some persistence on a young woman's part, in the end, the forums seem to largely accept that they cannot force her to do anything she does not want to do, and so the forums drop the matter. In these instances, the fact that many disputes go unresolved[86] and simply lapse because the vernacular forums cannot take the matter forward can be of some help to the more vulnerable women (faced with relatively strong husbands) in the disputes.

Adult men (26–59 years old)

The reader will have seen adult men's involvement in disputes threaded throughout the categories and examples that I have discussed thus far. For example, it was an adult male who attempted to rape his brother's young wife when he came across her on her return from collecting water.[87] Likewise, an adult male was responsible for the death – by culpable homicide, after an assault – of his adult cousin after the latter had allegedly raped the former's mentally disabled teenage daughter.[88]

As seen, it was an adult man who terrorised his neighbourhood by repeatedly attempting to severely assault his wife and daughter and then attempting to shoot his neighbour for giving his wife shelter.[89] The same protagonist, Cijimpi, was involved in another dispute when a different neighbour, Velelwe, initiated a claim against him for Cijimpi's saying, while intoxicated, that Velelwe had stolen his goat. (The protagonist apologised before the subward council, which encouraged the two men to forgive each other because they are kin.) Cijimpi, yet again, was involved in a dispute in which he had allegedly said of yet another neighbour, Qashiwe, that the neighbour was hired to kill him. (Cijimpi denied having said this, and because there were no witnesses that had heard him, the

86 Ibid.
87 Msukele/Walile.
88 Buhlungu: in re Sphiwo.
89 MaNovalo/Cijimpi.

council simply urged the two men to forgive each other.) Amidst all these disputes in which Cijimpi was involved, he brought a claim against one of his neighbours, Hlolela, for calling Cijimpi a witch. (Hlolela was found guilty and required to tender a goat as damages.)

What was interesting with respect to our protagonist, Cijimpi, was that, although his vernacular grouping genuinely objected to his conduct most of the time and although he was disturbing the peace in the subward, it seemed that his grouping was simultaneously afraid of him. In none of the disputes in which he was involved – though there were several – did the council members say to him, 'We are tired of you terrorising the neighbourhood'. He was the one that brought up in one of the matters brought against him the fact that he had a bad reputation, suggesting that he did not expect to receive justice in the vernacular forum because of a neighbourhood bias against him. One therefore gathers that he maintained significant status in the vernacular grouping – if only because of the fear that he attracts and cultivates.

Alongside this suggestion, one must wonder why the much-celebrated *iphini/igoso* system did not appear to take over intervention in this man's violent and threatening behaviour.[90] It seems possible to me that this protagonist was less of an exception than we outsiders might think. In other words, it is arguable that he was just at the far end of the spectrum of acceptability in a setting in which it is not uncommon for men to repeatedly and regularly get drunk, then get disruptive and violent. Furthermore, this problematic individual calls to mind the appeal made directly to us by the Nakudala Traditional Council for help with the difficulty of dealing with people who are a problem in the area but whom the council can no longer banish because of the Constitution. Banishment would have been the traditional solution but it is no longer available.

If we move away for a moment from the violent or potentially violent matters in which adult men were involved, this demographic seemed to get into the most conflicts over economic assets, and alcohol was usually involved there also. An example of such an economic conflict is that over a loan of approximately R200[91] between Nkonzo and Bolekile. Nkonzo had waited 14 years for Bolekile to repay the money he had borrowed to travel back home to KwaZulu-Natal when they had both worked in Johannesburg in 1997. He now claimed 10 goats in place of the one Bolekile had originally promised. Since neither of them now worked, the headman's council process yielded agreement on payment of three goats.

In one of the rare instances in which a dispute arose between two parties who were currently employed, the following case came before the chief's council. Mhleli had secured a municipal tender to build houses and invited Mhlanganyeli

90 It could have been because, as the headman in the same ward had had reported to him, *igoso* in this area was not fulfilling his responsibilities as the men in the ward expected.

91 The creditor could no longer recall the exact amount he had loaned his then colleague.

to join him on the project. In the midst of building a house, the tenderer found another job and thus left his recruited colleague in charge of the house that they were building. In the course of the case, Mhlanganyeli said that he had then told Mhleli to pay him R250 per day for his role substitution, but Mhleli denied this. With a witness corroborating the R250 per day, the chief's council found in favour of the recruit who was left with the job. Mhleli objected and said he wanted to take the matter to the Magistrate's court. To our knowledge, he did not do so.

Lest I give the reader the impression that the economic disputes in which adult men are involved are all innocuous or even relatively noble, let me refer to the dispute between Ngenzani and Muntu. The latter committed murder and was arrested for it. When the police interrogated him, Muntu claimed that his friend had perpetrated the offence with him. As a result, Ngenzani had to part with R4,000 in legal fees. Though the criminal case was not yet finalised in the Magistrate's Court, Ngenzani made a claim to get the money back from Muntu, on the basis that the accused had falsely implicated him. The subward council members concluded that the claimant was indeed wrongfully implicated but negotiated a reduction of damages to R3,000.

In another economic matter with dark overtones, readers may recall that a sum of money was outstanding on a car sale that had taken place years before between Babazala and his son-in-law, Mthengi. Babazala's daughter had since died, and this detail seemed very relevant to Babazala's claiming payment at this time. Likewise, a father named Yise developed 'sudden' tension with his son, Ndodana, over the fact that his son had not repaid the father's cow, which Ndodana had used for *lobolo* years before without his father's permission. It turned out that Ndodana had borrowed the cow while Yise was in prison for having assaulted Ndodana. They had not been in good terms since.

A similar conflict took place because of livestock (and an assault) between Yise's sons who fought over a goat. Bhutana claimed that his brother, Thengisile, had sold a goat belonging to him without his permission. Of course, goats were not the only livestock over which adult men fought. For instance, Mlingani had lent Buyisa a cow for *umsebenzi* (a ceremonial feast). They had agreed that Buyisa would replace the cow with another, but he did not do so. After a hearing, the headman's council agreed that Buyisa would repay Mlingani with four goats in the place of his cow.

Goats, and livestock in general, also came up in other ways, such as in an insult in which an adult man was accused of being a witch and stealing people's livestock.[92] This was not the only instance in which one adult male accused another of witchcraft.[93] In most instances, the matter went to a forum and, as in most witchcraft disputes, the witchcraft accusation failed there due to lack of evidence.

92 Thunukala/Thango.

93 Also see Cijimpi/Hlolela; Mzala/Mfowethu; Hlobene/Sakhelene.

Children (up to 14 years old)

After the numerous mentions of paternity disputes, it is obvious to say that children are the objects of those disputes. Yet, of course, in a culture that places a high premium on lineage and name, this is an important area of conflict – not only for the young and adult women who have children outside of marriage but also for the children's own identities and futures. This area of conflict is additionally impacted by the poor economic situation in Msinga, and the risks and dangers faced by children as they grow into young men and women. The seeds of these risks and dangers can perhaps be seen in the conflicts that children are engaged in while young.

Children tend to be engaged in regular instances of insults – especially against adults but also against each other and each other's families. In a place where reputation, family honour and, above all, the show of respect to older persons are still taken seriously as ideals, insults can lead to the need for dispute management. However, while moral commitment to family relations and the honour of the family name remain strong, the strength of family bonds as such is questionable.[94]

In the matter between Chukuluza and Deleliwe, the former girl said to the latter that the latter's younger brother carried witchcraft medicine (potions). Pursuant to the children's families discussing the matter before the headman, Chukuluza and her family were asked to make a public statement in school that her accusation had been false and publicly apologise. In a different dispute, an older man named Mkhulu brought a complaint against Ngane, a child who had insulted him. The child's parents had to make amends by paying damages to the old man. While witness evidence is typically still required in matters in which children are accused of insolence against adults, there does seem to be a modest presumption against the children. This, of course, is in keeping with the general view held by adults in Msinga that children are no longer very respectful of their seniors.

Insults aside, children get involved in assaults as well. Matshe and Hhuzukile, both boys on the cusp of becoming young men, got into a fight and Matshe injured his peer by throwing stones at him. Hhuzukile had to be rushed to the clinic, then on to the hospital, because he was so seriously wounded. As can be expected, amidst the high levels of gun violence, children are also often at real risk of being caught in the crossfires and being severely injured as a result. The example of Phutha – the man who, albeit accidentally, fired over his neighbour's yard while cleaning out the barrel of his gun – comes to mind. As was evident from his neighbour, Zihlalele's, emphasis on the fact that his children had been playing in the yard when this occurred, and that his son had been sitting under the tree through which the bullet travelled, Zihlalele was concerned that his children could have been seriously hurt.

94 See Campbell (above), Hunter (above) and Sathiparsad (above).

In our study, we did not come across any children who were injured except deliberately or in conflicts in which they were directly involved. The one semi-exception is the incident that occurred in a ward that we were not observing and that went directly to the police, in which the young father killed his wife and infant by pummeling them with rocks.[95] It was also mentioned to me repeatedly in the focus groups that when the police raid homes looking for firearms, they use excessive force and show indifference to who is there: 'They don't care – they just beat everything that is in their way: man, woman, child, dog'. I am unable to verify this repeated claim about brutality shown by the police. However, I would argue that what this claim reinforces is the concern that – whether they are the victims directly involved in violence or not – children are, nevertheless, exposed to plenty of violence and its aftereffects.

Group disputes

Finally, it is worth noting that there were instances of the kind of group conflict that Clegg argues is at the root of group violence in Msinga, and people live in heightened awareness of its persistent threat. Only a single boundary land matter explicitly arose in the time that we were doing our data collection. Nevertheless, there were several instances of inter-subward, inter-ward or inter-tribal conflicts and potential conflicts that were averted. Though the conflicts themselves began as interpersonal ones, people in the relevant areas (and especially, the headmen) were aware of the risk these conflicts posed of the outbreak of war.

One palpable illustration of the latter is the conflict – described in the previous chapter – that began with MaDlinzelwa and MaShonile fighting over a money debt in a bar, after which one of the women died (allegedly due to witchcraft by the other). In quick succession, several revenge killings took place, straddling two wards, and some persons involved in the conflict relocated out of fear of being murdered. The relevant chief's council intervened after three deaths had taken place. At this point, rumour pointed to the chief's council secretary and her family being suspected of accommodating supposed *persona non grata*. It was implicit that the secretary's family were next in line for harm. Indeed, her position may have contributed to the speed of the council's intervention. However, the council also had a separate reason for swiftly getting involved: this rapidly escalated conflict was quickly leading toward inter-ward war.

The Vakashile matter concerning the assault of the young man from a different nation when he was visiting his girlfriend is another example – albeit one that was handled in a manner much less consistent with the normative ideal. The matter was heard by the headmen of the two concerned areas together. But, as reported previously, other headmen in the vernacular grouping in which

95 Moshile/Limele.

it happened told me that they would have sent the matter directly to the chief's council, because of how 'delicate' it was. By 'delicate' they meant the risk it posed of the start of inter-tribal war.

I have discussed before the intra-subward war in Okunye that one of the headmen had to intervene in. There had been several instances of killings – by seeming assassins – in one of the subwards in the ward of which this headman was in charge. After a number of nighttime assassinations, he called a subward meeting and invited the police to attend to lend strength and support to this initial attempt at mediation (in case things got out of hand and hard intervention on the part of the police was required). He appealed to the men in the subward to put down their weapons. He felt relatively confident that he and his council's 'talking to' the men of the subward had yielded fruit. Again, unfortunately for the headman, before he could see whether the mediation had been a success, the police raided the homes of the subward's men looking for guns.

One potential land conflict in Kune came to our attention because of the preventative measures taken by one headman to avoid any future dispute with an adjacent ward. Some men had approached Headman Nyanga to ask him to grant them use of certain land for grazing their cattle. When the headman realised that the land requested bordered on another ward, he postponed the meeting so that they could have the headman of the bordering ward be part of the discussion. Headman Nyanga would demarcate the land for their cattle grazing only after consulting the other ward's headman.

When the relevant headman was invited to the next meeting and gave his approval, he expressed his gratitude for the initiating headman's consideration. He appreciated Headman Nyanga's taking such steps when the land at issue did not even form part of Headman Sivumele's ward but only bordered on it. He appreciated this preemptive action as sagacious. As the evidence I have presented shows, Headman Sivumele was right to remark at this approach because though aspired to, prevention or preemptive deterrence is not consistent in the Msinga dispute management space.

An explicit land conflict concerned the dispute around labour tenant land in Yisithupha ward. This was land that had not formed part of the Msinga tribal locations under apartheid but white-owned farms occupied, as labour tenants, by people who self-identified as part of Nezikhathi. These are the places that Alcock describes as causing some discomfort for 'tribal authorities' at the time because they did not have authority over the land but were responsible for accounting for and managing the disputes of those who lived on that land.[96]

After apartheid ended, some of this land was claimed back. However, chiefs (and their Traditional Communities) often thought that the land should be

96 Alcock, Creina in Cousins, Ben, Rauri Alcock, Ngididi Dladla, Donna Hornby, Mphethethi Masondo, Gugu Mbatha, Makhosi Mweli and Creina Alcock (2011) '*Imithetho yomhlaba yaseMsinga:* The Living Law of Land in Msinga District, KwaZulu-Natal'. PLAAS Research Report 43, Cape Town, University of the Western Cape at 24.

returned to the 'tribe'. According to Alcock,[97] in this particular area, the land was 'given back' to the former 'tribes'. In the process, some new Nezikhathi wards were created in May 2001 – Yisithupha was one. Yet, the historical record shows that some of the labour tenants[98] had started an organisation that was funded by the Swedish Free Church Aid (a Christian development agency) to support redistribution claims by former labour tenants in the area. They were successful in securing their area's participation in the Land Reform Pilot Project (March 1995–March 1997)[99] and claiming over 20 farms as residential farmland.[100] However, a land dispute had since ensued between the Wesizwe faction, who were of the view that the headman should place people on certain land in the ward, and the Wabantu faction, who were of the view that the land belongs to – and should be administered by – the former labour tenants.

This long-standing dispute presented the real risk of war but was still being negotiated through periodic meetings hosted by the chief. Unfortunately, the chief was old and sickly so there were many postponements, which caused plenty of frustration.[101] In the end, the chief decided largely in favour of the ward, and members of the labour tenant farm approached the government to try and get the satisfaction they sought. As I observed this dispute from a distance, it perplexed me that both sides were patient and willing to have the chief decide the matter. My reading of the situation was that the labour tenant people wanted to respect the chief – or, put in the negative, did not want to insult him – but did not genuinely expect that they would win the dispute before him.

That said, though, the chief did genuinely seem to try to mediate the dispute rather than adjudicate it. It is just that the mediation outcome seemed – at least, to many of the Wabantu faction – very much skewed in favour of the Wesizwe faction. In brief, his conclusion was that – because the labour tenant farm had been part of the 'tribe' before and its members continued to turn to the ward for some membership benefits, such as dispute management – the contested land was, in fact, to be administered as part of the ward. The headman who had been in place during that whole time was then replaced with a new headman who would not be covered with the stigma of the conflict.

97 Based on an interview on 9 June 2001 with the former Chief Headman of Nezikhathi.

98 See mention in Walker, Cheryl (2008) *Landmarked: Land Claims and Land Restitution in South Africa*. Johannesbury, Jacana Media at 194; Norborg-Jerkeby, Rachel Translated by Cash, Katherine (2006) 'People Changing the World: 40 Years of Diakonia' at 184–190 (accessible at www.diakonia.se/globalassets/documents/diakonia/about-diakonia/book-diakonia_40_years.pdf).

99 Coan, Stephen 'Taking Land Reform to a Village' *The Natal Witness*, 19 May 1998.

100 Ross, K. 'State Has Abandoned Us – New Farmers' *The Daily News*, 7 September 1998. In this article, Jotham Myaka claims that people who are impatient for government services to their acquired land build homes near natural resources like the river – a safety concern that has been named by headmen in other wards.

101 In the meantime, the main leader of the land redistribution movement in the area died. See Coan, Stephen 'Struggle and success' *The Witness*, 15 June 2011 (accessible at http://www.news24.com/Archives/Witness/Struggle-and-success-20150430).

On the positive side, in one of the headmen's reports of what he had done for the day, the headman shared that he had attended a celebration in which three wards were 'pouring water for each other' (*bethelelana amanzi*), meaning they were reconciling. He explained that there had been conflict between the wards in the past, even to the point of war, but they were putting this conflict behind them so that there would be peace between them. They had asked the chief to come, and bless and sanction their reconciliatory celebration.

Concluding remarks

I have argued that gender and age are key elements in the socio-legal space of disputing and the management thereof in Msinga. With that, gun violence is a defining element of the experience of living in Msinga and thus, by extension, a defining element of the disputing environment. This is exacerbated by the plausibility of violence as a conflict management tool and, as I will more fully demonstrate in the following chapter, an inability and ineptness of the available forums at effectively managing and containing some profound conflict.

The personal traits I have described frame the kinds of vulnerabilities and proclivities – and the fears attending to both – that accompany living in Msinga for certain demographic groups. Of course, they do not accomplish this exclusively – other factors certainly matter too. Yet these personal traits also frame the vulnerabilities and strengths that may sway forums toward or away from certain dispute management outcomes. I have, therefore, argued that these, as well as other, personal attributes can meaningfully influence the dispute management process. I showed that mainly social status – whether in terms of one's relationship to men or one's public position – can make a difference to the kind of outcome one gets from the process.

In an attempt to summarise the troubling risks that women in Msinga face, I would say that women are very vulnerable to substantial amounts of gender-based violence. Two additional considerations accompany this reality. First, men seem to carry a great sense of entitlement concerning women, such that even young men behave as though it is wrong for young women to whom they are attracted to reject their overtures. Second, physical violations of women's bodies are understood as wrongs performed against their families rather than personal violations. (Some wrongs – such as sexual harassment – are wholly disregarded.) As a consequence, women are often silent in negotiations over what should be done to address the wrong that they have suffered.

One young woman in a focus group said that she thought it was improper that, when rape cases are settled '*isikhaya*' (at home, between the families of the two parties), the money that is settled upon as damages and compensation goes to the family. She felt that the girl who has been violated should, at least, get the money. She also expressed that she held the unpopular preference that the young man go to prison for what he had done. I will return to the question of solutions in the final two chapters of this book. For now, I will simply flag this as a controversial set of issues needing to be addressed rather urgently.

To be considered with these issues is the reality that women do not know how to make effective use of the state resources that are supposedly available to them. Of course, there is a real question about how available these resources truly are to women in Msinga. It is clear that the police are only notionally available and that social support and counselling are largely absent when, for instance, women are abused or raped. But to the extent that the police and other social services[102] are contactable and should respond to women's concerns, women do not know how to access them in ways that will advance their interests.

For instance, MaNovalo – the older adult woman who was experiencing domestic violence but would not leave because she wanted to hold on to her property – should not have been in such a zero-sum situation. Moreover, in her attempt to scare her husband by once calling the police, the police came, did not find him home, left and did not return or follow-up to see if they could provide her with further assistance. Addressing this set of problems seems to require action on two fronts: first, improving institutional arrangements in place and repairing the existing, malfunctioning systems on the part of the state and the resources it is meant to provide; and, second, providing practical information, building capacity among, and empowering the women themselves.

In summarising the problems relating to men, I would argue that the most serious risk facing Msinga is the extent of young men's involvement in crime – especially that linked to guns and violence. There is a genuine crisis over young men and their futures for a multitude of reasons. They are poor and have little reason, if any, to believe that they will get out of poverty, even with education (a rather poor form of which they obtain in local schools). Gun violence is modelled to them as children and introduced to them while young. Also, the trend seems to be that young men who get involved in deviant conduct progress from delinquency to very large-scale offences. In addition, their families feel helpless to prevent these young men from getting trapped in the cycle of poverty and crime. The police either arrest or release them with no rehabilitation in sight; social services for them seem virtually absent; and once they leave school or are delinquent there, there seem to be no safety nets to catch them. All of this bodes ill for Msinga's future. Intervention is clearly and urgently needed. The question answered in the remaining two chapters is what intervention would succeed.

My primary concern in this project is to understand what role vernacular dispute management forums can realistically play. I began this book suggesting that they are important, especially in remote rural areas – primarily because of forums' accessibility in terms of proximity, cost, speed, form, and language or discourse. I also pointed out that there is much scholarly ambivalence about their benefits

102 For instance, the Family Violence, Child Protection and Sexual Offences Unit discussed by Smythe, Dee (2015) *Rape Unresolved: Policing Sexual Offences In South Africa*. Cape Town, University of Cape Town Press at 6–7, 206–207.

and risks for women.[103] Now it seems surprising that most scholarship does not reject these forums entirely as bearing no profit for women or anyone, except perhaps the adult men that presently compose them.

As often stated in vernacular forums' defence and expounded in the next chapter, the context in which these forums operate is one in which their key function is to enable members of the vernacular groupings they serve to live together well, as people depending on one another for security and often for survival. Those who hold this defensive view usually describe the forums' purpose as 'maintaining harmony'.[104] The picture I have presented in this chapter, however, is not one of harmony. Yet, perhaps, 'harmony' is not necessarily what people want from these forums. Sometimes people need and want the kind of 'justice' that the state courts might provide. Sometimes they want something that perhaps no 'court' can well – or individually – provide. The next chapter must therefore confront the questions of what kind of 'justice' are the vernacular forums asked to deliver and what kind of 'justice', if any, do (and can) they provide.

103 Whitehead, Alice and Dzodzi Tsikata (2003) 'Policy Discourses on Women's Land Rights in Sub-Saharan Africa: The Implications of the Re-Turn to the Customary' *Journal of Agrarian Change*, 3: 104; Nyamu Musembi, Celestine (2002) 'Are Local Norms and Practices Fences or Pathways? The Example of Women's Property Rights' in A. Ana-Na'im (ed.) *Cultural Transformation and Human Rights in Africa.* London, Zed Books at 126–150.

104 Holomisa, Phathekile (2011) 'Balancing law and tradition: The TCB and its relation to African systems of justice administration' 35: 17–22; Koyana, Digby S. and J.C Bekker (1998) *The judicial process in the customary courts of Southern Africa*, Umtata, University of Transkei. Also see Hinz, Manfred O. and Helgard K. Patermann (2006) *The Shade of New Leaves: Governance in Traditional Authority. A Southern African Perspective.* Berlin, Lit. Verlag.

7 Confounding objectives

What do people really want?

When your life may be on the line

A man by the name of Phutha fired a gun over the home of his neighbour, Zihlalele. When the matter came to a dispute management forum, it was quickly established that the firing of the gun had been an accident. Phutha had been cleaning out his firearm, when a bullet was unexpectedly released from its chamber and travelled over Zihlalele's yard.

Not initially knowing that the gun had been fired by accident, Zihlalele would have had a number of options immediately available on discovering that it was his neighbour who had fired the gun for what seemed to be mysterious reasons. First, Zihlalele could have confronted his neighbour directly to find out the reason for the gunfire over his house. Understandably, because Zihlalele would have known that most interpersonal violence happens between people who know each other and how quickly conflicts escalate to violence in his social setting, he elected not to. Zihlalele would have also known that firearms are widely available in his area – and he was certain that the gun had been fired from his neighbour's house and, more than that, by Phutha himself. For these reasons, in this case, Zihlalele evidenced the low social trust that I will argue is endemic as a result of this mix of contextual elements in Msinga.

The second option would have been for Zihlalele to call the police. However, the police were far away, and were known to take up to an hour to rumble over the dirt roads and arrive at any one crime scene. In general, the police are also feared as being an overly extreme solution, because calling the police often results in imprisonment for people with whose lives one's own life is often entwined. In fact, neighbours are commonly mutually dependent, and Zihlalele recalled that things had been good between him and his neighbour, which was why he could not imagine the reason Phutha fired the gun over the house. Zihlalele therefore did not call the police.

In the end, the option that Zihlalele went with was to approach the headman and ask him to mediate the dispute. Zihlalele asked the headman to bring the parties together and reconcile them. He hoped that whatever differences – of which he was unaware – existed between him and his neighbour, this mediation would successfully deter Phutha from further attempting violence.

In a separate matter, a patriarch of a family, Baba Mdala, was continuously being threatened by his nephew, Mshana. Whenever Mshana would see his uncle, he would tell him that he was going to hurt him. The options available to Mdala were similar to Zihlalele's. He could confront his nephew directly. Yet he shared the social knowledge that Zihlalele possessed about the context in which the dispute arose. In particular, Mdala knew that most interpersonal violence was between known entities, even family – and, with broader social trust already low, Mshana had eroded his uncle's personal trust by threatening him directly. Moreover, Mdala had already tried to reason with Mshana. Mdala had approached his nephew to ask why he was making threats, but the young nephew had proven stubborn. Mshana was unemployed and also known to be reckless after an alcoholic beverage. Drunken calls to his uncle's cellphone accounted for a notable number of instances when Mshana threatened Mdala.

For the same reasons as in Zihlalele's case, calling the police was an option but not a highly viable one in this context. Especially because the two men were family, Mdala's life and that of his nephew were very entwined. As the patriarch, Mdala was responsible for carrying out spiritual ceremonies that affected Mshana and the older man had to be present at all family occasions at which Mshana would likely be present also. Thus, pursuing the police as a solution seemed rather extreme. Besides that, the police were known to be quite unreliable and often unhelpful.

Mdala therefore elected to approach the headman for intervention, hoping that he would reason with Mshana and thus somehow deter Mshana from further threats and therefore protect Mdala from what he experienced to be the real risk of fatal harm. The headman was unable to provide this assistance, and the matter was referred to the chief's council for resolution. In the hearing of the matter by the chief's council, Mshana's brother, Zamile, acknowledged that Mshana had wronged their uncle and appealed to the chief's council to allow the matter to return to the family for the sake of peace. Zamile also hoped to avoid having a fine placed on his brother.

Differences between what is desired and what is delivered

As the reader will know from Chapter 2, I have elected to avoid the term, 'dispute resolution' in this project. I instead chose to refer to what is described here as 'dispute management'[1] because this shifted paradigm better takes account of the different milieu in which disputes occur in Msinga than that which is usually assumed when referring to dispute resolution. As detailed throughout this book, in the rural context under consideration, people's lives are deeply interwoven because of mutual dependence for survival and security.

1 This term is used by Merry, Sally Engle (1979) 'Going to Court: Strategies of Dispute Management in an American Urban Neighborhood' *Law & Society Review*, 13: 891 at 899–900.

Because relationships between people in Msinga are profound and interaction regular, and because of several social challenges, conflict occurs recurrently – varying between that which is minor and major.

I have already introduced the interplay between the socio-legal needs that arise in the local area and the judgments made on these needs by the forums that are asked to help meet them. I focused on how this interplay and judgments are informed by pragmatism and personality, and minimally determined by state law. Here, in Chapter 7, I am returning to this interplay between needs and judgments, now emphasising the social dimension – as these underlying socio-economic considerations are rarely articulated expressly when parties bring their disputes to the forums. I focus, here, on how this tension between parties' underlying needs and forums' express conclusions, as well as the forums' attempts at providing solutions, are limited by the forums' own circumstances and means.

In other words, Chapter 3 focused on the dissonance between the forums' legal jurisdiction and the subject-matters that the forums actually deal with. It also emphasised the forum authorities' own agency and its technical effects on the disputes. This current chapter centralises the substantive needs of the communities as they relate to the forums' means, and systematically demonstrates the incapacity of the forums to satisfy the bulk of those needs, as well as the reasons for this incapacity.

I previously suggested that part of the reason for this repeated occurrence – or re-presentation – of disputes might be the vernacular forums' limited capacity to provide the relief that is fundamentally needed by the parties.[2] Chapter 7 builds on this claim by searching beneath the surface of what Msinga people request from the vernacular forums, so as to ascertain why it is that people actually dispute. Put differently, this chapter examines the underlying purposes for which people bring their disputes to the vernacular forums. It is based on the hypothesis articulated in Chapter 2: when people bring their disputes to vernacular forums, they are pursuing objectives other than or more than what they superficially present.[3]

My thesis here is that while people in Msinga might approach the forum with a request for a guilty or not guilty verdict, declaratory order, interdict, repossession, damages or compensation, such is not often the entirety of what they want, if at all. I seek to understand what the parties really do want to get out of the dispute management process and how final of an outcome they wish to have arrived at through the proceedings. This thesis must be read against the historical and political economy background set out in previous chapters, namely, the fact that – despite what the 'harmony model' would have us believe of all

2 Also see Mnisi Weeks, Sindiso (2015–2016) 'Access to Justice?: Dispute Management Processes in Msinga, KwaZulu-Natal, South Africa' *New York Law School Law Review*, 60(1): 227–249.

3 Felstiner, William, Richard Abel and Austin Sarat (1980) 'The Emergence and Transformation of Disputes: Naming, Blaming, Claiming . . .' *Law and Society Review*, 15: 631.

vernacular groupings[4] – relationships in rural South Africa are under tremendous stress.[5] Relational proximity therefore does not prevent regular and often severe conflict from arising.

Violence is rife in Msinga and is partly motivated by the plausibility of violence as a conflict management strategy and wide availability of firearms and alcohol. This violence largely takes on a gendered nature, in the form of violence by men (especially young men) – against other men and against women. In the desperate economic conditions that prevail, the social fabric is tearing and is at risk of doing so irreparably. Disputes that are presented to the vernacular forums for management are therefore overlaid with all of these wider socio-economic issues and the social conflict embedded in them.

Of course, at times, when people approach the vernacular forums, they do say what they want – such as an apology or reconciliation with another. Yet at other times, the yearning underneath a petition needs to be determined by understanding the person's circumstances more broadly. Methodologically speaking, what is instructive in this regard is a combination of observing the transformations undergone by the dispute from its social inception and examining follow-up interviews with both parties after the vernacular management. A wide range of objectives motivating people to bring their cases[6] – or bring other external intervention into their long-standing disputes – emerges from such an assessment of Msinga.

Scholars have long recognised that people who initiate cases do not necessarily seek a single, final decision of the highest forum that issues judgment.[7] This is true of parties to disputes in Msinga, where different kinds of 'satisfaction' are often pursued by activating the vernacular dispute management process, beyond the mere finding of guilt or the absence thereof, or an order that property be restored or that damages and costs be paid. As already mentioned, people can approach vernacular forums in pursuit of publicity of a wrong they have suffered, acknowledgement of the wrong, or an apology. By initiating a formal dispute management process, they can seek to issue a warning to another or shame the other into doing what the complainant wants them to do.

4 Holomisa, Phathekile (2011) 'Balancing law and tradition: The TCB and its relation to African systems of justice administration' 35: 17–22; Koyana, Digby S. and J.C Bekker (1998) *The judicial process in the customary courts of Southern Africa*, Umtata, University of Transkei. Also see Hinz, Manfred O. and Helgard K. Patermann (2006) *The Shade of New Leaves: Governance in Traditional Authority. A Southern African Perspective*. Berlin, Lit. Verlag.

5 Cousins, Ben (2008) 'Characterising "Communal" Tenure: Nested Systems and Flexible Boundaries' in Aninka Claassens and Ben Cousins (eds.) *Land, Power & Custom: Controversies Generated by South Africa's Communal Land Rights Act*. Cape Town, UCT Press, 109–137 at 118 shows that the same is true regarding land administration.

6 Felstiner, Abel and Sarat (above) at 642–643.

7 Galanter at 26 writes of American disputing patterns: 'Many cases are withdrawn or abandoned because the mere invocation of the court served the initiator's purpose of harassment, warning or delay. . . . The invocation of official adjudicatory institutions does not necessarily express either a preference or an intention to pursue the dispute in official forums, to secure the application of official rules, or to obtain an adjudicated outcome. The official system may be invoked, or invocation may be threatened, in order to punish or harass, to demonstrate prowess, to force an opponent to settle, or to secure compliance with the decision of another forum.'

If parties allow the matter to be heard and discussed in the dispute management forum, they might be attempting to prevent fighting or violence, or they may be wanting to be proven right or affirmed. An appeal for a declaratory or monetary order may be intended to compel the other to take financial responsibility more extensively and, along with it, take relational responsibility too.

As is popularly and often exclusively assumed of a context like Msinga's, people might indeed approach a vernacular forum seeking to be reunified with another or to have their ability to continue living together with another re-established. In the socially presumed 'harmony model' of vernacular dispute management, this value is articulated in terms of the vernacular forums being petitioned to ensure (and predominantly achieving) 'harmony'. Another thing people can want to obtain is the simple re-articulation and re-affirmation of purportedly essential and shared values as being truly essential and shared by their vernacular social grouping, at whatever level of social organisation they petition it.

This is a long list and it is not a closed list. The reader can hereby see that there is a range of motives often underlying the initiative people take in bringing a matter. The request for a judgment may, in fact, harbour a significant amount of expectations that are unidentified. This multiplicity of objectives also relates to the motivations for one's performing an offence in the first place.

A question of great import that the study raises in relation to what people might anticipate that the vernacular forums can deliver is: to what extent are vernacular forums able to satisfy these weighty expectations of those who approach them for assistance in instances of dispute? The evidence collected in this study answers this question: the normative ideal claims that the vernacular forums can do more than they can actually do.[8] In fact, the evidence unequivocally points to the fact that vernacular forums can provide only a very small proportion of the relief that is desired – and, in practice, required – of them.

This observation raises critical follow-up questions: What relief can and do the vernacular forums provide? Additionally, what stands in the way of them delivering more of what is asked of them, both directly and indirectly? Furthermore, what are the implications of these forums being asked to deliver more than they are actually able to do?

Underlying motives: what are people really asking the forums for?

From the kinds of matters that come before the vernacular forums outlined in Chapter 3, we can deduce that the forums are asked for a range of things. These include interdicts and restraining orders, restoration of property, compensation and damages. They also extend to declarations of wrongdoing or guilt, rightful possession or ownership, debt, validity of marriage or divorce, custody or

8 See Mnisi Weeks (above) for details.

guardianship and orders of maintenance. Yet, hovering beneath the surface of the relief that parties to disputes in Msinga ask for is often – if not always – a deeper desire and/or need. Such is often unspoken.

Desired relief in bringing a matter

One portrayal of the unspoken need that brings people to dispute management forums is the marital claim in which a husband's family requests that the forum approached ensure the return of a wife who has left the marital home. The underlying desire here is for the restoration of relations that have broken down. The return of their wife is, unfortunately, beyond the purview of the forums to secure for the party that approaches the forum. Yet it is always the first request, and the forums inevitably pursue this as the first and preferred remedy. Scholars would also say that women, especially as wives traded for cattle, represent production – both material and procreative.[9] The economic considerations undergirding these and many other Msinga disputes are represented later in this chapter.

The same forum limitations pertaining to the desires and needs at the root of requested relief can also be observed with respect to paternity claims. On the part of the 'illegitimate' child's mother is a desire for validation. For her, the child must be acknowledged by the father's family in order for her child to bear the father's name and thus have access to and be protected by his ancestors. Moreover, as a woman who has had a child outside of marriage, socially speaking, she at least needs the father to take responsibility for the child and pay damages to her family. These forms of social acknowledgement give her some degree of dignity. Even if she does not win the case, bringing the matter at all gives her publicity, hence signalling her seriousness about the matter and thus her sincerity or certainty concerning the child's identity.

In one of the paternity disputes in our data,[10] there is obviously an underlying appeal for the vernacular forum to intervene in the breakdown of relationships within the family also – especially between the son, Kanankinga, and his mother, who denied her 'illegitimate' grandchild. This appeal shelters concerns regarding the respect that the young are traditionally required to show toward their elders, such as the son's allowing his mother to choose her daughter-in-law. Economic concerns play a role here also. Successfully refusing to acknowledge the child as legitimately part of the grown son's family means that the son is under no obligation to pay maintenance for the child. This could be the mother's way of preserving her son's wealth for herself rather than standing to lose it to the 'illegitimate' child.

9 See, for example, Guy, Jeff (1990) 'Gender Oppression in Southern Africa's Precapitalist Societies' in C. Walker (ed.) *Women and Gender in Southern Africa to 1945*. Cape Town, David Philip, 33–47.

10 Kanankinga/Landula; Nhlamba/Yala; Sukela/Fanele.

With the paternity cases one can align frequent occurrence of cases surrounding virginity or dating relationships. Similar to matters regarding paternity, such cases relate to the girl's dignity in the vernacular grouping. Even more important than having a child acknowledged and accepted by his/her paternal kin, a girl's being a virgin is of great significance and honour for her and her family.[11] Thus, if someone accuses her of being a 'wife', as in Ntombi's case, litigating the matter to defend the honour of the girl – and, it is supposed, to prove her innocence – is important. Likewise, if someone says that she is dating a young man,[12] especially another girl's boyfriend,[13] it is worth fighting over in order to send the message and purportedly prove that she is innocent and thus reclaim her public honour and dignity. Unsurprisingly in this context, the same set of expectations does not apply to young men.

A category of disputes where this issue of respect emerges more flagrantly is that of insults. These matters take a number of different forms. They often arise between young and older people when it is evident that the issue is one of breakdown in social fabric and intergenerational relations, especially regarding hierarchy, older people's authority, and related social expectations.[14]

This same set of concerns around respect, the authority of the elders, and expected social behaviour is embedded in a number of other disputes. One example is the intimidation case between Mdala and Mshana, in which the uncle who was actually the patriarch of the family was afraid of his nephew who kept threatening to kill him. Equally, these issues are at stake in the stock theft case in which older family members – and particularly the patriarch of the family, Baba Siphethe – were meant to intervene and stop the young men, Ginsa and Bambisene, from further thefts of other people's livestock but had thus far been unable to do so.

In the same way that witchcraft, whistleblowing, and stock theft accusations are brought to the public's attention, especially to 'smoke out' the guilty party, a person privately accused of such wrongs can use forums to try to defend him/herself. Thus, while witchcraft cases typically indicate the social marginality of the accused – and mostly that of women – these cases can still be used by both sides of the conflict to pursue something that either party needs. Albeit that the vernacular grouping often uses the formal initiation of a witchcraft dispute to reveal the guilt of the suspect or accused, the vernacular grouping is not necessarily the only one to use publicity as a strategy, and this purpose of fact-finding is not this strategy's only use.

A benefit that parties often try to get from the publicity that comes with bringing a dispute before a forum is increased security. A woman privately alleged to practice witchcraft can bring the matter to public attention in order to prevent the insidious spread of the rumour and take a stand for her

11 It also is a cultural and social reason for boys to try to win her.
12 Zifakile (and Sesheli)/Nqabile.
13 Sicabha/Sheliwe.
14 See, for instance, Biziwe.

innocence. Publicly denying the accusation against her, she can argue to the vernacular grouping that she is innocent and request that it assist her in finding the party that is truly guilty. By taking this stance as one who is a member of the grouping and even at its mercy, she can reduce her marginalisation and advocate for her protection by the vernacular grouping, rather than submit to her opposition and punishment by the same. While I did not see this strategy used in whistleblowing or stock theft cases, my reading of the data we collected is that it could be – though in the case of snitching and stock theft, it would be largely young men who were implicated.

As lengthily discussed in the previous chapter, another set of disputes that suggest a subtext of insecurity in Msinga are adultery and domestic violence (even that leading to death). The two kinds of disputes point primarily to women's heightened insecurity and vulnerability, both material and physical. In MaNovalo's case, discussed previously, she was the subject of severe domestic violence who refused to leave the marital property because, she said, she was not going to let this property for which she had worked so hard go to another woman, who was having an affair with her husband. MaNovalo was willing to risk her husband killing her. This stance supports what I have written elsewhere about the lack of material security women have if they become separated from their husbands.[15] Other instances that bear out women's physical insecurity include arson,[16] rape,[17] and other forms of sexual assault, many of which are discussed in the previous chapter.

A primary concern that runs through many requests for relief in Msinga disputes is that for compensation. In the estimation of the Nakudala traditional council secretary, a big motivation in bringing matters before the vernacular forums is that people want to be compensated for their loss, particularly in criminal matters. She reported instances when the chief's council would hear criminal matters only in terms of the parties having asked that damages be paid to them pursuant to a crime. She provided an example of a case in which the family claimed in the vernacular forum for compensation/damages in the form of funeral costs amounting to R8,000.[18] The evidence we collected bears this out. We recorded this kind of claim being made in the instance when Buhlungu (accidentally) killed his distant cousin in relation to the rape that his cousin had allegedly perpetrated against Buhlungu's daughter, Sphiwo.

15 Mnisi Weeks, Sindiso (2013) 'Women's Eviction in Msinga: The Uncertainties of Seeking Justice' *Acta Juridica*, 118–142. In the same article, I reflected that domestic violence is not uncommon in Msinga. Again, this offence is not separately reported in the police statistics.

16 Msinga police recorded 12 counts of arson as being reported to them in 2011 and 23 in 2012.

17 The police recorded 54 sexual offences in 2011 and 82 in 2012.

18 The secretary observed that, though the understanding is often that the damages are paid in lieu of charges being pressed, sometimes families will go on to have the case heard in the Magistrate's Court too and thus have the guilty party arrested also.

The repeated emphasis on the importance of compensation is a legacy of the precolonial past, when that was the primary way of dealing with disputes, even fatal ones – other than by capital punishment. However, this emphasis is so vehemently preserved partly because of the economic conditions of extreme poverty and unemployment in Msinga and the material needs of the families that suffer loss – especially in a context in which there are regular deaths and burials due to AIDS and crime. Most understandable is the case of a family that must bury the deceased family member who is killed and support his surviving dependents. But this is not the only instance in which claims for compensation are made, as the deceased need not have dependents.

Because of the living conditions in Msinga, commercial relationships are fragile, and for economic and other relational reasons, the social trust within which these relationships take place is low. For this reason many commercial disputes presented to the vernacular forums pertain to unsettled loans,[19] non-delivery of objects agreed for exchange, or non-payment of damages for another wrong. Examples include a car sale gone wrong,[20] and the non-delivery of the replacement cow agreed upon for a cow borrowed,[21] for instance. While it is obvious to say that people are definitely asking the vernacular forums for help apportioning and reapportioning the limited economic assets and resources, I would argue that there is more that is being asked of the forums also.

The commercial disputes are often surrounded by pettiness or envy. But often even non-commercial disputes are surrounded by similar pecuniary interests and the jealousies and resentments that seem to accompany them. This tendency is true whether the non-commercial disputes then later grow to encompass economic assets or not – for instance, when pre-existing tension between father and son is later transformed by the son using his father's cow for lobolo without his father's permission.[22]

One must remember that Msinga is a society that traditionally places great emphasis on symbiosis and, more than that, on mutual dependence. Furthermore, as previously discussed, the contemporary reality of people's lives harkens back to this tradition, at least rhetorically, and in many ways still by necessity. In these circumstances, the bitterness that undergirds many disputes points to more than Msinga's being a society in which economic want is significant and widespread. Such bitterness also signals that those who have more in Msinga are, in fact, envied and even resented – at least, by some. In other words, in keeping with what is argued by some of the literature on witchcraft accusations,[23]

19 For instance, Nkonzo/Bolekile.

20 Babazala/Mthengi.

21 Mlingani/Buyisa.

22 Yise/Ndodana. Also see Babazala/Mthengi; MaLwimi.

23 See, for example, Comaroff, Jean and John L. Comaroff (eds.) (1993) *Modernity and Its Malcontents: Ritual and Power in Postcolonial Africa*. Chicago, IL: Chicago University Press; Stewart, Pamela J. and Andrew Strathern (2003) *Witchcraft, Sorcery, Rumors and Gossip*. Cambridge: Cambridge University Press, West Nyack, NY, USA at 66.

these attitudes suggest that the difficult economic reality has a notable and fraught impact on the social compact and fabric. I would therefore argue that a way of understanding the needs often implicit in commercial (and related private, public and criminal) disputes is not only as a subdued attempt at redistribution of assets and wealth but also as a scramble to try to maintain a heavily degraded social compact.

People in Msinga often turn to the forums with more superficial – yet not unimportant – requests for relief, such as money and other possessions and punishments. Yet I think one can summarise the fundamental intangibles for which people in Msinga *really* appeal to the forums in three primary categories. First, people seek to shore up their public stature. As shown, the publicity given by the dispute management process through the vernacular forums is used to verify personal honour, demonstrate one's certainty and the truth of one's socially significant claim, as well as establish one's innocence and secure a modicum of dignity. This strategy is in large part a claim – or, in cases brought by those who are powerful, an assertion – of power. The paternity disputes are a key example of disputes in which those with diminished power, namely young women and their 'illegitimate' children, petition the forums to secure their dignity and status in their society.

Second, people petition the forums for peace and security. In a setting in which being marginal to one's vernacular grouping is a threat to one's safety, people at the margins appeal to the vernacular forums to overturn suspicion of their being a threat to the vernacular grouping and ask the forums to protect them from the consequent risk of mob justice performed by the same grouping. Again, publicity is the complainants' primary tool. Yet, beyond those at the margins, all people who turn to the vernacular forums, especially in the context of criminal disputes, seek for the forums to keep them safe in a situation in which people's lives are at near-constant risk. In the language used in the field of human development, people in Msinga turn to the forums in pursuit of 'freedom from fear'.

Adopting a more expansive notion of security and thus looking beyond physical security to include material security, one can say that a significant part of what people in Msinga seek – and ask the vernacular forums to help them attain in the contexts of their disputes – is 'freedom from want'. This need is evident from the multitude of cases that, ultimately, implicate economic assets or imply such concerns. Though both men and women seek this freedom, as demonstrated in Chapter 6, women are particularly, structurally vulnerable in this regard. Put simply, therefore, what is wanting in Msinga is 'human security' in its totality.[24]

24 The Human Development Report issued by the United Nations Development Programme (UNDP) in 2004 observes that both 'freedom from fear' and 'freedom from want' (thus referring to the human right of persons to have an adequate standard of living) compose the solution to global insecurity. (Also see Preamble to the Universal Declaration of Human Rights, 1948.)

Third, and perhaps most significant because it lies at the root of human insecurity – people in Msinga seek the restoration of their social fabric. One sees this desire in disputes over the legitimation of children born outside of marriage, for example. The 'illegitimate' children can be denied their rightful name, and family and spiritual connections, which everyone agrees are of paramount social and spiritual significance – often for reasons related to economic considerations, power plays, and other resentments. Practically, there is a palpable sense of relational breakdown and the felt need for repair. What this means, more expansively, is that the social compact that exists between people in Msinga has been eroded, and social trust is consequently low. The vernacular forums are therefore routinely asked, essentially, to re-establish social trust and restore the social compact.

Desired relief in committing an offence

Similar themes of underlying desires and needs being pursued by parties arise in the context of the offences that people commit. The reader will recall that I am taking a longer-term view of disputes in this project: one that is not confined to formal or institutionalised processes of dispute management. Thus, because wrongs are often committed in the form of self-help measures against prior wrongs, many offences are in fact transformations of disputes rather than originations of disputes. For instance, when the deceased husband's family denies a wife like MaLahlekelwe the ability to bury her husband where she sees fit, this usually follows from existing and even long-standing tensions.

In the context of disputes over material assets, such a step by the marital family can manifest as a way of holding on to long-lost power, if they have lost the battle over the pecuniary assets. Likewise, as in the example of MaSalelwe, if the wife died prior to her husband's family completing payment of her *lobolo*, her birth family can refuse her burial in the marital family's area. If the husband died first, as in MaSele's situation, her birth family can refuse that she wear mourning attire – a spiritually required show of respect in marking her husband's death. To the extent that social relations are relatively weak and the social compact is deficient by extension, in these instances, there is not much that the forums can do about it.

On the part of the perpetrator, a violent response to a perceived injurious experience (PIE) suggests either a lack of faith in the existing justice system or a conception of self-help in the form of violence as a legitimate part of this existing justice system,[25] or both. Louise Meintjes summarises this point well:

> When official institutions designed to control violence are insufficient, when the reach, degree, spread, integration, and mobility of violence, as well as the multiplicity of its sources, networks, and forms, leave the state

25 This is what I have termed the plausibility of violence as conflict management.

> incapacitated, citizens themselves develop practices of danger management through alternative institutions, communal organization, and personal commitments. Citizens implicated in violence manage the threat to their sense of moral order and to the order of their daily lives through discourse about violence, through performance, and through action.[26]

When people are faced with events or circumstances that threaten their own sense of security and well-being and the legally available means of addressing conflict are inadequate or unsatisfactory, people will turn to alternative – even illegal and violent – means to address the threat.

Consider MaThembile's case one last time. The step of attempting to kill the suspected goat killer suggests tremendous decline in social relations. This is so even if you accept that, as informants told me, 'a goat is like a person'. If the social compact was strong and MaThembile was not seen to be marginal or even an enemy to the vernacular grouping to which the compact applied – or, alternatively, if the mechanisms available in Msinga were thought adequate to the task of managing such disputes and if violence was not seen as a legitimate option – the attempted murder of MaThembile would likely not have occurred. This set of hypotheticals would hold even if MaThembile were known to be guilty of what she was suspected.

This same reliance on self-help as a legitimate and highly competitive alternative to the forums is evident in the matter concerning Gangile and Mngani. The two young men alleged that they were assaulted and, in the process, robbed by a minibus full of local men on the way back from a celebration in a different part of Msinga. These men told Gangile and Mngani that they were beating them up as retaliation for the public nuisance these young men caused through their own criminality.

What stands out in many of the matters in which people resort to self-help, especially in the form of violence, are two things. The first is a sense of helplessness. When one brings a matter to the vernacular forums and does not get real relief – either because the forum does not arrive at a conclusive resolution or seems unable to enforce the decision it has made – one is left with few options. In these cases, as previously discussed, people resort to self-help, alternative forums that do not form part of the vernacular dispute management system, or to vigilantism.

This was evident in the example of Webile's father who felt unable to stop his son from getting involved in ever-increasing delinquency, which had escalated to quite serious criminal activity. The father identified the issue as a problem of discipline and felt at his wits' end because he felt that he was without real control. The headman's council had recently found the unemployed father responsible for the son's theft of R50,000. The father had even gone to the

26 Meintjes, Louise (2017) *Dust of the Zulu: Ngoma Aesthetics after Apartheid*. Durham, NC, Duke University Press at 164.

police to ask them to take his son for some sort of intervention but they had said that this was not their job.

But I would argue that this sense of helplessness now pervades the climate in Msinga so much that it defines people's expectations before they even approach the vernacular forums – to the extent that they do not always even approach the forums first. If people do not employ endurance or avoidance, people may turn to the alternative (often vigilante) tribunals, mob justice performed by segments of the vernacular grouping or violent action taken by an individual. In light of the pervasive sense of helplessness, these methods are largely responses to and attempts to compensate for the system's deficiencies or even failure.

This kind of action occurred in Ntombi's case when she was accused of not being a virgin. As previously noted, after the matter had been appealed to the chief's council and the headman had attempted to enforce the order of damages for over a year and a half, the father of the defamed young woman took the matter to *isikebhe* for them to hear and resolve it. As it is generally known, *isikebhe* is strong on enforcement because it does not hesitate to use violence, which the vernacular forums are no longer permitted to do. If people can go to such lengths as to turn to *isikebhe* with its violent enforcement authority on a matter that is not one of life and death, how much more so can they when the matter is a life or death situation?

Of course, it is not a necessary consequence of people's frustration with the justice system that they resort to forms of violence that regularly lead to fatalities. Vigilantism and violent self-help in Msinga are surely also representative of attitudes towards violence and the reduced value of life, as already discussed in the previous chapter. This is therefore the second thing that stands out with respect to the use of violent self-help measures in Msinga: the speedy escalation in matters, from squabbles ('*imibango nje*') to violence that often results in serious injuries or casualties, shows how undervalued life is in some ways in Msinga. It also reflects the ready availability of arms that slots into a milieu in which fighting and feuding are part of the cultural store.

When the vernacular forums are deemed unable to deliver the desired relief – or not even given a chance – and matters turn violent, it is the fragility of life in Msinga that makes 'violence as conflict management' plausible. As argued, this frailty – or reduced value – of life must be understood in the context of life being cheapened by people having very little materially. Moreover, it is undergirded by people's burying loved ones with regularity due to the impact of AIDS and the high levels of human insecurity they experience which render violence part of the ordinary course of events in their lives. These factors make violence as self-help not only ordinary but also arguably compelling (and, hence, highly plausible) as a course of action.

It is in this context that retaliation by means of violence is not unusual. As retaliation, self-help measures can re-ignite dormant disputes. If the vernacular forums manage these self-help measures, they often fundamentally handle them as though they were original conflicts when they are, in fact, transformations of pre-existing, and frequently long-standing, conflicts. The forums do this, despite explicitly acknowledging that they are part of an extended and pre-existing conflict, by failing to address the problems systemically. This, arguably, further legitimates self-help measures and almost integrates them into the dispute management 'game'. Put differently, self-help becomes a complement to the system – a complement about which there is some uneasiness and ambivalence.

Possible relief: what can the forums deliver?

I have presented a rather dismal picture of what the vernacular forums are asked for and largely unable to deliver. Some readers may conclude that we should be rid of the forums entirely. I would not jump to such a conclusion before taking a look at what the forums *are* able to provide. I would argue that there are three primary things they can offer: a space for venting, affordability and improved relationships. However, they do not entirely achieve all three of these things as yet. As I will present more fully below, the vernacular forums are devoid of the tools necessary for them to effectively manage the degree and scale of social conflict and violence that is habitual in Msinga. Because of this, I would argue that the primary value they offer revolves around their role as mediated discursive spaces but they have yet to fulfil their potential for serving this role optimally.

Scholars note that disputants 'expect mediators to have goals of bringing about agreement . . . allowing the disputants to blow off steam . . . using efficiency/speed . . . and overseeing restitution.'[27] These goals are mostly accomplished in Msinga, though imperfectly so because, as I have discussed, the forums sometimes compel agreement in a manner that appears more like arbitration or adjudication than mediation. The goals are also imperfectly met because sometimes the solution is poorly or unsuccessfully enforced.

There are many potential goals of mediation that I would argue that vernacular forums presently barely meet, if at all. Particularly, these goals include

> improving the relationship between the disputants . . . attaining social justice . . . and social transformation . . . reducing sexual discrimination . . . preventing future conflicts . . ., solving problems . . ., forestalling future problems . . . reducing future costs . . . reducing violence . . . improving

27 Wall, James and Timothy Dunne (April 2012) 'State of the Art: Mediation Research: A Current Review' *Negotiation Journal*, 28(2): 217–244 at 226. Also see their references: Firestone, Gregory (2008) 'Empowering Parents in Child Protection Mediation: Challenges and Opportunities' *Family Court Review*, 47(1): 1–16; Bleemer, Russ (2009) 'The Rest of the Sept. 11 Cases–Those That Went to Court–Are Settled Via Mediation' *Alternatives to the High Cost of Litigation*, 27(5): 92–94; Umbreit, Mark. S., Robert B. Coates and Ann Warner Roberts (2000) 'The Impact of Victim-Offender Mediation: A Cross-National Perspective' *Mediation Quarterly*, 17(3): 215–229.

communication between the disputants . . . reducing stress . . . integrating relationships.[28]

A different way of characterising the various mediation objectives is in terms of the following categories: venting; improved communication and relations; agreement on problem solution; oversight and enforcement of agreed solution; prevention of repeat or future conflict; social justice and social change (including the reduction of systemic violence); efficiency and cost-effectiveness of process.

From these categories, what the vernacular forums unequivocally enable is easily accessible venting at very low financial cost – in other words, two of the three things I said that they could provide. Their primary means of delivering a place to vent is more-or-less inclusive,[29] participatory and deliberative discursive spaces in every vernacular grouping at whatever level of social organisation. As the reader will recall, publicity plays a significant role, and people can acquire that very quickly and economically by gathering their vernacular grouping to hear a matter of concern for them. In the context of the complexity of existing relationships the spaces provided for publicity by the vernacular forums are indispensible. The challenge is that they are not being used to optimal effect.

These same spaces are intended to facilitate better communication and generate highly enforceable – and effectively enforced – agreements. At present, vernacular forums modestly facilitate communication, though not necessarily improved communication; they generate agreement, though it is often mandatory or imposed agreement; and these authorities may provide some oversight of the implementation of presumptive agreements, but with limited actual

28 Wall and Dunne (above) at 226. Also see their references: Craig, Tara (2008) 'Firing off . . . ? Mediation' *Personnel Today*, 22 July: 9; Neves, Tiago (2009) 'Practice Note: Community Mediation as Social Intervention' *Conflict Resolution Quarterly*, 26(4): 481–495; Li-On, Lee (2009) 'The Politics of Community Mediation: A Study of Community Mediation in Israel' *Conflict Resolution Quarterly*, 26(4): 453–479; Stallworth, Lamont E., Thomas McPherson and Larry Rute (2001) 'Discrimination in the Workplace: How Mediation Can Help' *Dispute Resolution Journal*, 56: 35–44; Wort, Matthew (2009) 'How to Nip Conflict in the Bud' *Birmingham Post*, 15 July: 31; Zwier, Paul J. and Thomas F. Guernsey (2010) *Advanced Negotiation and Mediation Theory and Practice*. South Bend, IN, National Institute for Trial Advocacy; Kay, Julie (2009) 'Home Settling: Foreclosure Mediation Grows, but Some Wonder If It's the Best' *ABA Journal*, 95: 14–15; Kloppenberg, Lisa A. (2001) 'Implementation of Court-Annexed Environmental Mediation: The District of Oregon Pilot Project' *Ohio State Journal on Dispute Resolution*, 17(3): 559–596; Mazadoorian, Harry N. (2009) 'First (Mediation) Step: Stop the Shooting' *Alternatives to the High Cost of Litigation*, 27(2): 17–22; Portman, Tarrell Awe Agahe (2009) 'Faces of the Future: School Counselors as Cultural Mediators' *Journal of Counseling and Development*, 87(1): 21–27; Wiseman, Ellidh (2008) 'Make the Most of Mediation in Disputes' *Personnel Today*, 1 July: 9; Stimmel, Andrew (2002) 'Mediating Will Disputes: A Proposal to Add a Discretionary Mediation Clause to the Uniform Probate Code' *Ohio State Journal on Dispute Resolution*, 18(1): 197–224.

29 Readers will recall that they are less inclusive of women and young people.

enforcement. In keeping with the 'harmony model', the forums are also supposed to achieve improved relations, prevention of more conflict between the parties as well as broader social change and social justice (and, with it, human security). They scarcely achieve these things. In part, this is because they do not in fact catalyse genuine and fully voluntary agreement between the parties. Let me illustrate the point.

In the example of MaMakhe and MaMsolwa, visited in Chapter 2, the original conflict between the two women was over the fact that one was persuaded that the other's child had stolen her child's cellphone. When the suspected home of MaMsolwa was searched by surrounding neighbours, the cellphone was not found, yet this did not stop the aggrieved MaMakhe from continuing to hold the view that it was her neighbour's family that had stolen it. A while later, MaMakhe accused MaMsolwa of witchcraft. That dispute terminated at the chief's council, where it was concluded that the aggrieved MaMakhe had been wrong and should pay damages to her neighbour, MaMsolwa.

The dispute we were now witnessing at the headman's council was one in which MaMakhe's daughter had now accused the same neighbour of being a witch when she had seen MaMsolwa speaking to another neighbour outside her family's gate at dawn. This iteration of the dispute concluded with the headman's council asking MaMakhe to pay a goat (on behalf of her daughter) that would be slaughtered in a ceremony to cleanse MaMsolwa's name and home. The headman's council said that this would enable the parties to forgive each other and 'return to living alongside each other as neighbours as before'.

Without fully airing and effectively addressing the original source of conflict and the hurt it had left, however, the parties could not return to good neighbourliness. This was a conflict merely ready to find expression again in yet another dispute. In fact, the repeated punishments received by the initially aggrieved MaMakhe, who still believed that the cellphone had been stolen by MaMsolwa's family, only compounded the resentment that she and her children felt toward MaMsolwa and her family. Hence, the vernacular forums have perpetually failed to restore relations between these women and their progeny.

As I have already begun to do with particular attention to the process and strategies the vernacular forums use, let me share the broader systemic, socio-political reasons for why the forums are unsuccessful at providing the relief that people are really seeking when they approach them.

Obstacles to providing required relief: why can the forums not deliver the relief really being asked for?

The relief for which the vernacular forums are asked is not always easy for them to deliver. The primary reason for this is that the relief that they are asked for is often a proxy for some more significant systemic, socio-political intervention that they are not able to provide at all or can only provide with great difficulty and, even then, are dependent on the assistance of other institutions. I return to the two incidents described in the opening of this chapter, for illustration.

Besides the basic facts, what made the difference between the two cases of Zihlalele and Mdala? One significant difference was that the conflict between Zihlalele and his neighbour, Phutha, was a falsely perceived conflict, not a real one. By contrast, the conflict between Mdala and his nephew, Mshana, was very real, and though the chief and his council tried, they were unsuccessful at resolving it. Therefore, while both matters were potentially of deadly significance, and wholly rooted in the endemic socio-economic and political challenges of life and dispute management in Msinga, the realness of the one made it virtually impossible for the vernacular forum to remedy. This is what primarily led to the difference in outcomes.

In Zihlalele's case, the headman was able to facilitate a successful agreement. The neighbour said that he had been cleaning out the barrel of his gun in his yard when the shot accidentally fired. With that explanation, which was acceptable to Zihlalele, the matter was concluded by the headman instructing the two men to shake hands.

Quite different was Mdala's case, where no solution was – or could – be provided by the vernacular forums alone, if at all. First, the nephew denied that he had threatened his visibly fearful uncle. The chief's council thus threw up its hands and said there was nothing it could do. At Mshana's older brother's appeal, the council directed the two men to have the matter managed by their family council. Mdala objected to this suggestion because he was the patriarch of the family and was therefore the chair of the family dispute management council; if his nephew was threatening *him*, then the family council was clearly not a sufficiently authoritative forum to resolve their dispute.

In response to his objection, the chief's council then instructed Mdala to take his matter to the police. The difficulty, however, which Mdala did not seem to have the words to articulate, is that the police do not deal with matters that have not yet ripened. Though the police were unlikely even to suggest it to Mdala, all they could do for him is instruct him to get a restraining order. Yet, that would be difficult to enforce between Mdala and his nephew – given their deeply, socially embedded kinship ties and the regularity of their interactions, by necessity. Also contributing to the reduced likelihood of a restraining order's enforcement, in case of the order's violation by his nephew, was the distance between the place where their interactions occur and the police station.

Mdala left the forum adamant that his life was under threat and feeling helpless. Headmen interviewed after the hearing were frustrated at Mdala's dissatisfaction, as they said there was nothing they could do in this matter and seemed to think him unreasonable for not embracing this fact. As a final option, they invited Mdala to report to the council secretary with the outcome of the family discussions and told him that he could bring the matter back to the chief's council if discussions were unsuccessful.

While different, Zihlalele and Mdala's matters have a few key things in common. First, their problems are about personal safety and security threatened by another – that is, they are interpersonal problems. Second, their problems are embedded in broader socio-economic conditions that are beyond their individual control – that is, social justice challenges at local group and, more broadly, national level.[30]

Third, in light of these broader socio-economic conditions, and assuming for a moment that Zihlalele's matter was a *real* conflict rather than a perception error, each of Zihlalele's and Mdala's appeals to their local vernacular authorities are for more than the authorities can easily or effectively deliver, solely, in the context of the mediation that they provide. In other words, in both cases (if both were real) the vernacular forums alone would not be able to provide the full suite of services needed to resolve the matters presented to them. However, as I have suggested in the previous section, by improving their use of tested mediation strategies[31] to manage the disputes presented to them, forums could go further toward resolving the problems than they do.

What I am arguing is that there is a disjuncture between the ultimate goals sought of the mediation – namely peace and security – and the often-disappointing outcomes of local mediation. Vernacular forums cannot deliver security in the present context without greater support and willing collaboration from state organs. I would therefore argue that, beyond the mere dispute management processes used by vernacular forums, this disjuncture between the forums' mediation goals and the necessary outcomes is mostly to do with the ineffectiveness of the national cooperative governance model in existence in South Africa.

Without this support from the broader justice system (the state justice system), the vernacular forums are indeed devoid of the tools necessary for them to effectively manage the degree and scale of social conflict and violence that is habitual in Msinga. In this instance, I would still maintain that the primary value the vernacular forums offer in the form of mediated discursive spaces is meaningful and can become even more so with internal changes. Yet, I would be less optimistic about the possibility of the vernacular justice system in Msinga offering access to justice in the formal sense of the notion.

Concluding remarks

All of the implied weakness – and, really, failures – of the vernacular justice system are, in my view, encompassing of interpersonal and social justice problems. But, more than that, they are representative of systemic, institutional failure. I have argued that the failure is embodied in the vernacular forums' internal process as well as in the cooperative governance system supposedly in place in South Africa.[32] I would point to the severe, systemic resource limitations with which the vernacular forums are confronted. Additionally, I would

30 Crime in Msinga is not too much out of keeping with the rest of South Africa where, in 2015/16 murder happened at a rate of 33.9 per 100,000; rape at 77.43 per 100,000; common assault at 299.9 per 100,000 and assault GBH at 332.5 per 100,000.

31 See Wall and Dunne (above) at 226–229.

32 See Chapter 3 of the Constitution of the Republic of South Africa.

highlight the lack of cooperation between state and traditional authorities, largely because the police do not show – or are at least perceived not to show – real respect to the vernacular forums.

It would be too easy – and inaccurate – to attribute all blame to the failure of the cooperative governance system to provide the support necessary to make access to justice truly possible through the vernacular system, or at all, in Msinga. Part of the problem is that the vernacular forums themselves, partly because of historic sentiment that makes them position themselves competitively against the state institutions, feel the urge to do more than they actually can do. This sentiment is exacerbated by a lack of clarity about which authority belongs to whom. It is also partly founded on competing cultural values, in which the state system does not sufficiently understand or respect the vernacular value system, and vice versa.

I alluded in Chapter 4 to the turf wars taking place between the vernacular and state authorities as they attempt to defend their jurisdiction and, by extension, their very existence. The vernacular authorities also tend to act out this competition in unproductive ways, such as taking on an authoritarian stance in dispute management – acting more like arbitrators – when their strength is in providing a participatory, deliberative healing process to local people.[33]

But neither is the lack of cooperation all the fault of the vernacular forums. As I have tried to show, because of the relative incompetence of the police in approaching and managing problems in this particular context, as well as the inadequate presence or sheer absence of the state and its resources in Msinga,[34] vernacular forums are asked to try to do more than they can reasonably do.[35]

33 See Mnisi Weeks (2015–2016).

34 Msinga has fewer police personnel per 100 000 than Khayelitsha where a Commission of Inquiry found, at 315, that 'poor areas where the majority of residents are African or Coloured have the lowest numbers of police per population. Many of these areas have very high levels of serious violent crime.' See 'Towards a Safer Khayelitsha: Report of the Commission of Inquiry into Allegations of Police Inefficiency and a Breakdown in Relations between SAPS and the Community of Khayelitsha', August 2014, Commissioners, Justice Catherine O'Regan (Chairperson) and Advocate Vusumzi Pikoli at 260, 315–317 and 449–451 (accessible at www.khayelitshacommission.org.za/images/towards_khaye_docs/Khayelitsha_Commission_Report_WEB_FULL_TEXT_C.pdf).

35 Studies show that living in poor and crime-ridden settings can cause severe, chronic post-traumatic stress and depression. See, for example, Hong, Sunghyun and Inger Burnett-Zeigler (2016) 'The Frequency of PTSD and Subthreshold PTSD among African: American Women with Depressive Symptoms in a Disadvantaged Urban Neighborhood: Pilot Study' *Journal of Racial and Ethnic Health Disparities*; Lowe, Sarah R., James W. Quinn, Catherine A. Richards, John Pothen, Andrew Rundle, Sandro Galea, Kerry J. Ressler, Karestan C. Koenen and Bekh Bradley (2016) 'Childhood Trauma and Neighborhood-Level Crime Interact in Predicting Adult Posttraumatic Stress and Major Depression Symptoms' *Child Abuse and Neglect*, 51: 212–222. The headmen are expected to deal with their own trauma and also help other people manage their trauma and arrive at resolutions for their problems. This is an unfair and, arguably, impossible task for the government to leave on the shoulders of these men who, at the time of this study, were also unpaid for their work.

They are implicitly required to act as a hybrid between police, mediator, prosecutor, defender, arbitrator, judge, and *amicus curiae*.[36] This is an impossible task – not to mention, an exhausting task – largely put on the forums because of the inadequate training, or lack of training, of state police and other authorities to navigate this particular milieu.[37]

An additional challenge that contributes to the vernacular authorities' (especially the headmen's) wearing many hats is their degree of social embeddedness, which can often lead to a lack of impartiality and at least the appearance of bias. Impartiality is not an inherent and objective good.[38] However, partiality must be subjected to constraints as necessary in the context of trying to achieve fairness. If vernacular forums were equipped with the right skills and strategies, and if they did not have to straddle the many roles that are often simultaneously demanded of them, they could possibly be effective as mediation spaces even whilst being socially embedded.

My proposals may not entirely resolve the problems I have presented, but I think we can agree that the worst possible scenario for vernacular forums – which rely on social acceptance or local buy-in for success – is that both sides should feel that the headman has been biased in favour of the other side. The reader may recall that this was the case in the matter of Moyizela, the girl who lost her front teeth after being struck by Ngetshe, a boy who had seemingly tried to proposition her. Moyizela's mother believed that the headman had been bought off by the other side with alcohol, while Ngetshe's family felt that the matter had been so poorly handled, and their side so unjustly treated, that they were thinking of relocating to another area. I would say that this result was largely due to the headman's having played an adjudicative role that he was ill-placed and ill-equipped to play in this matter, rather than having the tools to mediate the dispute with long-term consequences being the main goal. Such a wholly unsatisfactory and unsustainable outcome should surely be avoided, and I would argue that if the forums were true mediation forums allowing both sides to fully air their views and were effectively managed in the context of wider social concerns, such conclusions to local disputes might be moderated, if not completely avoided.

In other matters one sees that the absence of wider structural support for the vernacular forums – especially the headmen and their councils – and what they are practically tasked with accomplishing in their broken material and social settings is also to blame. One can point to, for example, the effective absence of counselling services to support headmen in matters of gender-based violence

36 Friend of the court.

37 There are also compelling allegations that the police are corrupt and often side with the criminals, such as the stock theft syndicates.

38 See Cheyette, Fredric (1970) 'Suum Cuique Tribuere' *French Historical Studies*, 6(3): 287 at 290.

in its various guises. Additionally, intervention services specifically targeted at young men would be crucial, in my view.

In other words, I would say that, despite the temptation to conclude otherwise for simplicity's sake, I do not find vernacular forums to be without functional value. (This is setting aside the value they hold because they are culturally meaningful to the people who continue to use them.) However, I do find a perilous chasm between what assistance the forums need to provide the vulnerable people in Msinga, by virtue of necessity, and that which they presently have capacity to provide.

My argument is that, in order to have a chance at closing this gulf successfully, interventions that will address the weaknesses in both the vernacular forums' internal processes and the system within which they operate at large will have to be combined. These interventions would need to concentrate on improving the forums' capabilities for dispute management in specific proceedings and the environmental challenges that are primarily responsible for giving rise to repeated conflicts and undermining their effective management.

For the kinds of mediated spaces I propose that the vernacular dispute management forums would need to become, the key would be for them to allow the voices present – even those of people who are usually marginalised and silenced – to emerge and be heard. In this way, the forums would simultaneously allow for their dispute management processes to lead to genuine agreements that reflect the changing values of those with a primary stake, such as younger men and women. This approach would surely demand that the vernacular forums, rather uncomfortably, temper their own investment in the status quo – that is, patriarchy.

What would this change look like in practice? As an example, let us consider the disputes in which husbands claim the return of their wives. By understanding their own relative strength and comparative advantage in serving as a respectful, participatory process rather than ensuring a conservative substantive outcome, the vernacular forums would not have to emerge from the process as weak. Nor would women, for that matter.

Likewise, by applying tested mediation techniques, rather than throwing up their hands, in Mdala's case, the vernacular forum could have more likely facilitated real mutual appreciation of the respective concerns between Mdala and his nephew. They might even have helped the two men arrive at an understanding that would lessen the likelihood of violence between them, if not prevent it entirely. At the very least, they could have properly explored Mdala's claim that when his nephew threatened him, he often accused Mdala of doing something illicit with his grandmother's clothes – thus implying that Mdala had performed witchcraft on these belongings. This approach could not be accomplished in a formally adjudicative forum like the chief's council as it is currently structured.

This is what conflict resolution literature refers to as a 'win-win' solution: the fact that such an outcome – if arrived at by appropriate mediatory means – should allow all parties to emerge from the process feeling empowered, even if the agreement reached does not represent their first preference. In addition, what makes an outcome so reached a genuine 'win' for all involved is that the process that I am suggesting is not a new-fangled, modern, western invention. Rather, it has much in common with the customary process described in ethnographies and oral histories from the 19th and 20th centuries.[39] This fact raises the question, how might we possibly use contemporary legislation to recover – or reinvent – this vernacular system of law and justice?

39 See, for instance, Hammond-Tooke, William David (1975) *Command or Consensus: The Development of Transkeian Local Government.* Cape Town, David Philip at 67–68, 74 fn 13; Dutton, Major E. A. T. (1923) *The Basuto of Basutoland* at 59–60.

Section IV

Integrating access to justice and human security in rural South Africa

8 Conclusion

A vision of the South African legal order far beyond the Traditional Courts Bill

A social safety net

A young man, Webile, who had started with small criminal activity and steadily increased to larger offences, had now stolen R50,000 with a friend from a neighbouring family's home. Webile's friend, Balekile, had run away to Johannesburg and bought a car with the money. Webile's father, Wahlupheka, was tasked with repaying the stolen sum because his son was the only one linked to the offence by witness testimony. When interviewed, Wahlupheka told us that he had even taken his teenage son to the police, but the police released Webile because no case had been reported to them for which the young man was a (potential) suspect. Wahlupheka had really approached the police to see if they could arrest his son just to shake him up a little bit, but the police had turned the father and son away and said they could not help.

Wahlupheka was feeling helpless. He desperately wanted to save his son but did not know how. The headman, Nduna, also did not know how he could help the young man. When Nduna had chaired the dispute between Webile and the family Webile and Balekile had robbed, Nduna had tried to reason with the young man and caution him about his behaviour and where it would inevitably lead if he did not change course. But deep down inside, Nduna bore little hope, for he knew how little practical effect his caution would have. At some point, Nduna felt, Webile would steal from the wrong person and a contract would effectively be taken out on his life. If he got into serious crime like stock theft, the community might even agree that this young man was enough of a problem that they should 'take him out'.

Another young man in his area, by the name of Semncane, had recently been warned about this kind of serious consequence. Semncane had been called before Nduna by his father, Yesaba, who asked Nduna to warn Yesaba's son off continuing with pilfering marijuana. A man named Toho had accused Semncane of stealing marijuana from his field. Semncane denied that he did this, but Toho was adamant that he knew that Semncane was stealing his marijuana. Yesaba had brought the matter to Nduna because Toho had told Yesaba to warn his son, saying that if Semncane did not discontinue this crime, he would get hurt. Nduna told the parties that he could not weigh in on the matter (because it involved illegal activity) and said they should address it among themselves.

In reality, this is where these disputes ended – at least, for the time that we were present to witness their unfolding. But now I ask you to join me in imagining a different outcome.

Concerned, Nduna noted that these two young men were at-risk youths. He jotted these two disputes down in his notebook to discuss with the Msinga Multisector Conflict Management Collaborative (MCMC) when they next gathered, in two weeks. The MCMC is the joint body of representatives from the local police service, magistracy, social services, vernacular institutions, and Msinga residents that meets monthly to share knowledge and insights as well as strategise together on how to address local problems that lead to or manifest as interpersonal and social conflict. At the very least, the MCMC serves as a clearinghouse for knowledge concerning conflict management issues that straddle all of the representatives' spheres of responsibility. At its best, the MCMC is a space in which that shared knowledge and pooled resources are converted into collaborative action that is mutually agreed upon, then synergistically taken to produce positive results for the communities the MCMC representatives serve.

The two conflicts Nduna wanted to share (in a manner sensitive to the need to protect individual identities) had provoked a few key questions that were floating in the back of Nduna's mind. The MCMC helped him clarify, articulate, and feel more confident about addressing these questions: What systems of social support are failing to catch Webile and Semncane, and how? In what ways should the various systems of dispute management and social support ideally come together to address such a situation as this? What is the ideal strategy for preventing such situations (and worse) from arising – that is, for preventing steady escalation of the involvement of young men in crime?

When Nduna raised these concerns, it turned out that he was not the only one facing such disputes. The two other headmen and two headmen's policemen on the MCMC as representatives noted that they saw similar problems in the work that they do. The police representatives also confessed that they get requests like that made by Webile's father – to arrest their sons in order to shake them up – but do not have the capacity to satisfy these requests, as the prisons are already overcrowded and the police dockets full.

There was some discussion of the fact that imprisonment is not the only possible way – or even the best way – to deal with these troubled young men, especially because their social circumstances of poverty, poor education and chronic unemployment were part of what was driving their delinquency. The local magistrate expressed her displeasure at seeing so many young men between 16 and 25 years old appear before her as the accused in criminal cases that lead to severe sentences. She stated that she would like to see these young men's lives not wasted. One of the social service representatives reflected back to the group the agreement she had heard from its members: that they wanted to tackle the pipeline to prison in order to save these young men.

The other social service representative on the MCMC then said the most difficult thing of all. He observed that each of the institutions represented, including his own, had failed these young men. Given the silence in the room after this statement, the temptation to swiftly move on from this uncomfortable truth was palpable. The chair of the MCMC, Police Commissioner Gadile, then quickly grabbed the opportunity to skilfully direct the discussion into this discomfort for a bit longer. He seized on Webile's matter and publicly owned up to the fact that the police officers who had turned Webile and his father away – telling them that they could not help them – had acted with negligence. Gadile added that this response showed the extant need for continuous training for his officers on how to refer these matters to social services and on how to follow up to ensure that people are connected with the service officials most likely to provide the help they need. Though tempted to fall back on the excuse of how overstretched the police are in terms of time and resources, he insisted that this was a high enough priority that it was worth reassigning resources to it.

The commissioner's unprecedented move opened up the space for others to claim their share of responsibility. The headmen granted that they, in their helplessness concerning what they could do to save these young men, had largely given up hope on them and dealt with conflicts involving them rather perfunctorily. The headmen accepted the responsibility to work harder to bring in social services to help in individual cases, as well as the responsibility to engage in training for themselves, young men, and other members of their communities in order to make them all feel more empowered about alternative solutions to violence as a way to curb the young men's delinquency.

The courageous social service official who had opened this line of self-reflexivity acknowledged that his office was not as available to assist in these cases as he would like it to be. He observed that his office was very stretched, but he ended by agreeing with Commissioner Gadile in saying that it was ultimately a matter of priorities, and keeping young men from lives of crime had to be a priority. His colleague added that, with respect to what the headmen had said about acting pre-emptively, the social service officials had plans to put in place programs to help young people in the area, but these were slow in getting off the ground, partly for lack of sufficient funding. She too ended on a hopeful note that they wanted to help these young men and that this meeting was added motivation for their service office to do all they could and as quickly as they could.

When all officeholders had spoken, one of the community representatives, who appeared to be fighting back intense emotion (maybe even tears), spoke up, softly at first. She shared that her son had not been so lucky as Webile and Semncane might be in the wake of this meeting. After pausing, she added that many parents blamed the children's rights ushered in by the Constitution for young people's delinquency and parents' inability to discipline their children.[1] Yet, she said, at base in these statements was parents' genuine concern for their children's well-being, and she was confident that Msinga residents would be

1 See, for example, Smith, Nicholas Rush (2015) 'Rejecting Rights: Vigilantism and Violence in Post-Apartheid South Africa' *African Affairs*, 114(456): 341–360.

grateful to be empowered with any information on how to help their children when they are at immediate risk of falling into criminality as Webile and Semncane were. She and many women (and even some men) she knew, many of whom were unemployed, would be glad to help with any initiative that would save their children.

She then quickly thanked the officeholders for engaging in this process that showed they care, and she expressed her hope that they would act on the commitments they had made in that meeting. Using the community representative's closing statement as a segue, Commissioner Gadile invited the MCMC to talk about specific action steps they were each committing to taking. He asked them to be as specific as possible on what timeline was feasible for them so that the minutes could reflect this specificity to help them hold each other – and especially help the community representatives hold all the officeholders – accountable.

Traditional justice and the search for human security

This research project began with an interest in justice – narrowly construed as due process in law and fair outcomes as primarily obtained through the courts – and the avenues by which ordinary rural people in South Africa can gain access to something that resembles justice, especially using headmen's and chief's councils. Access to justice was the focus of the Traditional Courts Bill (B8–2008/ B1–2012) as provided in its Preamble.

This research project was intended as an assessment of the proposed legislative framework and content's viability in South Africa's poorest communities, the former homelands. The goal was to gather ethnographic data that would provide a more holistic understanding of how ordinary rural people use vernacular forums and how these forums dispense justice, so as to compare this reality to the vision of reform in the 2008/2012 Bill. The project therefore initially had the title 'Dispute Management in Vernacular Forums in Rural KwaZulu-Natal'.

As the book's title (*Access to Justice and Human Security*) reveals, this project has evolved into a more ambitious work. It is no longer about only access to justice through vernacular forums but the broader concern of human security as a precondition for any kind of justice that these forums (or state courts) could provide. The argument I have presented thus far is that the conflicts that come to the vernacular forums in Msinga are the product of severe material, social, and physical insecurity as well as weak (and sometimes corrupt) social services. The consequence is that of wider systemic failure that these vernacular forums cannot single-handedly address.

Yet, the vernacular forums too are part of the problem in that, when cases come before them, the methods of dispute management they use do not lead to long-term resolution. In fact, these forums often compound the conflict, if only by attempting to suppress it, as when the resolution headmen come to is telling people to forgive each other without creating space for them to be fully heard and their conflict histories and narratives thoroughly worked through.

This finding has meant that I can no longer focus solely – or even mainly – on whether the Traditional Courts Bill (TCB) or legislation of its kind could effectively regulate 'traditional courts', as it refers to vernacular forums. Neither can I focus on whether such legislation could ensure 'access to justice' – by which is meant reasonably accessible dispute resolution services that lead to reasonably effective relief – for ordinary rural people. The questions to be asked are much bigger than that. Consequently, the TCB, as a piece of legislation that was drafted (TCB-2008/2012) then redrafted (TCB-2017), does not warrant a clause-by-clause analysis in this chapter. Besides, such analysis has been exhaustively provided elsewhere.[2]

Rather, what is obviously needed is comprehensive social policy analysis and systems review far greater than I can provide in this last chapter of the book. I will therefore restrict myself to analysis and review of institutional arrangements (that is, systems) – their agents and forums – that ordinary rural people turn to and depend on for assistance or relief in the final instance of continued social conflict or crisis. After all, courts of any kind are typically the last institutional port of call in a seemingly intractable dispute.

This analysis focuses on the gaps in institutional arrangements and social policy implementation that exist in Msinga and that surfaced in the evidence presented in this book. It also spotlights how these gaps undermine the potential for any kind of justice for Msinga's residents, hence making the Traditional Courts Bill impotent, if it was truly intended to secure rural people access to justice. In other words, aside from the substantive problems with the Traditional Courts Bill when it is read in historical and contemporary context, its framework and the social and institutional assumptions on which it is based are shown to be fundamentally faulty.

The Traditional Courts Bill: invalid assumptions

Contrary to the 2008/2012 Traditional Courts Bill's troubled assumptions, Traditional Communities like Msinga do not operate according to the harmony model. The communities themselves – whose combined will the 'harmony

2 Himonga, Chuma and Rashida Manjoo (2009) 'The Challenges of Formalisation, Regulation, and Reform of Traditional Courts in South Africa' *Malawi Law Journal*, 3(2): 157–181; Himonga, Chuma, Thandabantu R. Nhlapo, I. P. Maithufi, Sindiso Mnisi Weeks, Lesala Mofokeng and Dial Ndima (2014) *African Customary Law in South Africa: Post Apartheid and Living Law Perspectives.* Cape Town, Oxford University Press; Mnisi Weeks, Sindiso (2011) 'Beyond The Traditional Courts Bill: Regulating Customary Courts in Line with Living Customary Law and the Constitution' *South African Crime Quarterly*, 35: 31; Mnisi Weeks, Sindiso (2012) 'Regulating Vernacular Dispute Resolution Forums: Controversy Concerning the Process, Substance and Implications of South Africa's Traditional Courts Bill' *Oxford University Commonwealth Law Journal*, 12(1): 133–155. On the TCB 2017, see Ubink, Janine and Sindiso Mnisi Weeks (December 2017) 'Courting Custom: Regulating Access to Justice in Rural South Africa and Malawi' *Law and Society Review*.

model' often fetishises – are prone to significant social conflict and upheaval, particularly as a result of misguided government intervention in the colonial and apartheid past. Among the problematic colonial policies that have had a disturbing impact on Msinga are the forced migrant labour system, the widespread possession of guns, the breakdown in family relations, and long-standing land and boundary conflicts. Without adequately considering the contemporary implications of the historical regimes' policy approaches, the present government seems unable to address the issues that it has attempted to tackle. For instance, pursuing state imposition as a strategy for resolving boundary disputes – which, in fact, abound – seems counterproductive. Unfortunately, the 2017 Bill does not depart from this strategy of fixing external boundaries.[3]

The disputes that vernacular forums are tasked with managing are not disembodied. They are embedded in a complex and challenging socio-economic environment, historical conditions, and close relationships. Therefore, a policy and legislation that addresses 'dispute resolution' as though all disputes were the same, regardless of context, and their resolution therefore similarly uncomplicated is unable to achieve 'access to justice'. As this book shows, we ought to take the particular socio-economic and relational context in which the vernacular forums operate seriously. Legislation that seeks to secure rural people justice ought then to address itself to their particular needs and the true capabilities of the local forums.

Vernacular forums, even if we call them 'traditional courts' as do both the TCB-2008/2012 and TCB-2017, cannot become tantamount to state courts. It is unreasonable to expect vernacular courts to take on a role for which they are ill-equipped, poorly resourced and unsupported. Furthermore, they have their own role to fulfil: managing social relations in such a way as to strengthen them. And I would argue that there is a need even for that. A side benefit of this focus for the forums is preserving their own internal legitimacy and thus not entirely losing their relevance and prospects of efficacy.

As things currently stand, institutions – whether state or vernacular – do not ensure ordinary rural people security. The development and proliferation of vigilante responses to social problems is one proof of this. Centralising and strengthening the power of institutions as the 2008/2012 Bill tried was unlikely to be the solution to people's insecurity and lack of access to justice. By taking on the character of state courts, 'traditional courts' would seem to lessen their own local authority, legitimacy and effectiveness. Hence, arbitration

3 Again, see Clegg, Johnny (1981) 'Ukubuyisa Isidumbu – "Bringing Back the Body" An Examination into the Ideology of Vengeance in the Msinga and Mpofana Rural Locations, 1882–1944' in Philip Bonner (ed.) *Working Papers in Southern African Studies, Vol. 2*. Johannesburg, African Studies Institute, University of the Witwatersrand 164 at 19 and Alcock, Creina in Cousins, Ben, Rauri Alcock, Ngididi Dladla, Donna Hornby, Mphethethi Masondo, Gugu Mbatha, Makhosi Mweli and Creina Alcock (2011) '*Imithetho yomhlaba yaseMsinga:* The Living Law of Land in Msinga District, KwaZulu-Natal'. PLAAS Research Report 43, The University of the Western Cape at 24.

and adjudication appear to be less effective modes of dispute management and governance than the seemingly more humble option of mediation.

Yet, by infiltration by western models of 'dispute resolution' – and, more than anything, adjudication – vernacular forums have been substantially robbed of their mediation processes. Muddled by expectations that vernacular forums function as state-like courts in order to be legitimate and authoritative in the state's eyes, vernacular institutions have become unskilled in effectively mediating local disputes, while local disputes have become increasingly more challenging to resolve.

Lack of clarity, communication and effective collaboration between the police and vernacular authorities (especially headmen) has undermined both the headmen's and police's ability to manage and reduce social conflict. In the context of competition, while trying to bolster their own position, authority and income (and in some instances to shade their corrupt dealings from view), both institutions show limited willingness to collaborate. The police are most guilty of this, as they tend to exclude and not effectively engage the headmen and appear to rather use them capriciously – and only when convenient – in order to shore up police authority. The police undermine the headmen's in some ways more-limited authority in the process.

Nevertheless, with all these gaping problems overlooked by the old (and, to a lesser but still substantial degree, the new) TCB, it seems to me that there are solutions for much of the breakdown that has and is continuing to take place in Msinga. I will therefore end with a discussion of what possibilities exist for short- and medium-term systemic reform to improve human security conditions for the people who live there.

In this respect, I will focus on two sources of local conflict management's institutional failure, which have continued to resonate through this project: the vernacular mediation system and the cooperative governance system. As I argue, a significant part of the solution is to intervene in these two systems that account for much of the continued interference with – and incapacity and repeated failure to address – human security in Msinga.

The factual case scenarios at the start of this chapter provide real-life examples of the necessity of both these interventions. Young men are in particular danger of falling between the cracks in places like Msinga. This danger has huge implications for women as well because they are often victims of the harm caused by the escalation of criminal involvement by young men.

In the end, intervention in only the vernacular dispute management system or only the cooperative governance system will not yield the desired results. Very necessary changes to the manner in which vernacular forums manage disputes, to place greater emphasis on mediation, will improve the outcomes of individual cases and have some impact on relationships and thus social conditions at large. However, without wider systemic changes to accompany better mediation, the vernacular forums cannot assure justice to ordinary rural people.

While the vernacular forums could better deal with conflicts involving young men at risk, these forums alone cannot handle the fallout. Several cases in this study involved young men, and the forums seemed helpless to address them effectively, systemically and preventatively. As shown by the examples of Webile and Semncane, this is clearly an instance where collaboration among institutional actors is critical. The fictitious and idealised ending of how the MCMC might go about strategising joint management of the complex issues at play is an attempt to illustrate this point.

Combined, local and systemic interventions would have a potent effect on Msinga society and the level of conflict and insecurity experienced by its people. Without either of them, regulatory legislation, like the TCB, that purports to try to make the 'traditional courts' operate better would be totally ineffectual at fulfilling its aimed purpose of ensuring 'access to justice'.

What is justice?

I have described what has changed during the course of this study. Readers might therefore wonder if anything has stayed constant. The thing that has remained with me almost from the start is a fascination with the concept of justice. I have been struck by the concept's ability to be so viscerally powerful that all agree on it as a patent good but so broad and vague as to allow for different conceptions of it to exist under the guise of the same name. Consider the decades-long debate that has taken place among legal philosophers about whether law's purpose is to ensure justice and, if so, what form that justice should take.[4] We can also go back even further to moral and political philosophy.[5]

Terms like 'traditional justice' (which is the subject area that the Traditional Courts Bill is intended to regulate), 'criminal justice' (presumed to be the domain, almost exclusively, of the police and particular state courts), 'social justice' (thought to be concerned with human rights as effected both inside and outside of the courts) are widely used and accepted. All are based on the noun 'justice', yet can it truly be said that the justice at the core of each is the same? This is assumed to be a self-evident truth, yet it is not at all clear to me that it is. Even while affirming that there are perhaps universally shared

4 Such scholars as Ronald Dworkin, John Finnis, Stanley Fish, Lon Fuller, HLA Hart, Neil MacCormick, Joseph Raz have taken part. For example, see Dworkin, Ronald (2006) *Justice in Robes.* Cambridge, Harvard University Press at 127–144; Hart, Herbert Lionel Adolphus, Penelope A. Bulloch, et al. (1997) *The Concept of Law.* Oxford, Clarendon Press; MacCormick, Neil (1986) 'Law, Morality and Positivism' in N. MacCormick and O. Weinberger (eds.) *An Institutional Theory of Law: New Approaches to Legal Positivism.* Dordrecht, D. Reidel.

5 Works such as those of Immanuel Kant, John Rawls, Frederick Nietzsche, Saint Augustine, Aristotle and Plato refer. See the review, analysis, and contemporary application by Sandel, Michael (2010) *Justice: What's the Right Thing to Do?* New York, Macmillan. Also see Rawls, John (1971) *A Theory of Justice.* Cambridge, MA, Harvard University Press.

aspects of what people refer to as justice,[6] the research presented in this book problematises the assumption that justice is itself universal.

I have already argued that the justice that is meant and intended by the legislature when it seeks to regulate 'traditional courts' through the mechanism of the TCB, as drafted, is a very narrow conception. 'Justice' in the Bill refers to access to courts that function efficiently and fairly in terms of process, as a result of which (it is assumed) the parties that come before the forums will obtain fair judgments that provide relief for the issues the wronged party has presented. Enforcement of those judgments is seemingly not considered essential, as the TCB-2008/2012 was virtually silent on this crucial point and the TCB-2017 insists that it will be achieved without assigning additional resources to the enterprise.

Certainly, the findings presented in this book support the idea that the forums to which people take their concerns should function properly. In fact, addressing the functional aspects of the vernacular forums is an important point of intervention in order to ensure just outcomes for rural people. However, the empirical evidence presented in this book decidedly refutes the idea that functional vernacular forums are the primary means by which people obtain just outcomes. In fact, I argue that the evidence shows that well-functioning vernacular forums are inadequate to the task.

Functional forums

Though functional vernacular forums could not provide all the necessary services for effective conflict management (let alone resolution) in Msinga, they could improve the quality and effectiveness of the services they do provide. I have previously argued that the vernacular forums would do better if they better understood their strengths and weaknesses. It is difficult for them to be completely objective adjudicatory forums because of how deeply embedded they are in their local communities. After all, they are composed of members of the local groupings.

It is even difficult for the vernacular forums to be purely arbitrational forums because of the ever-present need for people to be reconciled at a relational level in order to coexist in heavily mutually dependent arrangements. Because of the forums' limited ability to record and follow up on dispute outcomes, as well as to enforce forum decisions, it would be helpful to the forums if they could eliminate this oversight and enforcement function. Doing away with this expectation would reduce the impression of their ineffectiveness.

As socially embedded organisations, the forums have their greatest strength, it seems to me, in their ability to build on and enhance relationships.

6 Perhaps, as argued by Dworkin, Ronald (2013) *Justice for Hedgehogs*. Cambridge, Harvard University Press, the same value is ultimately at their core. But, in my view, it is still appropriate to distinguish these types of justice – at least, conceptually.

Strengthening the relational dimensions of the outcomes of the vernacular dispute management process might reduce some of the conflict that occurs between people who know each other well. It might even curtail the spiral effects of the bitterness people often experience as a result of poor outcomes from the vernacular dispute management process.

Another strength of vernacular forums is that they can provide parties with the opportunity to publicly air their concerns and vent their emotions. In this respect, a critical change would need to be made to the way in which they fulfil this function so as to prevent fallout from people's venting and publicising their conflicts (especially 'dangerous' accusations against them). In short, as I have argued, I believe that vernacular forums would do better in focusing on their functions as mediatory spaces.

What might functional vernacular forums look like? There is plenty of guidance from the conflict studies literature, especially on negotiation, mediation and arbitration. In the negotiation literature, the Harvard Negotiation Project based in the Harvard Law School has presented a seven-step model for successfully negotiating agreements that might be described as 'win-wins'.[7]

The Harvard model for negotiation emphasises opening up good channels of communication and building a strong relationship as a foundation before proceeding to substantive discussions. The authors advise focusing the substantive negotiations on interests rather than positions, and brainstorming all possible options that could result in mutual benefit before moving toward agreement. In attempting to come to an agreement, negotiators should determine the best options based on objective standards. The Harvard model encourages being ready with a 'best alternative to a negotiated agreement', in case there is an unavoidable need to reject a bad agreement.

This model can be used for mediation as well – the main difference being that the third-party mediator can be the one to manage the discussions and therefore take primary responsibility for ensuring that the parties stick to the process requirements. Indeed, scholars observe that mediators should strive to improve communication and relationships between parties, bring about agreement and reconciliation, and even prevent future disputes.[8] The Harvard negotiation model

7 Fisher, Roger, William L. Ury and Bruce Patton (2011) *Getting to Yes: Negotiating Agreement without Giving in*. New York, Penguin.

8 See Bleemer, Russ (2009) 'The Rest of the Sept. 11 Cases–Those That Went to Court–Are Settled Via Mediation' *Alternatives to the High Cost of Litigation*, 27(5): 92–94; Craig, Tara (2008) 'Firing off . . . ? Mediation' *Personnel Today*, 22 July: 9; Firestone, Gregory (2009) 'Empowering Parents in Child Protection Mediation: Challenges and Opportunities' *Family Court Review*, 47(1): 1–16; Portman, Tarrell Awe Agahe (2009) 'Faces of the Future: School Counselors as Cultural Mediators' *Journal of Counseling and Development*, 87(1): 21–27; Stimmel, Andrew (2002) 'Mediating Will Disputes: A Proposal to Add a Discretionary Mediation Clause to the Uniform Probate Code' *Ohio State Journal on Dispute Resolution*, 18(1): 197–224; Wort, Matthew 2009. 'How to Nip Conflict in the Bud' *Birmingham Post*, 15 July: 31.

prioritises the strengthening of communication and relationship as a preface for, and ongoing part of, the process of coming to an agreement.

Granted, in some ways mediation is a weak dispute management process solution to the severity of problems with which the people of Msinga are faced, and the personal risks with which the headmen are faced. I do not suggest that mediation is a complete solution. However, it is not as weak a solution as many assume, when we consider how much mediation is able to achieve. Mediatory processes have been recommended and used to address wide-ranging conflicts. For example, Donna Hicks writes of positive experience with mediation and dignity-based dialogue in addressing long-standing mutual contempt between different sides of the Irish conflict.[9]

Aside from allowing disputing parties to release the tension between them, improving parties' relationships and reaching agreement on a solution, mediation can be used to achieve goals such as social justice[10] and social transformation,[11] to reduce social ills such as sexual discrimination[12] and violence,[13] to resolve practical problems[14] and prevent future ones,[15] to provide efficiency and speed[16] while reducing cost,[17] to oversee delicate processes,[18] and to reduce the stress that is implicit in conflict.[19]

Ultimately, it is obviously important that the parties are satisfied with the outcome, leave with improved long-term relationships and feel empowered by the process in which they have just participated. I cannot overemphasise the importance of this side benefit of a successful mediation. As extensively discussed in the previous chapter, people in Msinga feel extremely disempowered and

9 Hicks, Donna (2011) *Dignity: The Essential Role It Plays in Resolving Conflict*. New Haven, CT, Yale University Press.

10 Neves, Tiago (2009) 'Practice Note: Community Mediation as Social Intervention' *Conflict Resolution Quarterly*, 26(4): 481–495.

11 Li-On, Lee (2009) 'The Politics of Community Mediation: A Study of Community Mediation in Israel' *Conflict Resolution Quarterly*, 26(4): 453–479.

12 Stallworth, Lamont E., Thomas McPherson and Larry Rute (2001) 'Discrimination in the Workplace: How Mediation Can Help' *Dispute Resolution Journal*, 56: 35–44.

13 Mazadoorian, Harry N. (2009) 'First (Mediation) Step: Stop the Shooting' *Alternatives to the High Cost of Litigation*, 27(2): 17–22.

14 Zwier, Paul J. and Thomas F. Guernsey (2005) *Advanced Negotiation and Mediation Theory and Practices*. South Bend, IN, National Institute for Trial Advocacy.

15 Kay, Julie (2009) 'Home Settling: Foreclosure Mediation Grows, but Some Wonder If It's the Best' *ABA Journal*, 95: 14–15.

16 Zimmer, C. (2010) 'The Brain: Memories Are Crucial for Looking Into the Future' *Discover*, April: 24.

17 Kloppenberg, Lisa A. (2001) 'Implementation of Court-Annexed Environmental Mediation: The District of Oregon Pilot Project' *Ohio State Journal on Dispute Resolution*, 17(3): 559–596.

18 Stimmel (above); Umbreit, Umbreit, Mark. S., Robert B. Coates and Ann Warner Roberts (2000) 'The Impact of Victim-Offender Mediation: A Cross-National Perspective' *Mediation Quarterly*, 17(3): 215–229.

19 Wiseman, Ellidh (2008) 'Make the Most of Mediation in Disputes' *Personnel Today*, 1 July: 9.

helpless, except when responding with violence. It is therefore important that local authorities find ways to reduce this sense of disempowerment and desperation, which can lead people to turn to destructive solutions to their problems. Often this destructive turn is what causes the biggest problems in Msinga, such as endemic violence.

Determining the goals of mediation is critically important, but at the centre of mediation is process. Several strategies can help mediators reach the goals that they have both implicitly and explicitly defined both on their own and with the parties coming to the forums for resolution. The mediation literature describes about a hundred possible strategies and techniques that mediators can use, which can be categorised into around 24 sets.[20] These sets can be boiled down even further to six key categories of strategies that can be used by mediators: namely, pressing, neutral, relational, analytic, clarification, and multifunctional strategies.[21]

Pressing (whereby the mediator nudges the parties toward a particular solution) seems to be the most used strategy in Msinga dispute management – often in the form of mediation-arbitration and power-political pressure (though the authorities actually have limited power). The forums are not that subtle in how they use this strategy. The forum will often tell the parties to abandon the dispute and simply forgive one another. The efficacy of this strategy is doubtful because forgiveness is something that occurs (or not) inside the individual parties.[22] Forum authorities cannot compel people to deliver forgiveness, and if the efficacy of the agreement reached from the proceedings is dependent on forgiveness, it seems unwise to compel people to say that they have arrived at a resolution.

This strategy seems to be overemphasised at the peril of both the disputing parties and whole communities, because this outcome seems rarely to lead to a final resolution; as a result, people turn to self-help interventions such as avoidance or violence, either prior or subsequent to the 'formal' management process.

The neutral strategy emphasises the mediator's role as maintaining interaction between the parties and limiting interference in the matter while sourcing and relaying information as objectively as possible. This is a strategy that is sometimes employed by the forum authorities (for example, some headmen and the chiefs will project neutrality in the proceedings) but rarely so. However, the authorities speak of their role in these terms; that is, they describe neutrality as defining of what they do. The way they describe this strategy reveals that neutrality is a value that they perceive as giving their processes legitimacy and validity. Indeed,

20 Wall, James A. and Timothy C. Dunne (2012) 'State of the Art: Mediation Research: A Current Review' *Negotiation Journal*, 28(2): 217–244 at 226–227.

21 Ibid. at 236–237.

22 It is for the same reason that it seems unhelpful that the TCB-2008/2012 and TCB-2017 both include this as an order that can be handed down by the 'traditional courts'.

the fact that the possible appearance of bias is given as a reason for headmen passing on disputes without hearing them reinforces the importance they place on neutrality as an ideal.

The relational strategy – prioritising clear expression of the emotions underlying the conflict, and improvement of communication and the relationship between the parties – is underutilised in Msinga. This is partly a result of the culture surrounding social expectations and performance of identity in Msinga. Men perform a kind of bravado in the public sphere, and women must perform a timidity as a way of showing respect. Moreover, feelings are not that highly valued, certainly not to the same extent that they are in the west. Events, relational connections (and the obligations that accompany them), as well as physical and spiritual reality are much more highly valued. Yet the relational strategy would be very useful in Msinga because it would surface underlying feelings and issues that tend to spring up again as different conflicts later.

The analytic strategy is often used in Msinga, but often the management forum is moved from such a strategy to another – mostly the pressing strategy – because other issues arise in the course of the settlement. This process is what I have previously referred to as transformation of disputes. As transformation takes place, it makes what initially presented as a relatively simple matter a much more complex one, and the forums do not prioritise keeping matters clear and singularly focused. By this, I do not mean to suggest that the vernacular forums should give up what is one of the elements that the people they serve value about their service: parties' ability to present messy disputes without having to define them in terms of the very narrowly defined civil law notion of a 'case'. However, the forums could continue to hear the 'messy' disputes that come to them but also break them down analytically, in order to address them systematically. In essence, the forums could improve on their ability, once they have identified the core issue causing the dispute, to make sure to mediate a mutually satisfactory resolution to that core issue, as the foundation for a long-term solution and avoidance of future conflict. The forums are not as skilled at the task of analysis (especially bottom-up analysis) as they could be. Frankly, they do not have enough means at their disposal to actually effectively resolve the fundamental problems with which they are presented, which makes it difficult for them to fully employ the analytic strategy.[23]

Clarification would also be a helpful strategy to use in Msinga because it would surface more plainly the shared objectives (and solutions) that people want at a macro-level. As demonstrated in the previous chapter, finding solutions is important to achieve in each case. But, beyond just a single case, it is important to clarify what people want at a personal and social level in the numerous cases that are presented to these forums. This clarification of the 'big picture' would help the Msinga forum authorities better grapple with the larger reality that they are tasked with rather than simply performing micromanagement – dealing

23 The limited education of the headmen and other residents may also be a barrier.

with '*imibango nje*'. This kind of clarification would help authorities move toward systemic reforms and increased security for everyone.

The multifunctional strategy – especially its tools of narrative and storytelling – is a combination of the previously mentioned strategies that is often used in Msinga. However, it is most singularly used to obtain agreement without doing much to effectively improve relationships or help the parties to clarify and understand their underlying goals, let alone actually achieve them. Moreover, the breadth of focus that comes with the clarification strategy and the narrow focus that accompanies the analytic strategy are not combined to achieve their greatest effect in the vernacular forums.

In summary, there is an overemphasis on settlement-oriented strategies in Msinga forums, though authorities are rhetorically committed to relationship-oriented strategies and a more-or-less neutral strategy approach. It would be immensely helpful if the vernacular forums more effectively applied Peter Coleman's observations that 'short-term interventions must be developed in light of long-term objectives . . . [and] intervention strategies must address issues rooted in the past, present and future.'[24]

Agreement rates tell us almost nothing about the quality of the agreements and the 'stickiness' of the resolutions arrived at, the long-term improvement in relations or long-term change for the parties, especially the weaker parties in the disputes. For this reason, the case method is useful as opposed to surveys based on self-reporting, by mediators especially. In Msinga, agreement rates are not exceptionally high but the impression is created that the sustainability of the agreements is extremely low.

Additionally, as James Wall and Timothy Dunne observe:

> Outcomes can accrue to third parties (other than the mediator) from the agreement as well as from the mediation process. The most heralded agreement outcome for third parties is peace when hostilities draw to a close. . . . As for other outcomes, several studies have indicated that mediation reduces the court docket . . . and case overloads for government agencies. . . . In divorce mediation, research indicates that the children benefit because mediation reduces the hostility between their parents and leads to agreements that are more favorable for the children. . . . Studies . . . have also indicated that gang mediation helps to provide safer neighborhoods for the residents.[25]

24 Coleman, Peter T. (2000) 'Intractable Conflict' in Morton Deutsch and Peter T. Coleman (eds.) *The Handbook of Conflict Resolution: Theory and Practice*. San Francisco, Jossey-Bass Publishers, 428–450.

25 Wall and Dunne (above) at 232–233. Also see their references: Koksal, Yonca (2006) 'Coercion and Mediation: Centralization and Sedentarization of Tribes in the Ottoman Empire' *Middle Eastern Studies*, 42(3): 469–491; Van Epps, Douglas A. (2001) 'The Impact of Mediation on State Courts' *Ohio State Journal on Dispute Resolution*, 17(3): 627–640; Swendiman, Matthew A. (2001) 'The EEOC Mediation Program: Panacea or

We might therefore ask what is the effect of lack of agreement – or the effect of forced agreement as a result of overt pressing by the vernacular forum – for the systemic nature of conflict in Msinga. I have demonstrated that the result is a failure to prevent the cyclical nature of conflict – and repetitive presentation of the same kinds of conflicts – that could be meaningfully mitigated by a systemic approach to conflict management. This pattern in local disputes should have substantial implications for the future strategies of the vernacular forums.

The trouble is, however, that in Msinga criticisms of the agreements produced by the forum process do not lead the authorities to alter their subsequent strategies.[26] Moreover, failure to reach agreement does not seem to provoke change of strategy either; rather it seems to motivate the authorities to force agreement, thus repeating the failed strategy of pressing.[27] In this sense, one might say that there is a failure of Msinga forums to effectively learn from prior experience. My assessment is that this inability to build on lessons from past failures is based on the forum authorities' faulty understanding of their role as being adjudicators and therefore having inherent authority and legitimacy that is virtually unchallenged. The authorities therefore perform what they believe they are supposed to be. Unfortunately, as the empirical evidence shows, this perception of their role fails to recognise the forums' proven strengths and weaknesses, which should rather orient these authorities toward conceiving of themselves as mediators.

However, as already suggested, it would be unfair to place the blame fully on the forum authorities' own poor judgment, or to suggest that adopting mediation strategies would guarantee that any injustice that might result from participation in vernacular dispute management would be eliminated. The vernacular authorities are faced with very real pressures on all sides and struggle, without adequate support, to withstand the pressure and overcome challenges. These pressures include the ever-present risk of being unduly influenced by the power, wealth and standing of a party to a dispute. They also include the constant turf war that has the authorities feeling beleaguered and thus constantly defending their position and sphere of authority through what they do, even enacting this contest in the context of managing individual disputes.[28]

Panicked Reaction?' *Ohio State Journal on Dispute Resolution*, 16(2): 391–408; Landsman, Miriam J., Kathy Thompson and Gail Barber (2003) 'Using Mediation to Achieve Permanency for Children and Families' *Families in Society*, 84(2): 229–239; Kotlowitz, Alex (2008) 'Is Urban Violence a Virus?' *New York Times Magazine*, 4 May: 52–59. Also see Buntin, John. (2008) 'Is Urban Violence a Virus?' *Governning: The state and localities*, 5 May (accessible at http://www.governing.com/blogs/view/Is-Urban-Violence-a.html).

26 Observing a lacuna in the literature on this question, Wall and Dunne at 232 ask whether mediators do.

27 Ibid.

28 Mnisi Weeks, Sindiso (2011) 'Securing Women's Property Inheritance in the Context of Plurality: Negotiations of Law and Authority in Mbuzini Customary Courts and beyond' *Acta Juridica*, 140–173.

The pressures the vernacular authorities face are not unique to them and would not necessarily be overcome by their approaching their task as mediation, because mediators face them also. For instance, Wall and Dunne observe that 'even when they access mediation, some groups (e.g., those with less power) are at a disadvantage in the process'.[29] Such a threat to the powerless would therefore have to be deliberately confronted, and overtly compensated for, in order to mitigate the damage it can cause to the credibility of the forum and injustice to the disadvantaged party.

Moreover, there is evidence that mediation in forums or organisational environments can develop a self-justifying and non-responsive culture that makes them immune to challenges to the way they do things and demands for them to change their approach.[30] Linked to the potential of an institution responsible for mediation to start serving its own interests more than those of the parties whose disputes it mediates is the concern that 'on occasion, [mediators] allow outsiders to influence the process . . . and infringe on the disputants' rights'.[31]

Taking a mediation approach to local disputes in Msinga therefore does not inherently guarantee that the vernacular forums will become highly responsive and learn from feedback on their successes and failures. This result would need to be intentionally institutionalised. A mediation approach also does not guarantee that forums will be immune to outsiders attempting to determine the process and affect the rights of the parties to the dispute. Just as intentionality is required to ensure that no parties are disadvantaged by their status or power, deliberation would be required to protect against undue influence from interested or influential outsiders to the conflict.

Human needs: relating social injustice and conflict

Emphasis on the functionality of the vernacular forums independent of the state system values the ability of Msinga people to productively air their concerns

29 Wall and Dunne (above) at 235. Also see Evans, Michelle R. (2001) 'Women and Mediation: Toward a Formulation of an Interdisciplinary Empirical Model to Determine Equity in Dispute Resolution' *Ohio State Journal on Dispute Resolution*, 17(1): 145–184; Kay (above); Mulcahy, Linda (2000) 'The Devil and the Deep Blue Sea? A Critique of the Ability of Community Mediation to Suppress and Facilitate Participation in Civil Life' *Journal of Law and Society*, 27(1): 133–150.

30 Wall and Dunne (above) at 235: 'Occasionally, . . . mediators can begin to serve their own needs or those of the system rather than disputants' interests'. See Bingham, Lisa B. (2004) 'Employment Dispute Resolution: The Case for Mediation' *Conflict Resolution Quarterly*, 22(1–2): 145–174; and Della Noce, Dorothy J. (2001) 'Mediation Theory and Policy: The Legacy of the Pound Conference' *Ohio State Journal on Dispute Resolution*, 17(3): 545–558.

31 Wall and Dunne (above) at 235. Also see Menin, Bruce. (2000) 'The Party of the Last Part: Ethical and Process Implications for Children in Divorce Mediation' *Conflict Resolution Quarterly*, 17(3): 281–293; Swendiman, Matthew A. (2001) 'The EEOC Mediation Program: Panacea or Panicked Reaction?' *Ohio State Journal on Dispute Resolution*, 16(2): 391–408.

publicly and to build a stronger social fabric through the dispute management process (or, at least, not to weaken the social fabric further through that process). This is a kind of justice – combining procedural and restorative justice.

If that was all people were looking for in approaching the vernacular forums that would be fine; however, most times people are looking for much more of an intervention than this. Ultimately, the disputes gathered through this research show security as people's main goal. Hence, for example, the common thread between Phutha's concern relating to a gun fired over his house (a wrongly perceived conflict that the forum manages to resolve) and Mdala's concern relating to his nephew's threat to kill him (a rightly perceived conflict the forums declare themselves unable to resolve).

But how do we guarantee people the physical protection that is the least that they should be able to expect to get from the justice system? Moreover, would giving Msinga people physical security (by whatever means, perhaps by bringing in the army) be enough to ensure them long-term security? Scholars have pondered this question and arrived at somewhat of a consensus. Based on extensive experience and study, John Burton put his representative findings thus: 'The only option, in politically realistic terms, was to resolve the social and behavioural problems that led to specific conflicts, and not try merely to suppress them or to settle them by coercion.'[32]

Burton is unsentimental about this finding. He goes out of his way to observe 'that there is no normative connotation in this alternative. There is no moral or idealistic basis.'[33] It just is the case that there are some basic human needs like security that, if not satisfied, will be pursued using 'all means'[34] available, including conflict-inducing ones. Addressing the conflict, in such instances, requires more than conflict resolution skills such as those discussed above; it requires addressing the root need. While Burton argues for addressing basic human needs over merely applying conflict resolution strategies, not on a moral basis but on pragmatic grounds, there is plenty of scholarship with which I agree that presents moral arguments for satisfying these human needs.

Morton Deutsch has famously argued that

> [i]njustice breeds conflict, and destructive conflict gives rise to injustice. It is well to realize that preventing destructive conflict requires more than training in constructive conflict resolution. It also necessitates reducing the gross injustices that characterize much of our social world at the interpersonal, intergroup, and international levels. Such reduction requires changes

32 Burton, John 'Conflict Provention as a Political System' *International Journal of Peace Studies* (accessible at www.gmu.edu/programs/icar/ijps/vol6_1/Burton2.htm).

33 Ibid.

34 Burton, John. (1987) *Resolving Deep-Rooted Conflict.* Lanham, MD and London, University Press of America at 15–16: 'subject only to constraints [these individuals] imposed on themselves in their need to maintain valued relationships.'

> in how various institutions of society – political, economic, educational, familial, and religious – function.[35]

Injustice can lead to conflict. And conflict, if it manifests in a destructive manner, can result in even greater injustice. The suggestion here is that if we are to ensure people long-term security, we must look at the causes of their present (and future potential) insecurity. We must also look beyond their physical insecurity, as important as that is, to the socio-economic dimensions of their insecurity and thus concern ourselves with social justice as part of the answer to addressing people's physical insecurity.

This study supports the fact that social injustice, in particular, is a source of conflict. As extensively canvassed, the social injustice that forms the roots of conflict in Msinga stretches back to the colonial and apartheid past and the political economy that was created on the backs of black men in migrant labour and their families, who were confined to arid and overcrowded rural lands. The impact of these socio-economic injustices committed by successive oppressive regimes had devastating, long-term effects on vernacular groupings like those in Msinga, effects still profoundly felt today.

The same injustices continue in contemporary South Africa, as the democratically elected government struggles and largely fails to address gross inequality. The result is the socio-economic exclusion experienced by people living under traditional institutions in the same deep rural areas that were denied citizenship by the apartheid government.[36] This social destruction births and sustains internal, interpersonal and social conflict that can only be fully addressed by tending to the fundamental human needs and deprivation that undergird it.

This study also shows that dispute management that fails to reduce social injustice, and that sometimes results in even greater injustice, undermines confidence in the institutions tasked with the management of conflict. Reactions to this system failure are, in many cases, self-help measures that are in fact aggressive and destructive, and that thus scale up individual conflict to a widespread social problem.

This book's findings point to a concept of human security that is based on Sabina Alkire's definition of human security as 'a subcategory of human

35 Deutsch, Morton (2006) 'Justice and Conflict' in Eric C. Marcus (ed.) *The Handbook of Conflict Resolution: Theory and Practice.* 2nd edition, San Francisco, California, John Wiley & Sons at 67.

36 See representation of inequality in Msinga by Budlender, Debbie, Sibongile Mgweba, Ketleetso Motsepe and Leilanie Williams (2011) *Women, Land and Customary Law.* South Africa, Community Agency for Social Enquiry; Cousins (above); Mnisi Weeks, Sindiso (2015) 'Contested Democracy and Rule of Law(s) in Pluralistic Societies: The Example of South Africa' in Galuppo, Marcelo C., Monica Sette Lopes. Karine Salgado, Thomas Bustamante and Lucas Alvarenga Gontijo (eds.) *Human Rights, Rule of Law and the Contemporary Challenges in Complex Societies.* Stuttgart, Franz Steiner Verlag.

development'.[37] In the introduction, I relied on Alkire's work to argue that there is a meaningful causal relationship between poverty and violence that must be understood and addressed using multilevel strategies relevant to the particular situation at issue.[38] As Alkire observes:

> Similar to human development, human security scrutinises the interconnections between dimensions and recognises that the core aspects of human development are of intrinsic value. Human security also locates the focal space in which to evaluate human security in the capabilities or freedoms that people enjoy.[39]

When Alkire refers to 'capabilities or freedoms', she is evidently relying on the capabilities approach that Amartya Sen[40] and Martha Nussbaum[41] are most famous for explicating. This approach generally requires that people be able to realise the fundamental moral right of achieving well-being. In other words, people should be able to avoid poverty and deprivation, be socially included,[42] and be able to pursue the social goods that they reasonably value. Only then can people be said to possess freedom, which is a primary moral and human right of all.[43]

37 Alkire, Sabina (June 2010) *Human Development: Definitions, Critiques, and Related Concepts*. United Nations Development Program Report at 60–61.

38 In assessing a context for intervention, it is important to appreciate both its assets and needs. On asset assessment, see Yosso, Tara J. (2005) 'Whose Culture Has Capital? A Critical Race Theory Discussion of Community Cultural Wealth' *Race, Ethnicity and Education*, 8: 69–91.

39 Alkire (2010) at 60.

40 Sen, Amartya (1984) *Resources, Values and Development*. Cambridge, MA, Harvard University Press at 307–324; Sen, Amartya (1993) 'Capability and Well-Being' in Martha Nussbaum and Amartya Sen (eds.) *The Quality of Life*. Oxford, Clarendon Press, 30–53; Sen, Amartya (1999) *Development as Freedom*. New York, Knopf; Sen, Amartya (2004) 'Capabilities, Lists and Public Reasons: Continuing the Conversation' *Feminist Economics*, 10(3): 77–80; Sen, Amartya (2005) 'Human Rights and Capabilities' *Journal of Human Development*, 6(2): 151–166. Also see Alkire, Sabina (2002) *Valuing Freedoms: Sen's Capability Approach and Poverty Reduction*. New York, Oxford University Press; Pogge, Thomas (2002) 'Can the Capability Approach be Justified?' *Philosophical Topics*, 30(2): 167–228.

41 Nussbaum, Martha (1992) 'Human Functioning and Social Justice: In Defense of Aristotelian Essentialism' *Political Theory*, 20(2): 202–246; Nussbaum, Martha (2000) *Women and Human Development: The Capabilities Approach*. Cambridge, Cambridge University Press; Nussbaum, Martha (2003) 'Capabilities as Fundamental Entitlements: Sen and Social Justice' *Feminist Economics*, 9(2–3): 33–59.

42 Sen, Amartya (June 2000) 'Social Exclusion: Concept, Application, and Scrutiny'. Social Development Papers No. 1, Office of Environment and Social Development, Asian Development Bank.

43 On the relationship that should be fostered between human rights and development, see Alston, Philip (August 2005) 'Ships Passing in the Night: The Current State of the Human Rights and Development Debate seen through the Lens of the Millennium Development Goals' *Human Rights Quarterly*, 27(3): 755–829.

Human needs theory, developed principally by Burton, helps us understand what those capabilities and freedoms might be in the context of conflict resolution.[44] Human needs theory is founded in behavioural theory in its perception of the behavioural sciences as essential to understanding conflict, analysing and predicting it, and ultimately resolving it. As briefly outlined above, the theory articulates that human beings have some essential needs that, if not met, cultivate deep and seemingly intractable, long-term conflict. Of these, Burton writes:

> there are certain human drives or needs that will be pursued, regardless of cost and consequences, which . . . cannot permanently be suppressed. Hence, in time, institutions must conform to human drives, and not, as has been assumed to be the case, the other way around.[45]

The human needs that are described as forming the basis of conflict are the following. The first essential is safety and security, as represented by the freedom from fear, and the reduced or lack of anxiety that comes with stability, predictability and structure.[46] It has been clearly demonstrated that this physical dimension is an element of human security that is severely wanting in Msinga, and is at the root of most appeals to the vernacular forums for assistance in managing disputes.

The second essential is a sense of belonging, love and acceptance within one's social circles (family, friends and identity group).[47] As demonstrated by this study, while the Msinga community is heavily built on embedded social relationships, these do not so much live up to the stereotype of the 'harmony model'. Instead, almost all conflict in Msinga (among which are violations of the worst kind) occurs between people who are in intimate relationships. This insecurity within the purview of one's core relationships – from which one draws one's identity and should find safety – substantially undermines any attempts at resolution of long-term conflict. The inverse is true too: when one's identity group holds a common value of 'retaliation' or 'revenge' against those outside the group, the social rewards of violence are difficult to resist, because one may need to perpetrate violence in order to earn one's acceptance among one's own.

While the third essential of self-esteem[48] may seem too soft to be of real significance for conflict, it is actually very important by virtue of Msinga residents' unfulfilled need to be seen to be strong and capable by those around them and, in turn, by themselves. Consider the fact that Msinga people are so materially insecure and socially excluded that they feel powerless to meaningfully

44 Burton, John, ed. (1993) *Conflict: Human Needs Theory*. Houndsmills, Basingstoke, Hamshire and London, Palgrave Macmillan.
45 Burton (*IJPS*). Also see Hicks (above) at 25–31.
46 Burton (*IJPS*); Hicks (above) at 27, 38 and 49.
47 Burton (*IJPS*); Hicks (above) at 33, 44.
48 Burton (*IJPS*); Hicks (above) at 59, 86.

influence or shape their circumstances.[49] Most Msinga residents predominantly experience being victims of their environment. This feeling is what I have referred to as helplessness (and hopelessness) in the previous chapter.

The fourth essential of identity is entwined with self-esteem.[50] Specifically, the sense of self one has relative to society and the world at large – especially the feeling of legitimacy concerning one's identity that one is denied or feels is threatened by the world – can lead one to feel inferior or threatened by others. Msinga residents (the men above all) feel, in part, that they must perform their identity in a world in which they perceive that their traditional ways are being imposed upon, compromised, and generally not respected.

Likewise, the fifth essential, cultural security – feeling that one's religious and cultural values and traditions, language, ideas and concepts are recognised and respected – is wanting for many in Msinga. Beliefs about embracing rights as being a form of rejecting traditional values inform this.[51] The attitudes and practices of the police which disregard and impose upon the headmen's ways of governing in their community are one representation of the absence of both the fourth and fifth essentials, as perceived and experienced by the headmen.

Deeply linked to the third, fourth and fifth essentials is Msinga residents' want of personal fulfillment, the sixth essential.[52] As I have discussed, all Msinga residents, but especially the young and adult men, experience hopelessness that they could possibly reach their potential in *any* areas of their lives, let alone *all* of them.

The final three essentials are interwoven in their absence in Msinga. Although, with apartheid ended, Msinga people are now physically, politically and civilly free of restraints, they can hardly be called completely free. Hence, they lack the seventh essential. That is, their freedom is significantly curtailed by their incapacity to make choices in all areas of their lives. This incapacity is largely due to people's lack of sufficient resources as a consequence of a lack of the eighth essential, distributive justice (fair allocation of resources),[53] in South Africa. Put differently, the people in Msinga are desperately poor, and this immensely limits the choices that they are able to make. This limited ability to make choices grossly limits their capabilities. Finally, they are not even able to participate effectively in civil society and influence decisions made concerning their circumstances and affecting their lives. The Traditional Courts Bill and

49 The importance of engagement and meaning are demonstrated by Schueller, Stephen M. and Martin E. Seligman (2010) 'Pursuit of Pleasure, Engagement, and Meaning: Relationships to Subjective and Objective Measures of Well-Being' *The Journal of Positive Psychology*, 5(4): 253–263; Seligman, Martin E. (2012) *Flourish: A Visionary New Understanding of Happiness and Well-Being*. New York, Simon and Schuster.

50 Burton (*IJPS*); Hicks (above) at 33, 44 and 63.

51 Smith (above).

52 Burton (*IJPS*). Also see Hicks (above) at 86; Schueller and Seligman (above).

53 Burton (*IJPS*). Also see Hicks (above) at 71; and Sen (1999).

how it came into being – without the ordinary residents of places like Msinga having meaningful opportunity to be consulted – is a case in point.

All of these unfulfilled human needs build upon one another. People feel very helpless and, thus, hopeless about the future. This degrades their self-esteem, and they consequently feel useless and lack personal fulfillment, not being invested in their social context because of a lack of faith that their investment will lead to results that would meet their needs. As we see, many men spend their days getting drunk, minor altercations are a common occurrence and are frequently accompanied by the risk of severe violence, and men's attendance of dispute management forums is often low.

Young men get into negative activities in their teenage years, and some go on to even worse forms of criminal and violent activity. Women are expected to be timid and left to do the hard work of trying to feed their families without much help from men; some of the women also turn to liquor for comfort. Many resort to more 'subtle' forms of violence than the men: unconstructive gossip that produces caustic rumours, such as witchcraft, rape and murder accusations.

These activities are obviously unconducive to the resolution of enduring conflict and securing long-term peace in the area. As I have argued, it is substantially due to their sense of helplessness and hopelessness about the options that are presented to them for the management of their conflicts – and the desperation they experience because of the basic human needs in which those conflicts are grounded – that Msinga residents fall prey to destructive modes of conflict management. When they do not endure violations or avoid conflict, such as by relocating, they may turn to violent self-help measures like arson and shootings (attempted murder) or enlist the services of hired assassins or local vigilante groups.

From individuals and communities to institutions and then systems

On the evidence, I must agree with Burton and Alkire that purely institutional interventions would obviously not be enough to address the problems I have named. As Alkire notes:

> Both human security and human development emphasise both the need to involve and empower people as agents and also the need to clarify the role and obligations of other institutions in protecting (for human security) or protecting and advancing (for human development) core capabilities.[54]

The ordinary people of Msinga themselves must be part of the solution. Not only that, but multilevel systems and strategies must be put in place to ensure society the ability to sustainably address complex problems in the long term.

Human needs theory as an indispensible element of conflict resolution emphasises the decision-making and problem-solving skills that individuals and groups

54 Alkire (2010) at 60.

need to acquire to effectively confront the conflict that is implicit in continuing intergroup relations. This constructive confrontation of conflict is termed 'provention', as distinct from 'prevention'. As Burton explains it:

> The significant and historical contribution that the theory of conflict resolution can make is to decision making – that is to the provention of conflict – and ultimately to providing a philosophy and a political-social system that could replace those presently dominant. Indeed, taking account of the magnitude of environmental problems, increasing levels of deprivation and violence at all social levels, and dramatically the falling quality of life, civilizations have no option but to substitute long-term problem solving for their traditional short-term policies of interest group expediency.
>
> It follows that research needs to be directed towards improved decision making (in all organizations including industry, and at all societal levels from the community to the international), rather than have an exclusive focus on interactive processes.[55]

What Burton is communicating is what I have observed of Msinga. Namely, the interactive processes that occur within forums are what is emphasised by the Traditional Courts Bill: the internal functioning of 'traditional courts' as dispute management institutions.[56] While certainly important, this focus is not where the solution to the existing problems is solely, or even primarily, to be found.

Rather, what is most needed is a shift from a focus on institutions as the primary power-holders to an emphasis on how systems structure, support or undermine people's interactions in institutions, communities and society at large.[57] Hence, the cooperative governance system that is nominally in place under the Constitution requires intervention. The system ought to be more pragmatically conceived, its terms should be more clearly articulated and systematised, and it needs to be more broadly construed as including a role for ordinary rural people.[58] In short, the underlying problems causing conflict must be addressed by

55 Burton (*IJPS*).

56 In this respect, the TCB-2008/2012 was worse than the TCB-2017 because it did not much concern itself with addressing the social injustices that bring parties to the forums and are replicated in the way the forums operate.

57 Burton (*IJPS*). Also see Foster-Fishman, Pennie G., Branda Nowell and Huilan Yang (2007) 'Putting the System Back into Systems Change: A Framework for Understanding and Changing Organizational and Community Systems' *American Journal of Community Psychology*, 39: 197–215.

58 See Burris, Scott, Michael Kempa and Clifford Shearing (2008) 'Changes in Governance: A Cross-Disciplinary Review of Current Scholarship'. 41 Akron Law Review 1 at 14, 24, 28–29, 33, 57 for a detailed discussion of the problems and how they affect most ordinary people the world over. Also see Von Benda- Beckmann, Franz, Keebet Von Benda-Beckmann and Julia Eckert. (2009). 'Introduction' in *Rules of Law and Laws of Ruling: On the Governance of Law*. Von Benda-Beckmann, Franz, Keebet Von Benda-Beckmann and Julia Eckert (eds). Surrey, Ashgate at 10, who observe that the decentralised and fractured

the parties involved, and supportive social and political institutions must be established around these parties in order to focus on problem-solving as opposed to narrow processes that are limited to adversarial or confrontational cases between individuals or interest-determined micro-groups.[59]

The ultimate point of all of this theory is this: To effectively address the existing long-term conflicts that are undeniably embedded in the very human needs of people in Msinga, much more is needed than is conceived of by the government or provided by the Traditional Courts Bill. But before we can even begin to discuss the best solutions to deal with these problems, agreement must be reached on the problems themselves. In other words, the government must acknowledge the range of problems and their relevance to its enterprise of providing 'access to justice'. While the TCB-2017 shows improvement in this respect, this acknowledgement has yet to fully occur;[60] hence, human needs theory is an important place to begin.

From faulty cooperation to real collaboration

If functional vernacular forums are inadequate to the task of providing access to justice to Msinga residents, then what is necessary? The evidence suggests that a more sophisticated and sensitive system of collaborative governance should be instituted. Chapter 3 of the Constitution of South Africa provides for a cooperative governance arrangement.[61] This chapter opens with section 40(1), which states, 'In the Republic, government is constituted as national, provincial and local spheres of government which are distinctive, interdependent and interrelated.' Section 41 then outlines the mutual obligations of the various spheres of government. These include the obligations to respect each other's 'constitutional status, institutions, powers and functions',[62] to not seize each other's constitutionally assigned powers or functions,[63] and to 'not encroach on

organisation of the state can have 'problematic consequences, especially for marginalized, poorly organized and poor sections of the population. The organization of these new governance structures is often highly unequal and dominated by powerful actors, while others are excluded.'

59 Burton (*IJPS*); also see Avruch, Kevin and Christopher Mitchell, eds. (2013) *Conflict Resolution and Human Needs: Linking Theory and Practice*. Abingdon, Oxfordshire, Routledge.

60 Ubink and Mnisi Weeks (above). Also see Hicks (above) at 59, 89.

61 See *Minister of Police and Others v Premier of the Western Cape and Others* 2014 (1) SA 1 (CC); *Premier of the Western Cape v President of South Africa and Another* 1999 (3) SA 657 (CC); *Glenister v President of the Republic of South Africa and Others* 2011 (3) SA 347 (CC) (Glenister II); *eThekwini Municipality v Ingonyama Trust* 2013 (5) BCLR 497 (CC); *City of Johannesburg Metropolitan Municipality v Gauteng Development Tribunal and Others* 2010 (6) SA 182 (CC); *MEC for Health, KwaZulu-Natal v Premier, Kwazulu-Natal: In re Minister of Health and Others v Treatment Action Campaign and Others* 2002 (10) BCLR 1023 (CC); *Independent Electoral Commission v Langeberg Municipality* 2001 (3) SA 925 (CC).

62 Section 41(1)(e) of the Constitution of South Africa.

63 Ibid., section 41(1)(f).

the geographical, functional or institutional integrity of government in another sphere'.[64] Finally, according to section 41(1)(h), the various spheres must

> co-operate with one another in mutual trust and good faith by
>
> (i) fostering friendly relations;
> (ii) assisting and supporting one another;
> (iii) informing one another of, and consulting one another on, matters of common interest;
> (iv) co-ordinating their actions and legislation with one another;
> (v) adhering to agreed procedures; and
> (vi) avoiding legal proceedings against one another.

While the Constitution does not explicitly include traditional authorities in this cooperative governance arrangement, the government has read section 212(1) to mean that traditional authorities can be considered part of the same arrangement. This section reads, 'National legislation may provide for a role for traditional leadership as an institution at local level on matters affecting local communities.' Judging from its practice, the government has read this section to mean that traditional authorities can be substituted for local government where it is lacking in capacity or effectively nonexistent.[65] While I think the government applies an incorrect reading of this constitutional provision, I do not focus on my challenge to it here.[66]

While brief, and manifestly incomplete, the constitutional provisions on cooperative governance form a good foundation. They place emphasis on the value of mutual respect, non-encroachment, mutual assistance and support, information sharing and mutual consultation, coordination, procedural agreement and adherence, and the avoidance of inter-sphere conflict. These principles constitute a decent basis for cooperation. Simply applying these principles between institutions involved in dispute management in the Msinga area – vernacular forums, police and the Magistrate's court – would improve outcomes for rural people. But so much more could be achieved than mere cooperation.

Kirk Emerson, Tina Nabatchi and Stephen Balogh present 'an integrative model for collaborative governance' that I find compelling. First, it is important to define what is meant by collaborative, as opposed to cooperative, governance. Specifically, Emerson, Nabatchi, and Balogh understand collaborative governance as:

> the processes and structures of public policy decision making and management that engage people constructively across the boundaries of public agencies, levels of government, and/or the public, private and civic spheres

64 Ibid., section 41(1)(g).

65 Oomen, Barbara (2005) *Chiefs in South Africa: Law, Power and Culture in the Post-Apartheid Era*. Oxford, James Currey; Mnisi Weeks (2015).

66 See Mnisi Weeks (*SACQ*), (2012), and (2015) for details of this critique.

> in order to carry out a public purpose that could not otherwise be accomplished.[67]

Just considering applying this understanding to dispute management in Msinga necessitates asking whether each of the spheres involved in the enterprise believe that the public purpose that they are fulfilling could not be completed without the assistance of the others.

The evidence we collected allows me to speak on only the vernacular forums and police. As presented in the early chapters, the competition between the two institutions strongly suggests that there is extreme ambivalence here. The typical attitude of the police seems to be that they can use the vernacular authorities in matters that fall under one or more of three categories: those that the police feel are too trivial to warrant their attention, those for which the police need only a piece of information in order to do the work themselves or those for which the police have exhausted all other possibilities for addressing the conflict themselves.

On their part, the headmen feel the value they add is vastly underappreciated and feel that their role and sphere of authority is disrespected. Hence, partly motivated by their striving to prove that they are foremost in resolving conflict locally, they will often seek to use the police to a limited degree. In those instances, partnering with the police is intended to shore up the headmen's own authority.

What would it mean to 'engage people constructively across the boundaries of public agencies, levels of government, and/or the public, private and civic spheres' for the purpose of creating a system for managing disputes effectively (in a manner that takes into account the imperative to address underlying human needs) in Msinga? What specific decision-making and management processes and structures are necessary to achieve this goal? And which additional actors ought to be engaged, other than just the vernacular authorities and police?

The integrative model that Emerson et al. propose considers three key nested dimensions,[68] starting with the general system context. This context represents the socio-economic, politico-legal, and ecological dimensions that present opportunities for or constrain what the collaboration can achieve both temporarily and persistently. From this context emanate what 'drivers' will launch and direct what Emerson et al. call the cooperative governance regime (or CGR).

The regime comprises what the scholars call collaborative dynamics and collaborative actions – the former (attitudes, skills, knowledge, resources and interactions) leading to the latter (outputs). Together, these result in impacts (otherwise known as outcomes) that can feed back into the collaborative

67 Emerson, Kirk, Tina Nabatchi and Stephen Balogh (2011) 'An Integrative Framework for Collaborative Governance' *Journal of Public Administration Research and Theory*, 22: 1–29 at 2.

68 Ibid. at 5–8.

dynamics and either positively reinforce these dynamics or negatively affect them. Adaptations to the context, regime or collaborative dynamics could therefore be necessary, as a response to the impacts. Contextual and external effects aimed at addressing existing or foreseeable contextual challenges could constitute further impacts of the collaborative dynamics and actions.

The drivers that instigate collaboration include 'leadership, consequential incentives, interdependence, and uncertainty'.[69] Collaborative dynamics include principled engagement, shared motivation and capacity for joint action.[70] Principled engagement points to exploration and then definition of the joint endeavour, as well as deliberation and determination in its pursuit. Shared motivation denotes the establishment of mutual trust and understanding, internal legitimacy and shared commitment. Capacity for joint action requires valid procedural and institutional arrangements, leadership, knowledge sharing and necessary resources.

Possibilities for collaborative governance in Msinga's dispute management

It would be unrealistic to expect that this breadth and depth of collaboration could be achieved in the context of Msinga's poverty and the government's institutional corruption and lack of resources.[71] Yet the fact that this model could not be fully implemented should not mean that we do not attempt to institute any of it. One strategy for identifying the ideas that can most pragmatically be tested is to focus on the factors that could be cultivated substantially by drawing on outside resources, and thus that do not require more internal resilience than the institutions actually possess. Below, I attempt to determine which factors in Msinga these are.

In my assessment, some such factors could also be capitalised on and implemented at a low cost of intervention relative to the moderately high returns in terms of impact. These elements include existing drivers (external motivation

69 Ibid. at 5.

70 Ibid. at 7.

71 In this regard, it is crucial to acknowledge and take seriously the need to address the depth of institutional dysfunction and incapacity, as well as entrenched negative attitudes, that Smythe, Dee (2015) describes of the South African Police Service at 48–54, 162–201. On the other hand, in keeping with the assets-oriented approach argued for in this chapter, the strategies and tools proposed by Froestad, Jan and Clifford Shearing (2012) *Security Governance, Policing, and Local Capacity*. Boca Baton, FL, CRC Press may be helpful. Their proposed approach is especially compelling as it relates to how to effectively mobilise the 'sense of justice' conceptualised by Dewey and Polanyi in ways that temper the urge for mob justice and thereby curb the rapid escalation of interpersonal conflict between individuals into intergroup conflict. See further, Dewey, John (1938) *Experience and Education*. New York, Touchstone; Polanyi, Michael (1951) *The Logic of Liberty*. Abingdon, Oxfordshire, Routledge; Aligica, Paul and Tarko, Vlad (2011) 'Polycentricity: From Polanyi to Ostrom, and Beyond' *Governance*, 25: 237–262.

for collaboration), the possibility of outsourcing the most important driver of all (convening and initiating leadership), and the possibility of cultivating collaborative dynamics with investment (thus producing the most important long-term driver, which also doubles as capacity for joint action, on the inside of the group of potential collaborators – namely, sustaining leadership). Let me illustrate the point.

The system context is desperately poor and has not manifested the main driver necessary to initiate collaborative action. But some important drivers exist that should inspire such action: for instance, consequential incentives such as the salience and urgency of the problem.[72] Yet the most powerful and resourced institutions that ought to initiate collaboration – the police and government social services – are largely ignoring these drivers. The headmen are unable to ignore their need for the police, though they imagine that they could fulfill the role of the police if the government were to give them the legislated powers and material resources necessary to do so. Interdependence is also an important potential driver, but since the police will not acknowledge the extent of their dependence on the headmen and local informants[73] to fulfill the police mandate of keeping communities safe, interdependence is not driving collaboration.

Similarly, the degree of uncertainty that exists around both the problems and solutions prevalent in this system context makes negotiated solutions the only realistic option. But this option has not yet been acknowledged by key government institutions, which often assume that they know what the problem is and which can hold the troubling belief that the local residents are victims of their own faults. Where corruption is an issue, government and police agents may avoid collaboration because their priority is not effective governance but personal benefit from their positions of power. These drivers (incentives like the salience and urgency of the problem, interdependence and uncertainty) consequently do not offer much of a basis for collaboration, but they could be leveraged if external impetus could form the primary driver of collaborative action.

What the inadequacy of the three drivers mentioned above – consequential incentives, interdependence, and uncertainty – on their own suggests is something that the Emerson et al. model does not adequately account for: leadership from an entity or individual with sufficient convening power and ability to marshal necessary resources is the most important driver for initiating collaborative governance, far outweighing the importance of the other drivers. In the way in which Emerson et al. describe this role, it is effectively a mediator – someone who manages relations within the group, does not push his or her

72 Ibid. at 9. Also see Gray, Barbara (1989) *Collaborating: Finding Common Ground for Multiparty Problems.* San Francisco, Jossey-Bass Publishers at 5–16, 21–25.

73 Beyond the creation and variable implementation of the Community Policing Forums.

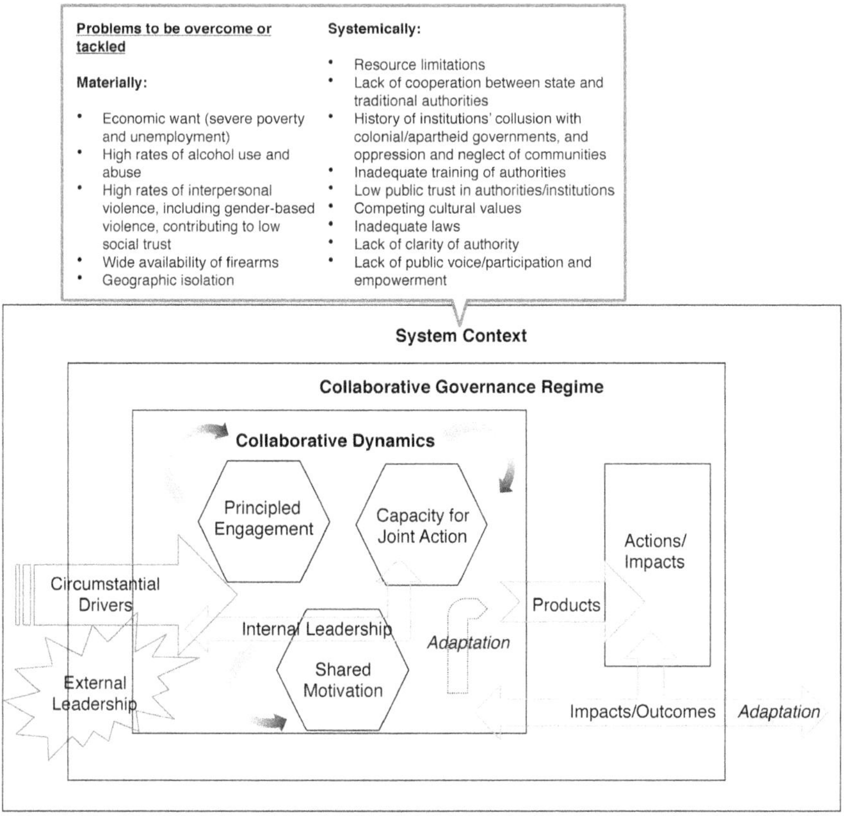

Figure 8.1 Integrative Framework for Collaborative Governance, Revised for Msinga

own views and interests, and manages the relative and composite power of the parties in order to facilitate agreements that have buy-in from all.[74]

This kind of compelling leadership need not be provided by a body or office-holder with authority within the governance system (not even a 'trusted boundary organisation', as Emerson et al. require).[75] But she or he must come from a

74 Emerson, Nabatchi and Balogh (above) at 9, 11. Also see Gray (above).

75 Ibid. Also see Bryson, John M., Barbara C. Crosby and Melissa Middleton Stone (2006) 'The Design and Implementation of Cross-Sector Collaborations: Propositions form the Literature' *Public Administration Review*, 66: 44–55; Selin, Steve. and Deborah. Chevez (1995) 'Developing a Collaborative Model for Environmental Planning and Management' *Environmental Management*, 19: 189–195; Schneider, Mark, John Scholz, Mark Lubell, Denisa Mindruta and Matthew Edwardsen (2003) 'Building Consensual Institutions: Networks and the National Estuary Program' *American Journal of Political Science*, 47: 143–158.

body with sufficient hard or soft power, and thus with influence, to gather the relevant actors to at least begin discussions on possible collaboration. I refer to this role as 'initiating leadership'.[76]

In the context of Msinga, it is hard to imagine this initiating leadership role coming from an internal source or even exclusively from a boundary organisation. In my adapted framework, I therefore refer to the leadership that builds on the other drivers to spark the collaborative initiative as 'external'. I imagine that it could be provided by a third-party organisation such as the Centre for Law and Society (CLS) at the University of Cape Town, with deep support from the trusted local boundary organisation Mdukatshani Rural Development Trust. The same could be stated in the reverse – that Mdukatshani could provide the leadership with extensive assistance from the CLS. The point is that, together, they have the experience and leadership capacity necessary to initiate this collaboration.[77]

Either way, the external leadership provides a holding space for positive interactions to occur, a goal of which must be to give rise to an internal leader for the sake of the sustainability of the collaborative governance regime. I therefore refer to this necessary product as 'sustaining leadership', which can be provided only by a strong and reliable insider to the collaboration. Granted, the initiating leader may only come to be persuaded and mobilised to initiate collaboration by the other drivers. Nonetheless, credible leadership (whether derived internally or externally to the governance system) would seem to be a *sine qua non* – in other words, that without which collaboration cannot begin to occur.[78]

76 The Provincial Registrar of Traditional Courts position created by section 10 of the TCB-2017 might conceivably play this role but it would be a stretch for it to do so. The role is presently crafted as a rather technical role of providing registration, oversight and enforcement akin to a Public Protector or Ombudsman on Traditional Courts – which is certainly needed. Unfortunately, with no additional funds intended for it (see the Memorandum of Objects on the Bill), the creation of this impoverished position in the TCB-2017 is a missed opportunity. Moreover, for the kind of initiating leadership I am describing to be provided by an internal government officer, a different and dedicated position would need to be created.

77 The Centre for Law and Society, formerly the Law, Race and Gender Research Unit, has a history of collaborating with and training government officials (especially magistrates) in improved and more contextually sensitive fulfillment of their dispute management role. With affiliated scholars like the author and other organisational partnerships – most notably Mdukatshani's long-standing relationship and deep commitment to the local authorities and communities – as well as capacity for fundraising to support such an initiative, the Centre could feasibly provide initiating leadership.

78 There are an abundant number of studies showing that leadership is the most vital determinant of successful change processes. See, for example, Heifetz, Ronald A., Alexander Grashow and Martin Linsky (2009) *The Practice of Adaptive Leadership: Tools and Tactics for Changing Your Organization and the World*. Boston, MA, Harvard Business Press; Gray (above); Hickman, Gill Robinson (2010) *Leading Change in Multiple Contexts: Concepts and Practices in Organizational, Community, Political, Social, and Global Change Settings.*

It is obvious that the collaborative dynamics that are needed to achieve the goal of establishing and implementing a system by which disputes can be effectively managed, giving cognisance to the basic human needs in Msinga, do not presently exist. But this is where it is possible for an external actor to intervene in a way that could help cultivate shared motivation, building on the potential drivers that do exist, to help produce mutual trust and cultivate mutual understanding.

I saw this kind of intervention happen in a workshop that I conducted in June 2015 with colleagues at CLS and Mdukatshani as part of CLS's Pathways to Justice research project. CLS and Mdukatshani brought together the vernacular authorities in Msinga and the magistrates to talk about challenges in the criminal justice system. The feedback we received was that the workshop was informative and empowering to all. Its greatest achievement was that together we all built goodwill between the participants. The participants themselves concluded from the workshop that these kinds of engagements need to happen on a focused and long-term basis and be expanded to benefit other communities as well.

This sort of process of enriching collaborative dynamics depends on getting the correct institutional representatives together to engage in principled ways,[79] in respectful communication that builds social capital between them.[80] However,

Thousand Oaks, CA, Sage; Homan, Mark S. (2011) *Promoting Community Change: Making It Happen in the Real World*. Belmont, CA, Brooks/Cole. Also see Bunker, Barbara Benedict and Billie T. Alban (2006) *The Handbook of Large Group Methods: Creating Systemic Change in Organizations and Communities*. San Francisco, CA, Jossey-Bass; Kegan, Robert and Lisa Laskow Lahey (2009) *Immunity to Change: How to Overcome It and Unlock the Potential in Yourself and Your Organization*. Boston, MA, Harvard Business School Publishing; Maton, Kenneth I. (2008) 'Empowering Community Settings: Agents of Individual Development, Community Betterment, and Positive Social Change' *Journal of Community Psychology*, 41: 4–21; Mills, Roger C. (2005) 'Sustainable Community Change: A New Paradigm for Leadership in Community Revitalization Efforts' *National Civic Review*, 94: 9–16.

79 Emerson, Nabatchi and Balogh (above) at 11, 17. Also see Ansell, Chris and Alison Gash (2008) 'Collaborative Governance in Theory and Practice' *Journal of Public Administration Research and Theory*, 18: 543–571; Carlson, Christine (2007) *A Practical Guide to Collaborative Governance*. Portland, OR, Policy Consensus Initiative; Carpenter, Susan L. and W. J. D. Kennedy (2001) *Managing Public Disputes: A Practical Guide for Government, Business, and Citizens' Groups*. San Francisco, CA, Jossey-Bass; Emerson, Kirk, Patricia J. Orr, Dale L. Keyes and Katherine M. McKnight (2009) 'Environmental Conflict Resolution: Evaluating Performance Outcomes and Contributing Factors' *Conflict Resolution Quarterly*, 27: 27–64; Susskind, Larry, Sarah McKearnan and Jennifer Thomas-Larmer, eds. (1999) *The Consensus-Building Handbook: A Comprehensive Guide to Reaching Agreement*. Thousand Oaks, CA, Sage Books.

80 See Dovidio, John F., Samuel L. Gaertner and Tamar Saguy (2009) 'Commonality and the Complexity of "We": Social Attitudes and Social Change' *Personality and Social Psychology Review*, 13: 3–20; LeBaron, Michelle and Nike Carstarphen (October 1997) 'Negotiating Intractable Conflict: The Common Ground Dialogue Process and Abortion' *Negotiation Journal*, 13(4): 341–361; Hicks (above).

as part of ensuring diverse representation, it would be similarly important for ordinary Msinga residents to be part of this collaborative, to represent on-the-ground experiences and the perspectives of their communities.[81] Institutional actors would have to include social services representatives, who would engage with the institutions tasked with conflict management, justice and security on how best the human needs and social injustice undergirding the endemic conflict in Msinga can be addressed, both on a case-to-case basis and at a systemic level.

The police would obviously also have to be among the institutional actors participating. They were invited to the Pathways workshops but declined to send representatives. This formal unwillingness to engage on the part of the police is a challenge that would need to be overcome for such an intervention to have any chance of becoming successful. A separate process of multilevel engagement would be necessary to cultivate this willingness and find more amenable and empowered parties within the police who can motivate for participation from within the police service. It goes without saying that headmen, headmen's policemen and the senior traditional leaders (formerly known as chiefs) of each vernacular grouping would have to buy into and actively participate in the process as well.

Emerson et al. describe what we can expect from such a process, if we were to get the right people in the room and manage the interactions effectively:

> Repeated, quality interactions through principled engagement will help foster trust, mutual understanding, internal legitimacy, and shared commitment, thereby generating and sustaining shared motivation. Once generated, shared motivation will enhance and help sustain principled engagement and vice versa in a "virtuous cycle."[82]

The most important driver of all could arise from this 'virtuous cycle': leadership. Unsurprisingly, this driver is also an essential component of capacity for joint action.

The sustained, positive interactive process might even birth agreement on the institutional arrangements that could support collaborative action, arrangements within the power of those engaging in the process to create. If no other form of collaboration – under the category of capacity for joint action – can be produced from the constructive discourse engaged in through the process, at least knowledge sharing could be. Emerson et al. call knowledge – as opposed to information and data – 'the currency of collaboration' when it is shared such that conclusions drawn from the information available to the participants benefits

81 Gray (above) at 11–16; Huxham, Chris. 2003. Theorizing collaboration practice. *Public Management Review*, 5: 401–423; Huxham, Chris, Siv Vangen, Christine Huxham and Colin Eden (2000) 'The Challenge of Collaborative Governance' *Public Management Review*, 2(3): 337–358.

82 Emerson, Nabatchi and Balogh (above) at 14.

from all their assessments of that information.[83] Strategies might also be generated for sharing very limited resources such as time, money, logistical and technical support, and particular skills and expertise. Opportunities could also emerge for acquiring external resources to support future collaboration, possibly even collaborative action and joint outcomes.

Ultimately, for collaborative action to follow on from this process of establishing and strengthening collaborative dynamics, a fundamental accompanying outcome must be 'a shared theory of action'.[84] Studies show that a problem for collaborative action is often that 'shared goals and an operating rationale for taking action are not made explicit.'[85]

I've already mentioned that the police and headmen do not recognise their mutual interdependence, incentive to collaborate and consequent need to do so because of the complexity and uncertainty presented by the situations with which they are faced. This unacknowledged yet self-evident set of realities obstructs arrival at a clearly defined, shared agenda. In turn, this lack of shared agenda prevents the possibility of effective, collaborative action that puts the cause of justice and security for local people above petty institutional differences or individual actors' interests in taking advantage of the system for their personal gain.

As Emerson et al. summarise the strategy for engendering collaboration, '[p]rincipled engagement and shared motivation will stimulate the development of institutional arrangements, leadership, knowledge, and resources, thereby generating and sustaining capacity for joint action.'[86] As their model also suggests, the outputs of the improved dynamics – that is, the actions they yield – will have consequences for the dynamics and wider context but will probably require continuing adaptation in order to maximise their positive impacts or outcomes in the long-term.

It is important to be realistic about the possibilities and limitations of such a process. It surely cannot be used to advance a one-size-fits-all solution. Those promoting the process must be open to each particular socio-economic, politico-legal and ecological context yielding different results.[87] This is a necessary

83 Ibid. at 16. Also see Ansell and Gash (above) at 544; Gray (above) at 8–14; Groff and Jones (2003); Agranoff, Robert (2008) 'Collaboration for Knowledge: Learning from Public Management Networks' in Lisa Blomgren Bingham and Rosemary O'Leary (eds.) *Big Ideas in Collaborative Public Management*. Armonk, NY, M.E., Sharpe, 162–194; Cross, Rob and Andrew Parker (2004) *The Hidden Power of Social Networks*. Boston, MA, Harvard Business School Press; Saint-Onge, Hubert and Charles Armstrong (2004) *The Conductive Organization Building beyond Sustainability*. New York, NY, Elsevier.

84 Emerson, Nabatchi and Balogh (above) at 17–18; Gray (above) at 13–15.

85 Emerson, Nabatchi and Balogh (above) at 17. Also see Huxham (above) at 404: 'common practice, however, appears to be that the variety of organizational and individual agendas that are present in collaborative situations make it difficult to agree on aims in practice'.

86 Emerson, Nabatchi and Balogh (above) at 16.

87 See, for example, Dwyer, Kathy, LdDonna Fowler, Tom Seekins, Carol Locust and Julie Clay (2001) 'Community Development By American Indian Tribes: Five Case Studies of

consequence of valuing the agency of participant actors and recognising that every context has its own particularities that are best understood by those who inhabit it.

This very iterative process constitutes slow, painstaking intervention and adaptation work. It is undeniably expensive too as human and other resources must be committed to the endeavour. But it is hard to see how this process is avoidable if sustainable results are to be achieved in the form of effective improvement in the dispute management in Msinga. Collaborative governance is therefore an important investment in the future of the people – especially the young people – in Msinga. Similar work is most likely necessary in other deep rural areas.[88] Government's limited resources, capacity and skills to do this kind of collaboration necessitates that outside funders support work that intervenes in these ways – at least as an interim measure to aid the building up of this capacity internally in government and in the affected communities over time.

Concluding remarks

The integrative model of collaborative governance that Emerson et al. provide is representative of a scholarship that essentially argues that democracy is a form of conflict resolution[89] – a complex exercise in resolving disparate and often competing interests among many stakeholders and governing bodies.[90] Collaborative governance is a subset of democratic practice – and therefore Msinga's conflict management problem is ultimately a democracy problem. This problem must therefore be resolved by means of democratic process. By this, I am not referring to simplistic answers like people going to the polls; rather I am suggesting directed, ongoing and iterative processes of participation, enquiry, problem-solving, decision-making, budgeting, implementation and adaptation that focus on the detail wherein the proverbial devil is to be found.

Embodied in all of the conflict that must be addressed through these deeply democratic processes in places like Msinga is disagreement over what is just. That is, what principle of justice should dominate in a context of scarce resources, where each individual seems to have little rational choice but to look out for his or her own immediate survival? And by what means should such a principle of justice be given effect when the most straightforward way of realising it would seem to be self-preservation at all cost?

Establishing Policy for Tribal Members with Disabilities' *Community Development: Journal of the Community Development Society*, 31(2): 196–215.

88 See, for example, Mnisi Weeks (*Acta Juridica*).

89 These two concepts are deeply interwoven in the work of Kew, Darren (2005) 'Building Democracy in 21st Century Africa: Two Africas, One Solution' *The Whitehead Journal of Diplomacy and International Relations*, 6(1): 149–161.

90 See Gray (above).

In previous chapters, I have illustrated that the slope toward a 'Lord of the Flies'[91] kind of situation is very slippery indeed, but in this concluding chapter, I have demonstrated that there is an alternative. What is needed in officials' confrontation of Msinga's prevailing conflict problems – from individual, interpersonal conflict to intra-community mediation by vernacular forums to security in and governance of Msinga and South African society at large – is a view of and approach to them as mutual problems that must be resolved collaboratively. It falls on all concerned parties to use their agency to choose this option. But it largely falls on those with the most power to support this as a viable choice. The police and other government officials can together move the culture away from one that says 'it's our turn to eat'[92] and institute a new culture focused on serving the needs of those with little other hope – first locally, then regionally, then provincially, and ultimately nationally. Police and other government officials can choose to focus on the basic human needs of local people and partner with all stakeholders and officeholders to tackle these needs effectively instead of protecting their own position.

To a lesser degree than the police, the headmen can do the same, turning their attention to building the legitimacy of the vernacular forums and institutions internally. The headmen can begin to achieve this goal by addressing the disconnect between what is asked of them by parties and what can actually be afforded by the vernacular forums, especially if the police and social services will not collaborate with the headmen. In other words, the headmen can invest substantial energy in developing a strong alternative to a collaborative agreement or systemic arrangement negotiated with their more powerful government counterparts.[93]

To do so, even within the desperate contextual factors that give rise to often intractable conflict, the vernacular forums can improve the success rates of their interventions. They can achieve this improvement by increasing the negotiability of all aspects of the process they employ and decisions available to parties, by engaging people through negotiation and mediation rather than more coercive strategies in the guise of arbitration or adjudication. This approach would most likely reduce the need for the headmen to bear the unmanageable burden of enforcement of decisions, while enhancing the enforceability of the agreements produced by the vernacular forums' processes. Parties who are satisfied with and invested in a decision that is mutually arrived at are more likely to honour it. In the process, vernacular forums would strengthen relationships and help people feel more empowered – all of which would yield the positive by-product of gradually strengthening the social fabric.

Outsiders like myself could help with skills training to empower the headmen and senior traditional leaders to turn the flexibility and uncertainty built into

91 Golding, William (1959) *Lord of the Flies*. New York, Penguin.

92 Wrong, Michela (2009) *It's Our Turn to Eat: The Story of a Kenyan Whistleblower*. London: Fourth Estate.

93 Emerson, Nabatchi and Balogh (above) at 10; Fisher, Ury and Patton (above) at 97–107.

the vernacular dispute management processes away from the disorganisation which currently manifests. In the process, we could help the headmen secure greater control of, and genuine confidence in, their role in local dispute management. This empowerment would partly involve helping vernacular authorities recognise and embrace the reality of competing values and objectives that are expressed by parties using the dispute management system, both intra-culturally and inter-systemically. Put differently, it is important for the headmen and senior traditional leaders to develop fuller appreciation of the reasons why people might choose one dispute management method (such as self-help over arbitration/adjudication in the chief's council), forum (like the headman's forum over the family council), or system (perhaps the state system over the vernacular system) at different times and in varying contexts. The outside trainer's task would also involve shining more of a spotlight on the systemic nature of the conflicts that are presented and their overwhelming gesturing toward parties' need for human security.

The support needed from us outsiders would also include helping the vernacular authorities grapple with the realistic consequences of their value assumptions in a context that advances different values and assumptions from their own.[94] For instance, the headmen may reasonably choose restraint, out of the commitment to the principle of honour that is in keeping with what they were taught by their grandfathers and what they want to teach their own grandchildren. However, when restraint leads headmen to commonly refer conflicts to higher forums that are less accessible to people and have lower success rates at finalising disputes, this action reduces faith in the vernacular system as a whole.

Finally, the vernacular authorities would need to continue to actively advocate for the government's collaborative assistance in addressing the gap between what is asked of them by the local community and what they can deliver to people for whom human security is the underlying need. This advocacy is something that I hope this book will make easier for the headmen of Msinga. In the end, the argument presented in this book is that the state should, first, support vernacular dispute management forums – and, in turn, the people they are meant to serve – in more targeted ways than mere regulatory legislation and, second, engage every stakeholder in shared, active solution-building and implementation.

In the meantime, the government's task of legislating in order to regulate vernacular forums in accordance with the Constitution should be premised on the reality that vernacular forums are not 'courts of law'.[95] The government should therefore regulate them in ways that will maximise their strengths rather than

94 Friedman, Victor J. and Ariane Berthoin Antal (2005) 'Negotiating Reality: A Theory of Action Approach to Intercultural Competence' *Management Learning*, 36: 69 at 83. The 'culturally shaped repertoire' of 'tacit knowledge' that the headmen are applying, taught to them by their forefathers, has lost effectiveness as Msinga has changed in the last decades.

95 Mnisi Weeks (*OUCLJ*); Ubink and Mnisi Weeks (above).

compel them to operate from a place of weakness, making them pretend to be state-like courts or the police.

As I have discussed, this approach requires regulating and supporting vernacular forums as alternative dispute resolution, or so-called ADR, forums – particularly mediation (and, only in exceptional circumstances, arbitration) forums. This regulatory approach requires going beyond the platitudinous language used by the Department of Justice and Correctional Services, which describes these forums as tribunals dispensing 'restorative justice',[96] 'maintaining harmony'[97] and manifesting a 'consensual nature'.[98] As I have shown, the vernacular forums studied are not particularly 'restorative', 'conciliatory' and 'harmonious' at present but have the potential to become so with appropriate assistance. Government should also model a 'restorative justice' approach by emphasising inclusion and collaboration with ordinary rural people in its legislative process.

As demonstrated at the start of this chapter, reasonable people can disagree on what 'access to justice' means. But we should not disagree on the primary moral requirement for all people to be able to live in safety, with basic material provisions to meaningfully sustain their lives and the capabilities to attain well-being, freedom, dignity, and such security as they are due. This is an uncontestable justice[99] which people in Msinga and deep rural areas throughout South Africa need. In adopting the solutions I have argued for, vernacular law and rural areas could set an example for the common law and urban areas of how to begin to address this generalised need for access to justice and human security in South Africa. If done right, these solutions would enable South Africa to meet the lofty standards of the Constitution and thereby set an example for the rest of the world, much of which is wrestling with similar challenges.

96 Preamble of TCB2008/2012; and sections 1, 2(a), 3(1)(b), and 6(2) of TCB-2017.
97 Sections 2(b)(i), 6(2)(c) and Memorandum of TCB-2017.
98 Sections 2(c)(i) and 6(2) of TCB-2017.
99 Dworkin (2011) at 2–3.

Index

Note: Page numbers in italic indicate a figure and footnotes are indicate by an "n" followed by number.

For Product Safety Concerns and Information please contact our EU representative GPSR@taylorandfrancis.com
Taylor & Francis Verlag GmbH, Kaufingerstraße 24, 80331 München, Germany

www.ingramcontent.com/pod-product-compliance
Ingram Content Group UK Ltd.
Pitfield, Milton Keynes, MK11 3LW, UK
UKHW010956180926
475701UK00004B/394
9780367889111